ENDORSEMENTS

There are numerous theological and philosophical works that address the relationship between divine sovereignty and human free will or responsibility. *The Wonderful Decree* explores a parallel and equally important issue: the compatibility of unconditional election and divine universal love. Campbell presents the various views fairly and with charity. He then argues that, by employing Thomistic categories, Reformed theology can affirm both unconditional election and a genuine, divine universal salvific desire. As someone who also makes a similar dual affirmation, I find *The Wonderful Decree* encouraging and refreshing (despite its standard Thomistic critique of Molinism!) This work makes a helpful contribution and should be read by all who are interested in issues related to our wonderful salvation.

—Ken D. Keathley, senior professor of theology,
Southeastern Baptist Theological Seminary

The Wonderful Decree is a book that is impressive in a number of ways. For one thing, it begins by removing any doubt that evil, as Travis Campbell treats it, is not just an abstract idea bandied about by philosophers. We confront evil directly in our personal experiences of suffering. The subsequent philosophical and theological discussion is very thorough as well as up to date by engaging with contemporary positions and the debate they have engendered. The technical discussions distinguish themselves by a mature and flowing writing style. I highly recommend this book to anyone who may question how a Thomistic metaphysics and a Reformed theology can (and should) go hand in hand in addressing pertinent issues of life. For others, who are not as concerned with conceptual issues per se, this book will open their eyes to the love of God in the face of life's hardships.

—Winfried Corduan, professor emeritus of philosophy and religion,
Taylor University

The Wonderful Decree is in my estimation one of the most significant contributions to Christian thought from the last century. Here the reader will find a sophisticated discussion of a whole range of issues relating to divine providence, predestination, and the nature of human freedom. It is written with a tremendous grasp of the big picture and sensitivity to the different possible strategies entailed in the church's attempt to work out the enigmas of divine revelation. Dr. Campbell writes with an unusual ability to bridge exegesis with sophisticated philosophical reflection. In my judgment he is a modern, Presbyterian version of the esteemed Réginald Garrigou-Lagrange! I highly commend this volume to anyone seeking a competent guide to exploring the mystery of God's wisdom and sovereignty.

—Paul L. Owen, professor of Bible and ministry, Montreat College

THE
WONDERFUL
DECREE

THE WONDERFUL DECREE

*Reconciling
Sovereign Election
and Universal Benevolence*

Travis James Campbell

LEXHAM PRESS

The Wonderful Decree: Reconciling Sovereign Election and Universal Benevolence

Copyright 2020 Travis James Campbell

Lexham Press, 1313 Commercial St., Bellingham, WA 98225
LexhamPress.com

Print ISBN 9781683593324
Digital ISBN 9781683593331
Library of Congress Control Number 2019950874

Lexham Editorial: Douglas Mangum, Claire Brubaker, and Joy Mosbarger
Cover Design: George Siler
Typesetting: Kathy Curtis

To

R. Edgar Campbell

My Father

My Mentor

My Friend

O Israel, thou hast destroyed thyself;

but in me is thine help.

Hosea 13:9 (KJV)

Contents

FOREWORD

An adept Christian theologian is able to navigate with skill through the various branches of theology: biblical, systematic, historical, and philosophical. Moreover, the best theologians also seek to practice the golden rule of apologetics—treating other people's beliefs the way they want theirs treated—with respect, care, and fairmindedness. Thus, noble Christian scholars pursue truth, unity, and charity in their writings, especially when the theological topics are controversial among the different branches and denominations within Christianity. I am very pleased to say that Travis Campbell has exemplified these admirable qualities in his insightful book, *The Wonderful Decree*.

For centuries Christian scholars and laypeople have hotly debated how God can be sovereign in choosing the elect in salvation and yet still have genuine love for all people in his providential plan of salvation. Theologians have proffered different answers to this provocative question; it is one of the challenging theological controversies that have divided Christianity into various groups and quarters. Campbell's book is a tour de force in making the case that God's decree of unconditional election is indeed compatible with his universal redemptive love. Yet Campbell is, refreshingly, not combative or confrontational in making his case. Rather he is fair and gracious in laying out the competing positions and quoting the best advocates, arguments, and sources for them. In the end I think this work contains the strongest critique of the popular position, known as "Molinism" or "middle knowledge," that seeks to reconcile God's sovereignty and libertarian human freedom.

Campbell's theological treatment is also a welcome work of Christian apologetics: it sets forth an intriguing philosophical theodicy. He also makes the case that a historic Reformed theology informed by a Thomistic metaphysic and aspects of St. Thomas's view of grace best explains and reconciles God's goodness and the enduring problem of evil.

I hope this fine book reaches a wide audience of readers. May it spark further discussion and dialogue in theological, philosophical, and apologetics circles. Christians need to take important doctrinal controversies seriously and yet reflect intellectual integrity and graciousness in doing so.

Tolle Lege ("Take Up and Read!")

Kenneth Richard Samples

Senior Research Scholar, Reasons to Believe

ACKNOWLEDGMENTS

There are quite a few people who deserve a word of thanks. First, I am so appreciative of Brannon Ellis for giving me the opportunity to present this work for Lexham's consideration. Brannon, few will know how hard this year has been for you and your family. Despite your struggles, you were available to receive my pestering phone calls, always there to give me sound advice. Thank you so very much! I would also like to thank the editing team at Lexham for helping me take a series of essays and turn them into an actual book. This was a first for me, and all of you made this process about as pleasant as it can get. I am also appreciative of the two reviewers who looked at this work in its earliest stages. The rave reviews of one were a great encouragement to me and inspired me to proceed; the rather harsh critique of another was also helpful, as it inspired me to improve my arguments—this is a much better work than it would have been without it.

I am also grateful for Ken Samples's gracious foreword. Our talks over the years, especially over the extremely intriguing doctrine of middle knowledge, which in many respects was the initial catalyst for our friendship, have gone far to mold my ideas on this matter. Appreciation also goes to others who commented on portions of this work: Hector Avalos, Matthew Butler, Jeremiah Pitts, Roger Kornu, and Kimbell Kornu. Special thanks goes to my good friend Paul Owen, who has read several versions of this work and made many helpful comments on it. Our many late-night discussions on all things theological are such a blessing to me; in fact, it is difficult to know where my ideas begin and his end on these matters. Again, thank you!

Kierkegaard once said that the problem with authors is that they're never home when they're home. My experience has proven this assertion to be uncomfortably true. To my wife, Jenny, and my son, Evan, thank you for your patience in dealing with this airhead. Your love and support mean more to me than words can express.

It is often said that a child's first impression of God comes from the lasting impression left by his or her father. As a child, my own father made it easy for me to believe that I had a loving heavenly Father who is easy to please and yet impossible to satisfy. When as an adult I encountered doubts about my faith, Dad became the parable of the Redeemer who simply would not let me go.

During the memorial service of my first wife, Lillian, I was virtually numb, having a hard time processing what was happening. As our family lined up for the funeral procession, my father stood behind me; and as the pastor asked me questions, Dad whispered the answers in my ear and I, like a parrot, simply repeated whatever he said. This is the lasting picture I have of my dad, my earthly rock and living parable, who has been my best friend, wisest mentor, and strongest support from the days of my youth until this very moment. This work is therefore affectionately dedicated to him.

ABBREVIATIONS

AB	Anchor Bible
BDAG	Walter Bauer, Frederick William Danker, W. F. Arndt, and F. W. Gingrich. *A Greek-English Lexicon of the New Testament and Other Early Christian Literature*. 3rd ed. Chicago: University of Chicago Press, 2000.
BDB	*The New Brown-Driver-Briggs-Gesenius Hebrew and English Lexicon*. Edited by Francis Brown et al. Peabody, MA: Hendrickson, 1979.
BECNT	Baker Exegetical Commentary on the New Testament
F&P	*Faith and Philosophy*
ICC	International Critical Commentary
JES	*Jonathan Edwards Studies*
LXX	Septuagint
NICNT	New International Commentary on the New Testament
NICOT	New International Commentary on the Old Testament
NT	New Testament
OT	Old Testament
SCG	Thomas Aquinas, *Summa Contra Gentiles*
ST	Thomas Aquinas, *Summa Theologica*
TDNT	Gerhard Kittel and Gerhard Friedrich, eds. *Theological Dictionary of the New Testament*. Translated by Geoffrey W. Bromiley. Grand Rapids: Eerdmans, 1972.
WBC	Word Biblical Commentary

Part 1

PROLEGOMENA

1

MUSINGS OVER A DARK PROVIDENCE

So what do you say to people (and I hear this all the time) who say,
"Everything happens for a reason"?
—*Bill Maher*

I say, this was not the coffee that I ordered.
—*Seth MacFarlane*

Have you ever found yourself traveling down the road of life thinking, "This is perfect! Life just couldn't get any better!"? As you were saying that, were you hit with a tragedy that seems too great to bear? That very thing happened to my wife, Lillian, and me.

In May 1999, Lillian and I discovered that she was pregnant. Most couples want to wait a few weeks, or even months, before letting people know. Not us! Lillian immediately began calling everyone she knew to announce the great news. Near the end of the month we left Philadelphia, where I was working on my PhD in theology, and went back to our original home in Dallas to visit with family and friends. Everyone was so happy for us. Things just couldn't have been better! In one year I would be finished with my coursework for the program and we would have a newborn baby, and so I looked forward to the summer of 2000 as the time when I would start my career and grow my family.

When we arrived back at our small apartment in Pennsylvania, we did what most people did back in the 1990s—we checked our answering machine. One message would change our lives forever. The doctor's office asked Lillian to call back to schedule more blood tests, as something didn't look right. The following day she called the office and was informed that her white blood cell count had reached thirty thousand. For one full month we spent most of our time ruling out possibilities. In July 1999 Lillian was diagnosed with chronic lymphocytic leukemia (CLL).

I really can't describe in words the depth of despair both of us sank into at that moment. My mother died of cancer when I was eight years old. I just figured, via some twisted sense of logic, that I had had my share of loss. Surely God would not allow my child to be raised without his mother since, after all, I had endured that already! Why would God bring a brand-new life into this world, only to snuff it out of existence? Why allow a child to grow up without a mother?

The total irrationality of the diagnosis was compounded even further when we learned just how "impossible" it was for a person like Lillian to have CLL. You see, there are three kinds of people who are rarely diagnosed with this form of leukemia: people under thirty, women, and Asians. Lillian was all three!

As you might imagine, I immediately began learning all I could about CLL. I learned that there are several kinds of leukemia. Acute leukemias are far more aggressive and so need immediate treatment. Had Lillian had an acute form of leukemia, she would have required immediate chemotherapy, in which case we would have surely lost our child. With a disease like CLL, one can potentially go years without treatment. So we began the process of month-to-month monitoring of her condition. Our hope was that she could at least give birth to our child before enduring chemotherapy.

Our prayers were answered when, in January of 2000, our beautiful baby boy, Evan, was born. And yet, as happy as I was about this wonderful gift, a certain foreboding sense of an imminent tragedy remained in my mind. Such fears were confirmed when one morning in February I awoke and, to my horror, saw very swollen lymph nodes around Lillian's neck. Due to Lillian's condition, I doubled my coursework to ensure that we could leave Pennsylvania in May.

I began applying for pastoral positions in Texas, thinking that we could move there to be with family for support as we sought treatment at M.D. Anderson Hospital. Unfortunately, no church would offer me an interview. To give one example of my bad experiences with various churches, a ruling elder of one congregation actually encouraged me, saying that I had made his short list of candidates—but within one week he reneged on that statement, saying I was unqualified for my lack of experience. So, with a newborn baby, a wife with cancer, and no prospects for a job, I heeded Lillian's advice that we should move in with her parents in Greenville, Texas.

Our family moved to Greenville in July, and within one month I landed a job as a security guard at Texas A&M University in nearby Commerce. Once again our prayers had been answered, as we now had absolutely no worries about medical costs. In October Lillian and I traveled to Houston to establish a relationship with the doctors at M.D. Anderson. By this time Evan was thriving and had even stopped breastfeeding in September. So, once again, the timing could not have been better, given our situation.

Just before Lillian traveled down to Houston to begin her first round of what was described as mild chemotherapy, her doctor informed her that the CLL had mutated into an aggressive lymphoma. Now there could be no delay; she had to begin treatment, and the chemo would be anything but mild. From November 2000 through April 2001 Lillian, our baby, and her parents lived in Houston while I worked five hours away as a security guard. She went through hell. While going through this horrendous experience, she told me that she never really felt like she had cancer until she was treated for it. And yet, though hellacious, the chemotherapy was worth it; for in April of 2001 we received the wonderful news that Lillian's cancer was in full remission.

We decided that the best choice we could make to ensure the cancer would not come back was for Lillian to undergo a bone marrow transplant. Unfortunately, no matches could be found among family members. So we opted for the next best thing, which (at the time) was quite revolutionary. Stem cells were proving to be a viable option, having the potential to accomplish exactly what we needed in a bone marrow transplant. We found a match in late May, and by late June the stem cell transplant had taken place. Lillian spent fifty days in isolation!

After moving back into our Houston apartment, Lillian had difficulty holding down food. She went back into the hospital, undergoing multiple tests to discover the source of the problem. In mid-September, just a few days after 9/11, the doctors talked us into performing a liver biopsy as a precautionary measure. Within a few days blood had seeped from Lillian's liver into her lungs. By September 17 Lillian had to go on a ventilator, as she had now acquired acute respiratory distress syndrome (ARDS). Lillian was a nurse, so when I gave her the news, she didn't say so, but I could see it on her face. She knew her days were numbered. Within days of going on the vent she was fully sedated, never to communicate again.

On October 4, 1996, I had asked Lillian to marry me. On October 4, 2001, I was informed by the doctors that there was nothing they could do. It was only a matter of time before Lillian passed away.

Our family and friends could not have been more supportive during this time! My father and sister, stepmother, aunts, uncles, and cousins, along with Lillian's extended family, all descended on Houston; and for one week we prayed for Lillian and comforted one another. I had asked one of the doctors to tell me when we passed from the point of "it's still possible she can make it" to "it's literally immoral for you to keep her on the vent," and on October 9 he informed me we had reached that moment. Lillian's parents, along with her brothers, were helping me with these decisions; and we decided to wait a few days to give as many people as possible a chance to say their goodbyes. On October 11, our family and friends gathered around Lillian while the doctors reduced her oxygen to around 20 percent. And she died.

I remember very little of the moments immediately following Lillian's death. I remember weeping over her corpse. I remember going to her parents and apologizing that this had happened, as no parent should ever have to bury a child. I remember a stupid nurse telling me, before even leaving the room, that I had a child to raise, as if to say, "Stop dwelling on this." I remember a pastor following me to the lobby telling me he loved me. I remember sitting in the lobby weeping, only to have a foolish lady tell me that I shouldn't cry. "What the hell do you expect me to do!" I yelled in retort. I remember going downstairs to the main lobby to see my friend Drew, who had been looking after Evan during this time, hugging my son, and then handing him off to a family member—as I just couldn't bear to see him. I remember lying in bed, crying, asking how in the world am I going to live without her and even raise a son by myself. I remember Drew lying next to me, saying, "You have tons of support, Travis. I know it's hard to hear now, but you'll find your feet."

The years 2001 through 2007 were not my best years, to say the least. The months immediately following Lillian's death can only be described as dark and numb. I had no desire to work or eat, and I simply could not sleep. Even though I would, several years later, finish my dissertation—on God's providence no less—I constantly entertained doubts about my faith. In many respects, I felt myself becoming a totally different person than I was before watching my wife die. In fact, starting around the fall of 2005 and going through 2007, for the first time in my life I totally opened myself to the thought that there simply was no god of any kind. After Evan would go to sleep, I would spend four to five hours most nights reading atheistic literature, watching debates between theists and atheists, or reading blog posts by those who lost their faith under circumstances similar to my own. If you were to have spoken with me during those years you may have heard me sounding like a Christian whose faith was strong, but inside I was a mess. Of course, I didn't always sound so Christian. As a teacher of comparative religion, I spend a great deal of time offering arguments from all sides of various religious questions, including the existence of God. I will never forget a student coming up to me with a perplexed look on her face. "I heard you were a Christian," she said. "I am," I answered. "Then why do you spend so much time offering arguments against your own religion?"

It wasn't just Lillian's death that made me doubt God's existence. It was, as it were, "the whole enchilada." Why answer all those prayers and illustrate such an intriguing, meticulous providence if, at the end of the day, she was going to die anyway? Examples of providence and answered prayer included things such as bringing about Evan's conception, which is the reason why Lillian had the bloodwork that revealed her high white-cell count; allowing her to have a chronic form of leukemia, so that she could carry her pregnancy to term; giving me a job that covered the medical costs; and even curing the cancer. You read that right! I was informed three days before her death that there was absolutely no trace of cancer in her body. The transplant was a success! Our situation was comparable to that Alabama versus Auburn game a few years ago. You know the one. In the final seconds of the game 'Bama not only missed a field goal, but it was caught by an Auburn player, who ran the ball back one hundred yards for a touchdown. We had won. We defeated the cancer. All we had to do was give Lillian's body time to adjust to the procedure. But the doctor's decision to do a liver biopsy led to the death of my wife and the mother of my son. I felt like I was the victim of a cosmic joke. It took two counselors to convince me that the biopsy wasn't my fault, and three law firms to convince me that I had no real case against the doctors who made that decision.

I did not entertain the notion that perhaps there is a God who is not as powerful or sovereign as the Bible portrays him to be. I had written a dissertation on one version of this perspective, and I believed then, as I believe now, that such conceptions render the deity more of an object of pity than worship. No, the old Epicurean argument against God's existence hit me hard during those moments: If God is all-powerful and all-good, then why is there evil? If he wants to rid the world of evil but cannot, then he is impotent; and if he can but does not, then he is not good.

The things people, even Christians, said to me, compounded my doubts even more. Within six months of her death, I was told that I should just get over it. A few years later I was told that I was not the one who suffered. I was told not to ask why. I was even given James 1:2: "Count it all joy, my brothers, when you meet trials of various kinds" (ESV). Sometimes I got the feeling that those who were offering words of assurance were trying to comfort themselves more than me. In the months following Lillian's passing I would sometimes walk into a room and feel eyes gaze on me, often wondering whether my presence wasn't a terrible reminder for them that life really does suck and the things we do to occupy our time are just acts of deception to bury that cold, hard truth. The words that came from these people often felt more like lectures to make me see reality as they saw it; and my silent nods seemed to confirm for them that, despite Travis's presence, all was ok with the world. I began to experience a strange emotional contradiction. I didn't want anyone to mention Lillian to me, because I didn't want anyone to feel sorry for me; I wanted everyone to stop whatever they were doing and mention Lillian to me, because I wanted everyone to feel sorry for me. So, if something was said, I was angry. If nothing was said, I was angry. I even began to make dumb and even (at times) immoral decisions, compounding my sin with the words "I deserve it." Knowing how stupid and irrational I was behaving and thinking, I thought it might be best that I not go out so much. So I became more and more nonsocial. When I wasn't trolling atheistic websites late at night, I was sitting at home, staring at the wall for hours on end.

During those moments when I was able to look beyond my own pain, the idea that there is an all-powerful and all-loving God became even more insane for me. A heightened sense of awareness of the suffering and evils of the world often hit me like a ton of bricks. After all, Lillian's death happened just one month after 9/11. Since then our nation has involved itself in two wars, has gone through a major economic recession, and has reeled in the wake of natural disasters such as Hurricane Katrina. The world as a whole has seen more of the same: tsunamis, radiation leaks caused by earthquakes, multiple deaths from war (often caused by the US), crimes against humanity on an unbelievable scale. My son at least has his father, along with a loving extended family. Millions of children have no parents, and millions who do are abused in ways we find difficult to imagine. As I processed all of this, mixing it together with my own experience, the words of one of my favorite comedians, George Carlin, rang true:

> But I want you to know something, and this is sincere. I want you to know, when it comes to believing in God, I really tried. I really, really tried. I tried to believe that there is a God, who created each of us in His own image and likeness, loves us very much, and keeps a close eye on things. I really tried to believe that, but I gotta tell you, the longer you live, the more you look around, the more you realize, something is f#@% up.
>
> Something is wrong here. War, disease, death, destruction, hunger, filth, poverty, torture, crime, corruption, and the Ice Capades. Something is definitely wrong. This is not good work. If this is the best God can do, I am not impressed. Results like these do not belong on the résumé of a Supreme Being. This is the kind of s#@^ you'd expect from an office temp with a bad attitude. And just between you and me, in any decently run universe, this guy would've been out on his all-powerful ass a long time ago. And by the way, I say "this guy," because I firmly believe, looking at these results, that if there is a God, it has to be a man. No woman could or would ever f#@% things up like this. So, if there is a God, I think

most reasonable people might agree that he's at least incompetent, and maybe, just maybe, doesn't give a s#@!. Doesn't give a s#@!, which I admire in a person, and which would explain a lot of these bad results.[1]

But there was something deeper bugging me, which nearly solidified my doubts into sheer antitheism. Up until Lillian's death I was a strong Calvinist. We both were. We sincerely believed that God was not only all-powerful and all-good, but that he had foreordained everything that comes to pass, even down to the death of my own mother. Not only so, God is the one who picks and chooses who will and who will not be saved from the eternal fires of hell. Remember the modern version of *A Christmas Carol*, titled *Scrooged*, starring Bill Murray? At the end of the film a young boy says, "God loves everybody." I remember watching that film after converting to Calvinism, and when the boy said those words I rolled my eyes, arrogantly thinking, "Wow, what bad theology!" I simply did not believe that God truly loved anyone unless they were elect. Lillian's death made me wonder about that. I wondered, Is my wife's death a good thing? Obviously not! But isn't love nothing less than willing and trying to accomplish a good thing for someone else? Some people told me that God allows people such as Lillian to die to make us love him more. I remember an atheist philosopher responding quite well to that kind of statement, saying that that's like a father physically abusing his son so that his son will love him more. Isn't God's providentially arranging Lillian's death proof that he doesn't love me? Or, if he does love me, perhaps he just doesn't love me as much as he loves others. After all, most of my friends are raising their children with their wives, and all seems well in their households.

Some Calvinists will interject at this point and insist that God loves me, and the proof of that is that I have placed my trust in Jesus Christ. Only the elect can do such a thing, and so my faith is proof that I am loved by God. But things are not so easy. For there are many who place their faith in Christ, only to later reject him. The options a Calvinist has at this point are painful. For example, one could say that anyone who apostatizes was never

---

a believer to begin with. Really? They sure looked, sounded, and acted like believers! If *all* of them were never believers, then what am I? Here I am, on the edge of losing my faith, learning that I possibly never had faith to begin with! Even worse, if God foreordains everything that comes to pass, then he clearly ordained that I would manifest a less-than-genuine faith in Christ, thereby deceiving myself. I spent years comforting myself with the thought that I belonged to God. Now I thought I was about to learn that such was never the case. True, we are all sinful and so do not deserve God's mercy. But why would God providentially lead me into thinking I am one of his, only to kill my wife and expose my false faith for what it is? Wouldn't it be easier, and even a little nicer, for him to just providentially arrange the world in such a way that I never came to profess Christ as my Savior in the first place? Is God up in his heaven getting his jollies playing with my emotions like this? It may be that such a God is just (though how such actions are consistent with justice is beyond me). But it is totally irrational to call such a God loving. Once again I found an ally in the cynicism of Carlin:

> When it comes to bulls@#!, big-time, major league bulls@#!, you have to stand in awe of the all-time champion of false promises and exaggerated claims—religion. No contest. No contest. Religion. Religion easily has the greatest bull@#! story ever told. Think about it. Religion has actually convinced people that there's an invisible man living in the sky who watches everything you do, every minute of every day. And the invisible man has a special list of ten things he does not want you to do. And if you do any of these ten things, he has a special place, full of fire and smoke and burning and torture and anguish, where he will send you to live and suffer and burn and choke and scream and cry forever and ever 'til the end of time.
> *But He loves you!*[2]

I began to think: If God exists and Calvinism is true, then if I do actually fall away from the faith my apostasy is, at the very least, a revelation of the fact that God never loved me to begin with. This thought haunted me for years.

---

2. www.youtube.com/watch?v=8r-e2wDSTuE&ab_channel=ChrissyA1.

In fact, if Calvinism, as I understood it, is true, there is no reason to think God loves *anyone*. If you believe in Jesus right now, you have no more reason to think you're one of the elect than any apostate out there. You have no genuine hope that a God of love has redeemed you.

Even more so, these disturbing questions do not merely apply to Calvinists. Indeed, can *anyone* who believes in an all-powerful God truly say he is all-loving? He makes a world knowing there will be people who go to hell. Think about that for a moment. *If God is sovereign, he makes people whom he knows will go to hell!* If he does not want them to go to hell, but they go anyway, then he is not sovereign. If he makes them for the purpose of burning in hell forever, then he is not all-loving.

Of course, it's been over ten years since I have entertained these doubts about God's love. I no longer doubt God's existence. Nor do I doubt his sovereignty. And, though I am still a card-carrying Calvinist, I no longer believe God loves only a select few.

What was it that convinced me to stay in the Christian fold and not apostatize? Well, for starters, I would like to share a few sentiments thrown at me that I found utterly unimpressive. First, I was wholly unimpressed with those who threatened me with hell if I ever were to abandon the faith. After all, if God were the sort of sadistic monster my former Calvinism had led me to embrace, then literally nothing I do, including remaining faithful, could ever assure me that I belong to God. Indeed, if God does not love everyone, then I have no reason to think he loves me, in which case my current faith in him may be nothing more than a silly game generated by a divine but sadistic sense of humor. Second, I was not impressed with Christians who told me that I should not ask why. If memory serves, the Psalms are replete with the saints of old who asked God "why" all the time; and Jesus himself asked that very question while he suffered on the cross. Third, I was not impressed with what other religions, with gods far less sovereign, had to offer. A few years after Lillian's passing, I remember some Mormons coming to my home, explaining that the reason they know the Book of Mormon is the word of God is because they feel a burning in their bosom concerning its divine truth. I cynically retorted, "How do you know that your 'burning bosom' is not just an acute case of gas?" Finally, I was not impressed with those who insist that it's all the devil's fault. Indeed,

God made the devil, knowing all along what he would do as well. So the problems raised are just pushed back one step when Satan is invoked as the ultimate solution to the problem of suffering.

A few very important aids were extremely helpful to me as I tried to reconcile Lillian's death with a God of power and love. First, while the truths of the Bible were not an immediate comfort to me, over time they became a balm for my soul. I spent many hours reflecting on the book of Lamentations. I imagined the prophet Jeremiah, watching the temple destroyed by the Babylonians as they razed the holy city to the ground. His suffering was virtually unimaginable. He wrote: "I am a man who has seen affliction under the rod of his wrath; he has driven and brought me into darkness without any light; surely against me he turns his hand again and again the whole day long" (Lam 3:1–3 ESV). I thought, What is greater proof that God is not real? The death of my wife? Or the destruction of the very temple that revealed YHWH's covenant with his people? What is greater proof that God is not real? Cancer? Or the utter destruction of all one takes to be good and holy? "In the dust of the streets lie the young and the old; my young women and my young men have fallen by the sword; you have killed them in the day of your anger, slaughtering without pity" (Lam 2:21 ESV). Jeremiah even watched women eat their own children during the siege of Nebuchadnezzar's armies (Lam 2:20). Am I greater or more privileged than a prophet of God? Then why should my suffering undo me, when his, which was so much greater, actually strengthened his faith? "Remember my affliction and my wanderings, the wormwood and the gall! My soul continually remembers it and is bowed down within me. But this I call to mind, and therefore I have hope: The steadfast love of the LORD never ceases; his mercies never come to an end; they are new every morning; great is your faithfulness. 'The LORD is my portion,' says my soul, 'therefore I will hope in him'" (Lam 3:19–24 ESV).

Second, I did remind myself that I am a sinner who has often disobeyed God. Do I deserve any of the gifts he gives me? Every good thing I have in this life is a gift of his grace. I don't deserve any of it. If the Lord gives it to me, then I should be grateful. If he takes it away, then I should be grateful that he once honored me with it. I am still sad over the loss of Lillian. But I can also honestly say that I would do it all over again for the privilege of loving her. I am so thankful to God for giving her to me for the short season we knew and loved each other. And, while I have suffered great losses in my life—e.g., my wife, my mother, a close friend through suicide, more recently a close uncle through cancer, and even more recently we lost Lillian's father to cancer—I have also enjoyed privileges and gifts most people in history never dared to dream of. The loss of my mother notwithstanding, I experienced a joyful childhood, mainly due to a strong and loving father, who never allowed me to want for anything. I have experienced the wonder of love, along with a beautiful child produced by it. I have lived to see that beautiful baby grow into a strong, intelligent, moral, handsome, and talented young man. I still have my father, who remains my strongest support and confidant. I have a wonderful extended family, including my sister and her family, my stepmother, an aunt, and even Lillian's mother and brothers, who have helped me with my burdens from the time Lillian passed away to this very moment. And I have found love again in a beautiful lady named Jenny, who years ago graciously decided to take me on—even with all of this baggage.

Third, while several Christians proved themselves morons as I mourned my loss, I can honestly say that most of the Christians I know were an immense comfort to me. Most of them are Reformed. I have touching memories of them singing hymns to Lillian in her last hours, calling me often to check up on me after her passing, and weeping with me as I shared my pain with them. They never once tried to defend the faith to me, or offer me words of encouragement, or (even worse) try to explain why this all happened. They simply sat with me and listened as I spoke, nodding their heads empathetically.

Fourth, my friends, both Christian and non-Christian, were eventually willing to give me some tough love after a few years of mourning. As I alluded to before, my mourning went from "oh my, what am I going to do" to "poor pitiful me." While we all need to give those who suffer tragedy some space to mourn, there does come a time when they need to be told, "Look, you've got to start living again." I am immensely thankful for some of those tough words!

Fifth, I read atheists. Yes, I devoured Dawkins's *The God Delusion*, Harris's *The End of Faith*, Hitchens's *God Is Not Great*, Dennett's *Breaking the Spell*,

Loftus's *Why I Became an Atheist*, Carrier's *Sense and Goodness without God*, and so on. Along with Loftus, I read and/or listened to, with great empathy, the deconversion stories of people such as Bart Ehrman and Robert Price. And I reread atheists whom I had read before my loss. I also read many atheistic essays on blogs and in journals. I can honestly say that I truly gave atheism a try. And I gotta say, I have rarely encountered a more incoherent philosophy than atheistic naturalism. The names I have just mentioned are all of people far more intelligent than me; and so I can only wonder why they have embraced such an irrational point of view. I will never forget the feeling I had as I read Dawkins's *God Delusion* for the first time. As I worked my way through his great proof that God was not real, where he triumphantly asks the great unanswerable question, "Who designed the Designer?" I remember thinking, "Is this the best they can do? Really? How embarrassing!" A common rhetorical point often made by the secularist community is, if you want to lose your faith in God then read the Bible. After reading their material I feel something similar: if you don't want to doubt naturalism, or if you think atheists are the rational ones while theists "just have faith," don't ever read a book by a naturalist. Few propositions are more irrational than the statement "God does not exist." Few attitudes are more unlivable than going through life as if there is no God.

Sixth, as I wrestled with the arguments from the secularist community, a thought occurred to me that I simply could not reconcile with the very notion of sanity. Atheists are beautiful people. So are Christians, Muslims, Jews, Hindus, straight people, gay people, black people, brown people, and whatever people. But what does that even mean in an atheistic universe? If there is no god of any kind, and all of reality is the result of space, time, and the meaningless collocations of atoms colliding with one another, then there really is no objective meaning in all of this. As one atheistic philosopher insisted, if there is no God, then there can be meanings *in* life even if there is no meaning *to* life. On this view, I derive meaning from, say, loving my wife in sickness and in health. Or I may choose some other meaning for me—e.g., dedicating my life to science, or medicine, or social justice, or whatever. But, if there is no god of any kind, and if all is the result of space and time and random atomistic collisions, then my choosing to do these things is no more significant than a person choosing to rearrange furniture on the Titanic. You may create some comfort for a few hours, but the ship is going down anyway. Indeed, loving a person, saving a person's life, or even finding a cure for cancer ultimately means nothing when we realize that human existence will eventually perish. I hate the fact that Lillian died. That has been a very troubling fact to deal with. But the thought that her life and death consisted of nothing more than the meaningless rearrangement of biological chemicals is even more disturbing. The thought that God took her is extremely painful. It sucks. However, the thought that she, my beautiful bride, is not really, objectively, beautiful at all, but is just a bag of chemicals that experienced a genetic anomaly, having been naturally selected for extinction, is just unbearable. How does one derive meaning from tragedy? Not through naturalism! If naturalism is true, life and death are "just so stories" that end in the extinction of the species. If naturalism is true, I will never see Lillian again. None of us will. Evan will never know his mother! At this point someone like Dawkins will say, "Too bad." And he has a point. Nothing I am saying here proves that God exists. But it does raise the question: If this is the end game of naturalism, then there really is no difference in belief and nonbelief. Pascal was right; if I reject God and he doesn't exist, then I am okay; if I reject him and he does, then I not only face his judgment, but I miss out on the opportunity to spend an eternity with those I love.

Seventh, I read Christians. I read and reread works by Augustine and Thomas Aquinas. I also read modern Christians such as Reginald Garrigou-Lagrange, Alvin Plantinga, William Lane Craig, Richard Swinburne, John Feinberg, Gary Habermas, Hugh Ross, Ken Samples, and C. S. Lewis. I also watched numerous debates on the existence of God, which featured many of these apologists' encounters with those in the secularist community. My own assessment is that, overall, these thinkers offered a more robust, intellectually compelling, and evidentially powerful case for Christian theism than did their atheistic counterparts for naturalism.

Finally, I have seen good come from Lillian's death. Here I would like to offer three examples of this. First, I have seen myself grow into a better person. I realize that this may sound arrogant for some readers. After all, none of us are perfect. But, though still extremely flawed, I am better. I have a better sense of who I am, as well as a better worldview—e.g., I no longer believe God only loves his elect. I have experienced the Lord's provision in the midst of my loss, including my acquiring a good job and a wonderful education for my son, and I have become a more grateful person because of it. Also, Lillian's brother, Kimbell, was still a college student as he watched his sister die. Just before her death the doctor who performed the liver biopsy spoke with our family. At one point in the discussion he said, "All I know is what goes on from 'here to here' (pointing to the area of the body containing the liver)." Kimbell was so angered at the detached and impersonal attitude of the doctor, who dissected his sister down to the liver (cutting the rest of her away), that he became interested in palliative care. His MD has given him the skills to work in the field of medicine; and his PhD in theology is allowing him to make contributions in the field of ethics—most notably, in setting forth a case for a more holistic approach to health care. And then there is Lillian's father, Paul Kornu. She always said that her death would be worth it if her parents came to know Christ as their Savior. After her passing, Paul began to reflect very seriously on his own mortality and often spoke in awe with his sons of the fortitude and grace Lillian manifested as she suffered. After years of reading portions of the New Testament, speaking with his sons and me, and reflecting on his beloved daughter, he finally informed his older son, Roger, that he had received Christ as his Savior. As I write these words, Paul's death occurred just over a week ago. On Monday, January 7 (2019), as he lay in bed—his body riddled with cancer—he informed his wife and sons that he would be dead within three days. On Wednesday, as he was letting go, his sons informed him that Evan would soon be at his side. Evan did arrive, at which moment Paul found himself with his immediate family—his lovely wife, Pia, Roger, Kimbell, and the spirit of Lillian through her son. He was truly at peace. Within one hour he was gone. God has truly drawn much good from a terrible evil. And the good news that gives me great joy is that Paul has been reunited with Lillian—a joyful reunion that will be surpassed when we all pass on to the next life, united once again in the covenantal bonds of God's unfailing love.

None of what I am saying, of course, answers the points I have made against the existence of a sovereign and loving God. But they hopefully explain, even if generally, how I retained my faith in God in the midst of tragedy.

So, how do I reconcile the existence of God with the evils and sufferings of our world? More particularly, how do I reconcile God's power with his love? This book seeks to answer that very question. At the end of this work, I hope the reader will have good reason to believe that God is an absolute sovereign who genuinely and savingly loves every human person.

2

COMING TO TERMS WITH TERMS

Finis origine pendet

One of the most important things a seeker of truth can do—regardless of the field of inquiry—is to master the terms, jargon, and nomenclature that have for some time guided the discussion under consideration. Both theology and philosophy involve conversations that have a long history, going back to the dawn of Western civilization—even back to the dawn of human existence itself. Given this history, labels for various viewpoints have come and gone. That said, while more than a few terms have changed over the years, the concepts conveyed through such terminology have largely stayed the same. For those not familiar with the subject we are about to address, I will offer a brief crash course on theological and philosophical terms. For more detail, any standard theological or philosophical dictionary can be helpful.[1]

THEISM

The term "theism" (aka "monotheism") is often associated with an overarching philosophy or worldview or way of seeing reality, shared by the three great monotheistic religions (i.e., Judaism, Christianity, and Islam). The term comes from the Greek word *theos*, meaning "God." Monotheism (i.e., *mono* [one] + *theos* [God]), simply refers to "the belief in one supreme reality, or God." Historically, theists have (at a minimum) maintained a belief in a single God who is a personal Spirit and possesses the attributes

---

1. For two examples in theology, see Sinclair B. Ferguson and David F. Wright, eds., *New Dictionary of Theology* (Downers Grove, IL: InterVarsity Press, 1988); Walter A. Elwell, ed., *Evangelical Dictionary of Theology*, 2nd ed. (Grand Rapids: Baker, 2001). For philosophy, see Robert Audi, ed., *The Cambridge Dictionary of Philosophy* (Cambridge: Cambridge University Press, 1995).

of omnipotence (i.e., the property of being all-powerful), omniscience (i.e., the property of being all-knowing), and omnibenevolence (i.e., the property of being all-good and all-loving). In addition, monotheists have maintained that God is the Designer and Creator of the entire cosmos from nothing; he continues to sustain or preserve the universe in existence; and he is himself the locus of all moral values.

There are actually two ways one can begin to get a handle on the concept of God maintained by monotheists. First, one can contrast the theistic view of God with its alternatives. Second, one can contrast schools of thought *within* theism itself. Both are helpful.

ALTERNATIVES TO THEISM

The way one thinks about God is front and center of one's outlook on life (i.e., one's worldview). Hence, we often name worldviews after the view of God expressed in them. The reader may be surprised to learn that there are only five worldviews humans have entertained throughout history, at least with respect to the nature of the divine—namely, polytheism, pantheism, panentheism, atheism, and theism.[2]

POLYTHEISM

Polytheism (i.e., *poly* [many] + *theos* [god]) is the belief that there are many gods out there—perhaps even an infinite number of them. These divine beings, having come into existence thousands (if not millions or billions) of years ago, are extremely powerful with respect to us humans. They are also incredibly intelligent. Some gods are quite moral, while others are immoral, and still others are a mixture of the two (similar to humans).

While polytheism and monotheism have a few common features, the differences between these two perspectives far outweigh the similarities. For example, like monotheism, the gods of the pantheon are personal. Like theism, the gods have been around for a long time. Like theism, the gods are interested in human interactions, and both require the worship of the deity from their respective adherents. However, unlike theism, the gods are finite with respect to power, knowledge, goodness, and even time (i.e., all gods are

---

2. To be sure, within each worldview one will find much diversity. So, for example, among monotheists one will find the debate between Judaism, Christianity, and Islam.

made by the forces of this universe). Hence, theists have often shied away from polytheism due to the paradox of worshiping a finite reality. For if a god is finite in power, then he or she cannot be fully trusted; and if a god is finite in goodness, then he or she cannot be fully adored; and since trust and adoration are the heart of any meaningful form of worship, it would seem that the gods themselves are simply not worthy of such devotion.[3]

PANTHEISM

Pantheism (i.e., *pan* [all] + *theos* [god]) is the belief that everything we encounter is either divine (or God) or one with the divine. That is to say, "all is God." Another label for this worldview is "monism" (from *mono* [one]), meaning "all is one." As God himself is eternal, the universe (since it too is divine) must be eternal as well. As God is necessarily existent (i.e., God must exist; or God cannot *not* exist), the universe *must* exist also. As God

---

3. Perhaps the most popular form of polytheism today is Mormonism, which actually advocates a form of henotheism (i.e., there are many gods, but humans are morally obligated to worship only one—namely, Elohim). Of course, Mormonism has evolved over the years, but even its most careful scholars are quick to insist that humans are only different in degree from God; they are not different in kind—hence Mormons explicitly deny the Creator-creature distinction. As Mormon apologist Stephen Robinson explains: "The soil from which the LDS doctrine of deification grows is the belief that humans are of the divine species and that the scriptural language of divine paternity is not merely figurative." Hence, "in our saved and glorified state we will be what God is through God's grace, even in God's so-called incommunicable attributes." Elsewhere Robinson writes: "Nothing I say here should be interpreted as denying the importance for Mormonism of God's corporeality and God's nature as an exalted man. Neither am I denying the importance of LDS belief that we humans are literally God's children and can become what God is. These are linchpins in LDS theology." Stephen Robinson, "God and Deification," in *How Wide the Divide? A Mormon and an Evangelical in Conversation*, by Craig L. Blomberg and Stephen E. Robinson (Downers Grove, IL: InterVarsity Press, 1997), 82, 91. For two helpful critiques of Mormonism, see Francis J. Beckwith, Carl Moser, and Paul Owen, eds., *The New Mormon Challenge: Responding to the Latest Defenses of a Fast-Growing Movement* (Grand Rapids: Zondervan, 2002); and Ron Rhodes and Marian Bodine, *Reasoning from the Scriptures with the Mormons* (Eugene, OR: Harvest House, 1995).

One line of argumentation supporting the notion that God and humanity, the human and the divine, are on a scale of being (or are of the same "divine species")—in which case one differs only in degree from the other—is found in a good number of OT studies wherein it is argued that the ancient Hebrews were originally polytheistic but eventually adopted an exclusively monotheistic worldview—chiefly via the mind-numbing and soul-forging experience of the Babylonian exile of the sixth century BC. For just one study defending such a thesis, see William G. Dever, *Did God Have a Wife? Archeology and Folk Religion in Ancient Israel* (Grand Rapids: Eerdmans, 2005). For a critique of this and other "religious evolutionary hypotheses," see John N. Oswalt, *The Bible among the Myths* (Grand Rapids: Zondervan, 2009); and Winfried Corduan, *In the Beginning God: A Fresh Look at the Case for Original Monotheism* (Nashville: B&H, 2013).

is infinite, the universe must be so as well. As God is absolutely one, the universe is as well. The question that naturally arises is, *If everything is God, then I am as well; but if I am God, how is it that I experience change, limitation, and diversity in my everyday experience?* The Eastern pantheist will say that such experiences are *maya*. The Western monist will say that your senses are deceiving you. In short, all manifestations of change, diversity, and finitude are illusions.

Theism and pantheism have several important similarities. For example, like pantheists, theists commonly believe that God is one, infinite, eternal, and necessarily existent. However, pantheists, unlike theists, reject the personality of God, as well as the real distinction between God and the cosmos—i.e., the Creator/creature distinction. For this reason, theists have rejected pantheistic monism precisely because it is difficult, if not impossible, to have an eternal love-relationship with something impersonal. Genuine worship also seems unlikely, if not utterly infeasible, on the monistic model. For if there is no real difference between myself and God, then at the end of the day there really is nothing to worship except myself. As nineteenth-century theologian Charles Hodge notes:

> Pantheism ... renders all rational religion impossible. Religion supposes a personal Being endowed not only with intelligence and power, but with moral excellence; and to be rational, that Being must be infinite in all his perfections. Pantheism, however, denies that an infinite Being can be a person; that is, intelligent, self-conscious, or possessed of moral attributes. It is just impossible to worship such a Being as it is to worship the atmosphere, or the law of gravitation, or the axioms of Euclid.[4]

---

4. Charles Hodge, *Systematic Theology* (New York: Charles Scribner's Sons, 1872–73), 1:333. For expositions of pantheism, one can do no better than Plotinus's *Enneads* and Spinoza's *Ethics*. For helpful critiques of pantheism, see David K. Clark and Norman L. Geisler, *Apologetics in the New Age: A Christian Critique of Pantheism* (Grand Rapids: Baker, 1990); Douglas R. Groothius, *Unmasking the New Age* (Downers Grove, IL: InterVarsity Press, 1986); and Groothuis, *Confronting the New Age* (Downers Grove, IL: InterVarsity Press, 1988).

PANENTHEISM

Panentheism (i.e., *pan* [all] + *en* [in] + *theos* [god]) is the belief that all or everything is in God and God is in everything. The idea here is that the world is just as dependent on God as God is dependent on the world. Or, in the words of one its greatest proponents, "It is as true to say that God creates the world as it is to say that the world creates God."[5] As this philosopher explains, many try to conceive of God as the grand exception to all of the change, procession, temporality, contingencies, insubstantiality, and uncertainty of our world—proffered in order to save the contingent cosmos from metaphysical collapse. However, according to panentheism, God is not the exception to these mundane properties but is rather their chief exemplification.[6] The world is insubstantial, so is God; the world is evolving, so is God; the world is in process, so is God. God does not stand in an absolute relationship to the world but is in fact relativized by it (and vice versa). God is really a *process*, not and *entity*. Hence, this perspective is also called "process theology" or "process philosophy" and even "co-relativism." This viewpoint is also known as dipolar theism, since on this model there are two poles in God—i.e., an actual pole, corresponding to the world; and a potential pole, corresponding to the ideals the world is striving toward. Hence, the divine-cosmos relationship is to be likened to the soul-body dynamic—i.e., God is to the world what the soul or spirit is to the body (or what the mind is to the brain). Just as the soul activates the body, and the mind gives the brain goals to strive for, so also God animates the universe and gives it its ideals.

Once again there is much theists have in common with panentheists. For example, like process theologians, theists believe that God infuses the universe with meaning, value, and goals to achieve. Like panentheism, theism insists that we can relate to God. And, like co-relativism, the theist thinks of God as immanent in the world. However, there are some important differences between these two perspectives, rendering them irreconcilable. For example, theists believe God creates the universe from nothing, while panentheists believe the universe (precisely because it is God's body)

---

5. Whitehead, *Process and Reality*, ed. David Griffin and Donald Sherborne (New York: Free Press, 1978), 348.

6. Whitehead, *Process and Reality*, 343.

is eternal;[7] theists believe God is omniscient, while panentheists think God's knowledge of the future is limited, and the trend among process theists is to assert the same about God's present knowledge;[8] and theists believe God is omnipotent, while process theologians reject the notion of an almighty

---

7. In the words of Griffin, "This idea does not entail that our particular universe, which evidently has existed for only ten to twenty billion years, exists naturally, but only that some world or other—some plurality of finite actualities—always exists." David Griffin, "Process Theology and the Christian Good News: A Response to Classical Free Will Theism," in *Searching for an Adequate God: A Dialogue between Process and Free Will Theists* (ed. John B. Cobb Jr. and Clark H. Pinnock; Grand Rapids: Eerdmans, 2000), 6.

8. In the words of Cobb and Griffin: "For example, to say that God is omniscient means that in every moment of the divine life God knows everything which is knowable at that time. The concrete actuality is temporal, relative, dependent, and constantly changing. In each moment of God's life there are new, unforeseen happenings in the world which only then have become knowable. Hence, God's knowledge is dependent upon the decisions made by the worldly actualities. God's knowledge is always relativized by, in the sense of internally related to, the world." John B. Cobb Jr. and David Ray Griffin, *Process Theology: An Introductory Exposition* (Philadelphia: Westminster, 1976), 47–48. Hasker sees this definition of "omniscience" (i.e., "knowing everything knowable" or "knowing whatever is possible for a perfect being to know") as a point of contact between process theism and so-called open-view theism (see William Hasker, "An Adequate God," in *Searching for an Adequate God*, 218).

The denial of an exhaustive present knowledge in God is only implicitly given among some panentheists, while it is explicitly given in others. That said, I tend to think this implication is a good and necessary consequence of several core panentheistic beliefs. Indeed, Griffin lists as a core process belief the notion that "all enduring individuals are personally ordered societies of occasions of experience" ("Process Theology," 4). As he goes on to say, "Each actual entity exists in two modes, first as a subject, then as an object. Its existence as a subject begins with its reception of efficient causation from prior actual entities (its physical pole) and ends with its exercise of self-determination (its mental pole). Then, with the perishing of its subjectivity, it exists as an object for subsequent subjects, which means that it exerts efficient causation on them" ("Process Theology," 4–5). Gruenler, himself a former panentheist, offers as an analogy "the one true ring" from J. R. R. Tolkien's *Lord of the Rings*. Whenever a character from Tolkien's universe (e.g., Bilbo Baggins) places the ring on his finger, he becomes invisible. *That* is your present moment of subjectivity. *That* is the moment when you are completely autonomous, when no one can touch you, and when you can act in a wholly self-determined manner. When a character takes off the ring, he becomes visible again. *That* is the moment of objectivity, when anyone can see you (at least in principle), and your efficient actions affect the world. Just as we can imagine a Tolkien character slipping the ring on and off in rapid succession, thereby becoming visible and invisible with the same rapidity, so also Griffin speaks "of the perpetual oscillation between subjectivity and objectivity" ("Process Theology," 5), where, presumably, we constantly perish as subjects, emerge as objects, perish as objects, emerge as subjects, etc. Gruenler then draws out the logical consequence of the process metaphysic: "What does God experience about us, then? He cannot experience our present while we are making our free decisions and he cannot experience the future we haven't yet met. There is only one segment of time left where God is free to poke about our affairs: the past. After we have made our decisions and chosen from several possibilities while wearing the ring of invisibility, then and only then are we willing to take off the ring and let our finished acts and words appear visibly before God." Royce Gruenler, "Reflections on a Journey in Process," in *Process Theology*, ed. Ronald H. Nash (Grand Rapids: Baker, 1987), 336.

God.[9] For precisely these reasons, theists reject the process model of God. And, just like pantheism and polytheism, panentheism has a difficult time reconciling itself to a genuine worship of the deity. For if God is constantly in process, then what exactly are we worshiping when we offer praise or prayer to him? If this process is, as Whitehead tells us, the chief exemplar of all the things we experience—including their mutability and insubstantiality—then worshiping God is no different from adoring a star, or a speck of dust, or a starfish. But if the divine process is distinct from all the other processes we experience, then how does it serve as the world's chief exemplification?

As we have seen, the tendency among process thinkers is to see God's knowledge of even the present as limited—for if God's knowledge exhausts the present moment, how can I be truly free if there is someone constantly watching everything I am currently doing? But then it would seem that panentheism places a rational religious experience beyond our grasp. Indeed, to have a genuine experience with the divine presupposes the possibility of God knowing me and me knowing God in the present moment. But this mutual experiential relationship between Creator and creature becomes impossible on the process model. For God is not truly our Creator, and he lacks a present knowledge of human activity. Hence, a relationship with God is virtually impossible if panentheism is true. In the words of one former process theologian:

> If God never knows us as we are in our lively moments of experiencing and choosing ..., then what he finally sees ... is not our complete self. The past he sees is minus all that former vitality of the living self. All he sees is a dead shell, a chambered nautilus. Everything vital has been lost forever. God can't remember it because he can't see it. ... [Panentheism] is indeed a tragic vision.[10]

---

9. In the words of Griffin, "I, following Hartshorne, have argued that 'the traditional conception of omnipotence is incoherent'" ("In Response to Hasker," in *Searching for an Adequate God*, 256). See also Charles Hartshorne, *Omnipotence and Other Theological Mistakes* (Albany, NY: SUNY Press, 1984).

10. Gruenler, "Reflections on a Journey in Process," 337. Perhaps the best exposition of panentheism or process theology is found in Cobb and Griffin, *Process Theology*. For helpful critiques of panentheism, see Nash, *Process Theology*; and Royce Gordon Gruenler, *The Inexhaustible God: Biblical Faith and the Challenge of Process Theism* (Grand Rapids: Baker, 1983).

ATHEISM

Atheism (i.e., *a* [no] + *theos* [God]) is the belief that there is no god or deity of any kind. The twentieth century saw atheists become quite sensitive over the matter of definitions, for the one we just gave suggests that atheists actually believe in something—i.e., that the proposition "God does not exist" is true. But, then, this places the atheist in a dilemma. That is, if one affirms such a proposition, is one not also obligated to bear some burden to prove that it is true? It would seem so. But, then again, proving the existence of a negative is notoriously difficult. How could one prove there is no gold in Alaska? How could one prove that invisible gremlins are not reading Hegel on the dark side of the moon? And so, most atheists are content to define their atheism as "a lack of belief in anything supernatural." An atheist, then, is not someone who believes there is no God; rather, an atheist is someone who simply does not believe anything about God, including the proposition "God exists." *Does God exist?* These atheists are known to say, "I have no idea!" *Do you believe there's a God?* "No!" In fact, it has become common to distinguish between two kinds of atheists. On the one hand, there is the negative atheist (aka *the implicit atheist*), who simply lacks theistic belief. All atheists are negative atheists. On the other hand, there is the positive atheist (aka *the explicit atheist*), who actually affirms the proposition "There is no god of any kind." Such atheists are known to actually offer arguments demonstrating, or (at least) strongly suggesting, that no god of any kind exists.[11]

Theists have shied away from atheism for obvious reasons. But this rejection is as much a *human* rejection as it is a theistic one. While religious believers and seekers of all stripes should commend atheists' commitment to rationality, science, exploration, and even skepticism,[12] with good reason they have a difficult time reconciling their own attitudes on how they are to conduct themselves in this world with the notion that there is absolutely no overarching plan, purpose, or person to which (or to whom) we owe

---

11. For what is perhaps the best articulation and defense of these distinctions, see George Smith, *Atheism: The Case against God* (Buffalo, NY: Prometheus, 1976), 3–28; see also Michael Martin, *Atheism: A Philosophical Justification* (Philadelphia: Temple University Press, 1990), 29–39.

12. At least, when defined as a reasonable stance whereby one will not accept a conclusion until there is good and sufficient evidence supporting it.

our existence. G. K. Chesterton made our point long ago in his now-famous quotation: "The worst moment for an atheist is when he is really thankful and has no one to thank." For example, after his nightmarish experience in the wake of a heart attack, atheist philosopher Daniel Dennett felt the pinch of Chesterton's point, going so far as to write an essay on the issue of thankfulness. His moving essay, "Thank Goodness," offers an account of how atheists can be truly thankful wholly apart from any religious or spiritual beliefs. At one point he writes:

> To whom, then, do I owe a debt of gratitude? To the cardiologist who has kept me alive and ticking for years, and who swiftly and confidently rejected the original diagnosis of nothing worse than pneumonia. To the surgeons, neurologists, anesthesiologists, and the perfusionist, who kept my systems going for many hours under daunting circumstances. To the dozen or so physician assistants, and to nurses and physical therapists and x-ray technicians and a small army of phlebotomists so deft that you hardly know they are drawing your blood, and the people who brought the meals, kept my room clean, did the mountains of laundry generated by such a messy case, wheel-chaired me to x-ray, and so forth. These people came from Uganda, Kenya, Liberia, Haiti, the Philippines, Croatia, Russia, China, Korea, India—and the United States, of course—and I have never seen more impressive mutual respect, as they helped each other out and checked each other's work. But for all their team-work, this local gang could not have done their jobs without the huge background of contributions from others. I remember with gratitude my late friend and Tufts colleague, physicist Allan Cormack, who shared the Nobel Prize for his invention of the c-t scanner. Allan—you have posthumously saved yet another life, but who's counting? The world is better for the work you did. Thank goodness. Then there is the whole system of medicine, both the science and the technology, without which the best-intentioned efforts of individuals would be roughly useless. So I am grateful to the editorial boards and referees, past and present, of Science, Nature, Journal of the American Medical Association, Lancet, and all the

other institutions of science and medicine that keep churning out improvements, detecting and correcting flaws.[13]

Dennett's words of gratitude for everyone who helped him in his struggles are an example for us all. How often do religious persons love to thank God without thanking others who offered their help in a time of need? And so, while reflecting on how kind Dennett's sentiments are, it is easy to pass over the strange line he delivers close to the end of the paragraph: "Allan—you have posthumously saved yet another life, but who's counting? The world is better for the work you did." Despite his atheism, his gratitude compels him to offer words of thanks to his dead friend—who, according to Dennett himself, does not exist anymore! Why is Dennett, who is literally going out of his way to demonstrate the rational superiority of "thanking goodness" rather than "thanking God," succumbing to such impulses? Indeed, at one point he even expresses his gratitude that his emergency occurred at the precise time it did, for if it had not done so, he would not be writing his words of thanksgiving.[14] This virtually irrepressible compulsion to thank forces outside of our control for our good fortune suggests a strong human tendency to worship. Theism accounts for Dennett's behavior by pointing out that he, like all of us, is made in the divine image, which compels him to be grateful to something bigger than himself.[15]

---

13. Daniel C. Dennett, "Thank Goodness," Huffpost, updated December 6, 2017, https://www.huffingtonpost.com/daniel-c-dennett/thank-goodness_b_33207.html.

14. Dennett, "Thank Goodness." In his own words, "Had I had my blasted aorta a decade ago, there would have been no prayer of saving me. It's hardly routine today, but the odds of my survival were actually not so bad (these days, roughly 33 percent of aortic dissection patients die in the first twenty-four hours after onset without treatment, and the odds get worse by the hour thereafter)."

15. I maintain that the best defenses of atheism, despite so many books that have been produced over the past decade or so by the so-called new atheists, are J. L. Mackie, *The Miracle of Theism: Arguments for and against the Existence of God* (Oxford: Clarendon, 1982); and, on a more popular level, Smith, *Atheism*. For two helpful critiques of atheism, see Edward Feser, *The Last Superstition: A Refutation of the New Atheism* (South Bend, IN: St. Augustine's Press, 2008); and Frank Turek, *Stealing from God: Why Atheists Need God to Make Their Case* (Colorado Springs: NavPress, 2014).

ALTERNATIVES WITHIN THEISM

The common theme we encountered while looking at the nontheistic worldviews was the issue of worship. Two questions confront us. First, why do humans feel compelled to thank invisible forces for their good fortune? Traditional theists answer that God has made all humans in his image, and so it is only natural for us to worship something greater than ourselves. Second, what conception of the divine or "that which is greater" is most appropriate for worship? In other words, is there a being "out there" who is truly worthy of our deep sense of gratitude for our own existence, as well as the good fortune we often experience? The theist answers in the affirmative, insisting that God is intrinsically worthy of our complete trust, commitment, obedience, and adoration.

As we have already noted, theists minimally believe in a deity who is all-knowing, all-powerful, and all-good. They also affirm God as Creator of the universe out of nothing (*ex nihilo*), Sustainer of the cosmos, and the supreme Moral Lawgiver. Beyond these basic beliefs, modern theists can be broadly distinguished into two schools of thought—i.e., *classical theism* and *theistic personalism*.

CLASSICAL THEISM

This tradition stretches back to the dawn of the common era, wherein first-century Jewish philosophers such as Philo began to integrate Hebrew theology with Greek philosophy. By the time we reach the second century, Christian apologists such as Justin Martyr were arguing that the highest ideals championed by the Greek philosophers were fulfilled by Christ, and hence what is most pure and perfect in the Greek mind comes from reflecting on truth offered in God's revelation in nature. Later theologians such as Athanasius (fourth century), Augustine (fifth century), Boethius (sixth century), Anselm (eleventh century), Aquinas (thirteenth century), and Scotus (thirteenth–fourteenth centuries) all adhered to this classical synthesis between Greco-Roman and Judeo-Christian thought. Still later, the Magisterial Reformers of the sixteenth century (e.g., Luther, Melanchthon, Zwingli, Calvin, Bullinger, etc.), along with their successors (e.g., Arminius, Beza, Owen, Turretin, and Limborch), and even their Catholic rivals (e.g., Cajetan, Báñez, and Molina), while disagreeing with one another on numerous important issues, nevertheless all affirmed the basic conception of God championed by the early Christian fathers—i.e., the classical conception of the divine.

WHAT IS THE CLASSICAL
CONCEPTION OF GOD?

Classical theists move beyond the minimalist affirmation of an all-knowing, all-powerful, and all-good deity, insisting that we should follow Anselm, who taught us that God is the "greatest conceivable being." For, if we were to conceive of anything greater than God, then *that* would be God. Indeed, Scripture itself confirms this intuition when it tells us that God can swear by no one greater than himself (Heb 6:13). For the classicist, the most fundamental of the divine attributes is God's self-existence or aseity. That is to say, God exists *a se* (i.e., from himself), being uncaused, uncreated, and independent of the creature. The aseity of the divine nature entails that God must transcend whatever pertains to the created order. So, for example, the created order is bound to time, where all moments are measured in accordance with a before and an after. God, then, is eternal precisely because he is atemporal or timeless and so does not experience a succession of moments. The universe exists within space. Hence God is literally spaceless. As a timeless and nonspatial being, God, precisely because he does not occupy a particular spatial location, must be omnipresent and hence immaterial. God must also be simple. In the words of Brian Davies, "classical theists" say "that God is entirely simple. They do not, of course, mean that he is stupid or unintelligent (one sense of 'simple'). What, then, do they mean? ... For the present," it means "in part that God is not a member of any genus or species."[16] The great Arminian systematician Philipp van Limborch describes simplicity as follows:

> By the *absolute simplicity* of God we mean his Freedom from all kind of Composition or Mixture, either of Principles or of Parts: For he is not only *One*, but as he is a *Spirit*, he is exempt from all manner of Composition whatever. Reason itself teaches us, that God

---

16. Brian Davies, *An Introduction to the Philosophy of Religion*, 3rd ed. (Oxford: Oxford University Press, 2004), 8–9.

cannot be compounded of any Principles, because the Principles and Ingredients which concur to the making of any thing, must be antecedent to that thing. And if the Divine Nature were compounded, it would follow that there must be something in Nature before him, which is inconsistent with his being the first Cause.[17]

---

17. Philipp van Limborch, *A Compleat System, or Body of Divinity, Both Speculative and Practical, Founded on Scripture and Reason*, trans. William Jones (London, 1702; repr., London: Forgotten Books, 2015), 1:56, italics original. A modern rendition of this argument, inspired by Plantinga, can be worded as follows (using one divine attribute for simplicity's sake): either God has the property of goodness or he does not; if he does, then he is not sovereign—for in order for him to possess the real property of goodness, goodness must exist independently of him (i.e., God is good because he conforms to the standard of goodness)—and if he does not, then he does not have a good nature. Indeed, if God possesses no properties, then he possesses no nature at all. The classicist way out of the dilemma is simplicity. God is simple in that he is his own goodness; or, goodness is not a property distinct from God but is wholly identical with the divine nature itself. Hence, God is both sovereign and has a nature. Nash, at least, concedes that, having rejected the divine simplicity, he lacks a full answer to this dilemma. See Ronald H. Nash, *The Concept of God: An Exploration of Contemporary Difficulties with the Attributes of God* (Grand Rapids: Zondervan, 1983), 96-97; Alvin Plantinga, *Does God Have a Nature?* (Milwaukee: Marquette University Press, 1980), 46-61.

Craig, in his impressive work on abstract objects, also inadvertently offers a strong argument for divine simplicity. In a chapter where he tries to show that God alone exists necessarily and uncaused, he gives "a powerful philosophico-theological argument against the existence of uncreated, Platonic properties" that exist alongside God. In other words, there are no abstract objects or universals (e.g., "goodness," the number two, or the laws of logic) that exist independently of God himself. They are either wholly nonexistent ideas or names we use to group objects of experience (i.e., nominalism), or they are ideas that inhere simply in the divine mind (i.e., conceptualism). Of course, other options are available. That said, here is Craig's argument: "Consider the cluster of divine attributes which go to make up God's nature [e.g., omnipotence, omniscience, omnibenevolence]. Call that nature *deity*. On Platonism, *deity* is an abstract object existing independently of God, to which God stands in the relation of exemplification or instantiation." To take our earlier example, there is the property of "goodness," which (on Platonism) God exemplifies just in case he is good. Craig continues: "Moreover, it is in virtue of standing in relation to this object that God is divine. He is God because He exemplifies *deity*. Thus, on Platonism, God does not really exist *a se* at all. For God depends on this abstract object for His existence. Platonism does not simply postulate some object existing independently of God—a serious enough compromise of God's sole ultimacy—but makes God dependent upon this object, thus denying the divine aseity. The implication? 'So deity/the Platonic realm, not God, is the ultimate reality.'" William Lane Craig, *God over All: Divine Aseity and the Challenge of Platonism* (Oxford: Oxford University Press, 2016), 43, italics original, quoting Brian Leftow (who is credited with the original version of this argument), *God and Necessity* (Oxford: Oxford University Press, 2012), 235.

But it gets even worse for the theist, if that were possible. As Craig argues: "Since aseity, like omnipotence, is one of the essential attributes of God included in *deity*, it turns out that God does not exemplify *deity* after all. Since aseity is essential to *deity* and God, on Platonism, does not exist *a se*, it turns out that God does not exist. On Platonism, there may [be] a demiurge, such as is featured in Plato's *Timaeus*, but the God of classical theism does not exist. Theism is thus undone by Platonism" (*God over All*, 43, italics original). This places us on the horns of a dilemma. We could follow Craig and deny abstract objects altogether, thereby

WHAT IS THOMISM?

Thomism is perhaps the most popular version of classical theism being promoted today. It gets its name from Thomas Aquinas (1224/5-74), a Dominican monk who sought to synthesize the thought of Aristotle (384–322 BC) with that of Augustine (354-430). Thus, while Thomas was fond of using Aristotelian language, his goal was to demonstrate the rationality of Augustinian theology by showing how easily it could be explained and defended using the terminology of the great philosopher. For example, Aristotle accounted for the distinctions between things using the categories of actuality and potentiality. That is, the things we see *actually* exist, but have the *potential* to be other than what they are. Thomas expanded on this idea, teaching us that, in the created realm, all of reality is composed of actuality and potentiality, and hence in all created things there is a real potential for differentiation. For Aquinas, God is distinct from the created realm precisely because he is not composed of actuality and potentiality. He is pure actuality with no potentiality. In fact, God is simple in that, as van Limborch points out, he is not composed in any way whatsoever. He is not composed of matter and form, since he is immaterial and thus pure form. He is not composed of essence and existence because his essence is to exist and thus he is pure *esse*. He does not have power. He *is* power. He does not have knowledge. He *is* knowledge. He does not have goodness. He *is* goodness. If God "had" any of his properties or attributes, he *could* lose them (at least in principle), which entails that he would be a being in potential and hence not pure act. Also, he would not be absolutely sovereign (as we

embracing a sort of "Christian nominalism" (see Craig, *God over All*). However, for those of us who think we are making an ontological commitment when we say, for example, "the law of noncontradiction is true," this kind of nominalism becomes problematic. On the other hand, we could embrace Platonism, but then we would have to reject theism (as Craig well argues). I think the best way out of this dilemma is the classical doctrine of divine simplicity and conceptualism (i.e., the doctrine that all truly existing abstract objects are ideas of the divine mind). It seems to be the only way to adopt all of the good insights of Plato, to affirm that God has a nature, and to also embrace the aseity of the divine essence. Note in this connection the words of Edward Feser: "From the classical theist point of view, to deny simplicity is implicitly to affirm atheism." Feser, *Five Proofs of God* (San Francisco: Ignatius Press, 2017), 195. For more on the issue of God and abstract objects, see *Beyond the Control of God? Six Views on the Problem of God and Abstract Objects*, ed. Paul M. Gould (New York: Bloomsbury, 2014).

have seen). Thus, he is whatever he "has." To give one more example, God does not have existence, he *is* existence. He is the *Great I AM* (Exod 3:14).[18]

THEISTIC PERSONALISM

This is a largely modern movement that, though inspired by much in the classical tradition, shies away from many of its convictions. Among the theistic personalists one will find some of the best twentieth- and twenty-first-century thinkers who have written on the issue of God's existence and attributes, including Ronald Nash, Alvin Plantinga, Richard Swinburne, William Lane Craig, Stephen Davis, Clark Pinnock, Gregory Boyd, Charles Hartshorne, and John Cobb. To be sure, there are more than a few differences between these thinkers on more than a few topics. For example, Pinnock and Boyd are open theists, claiming that God does not possess an exhaustive knowledge of the future—i.e., God lacks the property of omniprescience. Craig and Plantinga, on the other hand, are ardent defenders of omniprescience. Hartshorne and Cobb are process theologians, as we have seen. The other thinkers listed above would reject most, if not all, elements of process theology.[19] Craig and Plantinga adhere to Molina's doctrine of middle knowledge,[20] while the other thinkers listed reject it.

WHAT IS THEISTIC PERSONALISM?

Despite their diverse approaches to the divine nature, theistic personalists are labeled as such because of their insistence that it is the *personhood* of God that should be front and center in our thinking rather than, say, the divine aseity. To be sure, most theistic personalists would heartily affirm God's self-existence,[21] and yet they tend to analyze this conception of God via what it means to be a *person who is self-existent*. Most theistic personalists would affirm Anselm's insistence that "God is that than which none

---

18. See Thomas Aquinas, *De Ente et Essentia*; Aquinas, *ST* Ia.2–119.

19. For this reason, I follow those who see process theology as a different worldview altogether, wholly inconsistent with the essential tenets of theism. See Norman L. Geisler and William D. Watkins, *Worlds Apart: A Handbook on World Views,* 2nd ed. (Eugene, OR: Wipf & Stock, 2003), 107–46.

20. I.e., God possesses a knowledge of not only what *could* be and *will* be, but even of what *would* be if certain states of affairs were to obtain. For a full exposition of this doctrine, see chapter 5 of this work.

21. E.g., Craig, *God over All*.

greater can be conceived," but would shy away from the notion that God is simple. At least, God is not simple in the way medieval thinkers such as Aquinas would have it. God is a mystery, but he is not so mysterious that he is beyond the realm of human comprehension. As Davies explains, theistic personalists

> always concede that God is something of a mystery. But they frequently imply that we can have some sense of what it is to be God since we know from our own case what it is to be a person. They also sometimes suggest that words (especially adjectives) used by believers when speaking of God are most naturally to be construed in the same way as when they are applied to people.[22] Theists say that God is, for example, knowing, loving, and good. But we know what it means to say that people are knowing, loving, and good. So, reasons many a theistic personalist, we know something of what it means to say that God is knowing, loving, and good.[23]

I heartily take my stand with Thomas on the doctrine of God, believing that his version of theology proper is "theism come into its own," being the good

---

22. In other words, theistic personalists tend follow classical theists such as Scotus, who embraced univocity over analogy. Take the word "goodness" as an example. And take three propositions: "My dog, Winston, is good"; "My father, Edgar Campbell, is good"; and "God is good." We have three options in construing how the word "good" is used in these three sentences. First, it can be used *equivocally* (i.e., with a "different voice") in all three sentences, which entails that "good," when applied to Winston, Edgar, and God, means something *wholly different* in each case. This is largely rejected in the Christian tradition, for if we embraced equivocation God would become unknowable. Indeed, on this model we simply don't know what we mean when we say "God is good." Second, it can be used *univocally* (i.e., with the same or "one voice") in all three sentences, which entails that "good," when applied to Winston, Edgar, and God, carries with it the *exact same* meaning in each case. Thomists will want to point out here that it does seem counterintuitive to say that God is good in the exact same way humans and dogs are. Thus, while there is something to be said for consistency in our concepts across the board, as it were, it would seem that univocity mitigates the transcendence of God. Hence, while Scotus was a classical theist, most classicists follow Aquinas in his affirmation of analogy. That is, to follow our example, the word "good," when applied to Winston, Edgar, and God, carries a *similar*, though *not exact*, meaning, in each case. In other words, we are using the term *analogically* in all three instances. Thomists think that this doctrine preserves both the transcendence and knowability of God. For helpful discussions on this issue, see Thomas Aquinas, *ST* Ia.13.1–12; Davies, *Introduction to the Philosophy of Religion*, 139–54; and Norman L. Geisler and Winfried Corduan, *Philosophy of Religion*, 2nd ed. (Grand Rapids: Baker, 1988), 211–91.

23. Davies, *Introduction to the Philosophy of Religion*, 14.

and necessary inference from Scripture, as well as the best synthesis of all that preceded him in the Christian tradition. Hence, my goal will be to convince the reader that Thomas's solution to the perceived tension between sovereign grace and universal love is sound. That said, I also believe that several of the arguments in this work need not presuppose the Thomistic view of God (see chapter 4);[24] and, even when they do, I think those who disagree may benefit from my insights.[25]

THE ULTIMATE ARGUMENT AGAINST THEISM

Before we leave this topic we should introduce a major issue that will confront us throughout our study, which many think is the Achilles' heel of theism. I am speaking, of course, of *the problem of evil*. This problem comes in two forms—namely, *the experiential problem of evil* and *the intellectual problem of evil*. The former consists of the emotional strain evil and suffering can have on an individual, as in the case of my own experiences described in chapter 1. For this problem there are no easy answers. In fact, there really are no answers anyone can give a person undergoing such an experience to relieve them of their pain. The only real solution to the experiential problem is for us all to help one another bear our burdens with love, patience, and understanding.[26]

THE INTELLECTUAL PROBLEM OF EVIL

The intellectual problem of evil mainly consists in logically reconciling the idea of theism with the experience of evils in our world. Or, to put it another way, the intellectual problem of evil is the claim that theism and

---

24. Of course, one will notice, as we move through the argument of chapter 4, that a Thomistic metaphysic and theology proper give us the best solutions to potential objections.

25. So, for example, we offer, with some qualification, a defense of Thomas's general understanding of grace in this work. While the Thomistic view of grace is obviously strengthened by the metaphysics and theology proper of Aquinas, we see no reason why one *must* deny his view of grace if one denies his ontology or doctrine of God. Also, it should go without saying that one need not affirm every aspect of Thomas's view of grace before one can rationally affirm specific Thomistic affirmations about grace.

26. To name just two works on the experiential problem that were immensely helpful to me, see C. S. Lewis, *A Grief Observed* (1961; repr., San Francisco: HarperCollins, 1989); and Gary R. Habermas, *Forever Loved: A Personal Account of Grief and Resurrection* (Joplin, MO: College Press, 1997).

evil are logically incompatible. Nontheists of all stripes tend to use something similar to the following argument in an attempt to demonstrate the nonexistence of the theistic God:

a) The God of theism is said to be omnipotent, omniscient, and omnibenevolent.
b) As an omnipotent being, God is able to create a world without evil.
c) As an omniscient being, God knows how to create a world without evil.
d) As an omnibenevolent being, God wants a world to exist that contains no evil.
e) Evil exists.
f) God is either not omnipotent or not omniscient or not omnibenevolent or lacks all of these properties.
g) Therefore, the God of theism does not exist.

As we have noted, theism, at a minimum, is the belief that an all-powerful, all-knowing, and all-good God exists. Therefore, removing any of these properties from the package of divine attributes *just is* a rejection of theism. Hence, one must either embrace one of the alternatives to theism, along with a major problem we raised against each, or try to answer the problem within the context of a theistic worldview.

There are two broad strategies theists use in answering the intellectual problem of evil. Some offer what we call a "theodicy," which is a justification of why God creates a world with evil in it. People want to know why evil exists in a theistic universe. Theodicies attempt to give an answer. Others offer a "mere defense," which in this context is an attempt to show that theism and evil are *not* logically *incompatible*. Many who are willing to offer a defense have no clue as to why God allows evil to exist. For them, a theodicy is just too ambitious an undertaking for any human. That said, such defenders understand that, if it is even barely logically possible that both God and evil exist, then the logical argument from evil to nontheism is unsound.

A DEFENSE OF THEISM IN THE FACE OF EVIL

For most philosophers, the logical problem of evil has been answered. It was done so by Alvin Plantinga, who demonstrated that God and evil are logically compatible.[27] As Feinberg reports, "As a result of Alvin Plantinga's masterful elaboration and defense of the free will defense, there is a general consensus among atheists and theists alike that the logical problem of evil is solvable."[28] To be sure, this does not mean all aspects of the intellectual problem of evil are now resolved. Nontheists now tend to offer an evidential argument from evil, showing that, while there is no strict inconsistency between theism and evil, the former is nevertheless highly improbable due to the latter. Thus, Feinberg himself spends an entire section of his work dealing with the probabilistic version of the argument from evil.[29] Here we will look at two strategies that have been quite effective over the years in debates between theists and nontheists. The first strategy is what I call finding the missing premise. The second is what I call flipping the script.

FINDING THE MISSING PREMISE IN
THE ARGUMENT FROM EVIL

The idea here is that, if the theist can find at least one premise that is logically possible, consistent with theism, and stops the flow of the logical argument, then the argument from evil has been refuted. We need to emphasize here that, as Plantinga points out, the premise in question need not be true. In fact, the defender of theism need not even *believe* the premise. As long as the premise is possible, even barely so, then the argument from evil is unsound.[30]

We submit that the following three propositions are available to any theist (i.e., Jew, Christian, Muslim; classicist or personalist), since each is not only internally logically consistent and compatible with monotheism, but each is taught (even if implicitly) in all theistic traditions:

27. See Alvin C. Plantinga, *God, Freedom, and Evil* (Grand Rapids: Eerdmans, 1974).

28. John S. Feinberg, *The Many Faces of Evil: Theological Systems and the Problems of Evil*, 3rd ed. (Wheaton, IL: Crossway, 2004), 24.

29. Feinberg, *Many Faces of Evil*, 206–391.

30. Plantinga, *God, Freedom, and Evil*, 28.

Proposition 1: God has a good and sufficient reason for allowing
evil to exist.

Proposition 2: God will never allow evil to prevail over the good.

Proposition 3: God will one day utterly defeat evil.

If even one of these premises is just barely logically possible, then the argument from evil is defeated. Nontheists may respond to the first proposition as follows: "What, exactly, is God's reason for allowing evil to exist?" The theist may very well respond, "I don't know." At this point the nontheist may very well complain about not having an answer. The theist can surely sympathize with his nontheistic friend, and even complain with him. But this sad state of affairs in no way vindicates the nontheistic position. As Plantinga remarks: "The fact that the theist doesn't know why God permits evil is, perhaps, an interesting fact about the theist, but by itself it shows little or nothing relevant to the rationality of belief in God."[31] If the nontheist insists that God is only justified in allowing evil if and only if he explains to us what his reasons are, the theist will only wonder why he should accept this nontheistic standard. After all, Scripture itself reveals that God chooses not to tell us everything he knows (Deut 29:29); and, perhaps, God not only has a good and sufficient reason for allowing the evils he permits to occur, but even has a good reason for not giving us his explanation.

The second premise logically follows from the divine goodness. That is, God's goodness prevents him from permitting evil to ever prevail over the good. Evil may be pervasive; it may even seem at times that it will never be conquered; and yet good always comes to either mitigate evil or stamp it out for a season.

The third premise is explicitly taught in the three Abrahamic faiths, as each teaches that God will one day defeat evil. Because God will one day permanently defeat evil, Abrahamic theists are justified in their optimism about the future.

There is a fourth premise available to the Christian theist that is not available to either the Jew or the Muslim; namely, Christians believe that

---

31. Plantinga, *God, Freedom, and Evil*, 10.

God incarnated himself in the person of Jesus Christ. In this act of incarnation, God identified with the sufferings of humanity so as to redeem the world from its state of bondage to sin and evil. As the New Testament teaches us: "For we do not have a high priest who cannot sympathize with our weaknesses, but One who has been tempted in all things as *we are, yet* without sin" (Heb 4:15). The author of Hebrews explicitly tells us that Jesus is fully divine, being the Creator and Sustainer of the universe (Heb 1:1–14), and yet this same Christ is also fully human, a man who suffered for us in the days of his flesh (Heb 5:7): "Although He was a Son, He learned obedience from the things which He suffered. And having been made perfect, He became to all those who obey Him the source of eternal salvation" (Heb 5:8–9). Thus, while *any* theist is able to answer the logical problem of evil by appealing to our first three propositions, the Christian has a distinct advantage over other types of theists by offering yet a fourth premise illuminating the fact that God himself has personally identified with our sufferings in this life so that we can be redeemed for the next. Christians, in contrast to Jews and Muslims, can truly say, without qualification, that God not only *sympathizes* with us, but also *empathizes* with us in our suffering. Thus, putting it all together, the logical compatibility of both God and evil can be demonstrated as follows:

(a) The God of theism is said to be omnipotent, omniscient, and omnibenevolent.

(b)′ Evil exists.

(c)′ God has a good and sufficient reason for allowing evil to exist.

(d)′ As an omnipotent being, God is able to create a world wherein evil never prevails over the good.

(e)′ As an omniscient being, God knows how to create a world wherein evil never prevails over the good.

(f)′ As an omnibenevolent being, God wants a world to exist wherein good prevails, as well as one that eventually contains no evil.

(g)′ God will one day utterly defeat evil.

(h) God has already begun the process of defeating evil via redemptive incarnation.

(i) Therefore, theism is logically compatible with evil.

FLIPPING THE SCRIPT

Nontheists, especially pantheists and atheists, have had a difficult time reconciling the reality of objective moral values with their own systems. By
"objective moral values" I mean standards of value, character, ideals, and
behavior that are true independently of what anyone else might think of
them. Atheistic naturalists tend to think moral values are the product of
the human mind, along with millennia of socio-biological evolution. Hence,
they are an aid to survival and little, if anything, more. Monistic pantheists
tend to think that all distinctions are illusory, which logically includes the
distinction between good and evil. However, before one can be in a position
to call any action or state of affairs truly or objectively evil, one must have
an objective standard for adjudicating what is good and what is evil. In other
words, the claim that evil exists is meaningless in a world wherein objective
moral values do not exist. But neither pantheism nor atheism offers any
grounds for objective moral values. Therefore, theism is a more plausible
worldview, in light of the problem of evil, than either atheism or pantheism.

Of course, panentheism and polytheism could possibly be reconciled to
the existence of objective moral values. For it is *possible* that these truths
eternally exist as abstract and invariant laws of behavior, independent of
any divine nature, that all should follow, including the process deity and/
or the gods of the pantheon. To be sure, the gods may find themselves dis-
obeying the moral law from time to time, but that is another matter. The
point is that these worldviews can, in principle, allow for objective morality.
Theism, on the other hand, offers a transcendent anchor for these values.
In other words, on theism, the moral properties of justice and mercy, for
example, inhere within the divine essence itself. And this seems eminently more reasonable than both process theology and polytheism. For,
on theism, moral values exist as the properties of a personal God; however, on process polytheism, ethical norms exist as bare abstract objects.
As Craig notes, "It is hard to know what to make of this. It is clear what is
meant when it is said that a person is just; but it is bewildering when it is
said that, in the absence of any people, *Justice* itself exists."[32] Thus, given
objective morality, theism is the most plausible worldview.

---

32. William Lane Craig, "A Reply to Objections," in *Does God Exist? The Craig-Flew Debate*,
ed. Stan W. Wallace (Burlington, VT: Ashgate, 2003), 169. Helpful also is the discussion of

Hence, I offer the following argument *from evil* to *God's existence*:

a) If the theistic God does not exist, objective moral values either do not exist or exist as bare abstracta wholly disconnected from any mind.
b) Evil exists.
c) Thus, objective moral values exist, whereby one can distinguish good and evil.
d) Moral values are the properties of persons, and do not exist as bare abstracta.
e) Therefore, the theistic God exists.

A THEODICY FOR EVIL—NATURAL, MORAL, AND SOTERIOLOGICAL

Having shown that the theistic God is compatible with the reality of evil, and even seems to be (ironically) a rational inference from its existence, my goal in this work is to set forth a true theodicy, which is obviously more ambitious than a mere defense. Of course, if I fail, my defense is still secure. But, that said, I believe I can show why God allows evil to exist. More specifically, my work seeks to answer not merely the problem of evil, but even the *soteriological* aspect of this problem. "Soteriology" is "the study or doctrine of salvation." The soteriological problem is this: Why does God make a world containing persons he knows will not be saved? If we say that he could *not* avoid making such a world, then he is not omnipotent. In other

---

atheist philosopher Quentin Smith on this very notion—i.e., whether ideas such as *justice* can exist as bare abstractions or must be the property of a person(s). Smith's exposition actually underscores Craig's basic point insofar as he addresses the distinct but related issue of "propositions." Can a proposition exist in abstraction, or must it inhere in a mind? He finds the following premise reasonable, even though he harbors doubts as to whether it is actually true: "Necessarily, every proposition is an effect of some mind." If this premise is true, then it would entail that all objectively true moral imperatives—e.g., "Don't torture babies for the fun of it," "Do as you would be done by," "Do good and shun evil"—are the effects of a Mind, in which case God must exist as the anchor for these truths. For objective moral truths existed long before any human mind came into existence; therefore, these imperatives must exist in the eternal Mind of the Moral Lawgiver. To be sure, Smith finds this argument merely rational for one to accept; it is not rationally obligatory. Hence, he remains an atheist. See Quentin Smith, "The Conceptualist Argument for God's Existence," in *Philosophy of Religion: A Reader and Guide*, ed. William Lane Craig (New Brunswick, NJ: Rutgers University Press, 2002), 193–96.

words, he is not sovereign. If we say that he wanted a world with unsaved persons in it, then he is not omnibenevolent. At least, it would appear that God does *not* love all persons or that he is *not* genuinely trying to save them. Thus, we have a choice: God is either omnipotent or omnibenevolent. He cannot be both.

The Christian tradition has generally wanted to preserve God's absolute sovereignty as well as his genuine desire for universal salvation; and yet this same tradition affirms the sad notion that some will be damned. How can these presuppositions be reconciled? Answering this all-important question is the burden of this work.

MODALITY

"Modality" refers to the "mode or way something exists." There are several basic terms philosophers use to convey modality. First, there is the word "possible." Something is possible just in case it *could* exist. Of course, not all things possible are real. Examples of possible, but nonexistent, things are as follows: unicorns; gremlins reading Hegel on the dark side of the moon; Luke Skywalker; He-Man; Tatooine with its two suns; Krypton; the fortieth planet in our solar system; Travis Campbell's tenth daughter; and leprechauns. Why do we say these things are possible? Because no logical contradiction is entailed by these concepts. Whatever is logically coherent or noncontradictory *could* exist, even if it does not.

Of course, there are other logically possible things or concepts that *do* exist. To offer a few examples: President Trump; Hillary Clinton; Travis Campbell; the planet Mercury; and Alpha Centauri. The difference between a logically possible entity that does exist, such as Mercury, and one that doesn't, such as Krypton, is *reality*. The proposition "Mercury exists" corresponds to the way things actually are, while the proposition "Krypton exists" does not. To be sure, the opposite *could* have been the case—i.e., there could have been no Mercury, since it is possible that no planet with Mercury's size, shape, atmosphere, density, and so on ever existed; and it is possible that there could have been a Krypton. But it just so happens that things are as they are and not some other way.

Logical possibilities are what we call "contingencies." Something is contingent just in case it may or may not exist. I may or may not exist. Unicorns may or may not exist. Of course, it just so happens that I actually exist while unicorns do not. So we might say that the proposition "Travis Campbell exists" is a true proposition that contingently obtains, since there are various factors and causes that brought me into being (e.g., my parents) and continue to sustain me in existence (e.g., food and sunlight). On the other hand "unicorns exist" is a logically possible proposition that is actually false, since unicorns contingently fail to obtain. Indeed, no factor or set of circumstances has ever allowed for or caused such creatures to exist. Hence the falsity of this proposition.

But there are other truths that are not merely possible but *necessary*. That is, such propositions are not only logically consistent, but also *must* be the case. They *must* be true. Or, they *must* exist. So, for example, the law of noncontradiction (i.e., "two contradictory propositions cannot both be true at the same time and in the same sense") is *not only possible* or *plausible*, or even highly *probable*, but *necessary*. One way to state this point is to say that the law of noncontradiction is valid in every logically possible world. Any world that could exist will then be governed by the law of noncontradiction. Indeed, how could we even conceive of a state of affairs wherein the canon does not obtain without using this very law in our conception? Other candidates for logical necessities include numbers, sets, the laws of mathematics, and various abstract objects (e.g., justice and/or goodness). Most classical theists, along with many theistic personalists, would also insist that God is a necessary being since there is no logically possible world wherein God does not exist.[33] Some classical theists, along with many theistic personalists, will insist that God is *actually* necessary even if he is not *logically* necessary—i.e., God exists, and because he exists he cannot *not* exist. Thus, even if there is a logically possible world wherein there is no God, we happen to live in a world wherein the necessary being is.[34]

---

33. To be sure, the reader may think that such a position entails the soundness of at least one version of the ontological argument. Not true! The conclusion to an argument may be true, even if the argument is unsound.

34. Nash, *Concept of God*, 108. Unfortunately, Nash gives one definition of factual or actual necessity as follows: God is a necessary being in the sense that he is self-caused. In context, Nash is clearly indicating by this that he does not mean that God causes himself to exist—as if to say, God exists before he exists. But it is unfortunate that he did not avoid the term altogether and say, simply, that God is *uncaused*.

Finally, there is the impossible. Impossibilities are incoherent events, states of affairs, persons, or things that simply cannot exist no matter the circumstances. Examples include wholly red and nonred objects; square circles; worlds wherein 2 + 2 = 5; a man who is father and son at the same time and in the same sense; and an honest politician.[35] In other words, impossibilities consist of contradictories that are both unimaginable and inconceivable. They may be utterable or sayable, but they are nevertheless unaffirmable or self-defeating. So they do not exist in any logically possible world. Impossibilities, then, are not so much modes or ways a thing could be, but are just plain nonsense that cannot be conceived or imagined. Hence there are really only two modalities. That is, there are only two ways a thing could exist. Something is either *necessary* or *contingent*.[36] If necessary, then it cannot *not* obtain, and/or it exists in every logically possible world; if contingent, then it either does exist but could not, or does not exist but could.

HUMAN FREEDOM

Everyone intuitively realizes that if our activity is not our own then it is difficult, if not impossible, to think we are responsible for it. If I am standing near a cliff next to someone else, and an object hits me in such a way that I am pushed into the person standing next to me, who in turn falls off the cliff, most would agree that I am not to be held responsible for that person's death. I did push the individual off the cliff; but I did not choose to do so; I was, instead, moved to do so by another.

Since most of us recognize that our actions must be our own before we can be held responsible for them—and, since most of us recognize that humans, all things being equal, ought to be held responsible for their behavior—it is not very difficult to see why most of us believe that humans are free in the sense that their choices are their own. In short, humans are *free agents*, or have *free will* and/or the power of *free choice*.

---

35. The last example is a joke. The others are legitimate.

36. Those who do not believe there is a God may think we are begging the question here. But notice that this assertion does not commit one to affirming God's existence. Indeed, there may very well be no necessary beings or states of affairs. In any case, *if* something exists, it does so either *contingently* or *necessarily*.

As one may imagine, however, matters are not so simple, for there are at least two ways to construe the nature of human free will. Some philosophers embrace what is now most often called *libertarian* freedom, while others adhere to a *compatibilist* view of freedom.[37]

LIBERTARIANISM

This view insists that the very notion of freedom and responsibility is antithetical to any form of determinism. Hence, the older theologians coming out of the Reformation period referred to this kind of freedom as a "liberty of indifference." To be truly free, one must have control over one's will and action in such a way "that, given a choice to do A (raise one's hand and vote) or B (leave the room), nothing determines that either choice is made. Rather, the agent himself must simply exercise his own **causal powers** and will to do one alternative, say A (or have the power to refrain from willing to do something)."[38] Hence, a person who is free, in the libertarian sense of the term, "is the absolute originator of his own actions."[39] Thus, when "an agent acts freely, he is a **first** or **unmoved mover**; no event or efficient cause causes him to act. His desires or beliefs may influence his choice or play an important role in his deliberations, but free acts are not determined or caused by prior events or states in the agent; rather, they are spontaneously done by the agent himself acting as a first mover."[40] Moreland and Craig list the following thinkers who are widely recognized as libertarians: Thomas Aquinas, Thomas Reid (1710–96), William Rowe (1931–2015), Peter van Inwagen (b. 1942), and Timothy O'Connor.[41] As we will see in our study, Thomas Aquinas is more difficult to label here, since he does believe that in some sense God causes our actions. Yet God does not cause the movement

---

37. There are actually no less than four views of freedom, with two largely ruled out by the basic presuppositions of Christian theism. These views are anarchicism, libertarianism, compatibilism, and hard determinism. For more on this, see Travis James Campbell, "The Beautiful Mind: A Reaffirmation and Reconstruction of the Classical Reformed Doctrines of the Divine Omniscience, Prescience, and Human Freedom" (PhD diss., Westminster Theological Seminary, 2004), 179–200.

38. J. P. Moreland and William Lane Craig, *Philosophical Foundations for a Christian Worldview* (2nd ed.; Downers Grove, IL: InterVarsity Press, 2017), 303, emphasis original.

39. Moreland and Craig, *Philosophical Foundations*, 303.

40. Moreland and Craig, *Philosophical Foundations*, 303, emphasis original.

41. Moreland and Craig, *Philosophical Foundations*, 303.

of our will in anything like the mechanical or impersonal causes I earlier described (e.g., my accidentally pushing someone off a cliff). Much less is God the cause of our sins or immoral or evil actions. Also, it is safe to say that Pelagius (360–416), Augustine (at least in his early years), John Cassian (360–435), Desiderius Erasmus (1466–1536), Luis de Molina (1535–1600), Jacob Arminius (1560–1609), Simon Episcopius (1583–1643), and Philipp van Limborch (1633–1712), to name a few, were all libertarians.

COMPATIBILISM

For the compatibilist, human freedom and responsibility are *consistent* or *compatible* with at least *some* notions of determinism. Older theologians of the sixteenth and seventeenth centuries referred to this as "a liberty of spontaneity." Events or states of affairs that obtain prior to one's making a choice *cause* or *determine* the will, and yet the choice is still free in the sense that the agent causes it and so is to be held responsible for it. What events or states of affairs determine a person's choice? Compatibilists tend to locate these states within the agent himself and reject the idea that, say, the environment in which one is placed determines one's behavior— at least, when this sort of thing happens, the agent is not responsible for his actions. So, for example, if I am pushed into another by some outside force, I am not responsible for my action. However, I do have a character, set of beliefs, and desires that precede my action; and so if my strongest desire, for instance, at the moment of choice causes me to push another human being, then we have an example of a choice that is caused by a prior state that nevertheless arises wholly from within me. My choice is determined and yet free. Moreland and Craig list the following philosophers who are widely recognized as compatibilists: Thomas Hobbes (1588–1679), John Locke (1632–1704), David Hume (1711–76), Daniel Dennett (b. 1942), and Gary Watson.[42] Others include Martin Luther (1488–1546), Ulrich Zwingli (1484–1531), John Calvin (1509–64), Theodore Beza (1519–1605), William Ames (1576–1633), John Owen (1616–83), Blaise Pascal (1623–62), Francis Turretin (1623–87), and Jonathan Edwards (1703–58).

---

42. Moreland and Craig, *Philosophical Foundations*, 303.

As a personal note, I will simply state that my own view concerning the freedom of the will is currently being rethought. I see serious problems with both libertarianism and compatibilism as they are stated in the literature. That said, I think it is appropriate for me to state my firm conviction that humans are to be held responsible for their behavior, and so they do possess free will. As this work is not an exploration of divine sovereignty and human free will, but is rather and exploration of sovereign election and universal love, I offer no defense of either compatibilism or libertarianism in these pages.[43] Thankfully, nothing defended here stands or falls on a particular view of freedom. Indeed, while it is common for theologians to identify libertarianism as "the Arminian view of free will" and compatibilism as "the Calvinist view of free will," there are notable exceptions to this general rule (at least among Calvinists).[44]

GRACE

Grace is, by definition, "unmerited favor." There are three main branches of Christianity—i.e., Eastern Orthodoxy, Roman Catholicism, and evangelical Protestantism[45]—plus one—i.e., Oriental Orthodoxy (which includes

---

43. It should be reiterated that this work is *not* covering the age-old debate of how divine sovereignty is reconciled to human freedom. One recent example of how this might be done, from a Calvinistic perspective, is Guillaume Bignon, *Excusing Sinners and Blaming God: A Calvinist Assessment of Determinism, Moral Responsibility, and Divine Involvement in Evil* (Eugene, OR: Pickwick, 2018). For a different approach, which is also recent, see John C. Lennox, *Determined to Believe? The Sovereignty of God, Freedom, Faith, & Human Responsibility* (Grand Rapids: Zondervan, 2017).

44. For an example of a Calvinist libertarian, see J. Oliver Buswell, *A Systematic Theology of the Christian Religion* (Grand Rapids: Zondervan, 1962), 1:267. There are indeed several among the Reformed who embrace "a liberty of indifference," at least in a qualified sense—e.g., see William Cunningham, *The Reformers and the Theology of the Reformation* (1862; repr., Carlisle, PA: Banner of Truth Trust, 1967), 471–524; and William J. van Asselt et al., *Reformed Thought on Freedom: The Concept of Free Choice in Early Modern Reformed Theology* (Grand Rapids: Baker, 2010). See also the interesting debate between Muller and Helm on this issue: Richard A. Muller, "Jonathan Edwards and the Absence of Free Choice: A Parting of Ways in the Reformed Tradition," *JES* 1, no. 1 (2011): 3–22; Paul Helm, "Jonathan Edwards and the Parting of the Ways?," *JES* 4, no. 1 (2014): 42–60; Muller, "Jonathan Edwards and Francis Turretin on Necessity, Contingency, and Freedom of Will. In Response to Paul Helm," *JES* 4, no. 3 (2014): 266–85; and Helm, "Turretin and Edwards Once More," *JES* 4, no. 3 (2014): 286–96.

45. By "evangelical" I do not mean the modern Christian who votes Republican or takes take a prolife stance on abortion. The term goes deeper than that, having its roots in the sixteenth-century Reformation. At that time "Protestant" referred to one who protested the abuses of the Roman Catholic Church against the faithful and hence indicated what one was against. "Evangelical" was the positive term referring to what one was for—i.e., the gospel

Coptic, Ethiopian, and Eritrean Christians)[46]—and each one of them teaches that those who experience salvation do so by the grace of God. By "salvation" I mean "redemption from the ultimate consequence of our sins." By "ultimate consequence of our sins" I mean death, followed by an eternal separation between us and God in hell itself.[47] All good judges refuse to acquit those who are guilty. We are guilty of sin. Therefore, our sinful acts have rendered us blameworthy and hence wholly deserving of punishment

---

of justification by faith alone. The Reformed churches (e.g., the churches of Holland, the Presbyterians of Scotland), along with the Lutherans, Anglicans, and even some Anabaptist groups, can in this basic sense all be considered evangelical Protestant.

46. These communions split with the main branch of Christianity in the wake of the production of the Chalcedonian Creed. Today, Orthodox, Catholic, and Protestant Christians all accept the Chalcedonian Formula, which declares that Christ is one person with two natures that are never separated, though they are forever distinct—being neither fused nor intermixed with each other. Oriental Christians (e.g., Coptic Christians) reject this notion and embrace the Miaphysite Formula, declaring that Christ is one nature, human and divine. Sometimes this is confused with the Monophysite Formula, which also declared Christ to be of one nature. Properly understood, miaphysitism does not formally contradict the Chalcedonian Formula, as does monophysitism. Hence, no member of the three main communions should look on Oriental Christians as heretics (and vice versa).

47. Of course, the reality of hell would seem to exacerbate the soteriological problem of evil. For if God is loving, why would he punish anyone in the afterlife? At the risk of sounding glib, the answer to this question is easy. Retributive justice is fully justifiable, since those who commit crimes ought to be punished for them. Since humans have sinned against God, they deserve to be punished. If they refuse God's way of salvation, then they are in effect choosing to condemn themselves. Hence, as long as human beings are responsible moral agents, there is nothing unjust about God punishing those who deserve it in the afterlife. A more difficult question, however, concerns the *eternality* of hell. The traditional view of hell is that it is a place where reprobate sinners go to endure unceasing pain. Hell is eternal, and so consists of reprobates experiencing conscious torments forever, and ever, and ever ... and ever. Hence this traditional view of hell is referred to as the eternal conscious torment (ECT) view of hell. But isn't that overdoing it a bit? Doesn't it seem a little unjust, to say the least, to mete out an eternal punishment for a temporal crime? In our experience, finite crimes are given finite punishments. Humans who commit crimes either get time-out (jail) or total exile (death). No one endures an eternity of torture for bad decisions. So, while it does *not* seem unjust for God to send people to hell, and to even punish them for a season, it does seem unjust for God to literally torment them forever. It is precisely for this reason that many theologians of our day embrace a conditional immortality (CI) view of hell. According to CI, there is nothing about us that needs to exist forever. Since we are contingent beings, both our bodies and our souls *can* cease to exist. Hence whether one exists forever depends on whether or not one is saved. Those who are saved from hell spend eternity in heaven. Those who go to hell are indeed punished for their sins; but their punishment is not eternal. Eventually, they will be snuffed out of existence altogether by the mercy of God. To explore the issue of hell and its duration any further would take us far afield. Thankfully, nothing we say in this work stands or falls on whether ECT or CI is correct. For more on this topic, see Preston Sprinkle, ed., *Four Views on Hell* (2nd ed.; Grand Rapids: Zondervan, 2016); and William Crockett, ed., *Four Views on Hell* (Grand Rapids: Zondervan, 1996).

in hell. God, like all good judges, will not acquit us, precisely because we are guilty. He is all-powerful, and so is able to mete out his just punishment. He is all-knowing, and so it is impossible for us to avoid punishment by deceiving him in any way (e.g., as a lawyer might do for her client before a human judge). Notice, then, how Scripture describes sinful humanity:

> What then? Are we better than they? Not at all; for we have already charged that both Jews and Greeks are all under sin; as it is written,
> "THERE IS NONE RIGHTEOUS, NOT EVEN ONE;
>> ¹¹THERE IS NONE WHO UNDERSTANDS,
>> THERE IS NONE WHO SEEKS FOR GOD;
>> ¹²ALL HAVE TURNED ASIDE, TOGETHER THEY HAVE BECOME USELESS;
>> THERE IS NONE WHO DOES GOOD,
>> THERE IS NOT EVEN ONE."
>> ¹³"THEIR THROAT IS AN OPEN GRAVE,
>> WITH THEIR TONGUES THEY KEEP DECEIVING," "THE POISON OF ASPS IS UNDER THEIR LIPS";
>> ¹⁴"WHOSE MOUTH IS FULL OF CURSING AND BITTERNESS"; ¹⁵"THEIR FEET ARE SWIFT TO SHED BLOOD, ¹⁶DESTRUCTION AND MISERY ARE IN THEIR PATHS, ¹⁷AND THE PATH OF PEACE THEY HAVE NOT KNOWN." ¹⁸"THERE IS NO FEAR OF GOD BEFORE THEIR EYES." (Rom 3:9–18)

Elsewhere Christians are described according to how they used to be before they were saved from divine wrath:

> And you were dead in your trespasses and sins, in which you formerly walked according to the course of this world, according to the prince of the power of the air, of the spirit that is now working in the sons of disobedience. Among them we too all formerly lived in the lusts of our flesh, indulging the desires of the flesh and of the mind, and were by nature children of wrath, even as the rest. (Eph 2:1–3)

Notice that we are not only sinners, but *dead* in our trespasses, being *by nature* children of wrath. We are naturally wrathful or angry at ourselves, our neighbors, and God. In fact, we are dead to the things of God. Thus, our sins have earned for each of us a place in hell; and our sinful condition renders us unable to love God, obey God, or even seek after God, much less understand God. Our sins have placed us in bondage. As Jesus himself says, "Everyone who commits sin is a slave of sin" (John 8:34); or, in the words of Paul, the natural person who is dead in sin "does not accept the things of the Spirit of God; for they are foolishness to him, and he cannot understand them, because they are spiritually appraised" (1 Cor 2:14).

The "gospel" the world consistently teaches us is that we have the power to change ourselves. We can "make it work" (whatever that means). We can stop sinning and make the right choices. And, if we turn things around by doing our best to obey God and love our neighbor, God will not find fault with us. God will save us by our works. All we have to do is repent, stop sinning, and obey God. In the famous words of Benjamin Franklin, "God helps those who help themselves."

The reader needs to appreciate just how terrible the world's "gospel" is, which really isn't a gospel at all! No, the word "gospel" means "good news." But the world's news is bad news. This for three reasons. First, to be told that "we can do it" fails to appreciate the state we're in. We are in bondage to sin, lovers of self, and in no way want to do the things of God. How can we work our way to heaven when we have no desire to do so? How can we do the things of God when we don't love him, or want him, or even understand him? Second, given the state we're in, it does seem rather harsh and insensitive to be told that all we have to do is follow the commandments of God and we'll be okay. We can't follow the commandments, "because the mind set on the flesh is hostile toward God; for it does not subject itself to the law of God, for it is not even able *to do so*; and those who are in the flesh cannot please God" (Rom 8:7-8). Saying that we can merit the favor of God through our works righteousness is as illogical as saying that a dead man can walk out of his grave, or that a man with no legs can run, or that an infertile woman can give birth, or that a bachelor can kiss his wife. This is why the apostle Peter insisted that, as a means of salvation, the law of God is a burden too great for anyone to bear (Acts 15:10). Finally, even if a sinner could change his own heart and follow the law of God, such works could not, in principle, acquit him. A man accused of a crime will still have

to face his trial, even though he commits no more crimes, and even performs good deeds, before his court date. In the same way, a perfect life lived
after years of sinning cannot atone for the past. All sinners face a righteous
Judge at the end of their lives, and no good work will save them from the
just punishment they face because of their sins. For "by the works of the
Law no flesh will be justified in His sight; for through the Law *comes* the
knowledge of sin" (Rom 3:20).

It is precisely at this point where we sinners are in dire need of the
genuine gospel—a true word of good news for those who are perishing.
Peter, after speaking of the burden of trying to be saved by our own good
works, says that "we believe that we are saved through the grace of the Lord
Jesus" (Acts 15:11). Indeed, Christ followed the commandments of God perfectly, thereby doing what we could not do; and he then offered himself up
to God as an atoning sacrifice for our sins, thereby paying the just penalty
of our misdeeds. We owed a debt we could not pay; Christ paid a debt he
did not owe. As Scripture teaches: God "made Him who knew no sin to be
sin on our behalf, that we might become the righteousness of God in Him"
(2 Cor 5:21). Thus, after explaining the dire straits we are in through sin,
holy writ gives us the gospel:

> But God, being rich in mercy, because of His great love with which
> He loved us, even when we were dead in our transgressions, made
> us alive together with Christ (by grace you have been saved), and
> raised us up with Him, and seated us with Him in the heavenly
> *places* in Christ Jesus, so that in the ages to come He might show
> the surpassing riches of His grace in kindness toward us in Christ
> Jesus. For by grace you have been saved through faith; and that not
> of yourselves, *it is* the gift of God; not as a result of works, so that
> no one may boast. (Eph 2:4–9)

> For God so loved the world, that He gave His only begotten Son, that
> whoever believes in Him shall not perish, but have eternal life. For
> God did not send the Son into the world to judge the world, but that
> the world might be saved through Him. (John 3:16–17)

The good news is actually better than good. For it does not merely teach us that God sent his Son to save us. If that were not enough, the evangel is nothing less than a promise that *mere faith* in Christ saves us, wholly apart from doing any good works. "Believe in the Lord Jesus, and you will be saved" (Acts 16:31); "For we hold that one is justified by faith apart from works of the law" (Rom 3:28 ESV). By a simple act of faith, one does all one needs to do to attain a right standing before the eternal Judge.

However, if we are naturally unable to come to God in faith, how is it good news to be told that we are saved by faith? Is the gospel, then, not just another law or commandment of God? No! For the good news is that we "have been saved through faith; and that not of yourselves, *it is* the gift of God" (Eph 2:8). The best commentaries on this passage agree that when the text says "and that not of yourselves, it is the gift of God," it is pointing back to all of what pertains to salvation—i.e., salvation, grace, and faith.[48] In other words, God is not expecting us to conjure up faith for ourselves. We cannot do that, since we are naturally depraved and dead in our sins. Hence, God in his grace gives us not only salvation, but even the ability to have faith in Christ. "For to you it has been granted for Christ's sake ... to believe in Him" (Phil 1:29); "No one can come to Me unless the Father who sent Me draws him; and I will raise him up on the last day" (John 6:44); "And a certain woman named Lydia, from the city of Thyatira, a seller of purple fabrics, a worshiper of God, was listening; and the Lord opened her heart to respond to the things spoken by Paul" (Acts 16:14). Indeed, faith must be a gift of God; for if it were not a gift, it would be a work we must perform to merit his favor. Hence, God does not *merely* save us by grace, as if to say that he graciously offers his Son to us as the Savior and then waits on us to believe in him. No, God *only* saves us by his grace. He saves us by grace *alone*. He redeems us *sola gratia*. For "if it is by grace, it is no longer on the basis of works, otherwise grace is no longer grace" (Rom 11:6).

The doctrine of *sola gratia*, then, is no minor issue in the biblical worldview. It is a sine qua non of Christianity. If God does not save by his

---

48. See Andrew T. Lincoln, *Ephesians* (WBC 42; Dallas: Word Books, 1990), 112; Markus Barth, *Ephesians: Introduction, Translation and Commentary on Chapters 1–3* (AB 34; New York: Doubleday, 1974), 225; and Harold W. Hoehner, *Ephesians: An Exegetical Commentary* (Grand Rapids: Baker, 2002), 342–43.

unmerited favor *alone*, then we have no gospel, and Christ died needlessly (Gal 2:21). And so a *double* curse is pronounced on any teacher, whether human or angelic, who would rob the sinner of this wonderful news: "But even if we or an angel from heaven should preach to you a gospel contrary to the one we preached to you, let him be accursed. As we have said before, so now I say again: If anyone is preaching to you a gospel contrary to the one you received, let him be accursed" (Gal 1:8–9 ESV).

Throughout church history, there have been teachers who have attempted to tone down the clear biblical teaching that we are redeemed through grace *alone*. In many respects, the great theological controversies of the past have been between those who wish to recover the biblical understanding of grace and those who want to add human merit alongside grace as a basis for salvation. The most famous of these debates occurred during the fifth and sixteenth centuries, with the former being the controversy between Pelagius and Augustine and the latter consisting of the disputes between Rome and the Reformation.

In my own study of this issue, I have been greatly encouraged over the fact that, in the creedal statements of all branches of Christendom (i.e., Greek, Roman, and Reformational), we find the biblical teaching that salvation comes to us *solely* by the grace of God. To be sure, the affirmations are not always articulated in as clear and consistent manner as we would like to see. But in the representative creeds of these traditions, there is always an effort to deny human merit as the basis for salvation. Here we will briefly look at some representative examples of creedal and theological affirmations of the gospel from each branch of Christianity.

THE WESTERN (LATIN) CHURCH

In the Western tradition(s) the concept of grace has been dominated by Augustine's own understanding of the issue, which he developed in light of his controversy with Pelagius. The Western church sided with Augustine, condemning Pelagius's view at the Council of Carthage (418) and the Council of Ephesus (431). Yet, even a century later there were those who insisted that a person can believe in Christ apart from grace. Hence, the Council of Orange met in the year 529 to answer this antibiblical viewpoint.

Here are three canons produced by this council illustrating the point that all of salvation, from start to finish, is solely of grace:

> **Canon 5.** If anyone says that not only the increase of faith but also its beginning and the very desire for faith, by which we believe in Him who justifies the ungodly and comes to the regeneration of holy baptism—if anyone says that this belongs to us by nature and not by a gift of grace, that is, by the inspiration of the Holy Spirit amending our will and turning it from unbelief to faith and from godlessness to godliness, it is proof that he is opposed to the teaching of the Apostles, for blessed Paul says, "Being confident of this very thing, that He, who hath begun a good work in you, will perfect it unto the day of Christ Jesus" (Phil. 1:6). And again, "For by grace you are saved through faith; and that not of yourselves, for it is the gift of God" (Eph. 2:8). For those who state that the faith by which we believe in God is natural make all who are separated from the Church of Christ by definition in some measure believers.

> **Canon 6.** If anyone says that God has mercy upon us when, apart from his grace, we believe, will, desire, strive, labor, pray, watch, study, seek, ask, or knock, but does not confess that it is by the infusion and inspiration of the Holy Spirit within us that we have the faith, the will, or the strength to do all these things as we ought; or if anyone makes the assistance of grace depend on the humility or obedience of man and does not agree that it is a gift of grace itself that we are obedient and humble, he contradicts the Apostle who says, "What hast thou that thou hast not received?" (I Cor. 4:7), and, "By the grace of God, I am what I am" (I Cor. 15:10).

> **Canon 7.** If anyone affirms that we can form any right opinion or make any right choice which relates to the salvation of eternal life, as is expedient for us, or that we can be saved, that is, assent to the preaching of the gospel through our natural powers without the illumination and inspiration of the Holy Spirit, who makes all men gladly assent to and believe in the truth, he is led astray by

a heretical spirit, and does not understand the voice of God who says in the Gospel, "Without me you can do nothing" (John 15:5), and the word of the Apostle, "Not that we are sufficient to think any thing of ourselves, as of ourselves; but our sufficiency is from God" (II Cor. 3:5).[49]

Just over five centuries later we see Anselm affirm *sola gratia* without actually using the words. As he reflects on his own life, he realizes that Christ alone is his sole merit:

My life terrifies me. For when diligently examined, my whole life appears to me either as sin or as unfruitfulness. And if there seems to be some fruit in it, then it is either so counterfeit or imperfect, or in some way corrupt, that it can either fail to please or can actually displease God. It is certainly altogether either sinful and damnable or unfruitful and worthy of contempt. But why do I separate the unfruitful from the damnable? Certainly, if it is unfruitful, it is damnable. For every tree which does not bring forth good fruit will be cast into the fire. Therefore, O dry and useless wood, worthy of eternal fires! What will you answer on that Day, when an account is demanded of you, how you spent the whole time of life that was given you down to your last moment? I dread! On this side there will be the accusing sins, on that side terrifying justice; below appears the horrid chaos of hell, above the irate Judge; inside, the burning conscience, outside, the burning world. Hardly shall the righteous be saved. Where shall the sinner, thus caught, hide? To hide will be impossible, to appear intolerable. Where can I find counsel? Where salvation? Who is He who is called the messenger of the great counsel? It is Jesus. The same is the Judge, in whose hands I tremble. Revive, sinner; do not despair. Hope in Him whom you fear, flee to Him from whom you have fled. Jesus Christ, for the sake of this Thy name, do to me according to this Thy name. Look upon a poor man who calls upon Thy name. Therefore, Jesus, be Thou my Savior for

---

49. John H. Leith, ed., *Creeds of the Churches* (3rd ed.; Louisville: John Knox, 1982), 39-40.

Thy name's sake. If Thou wilt admit me to the all-embracing bosom of Thy mercy, it will not be more crowded on my account. It is true, my conscience has merited damnation, and my repentance does not suffice for satisfaction; but it is certain that Thy mercy overcomes every offense.[50]

Thomas Aquinas also affirms *sola gratia*, telling us "that God, **who hath predestined us**, has forechosen us *by grace alone* **unto the adoption of children**";[51] and so, commenting on Ephesians 2:8–9, he tells us that an error Paul is refuting in this passage

is that anyone can believe that faith is given by God to us on the merit of our preceding actions. To exclude this he adds **Not of** preceding **works** that we merited at one time to be saved; for this is the grace, as was mentioned above, and according to Romans 11 (6): "If by grace, it is not now by works; otherwise grace is no more grace." He follows with the reason why God saves man by faith without any preceding merits, **that no man may glory** in himself but refer all the glory to God. "Not to us, O Lord, not to us; but to thy name give glory. For thy mercy and thy truth's sake" (Ps. 113:1–2 or 9–10). "That no flesh should glory in his sight. But of him are you in Christ Jesus, who of God is made unto us wisdom, and justice, and sanctification, and redemption" (1 Cor. 1:29–30).[52]

Lest we think of Aquinas as some sort of semi-Pelagian who believed that God receives our self-generated faith by grace, Thomas also insists that free "will is inadequate for the act of faith since the contents of faith are above human reason." A few lines later he states: "For this reason he adds, 'for it is the gift of God,' namely, faith itself. 'For you have been granted, for the sake of Christ, not only to believe in him, but also to suffer for him'

---

50. Anselm, *Meditations*, quoted in Martin Chemnitz, *Examination of the Council of Trent: Part 1* (1578 Frankfurt ed.; trans. Fred Kramer; St. Louis: Concordia, 1971), 512.

51. Thomas Aquinas, *Commentary on Saint Paul's Epistle to the Ephesians* (trans. Matthew L. Lamb; Aquinas Scripture Series 2; Albany, NY: Magi Books, 1966), 47, italics added, boldface original.

52. Aquinas, *Commentary on Saint Paul's Epistle to the Ephesians*, 96, boldface original.

(Phil 1:29)."[53] Thus, we should be not surprised to see Aquinas elsewhere affirm that we are made members "of Christ through grace alone."[54]

Even the Council of Trent, which convened in the sixteenth century in order to oppose the Reformation, insists on the exclusion of merits as the basis for our justification before God:

> But when the Apostle says that man is justified by faith and freely, these words are to be understood in that sense in which the uninterrupted unanimity of the Catholic Church has held and expressed them, namely, that we are therefore said to be justified by faith, because faith is the beginning of human salvation, the foundation and root of all justification, *without which it is impossible to please God* and to come to the fellowship of His sons; and we are therefore said to be justified gratuitously, because none of those things that precede justification, whether faith or works, merit the grace of justification. For, *if by grace, it is not now by works, otherwise*, as the Apostle says, *grace is no more grace.*[55]

Unfortunately, Rome removes with her left hand what is granted with her right, insisting here and there that by our merits we can actually increase our justification.[56] Rome also teaches that "if anyone says that the sinner is justified by faith alone, meaning that nothing else is required to co-operate in order to obtain the grace of justification, and that it is not in any way necessary that he be prepared and disposed by the action of his own will, let him be anathema."[57] While a Protestant can, in principle, adhere to the

---

53. Aquinas, *Commentary on Saint Paul's Epistle to the Ephesians*, 96.

54. Thomas Aquinas, *Summa Theologica* (trans. Fathers of the English Dominican Province; Allen, TX: Thomas More, 1948), IIIa.62.1. For more on this, see Travis James Campbell, "Should Ole Aquinas Be Forgot and Never Brought to Mind: A Response to Dewey Roberts' 'Aquinas Not a Safe Guide for Protestants,'" https://www.the-aquilareport.com/ole-aquinas-forgot-never-brought-mind/.

55. Council of Trent (session 6, chapter 8), in Leith, *Creeds of the Churches*, 413, italics original.

56. E.g., "If anyone says that the justice received is not preserved and also not increased before God through good works, but that those works are merely the fruits and signs of justification obtained, but not the cause of its increase, let him be anathema" (Council of Trent [session 6, canon 24], in Leith, *Creeds of the Churches*, 423).

57. Council of Trent (session 6, canon 9), in Leith, *Creeds of the Churches*, 421.

second clause of this statement,[58] she cannot affirm the first. For if it is grace *alone* that grants us justification, then nothing should be required for our right standing before God except for faith (which is itself a gift of God). When Rome eschews human merit so as to preserve the exclusivity of grace, only to turn around and deny justification by faith alone and affirm human merits as the cause of the increase of justification, it does no less than offer an incoherent and obscure gospel. Indeed, the scriptural gospel is clear, telling us that we have full justification and peace with God by grace *alone* through faith *alone*: "But to the one who does not work, but believes in Him who justifies the ungodly, his faith is credited [or imputed] as righteousness" (Rom 4:5); "Therefore, having been justified by faith, we have peace with God through our Lord Jesus Christ" (Rom 5:1); "There is therefore now no condemnation for those who are in Christ Jesus" (Rom 8:1). And this was the gospel of the universal church from its inception into the sixteenth century. Trent changed all of that. As Pelikan writes: "What had previously been permitted (justification by faith and works), now became required. What had previously been permitted also (justification by faith alone), now became forbidden. In condemning the Protestant Reformation, the Council of Trent condemned part of its own catholic tradition."[59] Indeed, just before Trent first convened one could see the writing on the wall, as even sixteenth-century Roman Catholic theologian Albert Pighius observed: "We cannot hide the fact that this very chief part of the Christian doctrine [i.e., justification] has been obscured rather than made clear by men on our side by very many thorny questions and definitions from the Scholastics."[60]

Pelikan's and Pighius's words help illuminate many of the statements coming out of Reformational circles before the Council of Trent first convened in 1545. For example, the Lutheran Augsburg Confession (1530) is divided into two parts. Part one concerns "Articles of Faith and Doctrine,"

---

58. That is, if Rome is here saying that we are prepared by the movement of our will to receive the grace of justification, meaning that God in his grace is preparing our wills to receive salvation, then we affirm Rome's concerns here. But if by this Rome is saying that we initiate the movement itself, which would imply that faith is not a gift of God, then we deny even the second clause of this statement along with the sentiment that stands behind it.

59. Jaroslav Pelikan, *The Riddle of Roman Catholicism* (New York: Abingdon, 1959), 52.

60. Quoted in Chemnitz, *Examination*, 461–62.

while part two concerns "Articles about Matters in Dispute." Where does Augsburg place the doctrine of justification? In part one, indicating that justification by faith was a common doctrine among Christians on both sides of the Tiber! As we read in the opening sentence of part two: "From the above [i.e., part one] it is manifest that nothing is taught in our churches concerning articles of faith that is contrary to the Holy Scriptures or *what is common to the Christian church.*"[61] And what does the church commonly teach us about justification? "It is also taught among us that we cannot obtain forgiveness of sin and righteousness before God by our own merits, works, or satisfactions, but that we receive forgiveness of sin and become righteous before God by grace, for Christ's sake, through faith, when we believe that Christ suffered for us and that for his sake our sin is forgiven and righteousness and eternal life are given to us."[62] As a vindication of this claim, note well the words of what is perhaps the earliest Christian text outside the New Testament: "And so we, having been called through his will in Christ Jesus, are not justified through ourselves or through our wisdom or understanding or piety or works, which we have done in holiness of heart, but through faith, by which almighty God has justified all who have existed from the beginning, to whom be the glory for ever and ever. Amen."[63] Not only so, but the Reformational teaching that justification involves the glorious exchange between the believing sinner and Christ, so that the sin of the believer is imputed to Christ while the righteousness of the Savior is imputed to the sinner, is not a new teaching invented in the sixteenth century. Indeed, it is taught in Scripture (Isa 53:11; Jer 23:6; Rom 3:21–28; 4:1–8, 25; 2 Cor 5:21), and was even affirmed roughly one hundred years after Paul wrote his epistles: "In whom was it possible for us, the lawless and ungodly, to be justified, except in the Son of God alone? O sweet exchange, O the incomprehensible work of God, O the unexpected blessings, that the sinfulness of many should be hidden in one righteous man, while the righteousness of one should justify many sinners!"[64]

---

61. Augsburg Confession, in Leith, *Creeds of the Churches*, 79.

62. Augsburg Confession, in Leith, *Creeds of the Churches* , 69.

63. 1 Clement 32.3–4, quoted in Thomas Schreiner, *Faith Alone: The Doctrine of Justification* (Five Solas Series; Grand Rapids: Zondervan, 2015), 26–27.

64. *Epistle of Mathetes to Diognetus* 9.5, quoted in Schreiner, *Faith Alone*, 29.

THE EASTERN (GREEK) CHURCH

In 1054 the Orthodox Catholic Church formally split in two, with the Greek Orthodox Church residing in the East and the Roman Catholic Church residing in the West. While Orthodoxy formally upholds no creed beyond those produced by the first seven ecumenical councils, it has from time to time drawn up statements clarifying its stance on various doctrinal issues. On quite a few occasions the Orthodox Church has anathematized perceived abuses in the Roman Catholic Church.

In the wake of the Reformation, along with several important Greek teachers gravitating toward Reformed theology, Orthodox theologians met in Jerusalem in 1672 to give an answer to Reformational theology, which is commonly referred to as the Synod of Jerusalem. There the theologians in Jerusalem made statements affirming the structure of the Eastern church, along with denunciations of Calvinian predestination—which they interpreted as the doctrine that God elects and reprobates for no reason whatsoever. They also condemned justification by faith alone, insisting that salvation is also achieved through good works flowing from faith. This may lead one to think that the Eastern church, in principle, denies *sola gratia*. But that would be an overstatement. Indeed, what follows is a statement from the Russian-Orthodox Catechism, which is touted as the most authoritative standard of Eastern Orthodoxy:

> **[Question] 483.** May not a man, on the other hand, be saved by love and good works, *without faith?*

> It is impossible that a man who has not faith in God should really love him; besides, man, being ruined by sin, cannot do really good works, unless he receive through faith in Jesus Christ spiritual strength, or grace from God. ... *For by grace are ye saved through faith; and that not of yourselves: it is the gift of God: not of works, lest any man should boast* [Eph 2:8–9].[65]

---

65. http://www.pravoslavieto.com/docs/eng/Orthodox_Catechism_of_Philaret.htm#ii.xv.iii.i.p41.

What does the catechism mean when it says, "man ... cannot do really good works"? Does it mean that the good works unsaved persons perform are not good? Or are they not *really* good—meaning, they are good, but not for salvation? It seems that, either way, Orthodoxy officially rejects human merit as the basis for redemption. Or, to put it another way, whatever human merit might accomplish in the salvation of the soul, even this is all of grace. As we learn from one Orthodox theologian:

> Essentially, in Orthodoxy grace and free will are not separated or discussed in isolation, thus preventing doctrinal imbalance, as occurred with Pelagius. Free will and our cooperation with God is *always* understood to be an act of grace. Bishop Kallistos is again helpful here. His comments offer a response to [Protestant Douglas] Jones' question ..., in which he queries,—"how do the Eastern Orthodox attempt to explain that salvation is 'not of yourselves?'" His Grace would reply: "When we speak of 'cooperation,' it is not to be imagined that our initial impulse towards good precedes the gift of divine grace and comes from ourselves alone. We must not think that God waits to see how we shall use our free will, and then decides whether He will bestow or withhold His grace. Still less would it be true to suggest that our initial act of free choice somehow causes God's grace. All such notions of temporal priority or of cause and effect are inappropriate. On the contrary, any right exercise of our free will presupposes from the start the presence of divine grace, and without this 'prevenient' grace we could not begin to exercise our will aright. In every good desire and action on our part, God's grace is present from the outset. Our cooperation with God is genuinely free, but there is nothing in our good actions that is exclusively our own. At every point our human cooperation is itself the work of the Holy Spirit." This is a far cry from the assertion in [Jones] that in Orthodoxy "the beginning of salvation is purely by grace but the completion of the process is by human effort."[66]

---

66. Carmen Fragapane, "Salvation by Christ: A Response to Credenda/Agenda," http://orthodoxinfo.com/inquirers/frag_salv.aspx (accessed May 27, 2019).

Indeed, as one Coptic theologian puts the matter, "everything that God bestows on a human being is the work of divine grace."[67] Or as Orthodox theologian Marcus Eremita (fifth century) writes:

> (1) In the texts which follow, the beliefs of those in error will be refuted by those whose faith is well founded and who know the truth.

> (2) Wishing to show that to fulfill every commandment is a duty, whereas sonship is a gift given to men through His own Blood, the Lord said: "When you have done all that is commanded you, say: 'We are useless servants: we have only done what was our duty'" (Lk 17.10). *Thus the kingdom of heaven is not a reward for works, but a gift of grace* prepared by the Master for his faithful servants.

> (57) He who does something good and expects a reward is serving not God but his own will.[68]

Thus Letham is right when he says that, when all is said and done, the Orthodox "agree that on the day of judgment we will be unable to point to our works as a reason to enter heaven."[69]

Sola gratia is an essential doctrine of the Christian faith, so much so that if one self-consciously rejects this teaching then one is not a Christian. So I am thrilled that the best representatives of all branches of Christendom wish to eschew works-righteousness as the foundation of our redemption and rest *wholly* on the work of Christ for our salvation. In short, all branches of Christianity explicitly reject salvation by works and (at least) implicitly affirm *sola gratia*. However, I firmly believe that only the Protestant tradition in general, and Reformed Christianity in particular, advances the

---

67. Bishop Serapion, "The Divine Transforming Grace," *The Ecumenical Review* 56, no. 3 (July 2004): 312–21.

68. "On Those Who Think They Are Made Righteous by Works: Two Hundred Twenty-Six Texts," http://jbburnett.com/resources/mark_ascetic-righteousness.pdf (accessed June 22, 2018), italics added. I am grateful to Robert Letham for making this reference known to me. See Robert Letham, *Through Western Eyes (Eastern Orthodoxy: A Reformed Perspective)* (Fearn, Ross-shire, UK: Christian Focus, 2007), 251.

69. Letham, *Through Western Eyes*, 278.

doctrine of grace alone *consistently*.[70] Indeed, *sola fide* is a doctrine that guards what we as Christians all hold dear—*sola gratia*. As we move through our study, readers will hopefully see that Reformed theology, especially when it is enhanced by a Thomistic metaphysic and theology proper (i.e., Reformed Thomism), is able to emphasize, without qualification and without strain, that salvation is wholly from the Lord (Jonah 2:9). Indeed, "He saved us, not on the basis of deeds which we have done in righteousness, but according to His mercy, by the washing of regeneration and renewing by the Holy Spirit, whom He poured out upon us richly through Jesus Christ our Savior" (Titus 3:5-6).[71]

---

70. If we were saved by consistency, no one would be saved. Thankfully, we are all saved by grace *alone*.

71. For a helpful study of the development of *sola gratia* in church history, see Carl R. Trueman, *Grace Alone: Salvation as a Gift from God* (Five Solas Series; Grand Rapids: Zondervan, 2017). Even post-Tridentine Catholics, especially among the Thomists, recognize the absolute gratuity of salvation. For example, after citing Titus 3:5, Garrigou-Lagrange states: "Now, as it is a fact that He saves us, so He has predestined us to salvation. Foreknowledge of merits is therefore not the cause or reason of predestination which, as St. Thomas defined it ..., means predestination to glory." Indeed, as he goes on to say, all merit is excluded from being the basis for our salvation, whether it be merits acquired in a previous life, before justification, or after justification. In short, God's work of salvation is all of grace (i.e., *sola gratia*). Reginald Garrigou-Lagrange, *Predestination: The Meaning of Predestination in Scripture and the Church* (1939; repr., trans. Dom Bede Rose; Rockford, IL: Tan Books, 1998), 98.

But how can a Catholic affirm *sola gratia* if he denies *sola fide*? How can I merit salvation if redemption is wholly gratuitous? The common Thomistic answer is simple: "In the life of the predestined neither the good use of free will nor of grace can be given as the reason for predestination, *for they are its effects*" (Garrigou-Lagrange, *Predestination*, 99, italics added). As Craig explains, "On the Thomist view, the works are viewed as works of God to which He causally determines us, and therefore salvation by human works does not result. But then it is difficult to see either how man is genuinely free with regard to such works or how the merit wrought by such works can be attributed to man rather than to God." Thus, a more consistent approach is "to reject the Catholic doctrine of justification in favor of a Protestant understanding of salvation as a wholly unmerited and freely accorded gift of God's grace." William Lane Craig, *Divine Foreknowledge and Human Freedom: The Coherence of Theism; Omniscience* (Brill's Studies in Intellectual History 19; New York: E. J. Brill, 1991), 272. Elsewhere Craig notes that, if one wants to preserve the cardinal doctrine of *sola gratia*, "a Christian would therefore seem compelled to choose either Thomism or Protestantism" (*Divine Foreknowledge and Human Freedom*, 332n51).

How, exactly, does *sola fide* preserve *sola gratia* better than anything offered in Catholicism (e.g., Thomism) and/or Orthodoxy? It does so precisely because faith is the one act humans perform that explicitly recognizes the merit of another. In fact, the act of faith has a transitive property wherein its object does all of the work. For example, when I first jumped out of an airplane I climbed out on the wing and let go. The act of letting go was an act of faith in my parachute to bring me safely to the ground. I did nothing except fully trust in or rely on my canopy. The same is true in saving faith. When we trust in the Savior we let go of any and all merit or work that we are currently relying on to save us and depend wholly on Christ as

ELECTION

The doctrine of election is closely tied to the doctrine of grace. The word "election" means "choice," and "to elect" means "to choose." In the context of redemption, election refers to God's choice of persons for salvation. Notice that election is *not* salvation. Election is *unto* salvation. Hence, it is possible for a person to be elect and yet unsaved. Thus, Paul can say, "For this reason I endure all things for the sake of those who are chosen [i.e., the elect], that they may also obtain the salvation which is in Christ Jesus *and* with *it* eternal glory" (2 Tim 2:10). To be sure, if the doctrine of election is true, then all who are elect will be saved (John 6:37). Nevertheless, we must keep these notions distinct. Election is not salvation; it is unto salvation.

There are two views of election we will be discussing in this work—conditional election and unconditional election. If election refers to the

---

our sole merit. We submit that this very small act on our part, which recognizes the merit of Christ, is itself (in the words of Bob Marley) "light like a feather and heavy as lead," for our sinful hearts prevent us from seeing Christ for who he truly is. Hence, even the ability to do this one small act of letting go is a gift of God. Thus, as Sproul notes, "the Reformers strenuously objected to assigning any merit to our justification save the merit of Christ alone. Again, we see that the *sola gratia* of the Reformation was a true *sola*, without any mixture of any type of human merit. *Sola fide* meant that justification is by faith alone because it is a justification by the imputed merit of Christ alone." R. C. Sproul, *Faith Alone: The Evangelical Doctrine of Justification* (Grand Rapids: Baker, 1995), 151.

I have often spoken with Christians from other communions who say that their view of salvation is more plausible, since it seems counterintuitive to speak of oneself as "having been saved," as if to say that salvation is a done deal that is all in the past. Hence, they say, it is preferable to speak of my "being saved" continuously in the present from the bondage of sin. True, we Protestants often forget that there is more to our salvation than a past act of faith or justification ("having been saved"). We can only ask their forgiveness for being perhaps too excited over the glorious truth that we have been justified in Christ and that hence our right standing before God has been settled for all eternity. That said, we evangelicals are also able to speak of ourselves as "being saved" in the present, as our sanctification or growth in holiness is an ongoing process that will last a lifetime. Indeed, there is another sense in which we "will be saved" in the future, as our glorification in Christ is not yet accomplished. Hence, while we appreciate much of what Catholicism and Orthodoxy have to offer, even recognizing their desire to eschew works-righteousness, we think we can offer everything they are proclaiming and more besides; for, historically speaking, we alone can consistently maintain that we *have been saved* (justification), we *are being saved* (sanctification), and we *will one day be saved* (glorification). For a helpful work that develops these ideas from a Reformed perspective, see Anthony A. Hoekema, *Saved by Grace* (Grand Rapids: Eerdmans, 1989). For a modern defense of the Roman Catholic doctrine of justification, see Robert A. Sungenis, *Not by Faith Alone: The Biblical Evidence for the Catholic Doctrine of Justification* (Santa Barbara, CA: Queenship, 1997). For a modern defense of the evangelical doctrine of justification, see D. A. Carson, ed., *Right with God: Justification in the Bible and the World* (1992; repr., Eugene, OR: Wipf & Stock, 2002); and Schreiner, *Faith Alone*.

divine choice as to who will be saved, *conditional* versus *unconditional* election refers to *the basis* for that redemptive decision. That is, why does God choose a person for salvation? On what basis does he make that choice? The doctrine of *conditional election* states that the basis of election is faith (or some other action performed by the creature). In other words, the reason why God chooses some for salvation is that those so chosen trusted in Christ to be their Savior. Hence election is based on foreseen faith. The most common picture given to illustrate this view is the corridor of time. God looks down the corridor of time and foresees how everyone will respond to the gospel. Those whom he foreknows will respond positively, he elects unto salvation; those whom he foreknows will not respond positively (or, at least, those who explicitly reject the gospel), he reprobates unto damnation. Hence this view is also known as the prescient view of election, as well as conditional predestination.

In 1610 a group of Dutch theologians who were highly influenced by the thought of Jacob Arminius (d. 1609) drew up a document in protest of the Reformed Churches of Holland. The Reformed Churches followed the teaching of John Calvin, while Arminius and his students modified Calvin's teaching on predestination in order to make more room for faith. Their document was called the Remonstrantiœ, meaning "The Protest," and hence the Arminian theologians who drew up the document were often referred to as "the Remonstrants." The first article of their remonstration reads as follows:

> That God, by an eternal and unchangeable purpose in Jesus Christ his Son before the foundation of the world, has determined that out of the fallen, sinful race of men, to save in Christ, for Christ's sake, and through Christ, those who through the grace of the Holy Spirit shall believe on this his son Jesus, and shall persevere in this faith and obedience of faith, through this grace, even to the end; and, on the other hand, to leave the incorrigible and unbelieving in sin and under wrath and to condemn them as alienated from Christ, according to the word of the Gospel in John 3:36: "He that believes on the Son has everlasting life: and he that does not believe the Son shall

not see life; but the wrath of God abides on him," and according to other passages of Scripture also.[72]

Among Protestants, Wesleyans, along with most in the Anabaptist tradition(s), affirm this view of predestination. Conditional election is also affirmed by the Eastern Orthodox Church:

> We believe the most good God to have from eternity predestinated unto glory those whom He hath chosen, and to have consigned unto condemnation those whom He hath rejected; but not so that He would justify the one, and consign and condemn the other without cause. For that were contrary to the nature of God, who is the common Father of all, and no respecter of persons, and would have all men to be saved, and to come to the knowledge of the truth; but since He foreknew the one would make a right use of their free-will, and the other a wrong, He predestinated the one, or condemned the other. And we understand the use of free-will thus, that the Divine and illuminating grace, and which we call preventing [or prevenient] grace, being, as a light to those in darkness, by the Divine goodness imparted to all, to those that are willing to obey this—for it is of use only to the willing, not to the unwilling—and co-operate with it, in what it requireth as necessary to salvation, there is consequently granted particular grace; which, co-operating with us, and enabling us, and making us perseverant in the love of God, that is to say, in performing those good things that God would have us to do, and which His preventing grace admonisheth us that we should do, justifieth us, and maketh us predestinated. But those who will not obey, and co-operate with grace; and, therefore, will not observe those things that God would have us perform, and that abuse in the service of Satan the free-will, which they have received

---

72. Dennis Bratcher, ed., "The Five Articles of the Remonstrants (1610)," http://www.crivoice.org/creed-remonstrants.html (accessed June 25, 2018).

of God to perform voluntarily what is good, are consigned to eternal condemnation.[73]

Unconditional election, like conditional election, is a doctrine that affirms the notion that God chooses certain persons unto salvation. However, whereas Arminians insist that God elects on the basis of foreseen faith, Calvinists, whom the Remonstrants protested, insist that God does not elect on the basis of foreseen faith. Nor does God elect on the basis of any human merit. In fact, no human action or effort or choice or dispositions of any kind play a role in God's choice of election. God chooses persons unto salvation *wholly* from his mercy and nothing else. The Canons of Dort (1619), written in direct response to the Remonstrantiœ (and from which we get the so-called five points of Calvinism), give the following description of election:

> Election is the unchangeable purpose of God, whereby, before the foundation of the world, He hath out of mere grace, according to the sovereign good pleasure of His own will, chosen, from the whole human race, which had fallen through their own fault from their primitive state of rectitude into sin and destruction, a certain number of persons to redemption in Christ, whom He from eternity appointed the Mediator and Head of the elect, and the foundation of salvation. ...
>
> This election was not founded upon foreseen faith, and the obedience of faith, holiness, or any other good quality or disposition in man, as the prerequisite, cause or condition on which it depended; but men are chosen to faith and to the obedience of faith, holiness, etc.; therefore election is the fountain of every saving good, from which proceeds faith, holiness, and the other gifts of salvation, and finally eternal life itself, as its fruits and effects, according to that of the apostle: "He hath chosen us [not because we were but] that we should be holy, and without blame, before Him in love" (Eph. 1:4).

---

73. Acts and Decrees of the Synod of Jerusalem (1672) 6.3, http://catholicity.elcore.net/ConfessionOfDosithe-us.html (accessed June 25, 2018).

The good pleasure of God is the sole cause of this gracious election, which doth not consist herein, that out of all possible qualities and actions of men God has chosen some as a condition of salvation; but that He was pleased out of the common mass of sinners to adopt some certain persons as a peculiar people to Himself, as it is written, "For the children being not yet born, neither having done any good or evil," etc., it was said (namely to Rebecca): "The elder shall serve the younger. As it is written, Jacob have I loved, but Esau have I hated" (Rom. 9:11–13). "And as many as were ordained to eternal life believed" (Acts 13:48). (Canons of Dort 1.7–10)[74]

Nearly one hundred years before the Synod of Dort convened, the Lutheran churches advocated unconditional election. For while there are many differences between Lutheran and Reformed Christians on many important points, both branches of the Reformation deny, in the words of the Epitome of the Formula of Concord, "that there is also within us a cause of God's election, on account of which God has elected us to eternal life" (11.20). Indeed, "The predestination or eternal election of God …. is a cause of their [believers'] salvation, for he alone brings it about and ordains everything that belongs to it" (11.5).[75] Roman Catholics consist of a mixed group, though most of the great theologians associated with the Roman communion have embraced unconditional election (e.g., Augustine, Anselm, Aquinas, etc.).[76]

Few people are able to read the Scriptures and conclude that everyone will be saved. Indeed, it is clear that some persons will not ultimately be redeemed (Dan 12:2; Rom 2:6–11; Rev 14:9–11). For this reason alone, we must conclude that the Bible offers us a doctrine of *reprobation*. "Reprobation" is the act of God whereby he decides to allow some sinners to perish in his wrath. My contention, which is consistent with most Reformed theologians, is that the act of reprobation is not the same as the act of election in that the former is passive while the latter is active. That is to say, with

---

74. See Joel Beeke and Sinclair B. Ferguson, *Reformed Confessions Harmonized* (Grand Rapids: Baker, 1999), 28, 30, 32.

75. Theodore G. Tappert et al., trans. and ed., *The Book of Concord: The Confessions of the Evangelical Lutheran Church* (Philadelphia: Fortress, 1959), 497, 495.

76. For more on the history of election from a Catholic perspective, see Garrigou-Lagrange, *Predestination*.

respect to election, God actively selects a number of humans out of the mass of humanity to save. With respect to reprobation, God chooses to simply pass over some sinners and allow them to receive their just punishment. We say that election is active in that, had God not elected some unto redemption, everyone would perish. We say that reprobation is passive insofar as God does nothing against the reprobate sinner;[77] he is simply allowing a person to go to perdition without actively giving her the intrinsically efficacious grace that will certainly draw her to salvation. Again, God elects some unto salvation (those who will ultimately be saved are called "the elect"), and he *allows* or *permits* others to go to hell (those who will ultimately be damned are called "the reprobate"). Via election, the goodness that is God's *grace* is exalted; via reprobation, the goodness that is God's *justice* is exalted.

LOVE

Another term that is equally tied to the notion of grace is "love." A common definition of love is "the feeling of good will towards other things and persons."[78] To expand on this definition, *love is a deep and abiding affection one person (or personal being) has for another, which manifests itself in a compassionate feeling toward the object of affection, as well as acts of good will towards that same object.* In short, to love another is to possess an emotional attachment toward that other and to (attempt to) accomplish whatever is good or best for that other. Love, then, is both a feeling and an act; it is an emotion and a choice; it is a noun and a verb. Closely associated with love is the word "benevolent" or "benevolence." This term literally means "good or well (*bene*) wish or will (*volentia*)." Benevolence occurs when one wills the good of another. Hence, throughout our study I will be using the terms "love" and "benevolence" synonymously.

Most Christians wish to affirm the idea that God is not merely benevolent (i.e., good willing), but *omnibenevolent* (i.e., willing the good of all); he is not merely love (i.e., his essence is characterized by love) or loving (i.e.,

---

77. Technically, this is not the complete picture. God does many good things for the reprobate sinner, as I will illustrate throughout this work. My point here is that God is not actively pursuing the damnation of anyone.

78. *Webster's New World College Dictionary* (4th ed.; Cleveland: Wiley, 2002), 850.

he loves others), but he is also all-loving (i.e., he loves every single being other than himself). Not only so, most Christians throughout history have wanted to say that God's love is not merely expressed in a general benevolence given to everyone, but in actions performed for the purpose of saving every single person from eternal damnation. In short, most Christians believe, as we do, that God genuinely and savingly (or redemptively) loves every single human person.[79]

PELAGIANISM

This school of thought gets its name from Pelagius (ca. 360–418). He was a theologian, possibly even a monk, of great virtue who was disturbed by Augustine's famous prayer uttered in *The Confessions*: "Give what you command, and command what you will" (10.31, 45). Pelagius believed firmly that God would never command of us what we could not inherently perform in and of ourselves. His student Coelestius drew out the logical implications of Pelagius's sentiment, going so far as to deny that humans have inherited a sinful disposition from Adam. In short, the Pelagians denied original sin—which, in brief, says that we inherit a tendency to sin from our first parents. They also insisted that a special gift of grace, given to us supernaturally by God, is not necessary for salvation (though it is welcome). Humans, then, are saved by their own merits, according to the Pelagians. To summarize the difference between the Pelagians, Wesleyan Arminians, and Augustinian Calvinists on the issue of grace:

> Pelagianism = special grace is neither necessary nor sufficient in itself

---

79. One helpful study of the divine love by a formidable scholar, which is nevertheless fully accessible to the layperson, is D. A. Carson, *The Difficult Doctrine of the Love of God* (Wheaton, IL: Crossway, 2000). The few disagreements I have with him are mere quibbles, with one exception. Carson takes issue with the classical theistic doctrine of the impassibility of God, believing (as many do) that this doctrine affirms the very strange and unbiblical notion that God lacks any and all emotions. Near the end of his study, however, he affirms a revised understanding of impassibility as the notion that God's emotional life is in no way dependent on or determined by the creature (*Difficult Doctrine*, 28–29, 58–64), which is actually what the classical tradition has affirmed all along! See Richard A. Muller, *The Divine Essence and Attributes* (vol. 3 of *Post-Reformation Reformed Dogmatics: The Rise and Development of Reformed Orthodoxy, ca. 1520 to ca. 1725*; Grand Rapids: Baker, 2003), 310–11.

Wesleyan Arminianism = special grace is necessary, but not sufficient in itself

Augustinian Calvinism = special grace is both necessary and sufficient in itself

Historically, Christians have acknowledged both Wesleyan Arminians and
Augustinian Calvinists to be within the bounds of orthodoxy. Pelagianism,
as we have already noted, is a heresy precisely because it denies the necessity of grace. When we say that Wesleyan Arminians deny that grace is sufficient in and of itself, we are highlighting a feature of conditional election.
On conditional election, one must meet a single condition in order to be
elect—i.e., faith (or, in *some* Catholic circles, human merits). Grace is necessary for one to come to faith, for unless one is drawn by the Holy Spirit
one will never believe (see John 6:44; Acts 16:14). On the other hand, this
prevenient grace, which is given to all so as to draw them to the Savior, is
resistible (see Acts 7:51). Hence, in and of itself, it is not sufficient to move
a person to faith. Thus the sinner must cooperate with grace; the sinner
must make good use of the freedom given to one by God in order for prevenient grace to be sufficient for one's salvation. This Arminian view is called
"synergism," meaning that Creator-Redeemer and creature-sinner "work
together" for the accomplishment of one's salvation. In contrast, Calvinists
champion "monergism," meaning that there is only one who works for the
salvation of any person—namely, God, who gives a grace that fully accomplishes what it is given to accomplish (i.e., the redemption of the human
sinner). Hence Augustinians are known for emphasizing "efficacious or
effectual or efficient grace," meaning that divine grace, in and of itself,
is sufficient to accomplish the redemption of the sinner. Thomists, who
are Augustinian in their understanding of grace, emphasize a distinction
between *sufficient* and *efficient* grace—a point we develop in the seventh
chapter of this work.

Pelagianism, as we have seen, was condemned in the West. The Eastern
churches would not condemn Pelagius's teachings, feeling that the dispute
in the West between him and Augustine was over trivialities. To be sure,
Eastern Orthodoxy has often rebuked Pelagianism in its formal pronounce-
ments on grace, as we have seen, even though it has yet to condemn it as

heresy. B. L. Shelley offers the following summary of the heart of Pelagius's teaching:

> The keystone of Pelagianism is the idea of man's unconditional free will and his moral responsibility. In creating man God did not subject him, like other creatures, to the law of nature but gave him the unique privilege of accomplishing the divine will by his own choice. This possibility of freely choosing the good entails the possibility of choosing evil.
>
> According to Pelagius there are three features in human action: power (*posse*), will (*velle*), and the realization (*esse*). The first comes exclusively from God; the other two belong to man. Thus, as man acts, he merits praise or blame. Whatever his followers may have said, Pelagius himself held the conception of a divine law proclaiming to men what they ought to do and setting before them the prospect of supernatural rewards and punishments. If man enjoys freedom of choice, it is by the express bounty of his Creator; he ought to use it for those ends that God prescribes.
>
> The rest of Pelagianism flows from this central thought of freedom. First, it rejects the idea that man's will has any intrinsic bias in favor of wrongdoing as a result of the fall. Since each soul is created immediately by God, as Pelagius believed, then it cannot come into the world soiled by original sin transmitted from Adam. Before a person begins exercising his will, "there is only in him what God has created." The effect of infant baptism, then, is not eternal life but "spiritual illumination, adoption as children of God, citizenship of the heavenly Jerusalem."
>
> Second, Pelagius considers grace purely an external aid provided by God. He leaves no room for any special interior action of God upon the soul. By "grace" Pelagius really means free will itself or the revelation of God's law through reason, instructing us in what we should do and holding out to us eternal sanctions. Since this revelation has become obscured through evil customs, grace now includes the law of Moses and the teaching and example of Christ.

This grace is offered equally to all. God is no respecter of persons. By merit alone men advance in holiness. God's predestination operates according to the quality of the lives God foresees men will lead.[80]

This work will show that Pelagianism is actually an incoherent system insofar as its view of predestination cannot be reconciled with even a minimal commitment to theism.

THE PURPOSE OF THIS STUDY

My position on the issue of salvation is that of Reformed theology, which is mostly based on Augustine's view of grace. That is to say, I advocate unconditional election, as well as particular salvation (i.e., not all are saved) and reprobation (i.e., God does not elect everyone for salvation). The inference many want to draw from these three convictions—i.e., unconditional election, particular salvation, reprobation—is that God does not want everyone to be saved. On the contrary, my burden is to demonstrate that this conclusion simply does not follow from the doctrine of unconditional election and its concomitant teachings of particular salvation and reprobation. In short, sovereign election need not entail a denial of universal benevolence.

I believe that a Reformed theology that is informed by a Thomistic metaphysic, along with most of Thomas's views on grace, is the best way to reconcile God's goodness with the existence of evil. More particularly, Reformed Thomism is the best model for dealing with the soteriological problem of evil. That is, how can God savingly love all if he sovereignly elects some? My goal is to demonstrate that unconditional election is compatible with universal redemptive love. Contrary to many interpretations of Calvin, who famously said that divine election entailed a "horrible" or "dreadful decree,"[81] I instead see God's plan of redemption as a *wonderful decree* that ought to be celebrated by every Christian and taken seriously by all non-Christians.

The remainder of this work is divided into seven parts: the prologue attempts to set the tone of our study with two quotations of Charles

---

80. B. L. Shelley, "Pelagius, Pelagianism," in *Evangelical Dictionary of Theology*, 897–98.

81. John Calvin, *Institutes of the Christian Religion* 3.23.7. To be sure, in this same context he also calls the divine plan "wonderful." Hence the difference in interpretation.

Spurgeon. My quotations of him illustrate two points—first, he was a man who firmly believed that God sovereignly elects, but also genuinely loves all unto salvation; second, though a brilliant preacher, Spurgeon lacked the synthetic mind of an Aquinas, and so (to his credit) was willing to believe both truths, all the while owning up to the fact that he had no idea how to reconcile them.

Chapter 3 offers two exegetical arguments for unconditional election. There we explore passages from the Bible, showing how they teach this awesome truth. I will also answer objections to my exegesis of Scripture.

Chapter 4 offers a philosophico-theological argument for the doctrine of unconditional election. There I show that, if even a *minimal* understanding of God is granted, along with the classical doctrine of creation out of nothing, even a *Pelagian* must admit that election is not based on anything foreseen or foreseeable in the creature.

Chapter 5 explores what is perhaps the most popular way to get out of the argument presented in chapter 4. This way of modern Arminians is so-called middle knowledge, which presumably gives God the sovereignty necessary to control all events and humans the freedom necessary to render their choices a sufficient condition for election. There we will see that this doctrine in no way saves the theist from unconditional election.

Chapter 6 then expresses the ultimate protest against unconditional election—namely, if God unconditionally elects, then his love is not universal. There we will explore various passages of Scripture that seem to indicate that God really does desire the salvation of everyone. Attempts to refute this biblical truth will also be answered. This will leave us with Spurgeon's tension—how can God sovereignly elect and universally love at the same time?

Chapter 7 attempts to reconcile sovereign grace with universal benevolence by articulating one basic distinction found in the Thomistic and Reformed traditions, which includes the difference between sufficient and efficient grace. In articulating this distinction, we will also see how God is justified in creating a world wherein evil obtains and many experience damnation. If this distinction is even possible, then this thesis is secured. If it is true, then we have in Reformed Thomism a genuine theodicy. Indeed,

God sovereignly elects and universally loves, and yet he is fully justified in allowing some to perish.

I close with an epilogue. Spurgeon was a single man who lived in tension. But the Reformed tradition as a whole does not experience a dialectic but a divine reconciliation of these truths that is intellectually satisfying and spiritually comforting. In this dying world we are able to place our full confidence and assurance in a Savior who sovereignly loved us unto salvation; and we can also honestly look at any sinner and say that God genuinely and savingly loves him or her. In the church, which is the believer's "haven of revelation," we can look at any justified sinner and say that they have been redeemed by God's sovereign grace alone. To those who refuse the offer of redemption, their refusal does not come from God. Indeed, salvation is all of God's grace, while damnation is all of human sin and rejection. For "destruction is your own, O Israel; your help is found in me" (Hos 13:9).[82]

---

82. Author's translation from the Vulgate.

Part 2

THE WONDERFUL DECREE

A PROLOGUE

SPURGEON ON SOVEREIGN ELECTION

*But we are bound to give thanks always to God for you, brethren beloved
of the Lord, because God hath from the beginning chosen you to salvation
through sanctification of the Spirit and belief of the truth: Whereunto he
called you by our gospel, to the obtaining of the glory of our Lord Jesus Christ.*
(2 Thessalonians 2:13–14 KJV)

If there were no other text in the sacred Word except this one, I
think we should all be bound to receive and acknowledge the truthfulness of the great and glorious doctrine of God's ancient choice
of his family. But there seems to be an inveterate prejudice in the
human mind against this doctrine; and although most other doctrines will be received by professing Christians, some with caution,
others with pleasure, yet this one seems to be most frequently dis-
regarded and discarded.

...

[A] human authority whereby I would confirm the doctrine of election [is] the old Waldensian creed. If you read the creed of the old
Waldenses, emanating from them in the midst of the burning heat
of persecution, you will see that these renowned professors and con-
fessors of the Christian faith did most firmly receive and embrace
this doctrine, as being a portion of the truth of God. I have copied
from an old book one of the Articles of their faith: — "That God saves
from corruption and damnation those whom he has chosen from the
foundations of the world, not for any disposition, faith, or holiness
that he foresaw in them, but of his mere mercy in Christ Jesus his

Son, passing by all the rest according to the irreprehensible reason of his own free-will and justice."

I also give you an extract from the old Baptist Confession. ...

By the decree of God, for the manifestation of his glory, some men and angels are predestinated, or foreordained to eternal life through Jesus Christ to the praise of his glorious grace; others being left to act in their sin to their just condemnation, to the praise of his glorious justice. These angels and men thus predestinated and foreordained, are particularly and unchangeably designed, and their number so certain and definite, that it cannot be either increased or diminished. Those of mankind that are predestinated to life, God, before the foundation of the world was laid, according to his eternal and immutable purpose, and the secret counsel and good pleasure of his will, hath chosen in Christ unto everlasting glory out of his mere free grace and love, without any other thing in the creature as a condition or cause moving him thereunto.

It is no novelty, then, that I am preaching; no new doctrine. I love to proclaim these strong old doctrines, which are called by nickname Calvinism, but which are surely and verily the revealed truth of God as it is in Christ Jesus. By this truth I make a pilgrimage into the past, and as I go, I see father after father, confessor after confessor, martyr after martyr, standing up to shake hands with me. Were I a Pelagian, or a believer in the doctrine of free-will, I should have to walk for centuries all alone. Here and there a heretic of no very honourable character might rise up and call me brother. But taking these things to be the standard of my faith, I see the land of the ancients peopled with my brethren—I behold multitudes who confess the same as I do, and acknowledge that this is the religion of God's own church.[1]

---

1. Charles H. Spurgeon, "Election," in *Spurgeon's Sermons*, vols. 1–2 (Grand Rapids: Baker, 1996), 66, 69–70.

SPURGEON ON GOD'S UNIVERSAL LOVE

This is good, and it is pleasing in the sight of God our Savior, who desires all
people to be saved and to come to the knowledge of the truth.
(1 Timothy 2:4 ESV)

What then? Shall we try to put another meaning into the text than that which it fairly bears? I trow not.[2] You must, most of you, be acquainted with the general method in which our older Calvinistic friends deal with this text. "All men," say they,—"that is, *some men*": as if the Holy Ghost could not have said "some men" if he had meant some men. "All men," say they; "that is, some of all sorts of men": as if the Lord could not have said "all sorts of men" if he had meant that. The Holy Ghost by the apostle has written "all men," and unquestionably he means all men. I know how to get rid of the force of the "alls" according to that critical method which some time ago was very current, but I do not see how it can be applied here with due regard to truth. I was reading just now the exposition of a very able doctor who explains the text so as to explain it away; he applies grammatical gunpowder to it, and explodes it by way of expounding it. I thought when I read his exposition that it would have been a very capital comment upon the text if it had read, "Who *will not* have all men to be saved, nor come to a knowledge of the truth." Had such been the inspired language every remark of the learned doctor would have been exactly in keeping, but as it happens to say, "Who *will* have all men to be saved," his observations are more than a little out of place. My love of consistency with my own doctrinal views is not great enough to allow me knowingly to alter a single text of Scripture. I have great respect for orthodoxy, but my reverence for inspiration is far greater. I would sooner a hundred times over appear to be inconsistent with myself than be inconsistent with the word of God. I never thought it to be any very great crime to seem to be inconsistent with myself; for who am I that I should

---

2. "Trow" is an old English term for "trust, believe, or think." So here Spurgeon is saying, "I think not."

everlastingly be consistent? But I do think it a great crime to be so inconsistent with the word of God that I should want to lop away a bough or even a twig from so much as a single tree of the forest of Scripture. God forbid that I should cut or shape, even in the least degree, any divine expression. So runs the text, and so we must read it, "God our Savior; who will have all men to be saved, and to come unto the knowledge of the truth."[3]

3. "A Crucial Text—C. H. Spurgeon on 1 Timothy 2:3, 4," in Iain H. Murray, *Spurgeon v. Hyper-Calvinism: The Battle for Gospel Preaching* (Carlisle, PA: Banner of Truth, 1995), 150–51.

3

A BIBLICAL CASE FOR
UNCONDITIONAL ELECTION

But man's will is moved to good by God, as it says above: **all who are led by
the Spirit of God are sons of God** *(Rom 8:14); therefore, an inward action
of man is not to be attributed principally to man but to God: it is God who of
his good pleasure works in you both the will and the performance
(Phil 2:13).*
—Thomas Aquinas *(Commentary on Romans 9.16 [C.9, L.3])*

*G*od exercises his absolute freedom and sovereign grace by choosing to save
some sinners, thereby ensuring the redemption of those whom he has
chosen; and this choice is in no way based on the faith or merits of those sinners so chosen. This, in a nutshell, is the doctrine of unconditional election.
Here I will begin making my case for this teaching by examining two New
Testament passages: Acts 13 and Romans 8–9.

ACTS 13:48

This text gives us a picture of what is going on behind the scenes—that is,
it gives us the reason why people responded positively to Paul's message:
"When the Gentiles heard this, they *began* rejoicing and glorifying the word
of the Lord; and as many as had been appointed to eternal life believed."
This verse seems clear. The reason people believe is that they have been
appointed to eternal life (they are not appointed to eternal life because
they believe). As Calvin notes:

> And we need not doubt but that Luke calleth those τεταγμενους [*tetag-
> menous*], who were chosen by the free adoption of God. For it is
> a ridiculous cavil to refer this unto the affection of those which

81

believed, as if those received the gospel whose minds were well-disposed. For this ordaining must be understood of the eternal counsel of God alone. Neither doth Luke say that they were ordained unto faith, but unto life; because the Lord doth predestinate his unto the inheritance of eternal life. And this place teacheth that faith dependeth upon God's election. And assuredly, seeing that the whole race of man-kind is blind and stubborn, those diseases stick fast in our nature until they be redressed by the grace of the Spirit, and that redressing floweth from the fountain of election alone. ... Now, if God's election, whereby he ordaineth us unto life, be the cause of faith and salvation, there remaineth nothing for worthiness or merits.[1]

Objection. It would seem that the only way an advocate of conditional election can get around this text is to interpret it as somehow implying that election depends on faith. William MacDonald and Robert Shank are typical in this regard, arguing that the context of this passage suggests that τεταγμένοι (*tetagmenoi*, "had been appointed") should be taken as a perfect middle rather than a perfect passive participle and so should be translated as follows: "*and as many as were putting themselves in a position for eternal life believed.*"[2] An argument in favor of such a translation is an appeal to the immediate context, where Paul says the following to a group of unbelieving Jews: "It was necessary that the word of God be spoken to you first; since you repudiate it and judge yourselves unworthy of eternal life, behold, we are turning to the Gentiles" (Acts 13:46). Here is the point: If we are to understand Paul as saying that the Jews have rendered themselves unworthy of eternal life, then we should also understand that election was obtained by the gentiles because they, in contrast to the Jews, placed themselves in a position to receive God's free offer of salvation.[3] Hence,

---

1. John Calvin, *Commentary on the Acts of the Apostles* (trans. Christopher Fetherstone; ed. Henry Beveridge; 1844; *Calvin's Commentaries* 18; repr., Grand Rapids: Baker, 1996), 1:555–56.

2. William G. MacDonald, "The Biblical Doctrine of Election," in *The Grace of God and the Will of Man* (ed. Clark H. Pinnock; Minneapolis: Bethany House, 1995), 226–28, italics original. See also Robert Shank, *Elect in the Son: A Study of the Doctrine of Election* (Minneapolis: Bethany, 1989), 186–87.

3. MacDonald, "Biblical Doctrine of Election," 227. See also Shank, *Elect in the Son*, 183–84.

we can also translate Acts 13:48 as follows: "and as many as had ordained themselves to eternal life believed." Therefore, this text does not evince a biblical endorsement of unconditional election.

Response. We may respond to the above argument as follows: First, it is poor grammar; for Acts 13:46 is *not* a grammatical parallel to Acts 13:48. Here is why: In Acts 13:46 we read the following: καὶ οὐκ ἀξίους κρίνετε ἑαυτοὺς τῆς αἰωνίου ζωῆς, which is translated, "and [you] judge yourselves unworthy of the eternal life." The argument is that this verse serves as a sort of parallel to Acts 13:48 and hence verse 48 can be translated "and those who ordained themselves to eternal life believed." MacDonald and Shank correctly note that the word τεταγμένοι (*tetagmenoi*), found in Acts 13:48, can be translated as either passive or middle. If passive, then the gentiles of Acts 13 are being ordained unto eternal life *by God*—thus the translation "and as many as had been destined for eternal life became believers" (NRSV). In the middle voice, the subject of the verb performs and/or experiences the action of the verb—hence Mark 14:54, where we read of Peter "warming himself at the fire." If the word *tetagmenoi* is understood as middle rather than passive, Luke is saying that gentiles are the ones *ordaining themselves* to eternal life, not God. MacDonald and Shank, who both affirm conditional election,[4] will no doubt want to understand *tetagmenoi* as middle rather than passive for obvious reasons; but an appeal to 13:46 as a contextual vindication of this interpretation is misguided. Indeed, in verse 46 the verb being used is κρίνετε (*krinete*), from κρίνω (*krino*), meaning "judge." The Greek student will immediately recognize this verb as *active, being neither middle nor passive*. It seems obvious that one cannot vindicate an interpretation of the participle *tetagmenoi* as middle by appealing to a verb that is *not* middle. In short, the grammatical construction found in Acts 13:46 does not parallel that of 13:48. Therefore, any appeal to the grammar of verse 46 to make a case for a grammatical understanding of verse 48 is unwarranted.

Second, there are no clear examples of a participle in the middle voice throughout the book of Acts—the only exception being Acts 12:21, where we read of Herod clothing himself. In fact, the middle voice is rarely used

---

4. MacDonald, "Biblical Doctrine of Election," 228. See also Shank, *Elect in the Son*, 108–16.

in the New Testament as a whole.[5] The fact that verbs and/or participles in the middle voice are rarely found in the New Testament as a whole, and in Acts in particular, renders MacDonald's and Shank's contention suspect.

Third, a study of the word τάσσω (tasso), from which we get the participle *tetagmenoi*, warrants the conclusion that it is *God* who ordains persons unto eternal life, *not the persons themselves*. A study of this word, in both classical and New Testament literature, indicates that it never (or hardly ever) means anything other than "ordain," "appoint," or "determine" in the passive sense.[6] Hence F. F. Bruce notes:

> We cannot agree with those who attempt to tone down the predestinarian note of this phrase by rendering "as many as were disposed to eternal life." ... The Greek participle is from τάσσω [tasso], and there is papyrus evidence for this verb in the sense of "inscribe" or "enroll" (cf. "thou has signed a decree," in Theodotian's version of Dan. 6:12).[7]

Bock concurs:

> Those who have been ordained to eternal life believe. The word τάσσω (tasso, ordain) appears four times in Acts (13:48; 15:2; 22:10; 28:23; in the rest of the NT: Matt. 28:16–17; Luke 7:8; Rom. 13:1; 1 Cor. 16:15–16). In the other contexts of Acts, it means "appoint" or "assign" to something. Here it refers to God's sovereign work over salvation, where God has assigned those who come to eternal life. ... The passive voice indicates that God does the assigning. It is as strong a passage on God's sovereignty as anywhere in Luke-Acts and has OT Jewish roots.[8]

Keener, in his magisterial work on Acts, concurs with Bruce and Bock:

---

5. See Daniel B. Wallace, *Greek Grammar beyond the Basics* (Grand Rapids: Zondervan, 1996), 417–18.

6. See Delling, "τάσσω," in *TDNT*, 8:27–31.

7. F. F. Bruce, *The Book of Acts* (NICNT; Grand Rapids: Eerdmans, 1988), 267n111.

8. Darrell L. Bock, *Acts* (BECNT; Grand Rapids: Baker, 2007), 464–65.

The phrase "appointed" applies to "enrollment" in papyri, relevant in view of the perspective in Luke 10:20 [i.e., " ... do not rejoice in this, that the spirits are subject to you, but rejoice that your names are recorded in heaven"]. One may think of the Book of Life in early Jewish literature. Some scholars have argued that the people "appointed" themselves, but this interpretation is difficult to sustain. ... In this context, note the fairly conspicuous and perhaps deliberate tension with 13:46: "judge yourselves unworthy of eternal life," a contrast underlying the play between God's sovereignty and human choice.[9]

Fourth, MacDonald's and Shank's interpretation(s) seems to contradict Luke's theology as a whole. Throughout Acts, we see God's sovereign hand controlling every event that takes place. The predestinarian tone of the book is established early on with passages such as the following:

Jesus the Nazarene, a man attested to you by God with miracles and wonders and signs which God performed through Him in your midst, just as you yourselves know—this *Man*, delivered over by the predetermined plan and foreknowledge of God, you nailed to a cross by the hands of godless men and put *Him* to death. (Acts 2:22–23)

For truly in this city there were gathered together against Your holy servant Jesus, whom You anointed, both Herod and Pontius Pilate, along with the Gentiles and the peoples of Israel, to do whatever Your hand and Your purpose predestined to occur. (Acts 4:27–28)

It was the Lord who added the number of people being saved into the church on a daily basis (Acts 2:47). *It was the Lord* who granted the Israelites deliverance from the Egyptians (Acts 7:25). *It was the Lord* who sent Philip to the Ethiopian eunuch to give him the gospel (Acts 8:26). *It was the Lord* who

---

9. Craig S. Keener, *Acts: An Exegetical Commentary*, vol. 2, *3:1–14:28* (Grand Rapids: Baker, 2013), 2101–2. Fitzmyer's interpretation of this text is somewhat ambiguous, although he clearly translates 13:48 passively, as in "as many as were destined to eternal life became believers." Joseph A. Fitzmyer, *The Acts of the Apostles* (AB 31; New York: Doubleday, 1998), 521–22.

sovereignly called Paul out of the darkness and into new life and into his service, that he might take the gospel to the gentiles (Acts 9:15). *It was the Lord* who sent Peter to Cornelius (Acts 10:1–23), demonstrating that he had sovereignly granted "to the Gentiles also the repentance *that leads* to life" (Acts 11:18). In Acts 13 itself, the Holy Spirit set apart several men as missionaries (13:4), and, when Paul arrived in Antioch, he proclaimed God's sovereignty throughout his sermon to the Jews (13:17). And we learn at the end of the next chapter that it was God who opened the door of faith to the gentiles (14:27). I could go on, but in light of our survey of the first fourteen chapters of Acts, where God is always portrayed as the one who predetermines, initiates salvation, sets boundaries concerning where the apostles are to go, and grants faith (Acts 16:7, 11, 14), it is warranted to reject the middle voice rendering of 13:48; and, consequently, it is warranted to accept the translation advocated by the best New Testament lexicons and majority of modern translations (along with the prima facie interpretation that accompanies it).[10]

Fifth, the appeal to Acts 13:46 as a vindication of MacDonald's and Shank's understanding(s) of Acts 13:48 is, from the standpoint of theology, inconclusive at best. According to most Calvinists, there is an asymmetrical relationship between election and reprobation. God actively chooses some unto eternal life. But he merely passes over others and allows them to reject his gospel. God does not make anyone disbelieve, though he does elect and effectually call some. Hence, in the Reformed view, the reprobate truly render themselves unworthy of eternal life through their lack of faith (among other sins). But the elect do *not* render themselves *worthy* of eternal life for, if it were not for the God who chooses them, they would render themselves *unworthy* of eternal life just as the reprobates do. Hence, Acts 13:48 is one good biblical reason to think the doctrine of unconditional election is true.

ROMANS 8:29–30; 9:6–27

Paul's famous discussion of divine predestination in Romans 8–9 is a battleground between those who affirm and those who reject unconditional

---

10. See BDAG, 991; and ESV, NRSV, NASB, KJV, NKJV, NET, NIV, HCSB, etc.

election. Here we will first look at a few verses from Romans 8, and then we will follow up with an analysis of Romans 9.

ROMANS 8:29–30

Here the apostle writes: "For whom He foreknew, He also predestined to *become* conformed to the image of His Son, that He would be the firstborn among many brethren; and these whom He predestined, He also called; and these whom He called, He also justified; and these whom He justified, He also glorified."

This discourse on predestination is what many theologians call the golden chain of redemption. Indeed, *in this context*, there is no such thing as a person foreknown who is not also predestined, one predestined who is not also called, one called who is not also justified, one justified who is not also glorified. In the divine mind, it is all a done deal. As Schreiner observes: "The major objective of the text should be reiterated here. Believers are assured that everything works together for good because the God who set his covenantal love upon them, predestined them to be like his Son, called them effectually to himself, and justified them will certainly glorify them."[11]

---

11. Thomas R. Schreiner, *Romans* (BECNT; Grand Rapids: Baker, 1998), 455. Those who oppose this interpretation often appeal to Rom 8:29 (along with 1 Pet 1:2) in support of conditional election. The idea is that "those whom God foreknew *would believe in Christ*" are predestined to justification and to glory. See John Miley, *Systematic Theology* (New York: Hunt & Eaton, 1892–93), 2:261; Jack Cottrell, "Conditional Election," in *Grace Unlimited* (ed. Clark H. Pinnock; Minneapolis: Bethany, 1975), 62). Unfortunately, the words "would believe in Christ" are read into the sentence. Indeed, it is *persons* God is foreknowing in this passage, *not their activities* (e.g., belief). The overall context of both Rom 8:29 and 1 Pet 1:2 suggests that "foreknow" points to the intimate, covenantal love that God has for his people—e.g., "God has not rejected His people whom He foreknew" (Rom 11:2 HCSB; see Gen 4:1; Amos 3:2; Matt 7:23; 1 Pet 1:20). Thus, it would not be wholly inappropriate to (loosely) translate Rom 8:29 as "those whom He foreloved, He also predestined." Interestingly, John Laing offers an impressive defense of the intimate nature of the term "know," as it is used in both the OT and the NT; and yet, like Miley and Cottrell, reads a concept of conditional election into the text. See John D. Laing, *Middle Knowledge: Human Freedom in Divine Sovereignty* (Grand Rapids: Kregel, 2018), 304–17. Flowers agrees with me that "foreknew" is plausibly translated "foreloved," but wants to limit the scope of those "foreloved" to the OT saints known personally by God "beforehand" in redemptive history (e.g., Abraham, Moses, and David). See Leighton Flowers, *The Potter's Promise: A Biblical Defense of Traditional Soteriology* (N.p.: Trinity Academic Press, 2017), 84–91. However, this interpretation is implausible in the extreme, for Paul clearly identifies the saints as "we" and "us" in the immediate context of the passage (Rom 8:26–27, 31), and since there is little doubt that his audience was mixed, consisting of both Jews and gentiles (see Rom 1:7, 16; 2:17; 3:29; 11:13, 25–32; 16:1–15), we must conclude that those "foreloved" of God are those elected to be redeemed from among the Jews and the gentiles (Rom 11:2 ,7, 11). Notice also

ROMANS 9:6–27

Paul's elucidation of the golden chain of redemption is concluded with words of consolation and comfort:

> Who will separate us from the love of Christ? Will tribulation, or distress, or persecution, or famine, or nakedness, or danger, or sword? … But in all these things we overwhelmingly conquer through Him who loved us. For I am convinced that neither death, nor life, nor angels, nor principalities, nor things present, nor things to come, nor powers, nor height, nor depth, nor any other created thing, will be able to separate us from the love of God, which is in Christ Jesus our Lord. (Rom 8:35, 37–39)

The fact of our security in Christ raises yet another problem; namely, *Was not the nation of Israel chosen?* Of course! *Is the nation of Israel* (at least the majority of the people comprising that nation) *now lost?* Unfortunately, yes! For Israel has forsaken her Messiah (Rom 10:1–4)! *But if Israel has been lost even after being chosen, how shall our election unto salvation comfort us?* Indeed, can't we also be lost even after being predestined unto glory? Paul answers this question in his magisterial discourse in Romans 9:6–27 (the full text being quoted in note below).[12]

---

that Paul elsewhere locates God's election of the saints "before the foundation of the world" (Eph 1:4), indicating that it is unlikely that he would want to limit the scope of "foreknew" here in Rom 8:29 to a particular time in the past. Indeed, the election of the saints is anchored in eternity (see Titus 1:2; 2 Tim 1:9; Rev 13:8).

12. Paul, immediately following his discourse on the golden chain, first notes his sorrow over the disbelief of his Jewish brethren: "I am telling the truth in Christ, I am not lying, my conscience testifies with me in the Holy Spirit, that I have great sorrow and unceasing grief in my heart. For I could wish that I myself were accursed, *separated* from Christ for the sake of my brethren, my kinsmen according to the flesh, who are Israelites, to whom belongs the adoption as sons, and the glory and the covenants and the giving of the Law and the *temple* service and the promises, whose are the fathers, and from whom is the Christ according to the flesh, who is over all, God blessed forever. Amen" (Rom 9:1–5). Again, how can we hope in our security in Christ if those chosen beforehand have been cut off from him? Paul answers in what follows: "But *it is* not as though the word of God has failed. For they are not all Israel who are *descended* from Israel; neither are they all children because they are Abraham's descendants, but: 'THROUGH ISAAC YOUR DESCENDANTS WILL BE NAMED.' That is, it is not the children of the flesh who are children of God, but the children of promise are regarded as descendants. For this is the word of promise: 'AT THIS TIME I WILL COME, AND SARAH SHALL HAVE A SON.' And not only this, but there was Rebekah also, when she had conceived *twins* by one man, our father Isaac; for though *the twins* were not yet born and had not done anything good or

Perhaps the key verse that establishes quite conclusively the doctrine of unconditional election is 9:16: "So then it *does* not *depend* on the man who wills or the man who runs, but on God who has mercy." The "it" here probably refers to "God's purpose according to *His* choice" (NASB) or "God's purpose of election" (NRSV)—see 9:11.[13] The evidence for this contention is seen in the fact that "God's purpose of election" is the subject under consideration. God's purpose of election is not because of works, but because of God's calling. Paul's proof of this is that Scripture teaches that "the older shall serve the younger" (Gen 25:23) and "I have loved Jacob, but I have hated Esau" (Mal 1:2–3). As the Lord says to Moses, God has mercy on whomever he wills and hardens whomever he wills (Exod 33:19). Thus, verse 16 summarizes Paul's argument up to that point in his discourse—i.e., the Scriptures prove that God's purpose of election does not depend on human

---

bad, in order that God's purpose according to *His* choice might stand, not because of works but because of Him who calls, it was said to her, 'THE OLDER WILL SERVE THE YOUNGER.' Just as it is written, 'JACOB I LOVED, BUT ESAU I HATED.'

"What shall we say then? There is no injustice with God, is there? May it never be! For He says to Moses, 'I WILL HAVE MERCY ON WHOM I HAVE MERCY, AND I WILL HAVE COMPASSION ON WHOM I HAVE COMPASSION.' So then it *does* not *depend* on the man who wills or the man who runs, but on God who has mercy. For the Scripture says to Pharaoh, 'FOR THIS VERY PURPOSE I RAISED YOU UP, TO DEMONSTRATE MY POWER IN YOU, AND THAT MY NAME MIGHT BE PROCLAIMED THROUGHOUT THE WHOLE EARTH.' So then He has mercy on whom He desires and He hardens whom He desires.

"You will say to me then, 'Why does He still find fault? For who resists His will?' On the contrary, who are you, O man, who answers back to God? The thing molded will not say to the molder, 'Why did you make me like this,' will it? Or does not the potter have a right over the clay, to make from the same lump one vessel for honorable use and another for common use? What if God, although willing to demonstrate His wrath and to make His power known, endured with much patience vessels of wrath prepared for destruction? And *He did so* to make known the riches of His glory upon vessels of mercy, which He prepared beforehand for glory, *even* us, whom He also called, not from among Jews only, but also from Gentiles. As He says also in Hosea,

'I will call those people who were not My people, "My people,"
and her who was not beloved, "Beloved."
And it shall be that in the place where it was said to them, "you are not My people,"
There shall they be called the sons of the living God.'

"And Isaiah cries out concerning Israel, 'THOUGH THE NUMBER OF THE SONS OF ISRAEL BE LIKE THE SAND OF THE SEA, IT IS THE REMNANT THAT WILL BE SAVED'" (Rom 9:6–27).

13. Interestingly, Flowers agrees with us here: "Actually, 'it' refers back to 'God's purpose of election'" (*Potter's Promise*, 128). This concession is followed by the notion that it is an unconditionally chosen nation bringing about the divine plan of redemption that is the object of God's affection. I analyze this view in the pages to follow.

willing or exertion, but on divine mercy.[14] This is one of the great proofs that unconditional election is true, for Paul is explicitly denying the idea that election is based on or conditioned by any foreseen human activity (e.g., faith or good works)—that is, election is not based on human willing or working; and since it is the human will that chooses to believe, election is not based on foreseen acts of people willing to believe the gospel! Much less is it based on the good works of those persons.

Objections. More than a few New Testament scholars see Paul's argument in Romans 9 as a statement about God's sovereign purpose in electing certain nations as the recipients of God's (temporal) blessings in history. In other words, Romans 9 has nothing to do with the salvation of individuals for eternity; rather, it is about God's dealings with nations in time and/or his electing peoples for a particular service.[15]

Other New Testament exegetes insist that election has more to do with corporate groups than individuals. For example, while commenting on Romans 9:13 ("Jacob I have loved, but Esau I have hated"), Joseph Fitzmyer says that there "is no hint here of predestination to 'grace' or 'glory' of an

---

14. To be sure, some may insist that the "it" in v. 16 has as its immediate antecedent, "compassion"—as in "I will have mercy on whom I will have mercy, and I will have compassion on whom I have compassion" (v. 15). Hence, v. 16 should be interpreted as follows: "So, then, God's *compassion* does not depend on the person who wills or the person who runs, but on the God who shows mercy." But notice in this regard that, in the context of Rom 9:11-18, *election is the very expression of God's compassion.* So unconditional election still shines through Rom 9:16, regardless of whether the "it" refers to "God's purpose according to his election" or "compassion." For those who think the compassion expressed in election is given to everyone (even if potentially), Paul goes on to discuss Pharaoh, who (according to the Scriptures) was raised up for the very purpose of YHWH demonstrating the divine prerogative to harden whomever he wills (Rom 9:17, 18; see Exod 9:16); hence, "He has mercy on whom He desires, and He hardens whom he desires" (Rom 9:18). Thus, for Paul, some are not the recipients of election (actual, potential, or otherwise). This is confirmed for us in John (6:70; 17:12), where Judas obviously shares the same fate as Pharaoh!

15. See C. E. B. Cranfield, *A Critical and Exegetical Commentary on the Epistle to the Romans* (ICC; Edinburgh: T&T Clark, 1979), 2:479; James D. G. Dunn, *Romans 9-16* (WBC 38A; Dallas: Word Books, 1988), 539; Dunn, *The Theology of Paul the Apostle* (Grand Rapids: Eerdmans, 1998), 501; Leon Morris, *The Epistle to the Romans* (Grand Rapids: Eerdmans, 1988), 356-57. Another version of this viewpoint is found in Flowers, *Potter's Promise*, 107-9n103. For a survey of other authorities endorsing the "election unto service" viewpoint, see J. D. Myers, *The Re-Justification of God: An Exegetical and Theological Study of Romans 9:10-24* (Dallas, OR: Redeeming Press, 2017), 37-45.

individual; it is an expression of the choice of corporate Israel over corporate Edom."[16] Clark Pinnock concurs, writing:

> When the term predestination is used in relation to salvation, it concerns the believer's future destiny which is to be conformed to Jesus Christ, not to his becoming a Christian. ... There is no predestination to salvation or damnation in the Bible. There is only predestination for those who are already children of God with respect to certain privileges out ahead of them.[17]

Thus, election refers to "a class of people rather than specific individuals."[18] God elected the nation of Israel (Gen 12:1–3; Isa 42:1) as well as the church (2 John 1,13), but this does not prove that God has elected individuals unto salvation. It is the corporate entity that is unconditionally elected, not the individual sinner. Hence, God's election encompasses every single person potentially.

Still others see Paul as "arguing against the Jewish concept of 'unconditional' election (of all Jews by birth) and establishing, in its place, conditional election—election of believers."[19] Evidence for this interpretation is found in Romans 9:30–32, where the gentile (who has attained righteousness by faith) is distinguished from the Jew (who has failed to attain righteousness through works).[20]

In summary, then, Romans 9 cannot be used to support the doctrine of unconditional election—for (1) Paul is talking here about God's unconditionally electing a corporate people unto service, not salvation; (2) but even if it were salvation that is being discussed, we need to remember that it is a *corporate* entity (e.g., the church, made up of Jews and gentiles) that is being elected, not individuals—thus, the question remains, how does the

16. Joseph A. Fitzmyer, *Romans: A New Translation with Introduction and Commentary* (AB 33; New York: Doubleday, 1993), 563.

17. Jack Cottrell, "Introduction," in *Grace Unlimited*, 18.

18. Clark Pinnock, "From Augustine to Arminius: A Pilgrimage in Theology," in *Grace of God and the Will of Man*, 20.

19. Robert E. Picirilli, *Grace, Faith, Free Will—Contrasting Views of Salvation: Calvinism & Arminianism* (Nashville: Randall House, 2002), 73–74.

20. Picirilli, *Grace, Faith, Free Will*, 73.

individual enter the corporate body? Paul's answer: *by faith*! And (3) even if Paul is here discussing God's election of individuals unto salvation, we need to remember that God stresses faith at the end of the chapter. Thus, election is based on or conditioned by a person's faith after all.

Response. Two initial points need to be made before I answer the above arguments. First, I agree with those who see election as unto service. I also agree with those who see election as corporate. I take a both/and approach here—i.e., election is *both* corporate *and* individual; it is *both* unto salvation *and* unto service. Second, given the possibility of a both/and approach to this text, a fairly high burden must be placed on those who offer the either/or reading of the passage—e.g., Romans 9 is *either* about salvation *or* about service; it is about corporate entities *rather than* individuals; it is about temporal blessings, *not* eternal rewards; and so on.

The notion of corporate election is literally vacuous if it is not supplemented with a corresponding idea of individual election. For it seems odd, to say the least, to think that God elects a contentless corporation (e.g., the church) and then just leaves it up to us to decide whether we would like to join that body. As Myers, who rejects my interpretation, points out, choosing a corporate body *just is* the election of individuals to be a part of that body.[21] Besides, the Scriptures are replete with assertions and allusions to the intimate nature of the divine electing love. For example, Paul offers himself as a particular example of someone "foreknown" or "foreloved" by God (Rom 11:1-2). Elsewhere, he gives his own testimony of how God had set him apart, even while still in the womb (see Rom 9:11), and called him through grace to be his and to proclaim the gospel (Gal 1:15). Jeremiah, too, was known by God before he was even conceived and appointed to be YHWH's prophet to the nations (Jer 1:5); and John the Baptist was filled with the Holy Spirit while still in Elizabeth's womb (Luke 1:15). We cannot reduce God's choice of these individuals—Jeremiah, John the Baptist, and

---

21. In Myers's own words: "The stance taken here is that Paul is teaching both corporate and individual election. Since it is the purposes of God that determine who gets elected and to what form of service they are elected, then it is God who decides when He needs to call individuals and when He needs to call nations or groups of people to perform certain tasks. Of course, even when election is corporate, it is true that God's purpose for that group of people is carried out by individuals within the group, and so in this sense, we can say that even corporate election has an individual aspect" (*Re-Justification of God*, 48).

Paul—to *mere* service and not salvation, as some insist on doing, for not only is the redemptive-covenantal language in these texts strong, it makes little sense to elect someone to service if he is not first elected to salvation! On this point even Klein (who rejects unconditional election and defends corporate election) agrees: "Yet only in a theological discussion can we separate Paul's apostolic appointment from his acquisition of salvation, as the Acts speeches show [see Acts 22:14-16]. In Paul's thinking, if God appointed him from birth to be an apostle, was he not also appointed to salvation?"[22] Indeed, Paul explicitly connects his being set apart before his birth with his being called "through his grace" (Gal 1:15)—"grace" being a term used to denote salvation throughout the immediate context of the passage (see 1:6; 2:9, 21), and thus it should be so understood in Galatians 1:15. So it is clear that God chooses individuals unto salvation. Indeed, he elects groups of people unto redemption (see Acts 13:48; Eph 1:4), yet calls each person out "by name" (see Isa 43:1-7).

Picirilli points to Paul's appeal to faith in Romans 9:30-32 as suggestive of conditional election. However, what that text demonstrates is that *salvation* is based on faith. But it says nothing of the grounds for *election*. I contend that, while *salvation* is conditional ("Believe in the Lord Jesus, and you will be saved" [Acts 16:31; see Rom 10:8-9]), *election* is unconditional. Indeed, Paul elsewhere points out that there are those who are elect who have not yet been saved (2 Tim 2:10), which makes little sense unless these notions are clearly distinct.

Romans 9:16-18 tells us that the mercy of election is not based on human willing or running, but on the God of grace, who gives mercy and compassion to whomever he wills, and even hardens whomever he wills. John Piper gives three reasons why all forms of human willing and working, including the good will to exercise an act of faith, are excluded here as a basis for God's decision to show mercy. First, Romans 9:11 states that God's election of Jacob over Esau occurred before they were born, thereby establishing the point that God's choice obtained apart from their having done anything—whether good or bad. Second, Romans 9:16 is offered as an inference from what is written in the Torah—i.e., "I will show compassion

---

22. William W. Klein, *The New Chosen People: A Corporate View of Election* (Eugene, OR: Wipf & Stock, 2001), 195.

on whom I will show compassion" (Exod 33:19). This is clearly an affirmation of God's absolutely sovereign prerogative to show mercy to whomever he wills, which is precisely why Paul insists that it is not according to human will or works that God elects. "Third, the closest analogy in Paul to the phrase οὐ τοῦ θέλοντος οὐδὲ τοῦ τρέχοντος in Rom 9:16 is Phil 2:13: 'God is the one who works in you both the willing and the working' (τὸ θέλειν καὶ τὸ ἐνεργεῖν)."[23] Thus Philippians 2:13 serves as the positive counterpart to Romans 9:16. Hence, human "willing and running do not determine the bestowal of God's mercy (9:16); on the contrary, God's mercy determines man's willing and working (Phil 2:13)."[24]

Given the unconditional nature of election, along with the mutual entailment between the individual creature and the corporate body to whom he belongs, one can see why the exegesis of Romans 9 hinges on its soteriological character. In other words, is Paul speaking about election for *salvation* or election for *service*? My answer is that Paul is speaking about both, which (if true) secures the unconditional nature of the divine choice of individuals for salvation. Those who disagree bear the burden of showing that Romans 9 is speaking of election unto service *to the exclusion of* election unto salvation. I have every reason to think this burden will never be met. Indeed, beyond the evidence I have already offered for this point, there are three good reasons to think Romans 9 teaches that individuals are unconditionally elected for *salvation*. First, Romans 1–8 has concerned itself with little more than the issue of salvation from eternal judgment (see Rom 1:16–17; 2:5–16; 3:21–31; 4:5, 25; 5:1, 8–10; 8:1, 29–39). Are there any transitional markers in Romans 9:1–33 to suggest that Paul has changed the subject from salvation to temporal blessings or services to be rendered in history? We don't see any! We do see Paul ending Romans 8 with the comforting words concerning our security in Christ: no "created thing, will be able to separate us from the love of God, which is in Christ Jesus our Lord" (Rom 8:39). This comes at the end of Paul's golden chain of redemption (Rom 8:28–30) which, in turn, comes at the end of Paul's discussion of our future glorification (8:18–25) which, in turn, is part of a discussion that

---

23. John Piper, *The Justification of God: An Exegetical and Theological Study of Romans 9:1–23* (2nd ed.; Grand Rapids: Baker, 1993), 153–54.

24. Piper, *Justification of God*, 154.

speaks of our justification in Christ (8:1; see 5:1). How does Paul's discussion in Romans 9 end? It ends with the doctrine of salvation—i.e., how gentiles are able to inherit the promise, thereby becoming a part of the people of God through faith (9:24-30)—where Paul goes on to pray, "Brethren, my heart's desire and my prayer to God for them [the Jews] is for *their* salvation" (10:1). Between 8:39 and 10:1, both of which speak of our redemption (or salvific security) in Christ, we see nothing in Romans 9:1-33 that would suggest salvation is no longer being discussed.

Second, in the midst of his discussion in Romans 9, Paul is also refuting a common Jewish doctrine of unconditional election. We saw Picirilli note that the Jews of Paul's day held to an unconditional election for salvation grounded in their ethnic identity as Jews. He suggested that Paul is replacing this pharisaical doctrine with a doctrine of conditional election based on faith. I have already refuted Picirilli's exegesis on *that* point. However, there is good reason to think that Picirilli is correct about the historical circumstances in which Paul wrote his epistle. As Moo reports: "Paul is engaged here in a discussion of the Jewish doctrine of election. Mainstream Jewish teaching held that all Jews were elected to salvation by virtue of their inclusion in that people with whom God had entered into covenant relationship. Only by apostatizing did the Jew forfeit that salvation."[25] Moo's statement is corroborated by Scripture (see Luke 3:7-9). Paul, then, is not replacing the common Jewish doctrine of unconditional election based on ethnic identity with a conditional election based on faith, since Romans 9:16 speaks of the divine choice as *unconditional*; rather, he is replacing an unconditional election *based on ethnic identity* with an unconditional election *based on the mercy and compassion of God.* By pulling the foundation of their election out from under Jewish feet, Paul is able to do many things at once. For example, he is able to show that God has always been faithful to his people, since everyone of (ethnic) Israel is not of true (spiritual) Israel; for rather than committing himself to an ethnic people, God has always and only been committed to a remnant within that people (see Rom 2:28-29; 9:7-13, 27; 11:1, 5; compare Isa 10:21; 11:1; 46:3; Jer 31:7). Hence, no created thing can come between God and his elect! He is also able to explain

---

25. Douglas J. Moo, *The Epistle to the Romans* (NICNT; Grand Rapids: Eerdmans, 1996), 569n2.

how it is that gentiles have become the heirs of God's promises—i.e., God gives mercy to whomever he wills and has obviously decided to give it to many Jews (Rom 9:23–24; see Isa 52:15), which entails that, currently, gentile heirs of the promise greatly outnumber Jewish heirs (Rom 11:11–32; see Acts 13:46–48). It is God's prerogative to do this, for he is sovereign (Rom 11:33–36; see Dan 4:34–35), and hence he is the God of both Jews and gentiles (Rom 3:29–30; see Ps 87:1–7).

Finally, throughout Romans 9, Paul uses the terms "calling" (vv. 11, 24), "election" (v. 11), "wrath" (v. 22), "mercy" (v. 16), "righteousness" and "justice" (vv. 14, 30), "faith" and "works" (vv. 11, 16, 30, 32); and it is clear that throughout the epistle to the Romans these terms are used as references to eternal salvation (see Rom 1:16, 18; 2:7–8, 13; 3:28; 4:2, 5; 5:1, 9; 8:28–39; 10:1–10). In fact, these are common soteriological terms used by Paul throughout his letters (see 1 Cor 1:9, 24, 26; Gal 1:6, 15; 5:8; Eph 4:1, 4; Phil 3:14; 1 Thess 2:12; 4:7; 5:24; 2 Thess 2:14; 1 Tim 6:12; 2 Tim 1:9). Now, if Paul is using these terms to refer to eternal salvation elsewhere, and even in the immediate context of the passage (e.g., Rom 8:39; 10:1), then we have every reason to think he is using these terms in the same way in Romans 9 itself. In this light, Pinnock's claim that there "is no predestination to salvation … in the Bible" becomes preposterous. Indeed, we clearly see God electing and/or appointing and/or predestinating persons unto redemption throughout the Bible (Eph 1:1–11; Rom 8:28–9:24; Acts 13:48; etc.), "because … God has chosen you [i.e., persons] for salvation" (2 Thess 2:13 HCSB). In Romans 9 itself, the key "words in the paragraph—'children of God' (v. 8), 'descendents' (vv. 7 and 8), 'counted' (v. 8), 'children of promise' (v. 8) 'name' or 'call' (vv. 7,12), and 'not of works' (v. 12)—are constantly applied by Paul elsewhere to the salvation of individuals."[26] In fact, "The continuation of vv. 6b–13 in vv. 24–29 shows that Paul's point is to demonstrate how God has called *individuals* from among both Jews and Gentiles to be his people and that those Jews who are called … constitute the 'remnant' that will be 'saved' (v. 27)."[27] Thus, when Paul quotes Exodus 33:19 (i.e., "I will be gracious to whom I will be gracious, and I will show compassion on whom I will show

---

26. Moo, *Romans*, 572; see Gal 1:13–17; 2:15–21; 3:10–14; Eph 2:8–10 (see also Moo, *Romans*, 572–88).

27. Moo, *Romans*, 572, italics original.

compassion"—9:15), the Greek word ὅν, which is translated "whom," is singular (not plural). Notice also the singular expression in 9:16—literally, "So, then, not of the one willing nor of the one running, but of the mercy of God" (my translation). The singular is used again in 9:18—"So then He has mercy on whom He desires, and He hardens whom He desires." When Paul goes on to ask, "Why does He still find fault? For who resists His will?" (9:19), the "who" (τίς) in that second sentence is also singular. Last, in 9:21 we find another cache of singular terms—"Or does not the potter have a right over the clay, to make from the same lump one vessel for honorable use and another for common use?" After surveying this evidence, Schreiner concludes: "Those who say that Paul is referring only to corporate groups do not have an adequate explanation as to why Paul uses the singular again and again in Romans 9."[28] Hence, there is little doubt that Paul is addressing the salvation of individuals in Romans 8-9. So Romans 8-9 clearly teaches (among other things) the doctrine of unconditional election.

SUMMARY AND CONCLUSION

The doctrine of unconditional election states that God's choice of those whom he will save is in no way based on anything they do—whether it be faith or good works or any other action they may perform. Rather, election is based wholly on God's mercy. Jesus himself taught this very truth, saying: "All that the Father gives Me will come to Me, and the one who comes to Me I will certainly not cast out" (John 6:37). The second clause is the promise that anyone who comes to Christ in faith will not be rejected. The first clause gives us the reason they will not be rejected—that is, the Father has given a particular people to his Son, who will most certainly come to him in faith and never be rejected. "This is the will of Him who sent Me, that of all that He has given Me I lose nothing, but raise it up on the last day" (John 6:39). Notice here that *everyone* given to the Son *is* redeemed—*none* are lost. But many there are who do not believe in the Son, and so are *not* redeemed (John 6:30, 41-42, 64-65, 70-71). Therefore, it is *not* the case that everyone is given to the Son by the Father. For had they been so given, they would

---

28. Thomas R. Schreiner, "Does Romans 9 Teach Individual Election unto Salvation," in *Biblical and Practical Perspectives on Calvinism* (vol. 1 of *The Grace of God, The Bondage of the Will*; ed. Thomas R. Schreiner and Bruce A. Ware; Grand Rapids: Baker, 1995), 99.

have certainly come to Christ in faith. Nor can we say that those given to the Son come to him of their own accord. Indeed, "No one can come to Me unless the Father who sent me draws him; and I will raise him up on the last day" (John 6:44). In the words of Leon Morris: "People do not come to Christ because it seems a good idea to them. It never does seem a good idea to sinful people. Apart from a divine work in their souls (cf. [John] 16:8) people remain more or less contentedly in their sins. Before they can come to Christ it is necessary that the Father give them to him."[29] In short, God is the one who elects us for redemption, not us. Or, in the words of Jesus himself, "You did not choose Me but I chose you" (John 15:16a).[30]

In this chapter we have looked at two biblical passages that explicitly teach the unconditional nature of redemptive election—namely, Acts 13:48 and Romans 8-9. Those who object to our interpretation of Acts 13:48 insist that it is the people being saved, and not God, who appoint themselves unto eternal life. However, a closer examination of the text demonstrates that, on the contrary, God is the one doing the appointing, not the people being saved.

Those who oppose our interpretation of Romans 8-9 have, more often than not, attempted to either ground election in faith or insist that the

---

29. Leon Morris, *The Gospel according to John* (2nd ed.; NICNT; Grand Rapids: Eerdmans, 1995), 325.

30. The entire verse reads: (Jesus speaking) "You did not choose me but I chose you. And I appointed you to go and bear fruit, fruit that will last, so that the Father will give you whatever you ask him in my name" (John 15:16 NRSV). Many insist that this verse is not talking about election for salvation, but merely election for the office of apostleship and/or the task of preaching the gospel (e.g., see Klein, *New Chosen People*, 132). No doubt the election spoken of here includes the specific task given to the apostles; and yet, in "speaking of those whom he has chosen the Johannine Jesus is undoubtedly addressing himself to all Christians who are 'elect' or 'chosen' of God (Rom viii 33; Col iii 12; 1 Pet ii 4). ... If elsewhere in Johannine thought the Twelve are apostles par excellence (Rev xxi 14: 'the Twelve Apostles of the Lamb'), the Twelve are being given a mission that all Christians must fulfill. By stressing that the *fruit* that they bear must *remain*, John achieves in 16 an inclusion with the themes of 7 and 8 [i.e., "If you abide in me, and my words abide in you, ask for whatever you wish, and it will be done for you. My Father is glorified by this, that you bear much fruit and become my disciples" (John 15:7-8 NRSV)], and at the end of the explanation ... brings back once more the prominent vocabulary used to describe the vine and the branches." Raymond E. Brown, *The Gospel according to John (XIII-XXI)* (AB 29A; New York: Doubleday, 1970), 683-84, italics original. Therefore, far from being a mere statement about service or apostleship, "this saying speaks of Christ's sovereign freedom to choose whom and what he will—and of the privilege of being called out of the world (v. 19) to be Jesus' disciples and friends." Herman N. Ridderbos, *The Gospel of John: A Theological Commentary* (trans. John Vriend; Grand Rapids: Eerdmans, 1997), 521.

election being discussed in these texts has nothing to do with salvation. Others insist that it is a corporate entity God chooses, not individuals. But a close look at the passage will not allow such maneuvers. Indeed, those who insist on a choice for service to the exclusion of an election for salvation have failed to meet the very high burden placed on them. On the other hand, the doctrine of an *individual* election unto salvation easily emerges from Paul's tightly argued discourse in Romans. Paul, along with Luke and Jesus, teaches us that election is wholly gratuitous, being based on God's prerogative to show mercy to whomever he will, and so is in no way based on human merit or human faith.

Humans have a tendency to make God in their image, and so it is quite natural for them to construe election as a divine choice that is conditioned by or based on the actions of the creatures he wishes to save. However, Scripture offers us a God who transcends us, being qualitatively infinitely other than us, and (thus) simply does not think in the same manner we do (Isa 55:7–8). And so, when it comes to the reasons God chooses one person and not another, we should not be surprised to see him defying our own categories as to how it should be done. In the words of Aquinas:

> Election and love, however, are ordered differently in God than in man. For in men, election precedes love, for a man's will is inclined to love a thing on account of the good perceived in it, this good also being the reason why he prefers one thing to another and why he fixed his love on the thing he preferred. But God's love is the cause of every good found in a creature; consequently, the good in virtue of which one is preferred to another through election follows upon God's willing it—which pertains to his love. Consequently, it is not in virtue of some good which he selects in man that God loves him; rather, it is because he loved him that he prefers him to someone [else] by election.[31]

And so, when speaking of the divine electing love, Thomas says, "For it is called God's love, inasmuch as he wills good to a person absolutely; it is

---

31. Thomas Aquinas, *Commentary on the Letter of Saint Paul to the Romans* (trans. F. R. Larcher; ed. J. Mortensen and E. Alarcon; vol. 37 of The Latin/English Edition of the Works of St. Thomas Aquinas; Lander, WY: The Aquinas Institute for the Study of Sacred Doctrine, 2012), 255.

election, inasmuch as through the good he wills for a person, he prefers him to someone else."[32] Indeed, God does not love us because we first loved him. Rather, we love God "because He first loved us" (1 John 4:19; see Rom 5:8).[33]

---

32. Aquinas, *Commentary on the Letter of Saint Paul to the Romans*, 255.

33. Many Christians believe God's love is unconditional. True! But how can this be if his election of us, which is an expression of divine love if there ever was one, is conditioned by our faith?

4

THE ARGUMENT FROM MINIMAL THEISM TO UNCONDITIONAL ELECTION

*This is all that follows from an absolute, unconditional, irreversible decree,
that it is impossible but that the things decreed should be. The same exactly
follows from foreknowledge, that it is absolutely impossible but that the thing
certainly foreknown should precisely come to pass.*
—Jonathan Edwards (Miscellanies, "Entry 74")

G od exercises his absolute freedom and sovereign grace by choosing to save
some sinners, thereby ensuring the redemption of those whom he has
*chosen; and this choice is in no way based on the faith or merits of those sinners
so chosen.* In the previous chapter I offered biblical evidence suggesting
that this doctrine of unconditional election is true. In fact, I believe the
exegesis offered there is alone sufficient to secure the point quite conclusively. However, beyond the explicit assertions of Scripture, there is a
strong philosophical argument to be made in favor of sovereign election
that in no way presupposes the argumentation offered in chapter 3.

Let us concede the Pelagian heresy (for *argument's* sake)—thereby
believing that human beings are as good and free as Pelagius said they are.
No doubt this means that I (and everyone else) was born into this world *neu-
trally,* and formed my character through the use of my free will. By doing
my best to do what is right, as well as believe divine truth (as far as I can
ascertain), I can achieve salvation for myself. God's guidance and help are

most welcome in my endeavors—but by no means are they necessary (let alone sufficient) for the achievement of my own salvation.[1]

One premise we will not concede is universalism. Pelagius himself was not a universalist (i.e., he did not believe that everyone will inherit the world to come), and his position on the matter is backed up by more than a few biblical texts (Dan 12:2; Matt 25:46; Rom 2:5-8; Rev 14:9-11; 20:11-15).[2] He believed—and so shall we, *for the sake of argument*—that those who freely choose the right path are going to heaven, and those who freely choose the wrong path are going to hell.[3]

Another premise we will not concede is (*at least*) a minimalist, bare-boned, theism—i.e., the belief that an all-knowing and all-powerful God exists, who is the Creator and Sustainer of the universe. Pelagius was a theist,[4] even if many who accept his presuppositions now tend to embrace various forms of pantheism and/or panentheism.

Traditionally, Jews, Christians, Muslims, and *some* pagans embrace (*at least*) a minimalistic version of theism. The belief that an omniscient and omnipotent God exists who creates the universe from nothing is, we contend, provable via natural theology (i.e., the art and science of establishing the existence of the theistic God through a study of nature)[5] and/or simply reflecting on creation (see Ps 19:1-6; Rom 1:20). In any case, these

---

1. Pelagius, *Commentary on St. Paul's Epistle to the Romans* (Oxford Early Christian Studies; Oxford: Clarendon, 1993), 103-4, 117.

2. Pelagius, *Commentary on St. Paul's Epistle to the Romans*, 68-73.

3. Pelagius, *Commentary on St. Paul's Epistle to the Romans*, 71, 117.

4. Pelagius, *Commentary on St. Paul's Epistle to the Romans*, 64-65, 112.

5. See Russell Re Manning, ed., *The Oxford Handbook of Natural Theology* (Oxford: Oxford University Press, 2013); William Lane Craig and J. P. Moreland, eds., *The Blackwell Companion to Natural Theology* (Chichester, West Sussex, UK: Blackwell, 2009); William Lane Craig, ed., *Philosophy of Religion: A Reader and Guide* (New Brunswick, NJ: Rutgers University Press, 2002); William Lane Craig and J. P. Moreland, eds., *Naturalism: A Critical Analysis* (London: Routledge, 2000); Paul Copan and Paul K. Moser, eds., *The Rationality of Theism* (London: Routledge, 2003); Brian Davies, ed., *Philosophy of Religion: A Guide and Anthology* (Oxford: Oxford University Press, 2000); and Norman Geisler and Winfried Corduan, *Philosophy of Religion* (2nd ed.; Grand Rapids: Baker, 1988). For a classic defense of natural theology, along with a rigorous articulation of the Thomistic proofs, see Reginald Garrigou-Lagrange, *God: His Existence and Nature (A Thomistic Solution to Certain Agnostic Antinomies)* (2 vols.; 5th ed.; trans. Dom Bede Rose; St. Louis: B. Herder, 1945). The biblical claim that human beings were originally monotheistic but then devolved into embracing alternative worldviews and worshiping other kinds of gods has recently been given an impressive defense by Winfried Corduan in his *In the Beginning God: A Fresh Look at the Case for Original Monotheism* (Nashville: B&H, 2013).

presuppositions are clearly maintained in Scripture (see, e.g., Gen 1:1; 17:1; Neh 9:6; Ps 147:5; Luke 1:37; John 1:3; Rom 4:17; Heb 11:3; 1 John 3:20).[6]

So consider the following argument, which reasons from minimalistic theism to unconditional election:

> (A) If an omnipotent and omniscient God creates the universe from nothing, then the doctrine of unconditional election is true.
>
> (B) An omnipotent and omniscient God creates the universe from nothing.
>
> ∴ (C) The doctrine of unconditional election is true.

Premise (B), as we have seen, can be justified through natural theology as well as biblical revelation. In short, premise (B) is nothing more than classical theism (or, at least, bare-boned theism)—which even Pelagianism has traditionally upheld.

---

6. There are strong exegetical and philosophico-theological arguments for so-called classical theism, which is the theology proper broadly articulated by the early church fathers, Augustine, Anselm, Aquinas, and the Reformed tradition (among others). For a popular treatment of the issues, see Norman L. Geisler and Wayne House, *The Battle for God: Responding to the Challenges of Neotheism* (Grand Rapids: Kregel, 2001). For more scholarly defenses of classical theism, see Thomas Aquinas, *Summa Theologica* Ia.3–119 (trans. Fathers of the English Dominican Province; Allen, TX: Thomas More, 1948); Reginald Garrigou-Lagrange, *The One God: A Commentary on the First Part of St. Thomas' Theological Summa* (trans. Dom. Bede Rose; St. Louis: B. Herder, 1946); Richard Muller, *The Divine Essence and Attributes* (vol. 3 of *Post-Reformation Reformed Dogmatics*; 2nd ed.; Grand Rapids, Baker Academic, 2003); and Herman Bavinck, *God and Creation* (vol. 2 of *Reformed Dogmatics*; 2nd ed.; trans. John Vriend; Grand Rapids: Baker Academic, 2004). In my estimation, the best contemporary philosophical defense of classical theism is Edward Feser, *Five Proofs of God* (San Francisco: Ignatius Press, 2017); and the best contemporary biblical-theological defense of classical theism is James E. Dolezal, *All That Is In God: Evangelical Theology and the Challenge of Classical Christian Theism* (Grand Rapids: Reformation Heritage Books, 2017).

On the traditional belief that Gen 1:1 teaches creation out of nothing, see C. John Collins, *Genesis 1–4: A Linguistic, Literary, and Theological Commentary* (Phillipsburg, NJ: Presbyterian & Reformed, 2006), 50–55. For other biblical, philosophical, and scientific defenses of *creatio ex nihilo*, see Mark William Worthing, *God, Creation, and Contemporary Physics* (Minneapolis: Fortress, 1996); Paul Copan and William Lane Craig, *Creation Out of Nothing: A Biblical, Philosophical, and Scientific Exploration* (Grand Rapids: Baker, 2004); Hugh Ross, *The Fingerprint of God* (2nd ed.; New Kensington, PA: Whitaker House, 1989); Ross, *The Creator and the Cosmos* (4th ed.; Covina, CA: Reasons to Believe, 2018); Augustine, *Confessions* 11–12; Aquinas, *De Potentia Dei* I.3.i–xix. For a helpful reconciliation of Genesis with the discoveries of modern (conventional) science, see Hugh Ross, *Navigating Genesis: A Scientist's Journey through Genesis 1–11* (Covina, CA: Reasons to Believe, 2014).

Premise (A) can be justified in a number of ways. First, ask yourself this question: *Could the universe be different than it is now?* In other words, is it *logically possible* for the grass to be blue instead of green; for the sky to be green instead of blue; for gravity to be a little stronger or weaker than it is; for the Earth to be a little closer to or farther away from the sun than it is; for there to be no sun; and so on? I have a hard time believing that anyone will say no to any of these possibilities. *Surely* they are all logically *possible*, and so surely they are all ways in which the universe *could* have existed. They are all logically possible worlds.

By a "possible world" I do not *merely* mean a universe and its physical parts. Rather, I mean an entire story of how a world could be—which includes not only its physical parts (if such exist in that possible world), but every single event making up that world (e.g., moments, thoughts, feelings, dispositions, statements, etc.). A possible world is a completely consistent world-ensemble or set of "states of affairs" (i.e., a description of any particular situation).[7] Synonyms for a possible world can include "possible cosmos," "alternative universe," "logical story," "possible metanarrative," "ways the world could be," or "ways the cosmos could have been," and so on.[8]

In the logical moment before[9] God creates this universe—or, better still, logically prior to bringing this world-ensemble (which includes the physical cosmos) into being—it is just one of an infinite number of possible

---

7. John Laing, *Middle Knowledge: Human Freedom in Divine Sovereignty* (Grand Rapids: Kregel, 2018), 54.

8. Standard works exploring the issue of possible worlds include Robert C. Stalnaker, *Ways a World Might Be: Metaphysical and Anti-Metaphysical Essays* (Oxford: Clarendon, 2003); David Lewis, *On the Plurality of Worlds* (Oxford: Blackwell, 1986); Lewis, *Counterfactuals* (Oxford: Blackwell, 1973).

9. The word "before" can be used temporally and/or logically and/or ontologically—i.e., as referring to events/persons in time (e.g., Julius Caesar exists *before* Tiberius Caesar) or as referring to logical relationships (e.g., if p then q) or as referring to an ontological hierarchy (e.g., angels are *before* men in their *respective natures*). Now, clearly any "moment" before the creation of the universe must be construed logically and/or ontologically rather than temporally, for the creation of the universe *just* is the creation of *time*—and, hence, there are no temporal moments before the beginning of time (see Titus 1:2; Jude 25). Or, in the words of Stephen Hawking: "Almost everyone now believes that the universe, and time itself, had a beginning at the big bang" ("Classical Theory," in Stephen Hawking and Roger Penrose, *The Nature of Space and Time* [Princeton Scientific Library; Princeton, NJ: Princeton University Press, 1996], 20).

ways the world could be. In the (logical) moment before God creates this universe, this world-ensemble is merely a logically possible thought in the divine mind. Notice that God, because he is omniscient, knows everything that happens in our logically possible world. He knows everything in our world, from the laws of physics to the positions of the planets to the species living on planet Earth (as well as which species will go extinct) to the activities of human beings. And what is true of our world, the actual world, is equally true of any and all logically possible world-ensembles. His knowledge of a logically possible world, since it is infinite, comprehends the entire history of that world—including every free action of every free creature. Notice that, for any activity that happens in a logically possible world, there is its corresponding opposite that could also happen. For example, in our world Caesar freely chose to cross the Rubicon River in 49 BC and, after crossing it, he freely chose to say the words *alea iacta est* ("The die is cast"). In the (logical) moment before God brings this world-ensemble into being, those free actions of Caesar are a *mere* possibility; and Caesar's choosing not to cross the Rubicon and/or not to utter his famous words are equally possible (i.e., in the moment before creation). Take any free action you like, and there is a corresponding opposite—e.g., administrators in several Vienna art academies rejected the application of Adolf Hitler (they could have accepted him), who could have chosen not to go to art school upon being accepted; Socrates chose to drink the hemlock (he could have chosen the opposite);[10] Judas freely chose to betray Christ (he could have chosen the opposite); Peter freely chose to deny Christ (he could have chosen the opposite); and so on. We could go on and on; for what we have

---

10. Let's unpack this particular example to illustrate the point. What do I mean by saying Socrates could have chosen the opposite of the hemlock? What were his options in place of hemlock? An antidote? Water? Dr. Pepper? By "could have chosen the opposite" I obviously do not mean that Socrates had any and all options available to him at the moment of his choice. In the history of our actual world, Socrates could have chosen the opposite insofar as the Athenians gave him a choice—i.e., either drink the poison or leave the city permanently. Of course, there is a logically possible world wherein Dr. Pepper was invented by the Athenians ca. 400 BC, just in time for that to be a genuine option for Socrates. For there is an infinite number of possible worlds Socrates could find himself in, in which case there is an infinite number of options Socrates can choose; however, in no particular logically possible world is Socrates faced with an infinite number of options—rather, his options are limited by the states of affairs surrounding his choice (e.g., the time in which he lives, the inventions accomplished at that time, the options given to him by the Athenians, etc.).

here is a mind-boggling idea—infinities on infinities of logically possible states of affairs and world-ensembles[11] timelessly comprehended in the divine mind in one eternal act of intuition. What we have here is the first (logical) moment in the life of God.

THE FIRST LOGICAL MOMENT (NATURAL KNOWLEDGE, OR THE KNOWLEDGE OF SIMPLE INTELLIGENCE)

Traditionally, Christian theologians, both Reformed[12] and Arminian[13] (Thomist and Molinist),[14] call the first moment in the life of God his natural knowledge (Thomas called it God's *knowledge of simple intelligence*).[15] God's natural knowledge is his comprehension of everything that *could be*.

---

11. There is some dispute as to whether the possibilities of the ways a world could be are infinite. Some may argue that these are only virtual infinities rather than actual infinities. Laing asks us to consider molecules as a case in point. While it may seem that there is an infinite number of ways molecules could be arranged before we consider changing the molecules themselves or adding/subtracting new ones, there is actually only a finite number of possibilities. "Put differently, anything composed of finite items must be finite, and therefore, the universe and possibilities of universes, are finite. Conversely, anything infinite cannot be composed of finite items (or attributes)" (*Middle Knowledge*, 54–55n12). Laing rightly notes that how one addresses these issues is largely determined by one's presuppositions in other areas. To use my own example, consider the issue of whether one thinks it is logically possible for the universe to have never had a beginning. Consider also the possibility that God could have brought it about that an eternally existing universe obtains. If one thinks, as I do, that both states of affairs are logically possible, then it would seem that the possible ways a world could be really are infinite. Take our actual world as an example. It had a beginning. But it is logically possible that God could have chosen to eternally will that this cosmos, even with all of its physical laws, exists without a beginning. To be sure, whether such a state of affairs is *metaphysically* possible is a different issue (see William Lane Craig and James D. Sinclair, "The *Kalam* Cosmological Argument," in *Blackwell Companion to Natural Theology*, 105–6). On this possibility, there are an infinite number of ways any molecule or set of molecules could be arranged, for arrangements do not merely concern spatial relationships, but temporal ones as well and, the timeline now being infinite, the possible arrangements are also limitless. But, be that as it may, if the reader is not convinced, my argument does not stand or fall on this particular issue. Whether virtually or actually infinite, the point is that God had quite a few options before bringing this particular world-ensemble into being.

12. E.g., see John Owen, *A Display of Arminianism* (vol. 10 of *The Works of John Owen*, ed. John Goold; Carlisle, PA: Banner of Truth Trust, 1967), 23; and Louis Berkhof, *Systematic Theology* (rev. and enl. ed.; Grand Rapids: Eerdmans, 1996), 66–67.

13. James Arminius, *Private Disputations* (vol. 2 of *The Works of James Arminius*, trans. James Nichols and William Nichols; Grand Rapids: Baker, 1986), 342. See Richard A. Muller, *God, Creation, and Providence in the Thought of Jacob Arminius* (Grand Rapids: Baker, 1991), 150–53.

14. See Garrigou-Lagrange, *One God*, 464; and Kirk R. MacGregor, *Luis de Molina: The Life and Theology of the Founder of Middle Knowledge* (Grand Rapids: Zondervan, 2015), 91–92.

15. See Aquinas, *ST* Ia.14.9.

As we have seen, what could be includes a lot—an infinity of an infinity of possible worlds, each possessing states of affairs, creatures, activities, and laws that we cannot even begin to imagine. One way to picture God's natural knowledge is through the following analogy:[16] Imagine that there are an infinite number of DVDs at God's disposal, each one representing a way a world could be; and that God, from all eternity, has watched each and every one. Some DVDs only last a few seconds (or less)—for it is logically possible for a world-ensemble to come into being, exist for a second or two, and then perish into oblivion. Other DVDs last for billions on billions on billions of years, each containing entire histories of various species. Each DVD comprehends both the "big picture" (e.g., the laws of physics in each world; the histories of groups of species; the number of stars; etc.) and the "little picture" (e.g., the entire life of each individual creature, including its actions and/or thoughts and/or free decisions throughout its life—even if that created life comprehended by the divine mind is itself immortal). And so, after God finishes watching a DVD, he possesses an exhaustive knowledge of everything (from the place of the stars to the histories of the races to the life of a fly) that happens in that possible world.

Now, of course, our analogy is terribly anthropomorphic. In reality, God does not need to *take time to watch* the DVDs since he is literally timeless, and so does not experience a succession of moments. Nor does he need to even *watch* or *observe* such worlds, since he is a pure Spirit who in no way relies on sensation to know what he knows.[17] And these DVDs are not *extrinsic* to God, but are *intrinsic* to him. They are *of his essence*—they are his *natural* knowledge, which, again, comprehends everything that could be in one simple and eternal act of intuition.

---

16. I am grateful to Bobby Joiner for giving me the original version of this analogy via personal correspondence.

17. In saying this, we side with those who endorse a conceptualist, as opposed to a perceptualist, notion of divine cognition. That is, in his natural knowledge, God knows *ideas*, not *images*. For helpful expositions on the mode of divine cognition, see Garrigou-Lagrange, *One God*, 416–27; and Berkhof, *Systematic Theology*, 66–67. For an exposition that explicitly uses these categories, see J. P. Moreland and William Lane Craig, *Philosophical Foundations for a Christian Worldview* (2nd ed.; Downers Grove, IL: InterVarsity Press, 2017), 527–28.

THE DIVINE CREATIVE DECREE

God knows exactly what happens in any logically possible world, and he alone is the only power able to choose one logically possible world over another, as well as bring it into being from nothing.

As we have said, this actual world is merely a logically possible world in the first moment of God's life. With an exhaustive comprehension of everything that happens in every logically possible world, God selects which world will be actual, thereby decreeing that a particular world exists and, because his knowledge of that world is exhaustive (i.e., comprehending that world's history [its past, present, and future]), he, in effect, foreordains everything that will happen—from the necessary consequences of some physical laws to the contingent acts of free creatures to quantum events, and so on—in the actual world.

THE SECOND LOGICAL MOMENT (FREE KNOWLEDGE, OR KNOWLEDGE OF VISION)

Christian theologians have traditionally referred to this logical moment in the life of God as his "free knowledge" (Thomas Aquinas called it God's "knowledge of vision").[18] As we have just seen, God's natural knowledge comprehends every possibility—everything that *could* be—and describes the divine cognition logically prior to the divine creative decree. We call it "natural knowledge" because it is natural to God's essence, existing "before" God's decision to create the universe—that is, the *scientia naturalis* just *is*, sans *any* choice by God.

We call the final (logical) moment in the life of God his free knowledge because it occurs "after" (or in light of) God's free decision to make this world and not another. God's free knowledge, then, is his exhaustive comprehension of everything that *will* happen in this actual and contingent world. Since God chooses what he knows via his *scientia libera*, and since God is omniscient, we must conclude that God foreordains everything that comes to pass (from the laws of physics to the life of a snail) via his creative decree.

---

18. Aquinas, *ST* Ia.14.9; see also Owen, *Display of Arminianism*, 23; Garrigou-Lagrange, *One God*, 464; MacGregor, *Luis de Molina*, 95. "Knowledge of vision" is clearly an anthropomorphism for Thomas.

And how do we know that this doctrine is true? How do we know that God foreordains everything that comes to pass? First of all, we know that it is true because it is explicitly taught in Scripture. Indeed, there are plenty of passages that explicitly state that God foreordains everything that obtains in the actual world (1 Chr 29:13, 14; Job 12:7–23; 14:1–6; Pss 31:15; 39:5; 139:16; Lam 3:37; Prov 20:24; 21:1, 30–31; 16:1, 4, 9, 33; 19:21; Isa 14:24, 27; 46:9–10; Amos 3:6; Mark 14:21; John 19:11; Rom 11:33–36; Eph 1:11).

Beyond the direct biblical testimony, the doctrine of the exhaustive divine creative decree logically follows as a good and necessary consequence from everything we have said so far. Indeed, God is omniscient and omnipotent; and, in light of an (virtually) infinite number of options, brings the actual world into existence from nothing. Hence the argument suggested by Jonathan Edwards:

(1) God foreknows all events that ever obtain.

(2) God either wants whatever happens to obtain or he does not want whatever happens to obtain.

(3) If the latter, then the event would not have obtained.

(4) If the former, then the event obtains because God wants it to obtain.

(5) An event obtaining due to the wants of a person is the same as an event obtaining by decree.

(6) God foreknows whatever obtains because he wants whatever obtains to obtain.

∴ (7) God decrees all events that ever obtain.[19]

---

19. To be sure, the argument is not wholly complete as Edwards states it. In his own words: "*u*. DECREES: whether God has decreed all things that ever come to pass, or no. All that own the being of a God own that he knows all things beforehand. Now it is self-evident, that if he knows all things beforehand, he either doth approve of them, or he doth not approve of them; that is, he either is willing that they should be, or is not willing they should be." In another section he writes: "Contingency, as it is held by some, is at the same time contradicted by themselves, if they hold foreknowledge. This is all that follows from an absolute, unconditional, irreversible decree, that it is impossible but that the things decreed should be. The same exactly follows from foreknowledge, that it is absolutely impossible but that the thing certainly foreknown should precisely come to pass." A few lines later he states: "Again, let it be considered whether it be not certainly true, that everyone that can with infinite ease have a thing done, and yet will not have it done, wills it not; that is, whether or no he that wills not to have a thing done, properly wills *not* to have a thing done. For example, let the thing be this, that Judas should be faithful to his Lord: whether it be not true, that if God could with

Premise (1) is one of our presuppositions going into this argument. Premise (2) is true given the personhood of God and the law of excluded middle.[20] Premise (3) is true given the omnipotence of God—for if an event obtains that God does not want to happen, then it is out of his control. Premise (4) is self-evident—for if God can prevent any event from obtaining, then if an event occurs it does so because God either causes or allows it to do so and, hence, *in some sense*, God wants it to occur. Premise (5) is also self-evident—for if the wants of someone are determinative of whether the event happens or not, then when such an event happens it does so because the person in question determined that it would occur. And this *just is* an order or decree on the part of the one wanting the event to obtain. But then (6) automatically follows from (5), since God's foreknowing an event is due to his wanting it to happen, which is a way of saying (7) that God decrees all events in time.

The fact that God creates this world, knowing all along everything that will happen (*if he creates it*) before actually doing so, entails that he decrees (or foreordains) everything that happens in this actual world. It is as if he had watched a DVD showing him everything that happens in this possible world in exhaustive detail and then said *"BE"*—a word so powerful that a merely possible world obtained, thereby becoming the actual story we are acting out even in this very moment. Thus, given the two premises of our argument, it is virtually undeniable that God foreordains whatsoever comes to pass.

SOVEREIGN ELECTION

Having demonstrated that God foreordains whatever comes to pass, I am now prepared to offer a fuller defense of the major premise—namely, (A) *if there is an omniscient and omnipotent God who creates the universe out of nothing, then the doctrine of unconditional election is true.* By "God" I

---

infinite ease have it done (if he would), but would not have it done (as he could if he would); whether it be not proper to say, that God would not have it be, that Judas should be faithful to his Lord." Jonathan Edwards, *The "Miscellanies" (Entry Nos. a-z, aa-zz, 1–500)* (vol. 13 of *The Complete Works of Jonathan Edwards*, ed. Thomas A. Schafer; New Haven, CT: Yale University Press, 1994), 175, 243.

20. The logical principle of excluded middle states that between two contradictions there is no third option.

mean, minimally, an omniscient, omnipotent, and personal being who is the Creator and Sustainer of the universe out of nothing. Omniscience is the property of knowing any and all truths. Omnipotence is the property of being able to control whatever exists distinctly from oneself, as well as perform any action that is consistent with one's nature. A personal being is one who is alive, and possesses a mind, a will, and emotions. To create something is to cause it to come into existence. To create out of nothing is to bring something into existence sans any material causes apart from oneself. In other words, God is the efficient cause of the universe who needs no raw materials to make the world. He is the Sustainer of the universe in the sense that, if he were to stop causing the universe to exist, the cosmos would perish into oblivion.

Redemptively speaking, "election" is the act of God whereby he chooses p unto salvation; and election is "unconditional" just in case God's choice of p has nothing to do with p's choices, personality, character, intelligence, and so on. In other words, p does not have to meet any conditions in order to be "elect" or "chosen" by God (in fact, p cannot meet any conditions to be chosen by God!) — hence the term "unconditional election."

To go back to our DVD analogy: In the logical moment before creation, there is an infinite number of DVDs; in that infinite set, there are DVDs that contain all the logical possibilities pertaining to the human race. Many DVDs, no doubt, describe worlds wherein every single person rejects God's truth and goes to hell; there are also many DVDs, no doubt, describing worlds wherein some persons freely choose God's truth and are thereby saved, while others reject it and are thereby lost; and there are yet other DVDs — many, of course, describing worlds wherein everyone freely chooses to believe in the truth of God and do good works and is thereby saved. The question that immediately confronts us is, Why didn't God choose to actualize a DVD wherein everyone freely chooses his truth and/or does good works and gets saved? The answer cannot be that he did so because he wanted to give everyone free will — for that is the very thing we are presupposing in this argument! There is a logically possible world wherein everyone freely[21] chooses salvation.[22] So, why did God not choose that world and/or one of the many world ensembles in which everyone freely believes and/or does good works to be saved? The answer that is immediately available to us is that, in some sense, God did not will or want a world to exist wherein everyone is saved, and then chose a world in which, for example, Bonhoeffer freely chooses God's plan of salvation while Hitler freely rejects it. However, if that immediately available answer is, in fact, the correct one, then one has (in effect) concluded that the reason a person finds himself in a world in which he either freely believes or freely rejects the gospel is that God determined that such a world would exist, which in effect entails that God is the one who determines which free choice a person makes—i.e., the choice either for or against God's offer of salvation is grounded in God's prior determination that this world will obtain and not another.

Notice that God's decision concerning which logically possible world will obtain had nothing to do with his estimate of any creature—i.e., before anyone is born, and before the world in which anyone exists had even been created, God determined that each would be a person living in a world that

---

21. The freedom here being granted is the Pelagian view of freedom, which many would describe as "libertarian." But an even more basic point is this: *Embrace any view of freedom you please.* It really does not matter. Our contention is that, regardless of the view of freedom one adopts, a minimalistic account of theism entails the doctrine of unconditional election. To be sure, many will complain that this argument has caused them to doubt their own understanding of free will. If so, that may very well suggest a fault in their view of freedom, not in this line of reasoning!

22. This assertion—i.e., "there is a logically possible world wherein everyone freely chooses salvation"—appears to me to be self-evidently true, for all one has to do is pick any unbeliever in history and ask, Was it possible for this person to believe and be saved? I can in my own mind imagine Hitler embracing Christ as his Savior while suffering from a gas attack on November 11, 1918, and then spending the rest of his life in humble obedience to his Lord. History, of course, records something else—i.e., in light of the armistice between the Allies and the Germans, Hitler decided to go into politics, joining the German Workers Party (later called Nazis) some nine or ten months later. Now, the fact that I can imagine Hitler being saved is proof that God can, for my imagination cannot be greater than his! In fact, there is no single human person who has ever lived whom God cannot imagine embracing the Savior. For no logical contradiction is entailed by such a thought. Hence, there is at least one logically possible world wherein everyone free embraces the Savior. Indeed, what we are claiming here is embraced not only by Calvinists and Thomists, but Arminians and Molinists as well. God's *scientia naturalis* comprehends countless worlds wherein everyone freely chooses salvation. Of course, the Arminian and Molinist way out of this dilemma is to advocate a distinction between what is logically *possible* and what is *feasible*. I take up this subject, and more besides (e.g., "transworld depravity") in the next chapter.

has, as a part of its "story," his acceptance of the salvation (or rejection of it, as the case may be). In short, God's choice concerning which person is to be saved is in no way conditioned on anything any person does. In other words, *God's choice of a person is unconditional.* Indeed, history records that, as a part of our story, Adolf Hitler freely rejected the gospel, while Dietrich Bonhoeffer freely received it. But there is another logically possible world wherein Hitler is freely saved and Bonhoeffer is freely lost. So, by choosing a world wherein the latter is saved and the former is lost—*even a world wherein free will makes the difference*—God has, in effect, unconditionally chosen one person over the other.

This argument is a strong challenge to both Pelagianism and Arminianism—i.e., two theologies that affirm *conditional* election (i.e., God foresees the choices we make and elects us to salvation [or refrains from doing so] *on that basis*). For even if the standard Arminian interpretation of various biblical passages is correct—e.g., even *if* texts such as Romans 8:29, 1 Peter 1:2, and Ephesians 1:4 *are* affirming conditional election (which we have seen to be far from obvious!)—we are still left with a God who has determined which person will meet the conditions necessary to obtain election. Election may be based on foreseen faith, but the foresight itself is based on God's decree that this world obtain and not another. God would not have foreseen Bonheoffer's faith had he not first decreed that Bonheoffer would find himself in a world in which he believes!

OBJECTIONS

This argument is, perhaps, not new—even if its particular structure and application is somewhat unique.[23] In any case, there are a few (potential) objections we may need to answer before moving forward.

---

23. While I have never seen or heard a case for unconditional election stated in the way it's been articulated in this chapter, my argument was inspired by the insights of R. C. Sproul, who once argued with his students, saying "that the idea that God foreordains whatever comes to pass is not an idea unique to Calvinism. It isn't even unique to Christianity. It is simply a tenet of theism—a necessary tenet of theism." R. C. Sproul, *Chosen by God* (Wheaton, IL: Tyndale House, 1986), 26.

THEISM MAY NOT BE TRUE

One alternative a critic of this argument may embrace is a simple rejection of theism. In fact, we tend to think that a major reason many reject theism is precisely due to the kinds of conclusions one must come to if one believes that an all-powerful and all-knowing God really does exist—e.g., unconditional election is true.

Response. While I will not offer a full defense of theism here, we can only wonder where the critic of our argument will go so as to avoid the conclusion. Her options are atheism, polytheism, pantheism, and panentheism.[24] Of course, as I point out in chapter 2, these alternative worldviews themselves have their own set of problems—most notably the fact that none adequately accounts for objective morality, much less the genuine human need to worship something greater than ourselves. For us the intellectual price to pay for the rejection of unconditional election is just too high.

THERE ARE ALTERNATIVES WITHIN THEISM

Of course, one could reject the version of theism set up in this chapter and embrace a different understanding of God—i.e., one that is consistent (even if only in spirit) with traditional monotheism that allows one to reject sovereign election. For example, one could embrace the open view of God, or Boethianism[25] and/or "simple foreknowledge," or even Origen's solution to the problem.

OPEN-VIEW THEISM

This model suggests that, while God is indeed all-powerful and all-knowing, and even creates *ex nihilo*, he lacks an exhaustive view of the future. For the open-view theist, God is omniscient in the sense that he justifiably believes all true propositions—where a true proposition is defined as a declarative statement that corresponds to reality (to the way things really are). But the future does not exist. Hence, there is literally nothing corresponding to any future-tensed proposition. This entails, of course, that no

---

24. For a brief exposition of these alternatives, see chapter 2 above.

25. After Anicius Boethius (ca. 480–524), who advocated an atemporal God who timelessly comprehends all truth. See Boethius, *The Consolation of Philosophy* (2nd ed.; trans. Victor Watts; New York: Penguin, 1999), 132–37.

future-tensed proposition is either true or false. All such statements lack a truth-value. In the words of Pinnock, decisions "not yet made do not exist anywhere to be known by God. They are potential—yet to be realized but not yet actual." Hence, "God can predict a great deal of what we will choose to do, but not all of it, because some of it remains hidden in the mystery of human freedom."[26] Obviously, if God lacks omniprescience, he cannot have foreordained all that comes to pass, in which case our argument for unconditional election is unsound.[27]

Response. First, there are quite a few problems with the argument for open-view theism given in the previous paragraph. To offer just two examples: (1) The argument proves too much, for the past does not exist either, in which case there is nothing corresponding to any past-tensed proposition—hence, no such statement is true (or false), and thus the past is wholly unknowable to anyone (including God). In any case, (2) the above consideration is just a denial of the principle of bivalence with respect to future-tensed propositions.[28] This logical move, however, pays quite a high philosophical, theological, and biblical price. *Philosophically*, it seems intuitively obvious that any proposition a person utters is either true or false. If it is a future-tensed proposition, while we may not know its truth-value in the present, its truth or falsity will be confirmed when the future

---

26. Clark H. Pinnock, "From Augustine to Arminius: A Pilgrimage in Theology," in *The Grace of God and the Will of Man* (ed. Clark H. Pinnock; Minneapolis: Bethany, 1989), 25. Perhaps the best expositions and defenses of open-view theism are Clark Pinnock et al., *The Openness of God: A Biblical Challenge to the Traditional Understanding of God* (Downers Grove, IL: InterVarsity Press, 1994); Gregory A. Boyd, *God of the Possible: A Biblical Introduction to the Open View of God* (Grand Rapids: Baker, 2000); and William Hasker, *God, Time, and Knowledge* (Cornell Studies in the Philosophy of Religion; Ithaca, NY: Cornell University Press, 1989).

27. We should point out that, even if open-view theism is true, such would only entail that our argument for unconditional election is not sound. It would not entail that the doctrine of unconditional election is false. For perhaps God unconditionally elects on multiple occasions as he experiences history rather than in one eternal "moment." Thus, an open-view theist may avoid our argument in this chapter, but may still have to embrace unconditional election in light of our exegesis in the previous chapter.

28. "Bivalence" (literally "two values") is an extension of the principle of excluded middle, stating that every proposition must be either true or false. Some standard textbooks see no difference between excluded middle and bivalence. For example, see Irving M. Copi and Carl Cohen, *Introduction to Logic* (12th ed.; Upper Saddle River, NJ: Prentice Hall, 2005), 356. As far as I can tell, the first thinker to deny bivalence with respect to future-tensed propositions is Aristotle, *De Interpretatione* 9.

arrives. Abandoning our intuitions on this score just to avoid an unsavory conclusion seems ad hoc.

Theologically, while it may be problematic to think God knows non-existent events on a perceptualist model of divine cognition, most theologians reject perceptualism in favor of conceptualism.[29] Embracing such a model allows us, in keeping with the traditional conception of God as "the greatest conceivable being," to simply embrace the notion that God is an omniscient being precisely in the sense that he knows any and all truths (past, present, and future).[30]

Biblically, we have both implicit and explicit scriptural testimony to the divine omniprescience. Take, for example, the test of a true prophet in Deuteronomy 18. If a prophet does not speak a word given to him by God, that false prophet shall be put to death (v. 20). How does one know the difference between a true and a false prophet? "When a prophet speaks in the name of the LORD, if the thing does not come about or come true, that is the thing which the LORD has not spoken" (v. 22). However, if God does not know the future, the test offered here is vacuous, since even a word from YHWH may very well not come to pass. In any case, the Scriptures explicitly tell us that the divine knowledge is infinite. In fact, God is said to know all things (1 John 3:20), for his understanding is without limit (Ps 147:5). Or, in the words of King David: "in Your book were all written The days that were ordained *for me*, When as yet there was not one of them" (Ps 139:16).[31] Indeed, the notion of an omniprescient deity is embedded deep within the Judeo-Christian tradition—as we read in the apocryphal addition to Daniel: "O eternal God, you know what is secret and are aware of all things before they come to be" (Sus 42 NRSV). So C. S. Lewis speaks for nearly every Christian when he says, "Everyone who believes in God at all believes that He knows what you and I are going to do tomorrow."[32] Therefore, I cannot see any good reason to embrace open-view theism.[33]

---

29. William Lane Craig, *Time and Eternity: Exploring God's Relationship to Time* (Wheaton, IL: Crossway, 2001), 264. For a brief exposition of the difference, see page 107n17 above.

30. Craig, *Time and Eternity*, 264.

31. For the open-view theist who believes this verse only applies to David, see Job 14:5.

32. C. S. Lewis, *Mere Christianity* (2nd ed.; New York: Macmillan, 1952), 148.

33. For a full critique of open-view theism, see Campbell, "The Beautiful Mind"; John Piper, Justin Taylor, and Paul Kjoss Helseth, eds., *Beyond the Bounds: Open Theism and the*

BOETHIANISM AND SIMPLE
FOREKNOWLEDGE

Another option for the theist is to abandon talk of natural versus free knowledge altogether and just affirm, in the words of David Hunt, "that God simply *knows the future* (leaving open the question of how he does it)."[34] Hunt goes on to offer a concise, scholarly account of his own position. Popular writer Dave Hunt agrees with both (former) Hunt and Boethius, writing:

> We have already seen why God's foreknowledge has no causative effect upon man's free choice. God, being timeless, lives in one eternal now. He sees what to us are future events as though they had already happened—thus His knowledge has no effect on man's will. There is no reason why in His omniscience God cannot know what man will freely choose to do before he chooses to do it.[35]

Response. The problem with either of these suggestions—i.e., a simple-foreknowledge view that offers no account of how God knows or a timeless-eternity view that portrays God as seeing all events transpire in his "eternal now"—is that they end up with a fatalism that is worse than the Calvinism they are trying to avoid.[36] If we imagine that God *just knows* what is to be, without in any way causing it, then he has no more control of the future than humans do. God is now in a dilemma. If he uses his omnipotence to change the future, then he has falsified his foreknowledge—in which case he is neither infallible nor omniscient. If he refrains from preventing any future event from happening, then he does so either because he truly wants the event to happen or he does not want it to happen while allowing it to happen anyway. If the former, then we are back to exhaustive

---

Undermining of Biblical Christianity (Wheaton, IL: Crossway, 2003); John M. Frame, *No Other God: A Response to Open Theism* (Phillipsburg, NJ: Presbyterian & Reformed, 2001); and Bruce A. Ware, *God's Lesser Glory: The Diminished God of Open Theism* (Wheaton, IL: Crossway, 2000).

34. David Hunt, "The Simple-Foreknowledge View," in *Divine Foreknowledge: Four Views* (ed. James K. Beilby and Paul R. Eddy; Downers Grove, IL: InterVarsity Press, 2001), 67.

35. Dave Hunt, *What Love Is This?* (Sisters, OR: Loyal, 2002), 160.

36. To be sure, David Hunt embraces Augustine, thinking that others in the Calvinistic tradition (e.g., Jonathan Edwards) have departed from the great master (David Hunt, "Simple-Foreknowledge Response," in *Divine Foreknowledge: Four Views*, 196).

foreordination. If the latter, then we are also back to exhaustive fore-ordination, since God is still allowing all events (tragic or otherwise) to happen, albeit with the following proviso: we are now embracing a sort of "Cassandra theism,"[37] wherein God foresees what is to come, but can do nothing to change what will be (as a matter of principle or from a lack of power). In any case, divine power becomes vacuous, and God is himself subject to fate.

But perhaps God is timeless and hence never really *foresees* anything. Rather, in his eternal vision his knowledge of the future is no different from my knowledge of the present. Like a man standing on a building and watching a parade, seeing the beginning, and middle, and end of the procession at a glance, God sees the whole of time, from beginning to end, in a single instant. Just as it would be foolish to think that my present knowledge of, say, a person sitting down has anything to do with her freedom to sit, so also it is positively bizarre to think that God's eternal knowledge of a person's faith has anything to do with her so exercising it.

However, while I agree that God is atemporal, I do not believe this option allows anyone to completely avoid either the universal decree or the sovereignty of election. Like the simple-foreknowledge viewpoint, the timeless-vision alternative, if not supplemented with a distinction between natural and free knowledge, leads one to embrace fatalism. For if God sees all events at a glance, so that the past, present, and future all exist before the timeless vision of God, then whatever will happen is happening right now. God sees the event right now and has done nothing to cause it. Take, for example, the 2020 election—which, at the time of this writing, is more than two years away. On the timeless-vision viewpoint, God is no more in control of the event than I am. Yet, unlike me, God sees it taking place, and this entails that it *is* taking place. Two major problems immediately follow from this. First, it is counterintuitive to think that, as I type these words, Jesus is being crucified, Hitler is ruling Germany, J. F. K. is being assassinated, and the forty-fifth/forty-sixth president is being sworn into

---

37. Named after the Trojan prophetess who was cursed with a knowledge of future events, yet no one would believe her as she uttered her true prophecies. This rendered her impotent to help those whose fates she foresaw.

office![38] In short, this viewpoint tends to render time timeless! Second, on this view, I do not really have a free choice to perform any future action. For if my future self is already there, in the future, performing that act, then there is no genuine sense in which my present self can, at least in the libertarian sense, freely choose that action. Indeed, if in the future my choices have *already been made*, then whatever alternatives I think I have are completely illusory.[39]

ORIGEN'S SOLUTION

A final answer to our argument was made popular by Origen during the third century AD. It goes something like this: The argument for unconditional election presupposes that we do what we do because God foreknows and foreordains our actions; however, the opposite is actually true—i.e., God foreknows what he does precisely because he sees us performing those actions; therefore, the argument for unconditional election is unsound. In other words, God's foreknowledge does not determine our actions; rather, our actions determine God's foreknowledge.[40]

Response. This solution actually compounds the very problem its proponents are trying to avoid, thereby inheriting and exacerbating the difficulties we have already seen in the simple-foreknowledge and timeless-vision perspectives. For if God foreknows what I am going to do because I am going to do it, then we must conclude that the present can cause events to obtain in the past; and yet, I submit that this sort of backwards causation contradicts our experience of the flow of time. Also, this solution once again raises the specter of fatalism, for no effect can exist without its cause. But if the effect (God's foreknowledge) has obtained, then the cause (my actions) *must* occur, in which case I do not have the power to choose the opposite of what I have chosen.[41]

The problems raised by these alternatives to traditional theism illustrate why so many Christian theologians have followed the lead of thinkers

---

38. A point well made by Anthony Kenny, *God of the Philosophers* (Oxford: Clarendon, 1979), 38–39.

39. See Jonathan Edwards, *Freedom of the Will* (vol. 1 of *The Works of Jonathan Edwards*, ed. Paul Ramsey; New Haven, CT: Yale University Press, 1957), 266–69.

40. See Origen, *Contra Celsum* 2.20.

41. See Edwards, *Freedom of the Will*, 266–69.

such as Aquinas, Molina, Arminius, Owen, and Turretin in their distinction between natural and free knowledge. Indeed, justification for this theological construct *may* be found in the prophetic word of Isaiah himself.[42] In any case, by making a distinction between necessary and free knowledge, we are able to embrace many things at once. For example, we can truly say that God has genuine options in creation, and so history, being the result of divine free will, is not subject to the horrors of fate; there is a real sense in which all things in this world are contingent (i.e., they need not be), and hence that fact alone makes room for creaturely freedom (however construed); we can truly say that we are wholly dependent on our Creator, who depends on no one for anything (including his knowledge).[43]

THE ARGUMENT TO UNCONDITIONAL ELECTION TURNS GOD INTO A MORAL MONSTER

Indeed, the very idea that God would pick and choose who is to be saved and who is to be damned simply cannot be reconciled to the notion of an all-good and all-loving being. The God who is love (1 John 4:16), who loved the world so much that he sent his Son to save it (John 3:16), cannot be a God who unconditionally elects some people for redemption and passes over others.

Response. Up to this point in our discussion, very little (if anything at all) has been said about the goodness of God. There is a specific reason for this—namely, had we added the term "omnibenevolence"[44] to our major premise,[45] then things would begin to look even worse for the Pelagian. Indeed, the Pelagian insists that *the doctrine of unconditional election is*

---

42. E.g., see Isa 41:23; 48:4. For a helpful discussion on this issue, see Sze Sze Chiew, *Middle Knowledge and Biblical Interpretation: Luis de Molina, Herman Bavinck, and William Lane Craig* (Contributions to Philosophical Theology 13; Frankfurt am Main: Peter Lang, 2016), 60–62.

43. Notice that the Origenist solution, Boethian timeless-vision model, simple-foreknowledge-view, and open-view perspectives all render God dependent on creation for his knowledge. But to affirm the Creator's dependence on creation for his knowledge contradicts his aseity or self-existence. Hence, classical theists have yet another reason to reject these alternatives. We return to the issue of aseity in the next chapter.

44. I.e., God is omnibenevolent in the sense that he wills goodness for every creature. In short, he loves all.

45. As in "If there is an omnipotent, omniscient, *and omnibenevolent* God who creates the universe from nothing, then the doctrine of unconditional election is true."

unjust, for it is unfair for God to give grace to some that he does not give to others. There are two vantage points from which one can lodge this objection—(a) from the vantage point of the first (logical) moment in the divine life and (b) from the vantage point of the second (logical) moment in the divine life.

NATURAL KNOWLEDGE

The reader will recall that, in the first moment of his life God (via his *scientia naturalis*) comprehends every logically possible world and/or state of affairs and, via his omnipotence, is able to select any world he (ultimately) wills to become actual. But God is not merely all-powerful and all-knowing; he is also all-good. As any good theist will insist, goodness is an essential and necessary attribute of the deity. Given the necessity of the divine goodness, one is led to the embracement of an important qualifier in possible-world semantics—namely, the distinction between *possibility* and *conceivability* or, better still, the distinction between broad and narrow possibility. In this context, a world is *narrowly possible* if, *per impossible*, God did not exist, and yet it still remains attainable or possible. For example, *narrowly* construed, there is no contradiction in the idea of evil prevailing over good; hence, such a world is *narrowly logically possible*. However, when we broaden our perspective, and add an all-powerful, all-knowing, and all-good God into the mix of our basic presuppositions (or, better still, when we recall that these presuppositions were a part of our basic beliefs all along), a world wherein evil prevails over good is *broadly logically impossible*. Given this qualifier, we submit, along with Thomas Morris, that

> no state of affairs whose actualization would be prohibited to just any moral agent, which would be such that God would be blameworthy in intentionally bringing it about or allowing it, represents a genuine possibility. Thus, on any careful definition of omnipotence, God's inability to actualize such a state of affairs no more detracts from his omnipotence than does his inability to create spherical cubes or objects which are green yet uncolored. And none of God's

creatures has the power to trespass beyond the bounds set by the necessities of the divine nature.[46]

Now, the reader will recall that our original argument for unconditional election presupposes the Pelagian heresy. However, once the divine benevolence is taken into account, our argument from a minimalistic version of theism to unconditional election entails a contradiction; for one is being illogical if he is both a theist and a Pelagian. For, on the Pelagian anthropology, human beings are not fallen (i.e., there is no original sin[47] in the Pelagian universe).[48] And, in the logical moment before the divine decree, no human being is more worthy of election than another. Also, in the logical moment before the divine creative decree, *no human being is worthy of reprobation!* Indeed, since there are just as many logically possible worlds in which Hitler freely chooses salvation as there are wherein Bonhoeffer does—and the divine mind can surely contemplate an (virtually) infinite number of circumstances wherein both choices obtain—we are confronted with a situation in which the Pelagian god chooses one good person (to be saved) over another good person (to be damned). However, it is unjust for one good person to be chosen over another and, since one cannot be considered omnibenevolent unless one is also just or fair, the god of Pelagianism is not all-good. In short, Pelagian theism entails a contradiction—for omnibenevolence, omnipotence, and omniscience are all essential attributes of the deity; but Pelagian theism entails a rejection of one or all three of these attributes; therefore, one can be either Pelagian or theistic, but not both.

Of course, rejecting theism is an option. Once a person is convinced that theism entails unconditional election, which, to her, may be unfair, one may turn the tables back on a traditional theist and say, *tu quoque.* Indeed, how does a traditional Christian, for example, reconcile the concept of justice with a God who, in his first moment, could decree any world he wants? Why not make a world wherein everyone chooses salvation? This

---

46. Thomas V. Morris, *Anselmian Explorations: Essays in Philosophical Theology* (Notre Dame, IN: University of Notre Dame Press, 1987), 47–48, taken from a chapter originally published as "The Necessity of God's Goodness," *New Scholasticism* 59 (1985).

47. For a brief exposition and defense of this doctrine, see appendix 1.

48. See Pelagius, *Commentary on St. Paul's Epistle to the Romans*, 95–96.

question will occupy our attention for chapters 6–7. For now, I will simply assert, somewhat ambiguously (I admit), that God is somehow glorified in a world in which some do not receive salvation.

Yet our ambiguous answer should not be accepted so easily. For the question can be pressed even further: *How is it even possible for an all-good being to be glorified in the damnation of his creatures?* While a full answer (again) awaits more development in succeeding chapters, I present a thumbnail sketch of an answer here.

Because he is all-powerful, God can create any world he wants; but because he is all-good, God does not want a world to obtain that is inconsistent with his justice. Such a world is conceivable or narrowly possible, but not broadly possible. Indeed, righteousness and justice are the foundation of God's rule (Ps 89:14a). Thus, whatever his justice demands, his righteousness executes. This entails, of course, that God (because he is infinitely just) cannot elect one good person over another good person. Also, because he is all-good, he cannot desire what is evil as such.

So, how can an all-good and all-powerful God bring it about that (1) he is glorified in a world wherein only some are saved and others are damned, (2) he never engages in the business of choosing one good person over another, and (3) he, as an all-loving being, sincerely desires that all of his creatures *qua creatures* inherit salvation? The answer to this question is found in the divine natural knowledge, tempered as it is by his goodness. That is to say, God naturally comprehends an (virtually) infinite number of worlds, and among this infinity of world-ensembles are (4) those in which everyone freely chooses salvation, (5) those in which some choose salvation and others choose damnation, and (6) those in which every single human being chooses damnation. In order to fulfill conditions (1)–(3), God selects (6). In other words, God chooses to bring into existence (6) a world-ensemble wherein every single human person sins and rejects God. There is an (virtual) infinity of possible worlds consistent with (6), with no possibly fallen world better than another. Among this infinite ensemble of worlds is our logically possible universe, one wherein everyone chooses to rebel against God, thereby ensuring his own damnation.

Hence, God chooses a world that is of the most destitute in order to magnify his wisdom, justice, power, and grace—*wisdom*, since he devises

a plan to redeem many from their fallen estate; *justice*, since he justly condemns those who deserve it; *power*, since he is able bring so much good out
of so much evil; *grace*, since those who are redeemed in no way deserve his
good favor. *Selecting* such a world cannot be evil, since God's intention is not
the existence of sin, evil, and rebellion as such, but for his goodness and
grace to be magnified in the fallen world.[49] *Creating* such a world is not an
evil act of God, for such a world is originally good, and yet corrupts itself.
Condemning those who rebel cannot be unjust, for the world he chooses is
one in which every single person *freely* chooses to rebel against God and
resist his grace (i.e., their fault lies within themselves, not God). All evil
obtains via the divine permission, not promotion.

Going back to our DVD illustration, God simply sees everyone freely
condemning themselves through their own sins, being under no compulsion or influence in any way by God to commit evil. No one in this hypothetical world can gainsay God by insisting that it is his fault that they
commit their sins; on the contrary, a fundamental principle laid down in
this world-ensemble is that every *sin* committed by the creature is *wholly*
from the creature, and in no way is their *evil* compelled or caused *in any*
way by God.

But the situation is actually simpler than we have described, for it turns
out that God, in order to ensure that one Savior would be sufficient for
all humankind, selected a world wherein there is a corporate solidarity
within the human species. It is a world wherein the first humans are created good and innocent (though mutably so), and who are placed in a paradise wherein they are given every opportunity to accept or reject God's
covenantal love. However, they choose to rebel against God. To go back
to our analogy, as God watches the DVD describing this logically possible
world, he does not see himself causing the fall—he simply sees it happening. By selecting this world over others, and then merely allowing events

---

49. The law of double effect may be of help here. Catholic ethicists have traditionally
invoked this law in cases where an evil result is unavoidable. For example, imagine a woman
who is diagnosed with cancer while being two months pregnant. Imagine also that she is given
only a few weeks to live. It would be moral for her to undergo chemotherapy with the hope
of going into remission, even though such a procedure would surely kill the unborn child
within her. Her intent was not to kill the child, even though the child's death is an inevitable
result of her choice. In a similar (albeit imperfect) way, God never intends the evil (as such)
he allows to obtain. What he does intend is the manifestation of his grace and mercy.

to take their course, God permissively decrees that all of his human creatures fall into sin via their first parents.

FREE KNOWLEDGE

The preceding insights, in turn, destroy this overall objection—i.e., that God is unjust if he unconditionally elects—when articulated from the vantage point of God's *scientia libera*. For God's electing love is not given to *hypothetical good essences* awaiting instantiation in a real world, but rather manifests itself towards *actual destitute sinners* in dire need of redemption. Hence, God does not choose one good person over another good person; rather, God chooses one evil, totally depraved sinner over another evil, totally depraved sinner. God is just in that he never deprives anyone of a good that is owed; but God does not owe the sinner grace—for a grace that is owed is not grace, but a debt that is one's due to another. Indeed, the idea that *anyone—let alone God—owes* anyone else *grace* is a contradiction in terms. Grace is, *by definition, unmerited* favor. So the sinner who is given grace from God receives mercy—which, while a form of the good, is also form of *nonjustice*. But mercy or grace is not a form of *injustice*.[50] Hence, the reprobate receive *justice* due to their condemnation of their own selves, while the elect receive *mercy* due to the free and sovereign grace of God. But no one receives injustice. Therefore, the objection that the doctrine of unconditional election is unjust has no teeth to it. Also, far from making God into an unjust judge, the doctrine of original sin ensures that God can be both sovereign and just. Pelagianism, in turn, cannot be reconciled to biblical theism, for insofar as it is theistic it turns the great being into a moral monster.

Summary and conclusion. We will build on the points established in this response over the course of this work. Suffice it to say here, by way of summary, that in the first moment of the divine life God desires to create a world that manifests his own goodness in all of its splendor insofar as such is possible for a creature. The only kind of world that could possibly fulfill such a desire is one that emerges from the creative act wholly good, but is also one wherein every single person made in God's image freely chooses

---

50. See Sproul, *Chosen by God*, 38.

to damn himself or herself via his or her own sin. This is consistent with what we read in Scripture: "For God has shut up all in disobedience that He might show mercy to all" (Rom 11:32). In the words of Aquinas: "For since all men are born subject to damnation on account of the sin of the first parent, those whom God delivers by his grace he delivers by his mercy alone; and so he is merciful to those whom he delivers, just to those whom he does not deliver, but unjust to none."[51] But, some will insist, the doctrine of unconditional election denies the universality of divine grace, which is clearly affirmed in the text we just read in Romans. Again, we will explore this issue in more detail later in this work. For now we simply note that Thomas, at least, did not see any contradiction between unconditional election and the universality of grace, especially since the latter is not evinced in Romans 11:32. As Aquinas comments on this text:

> **That he may have mercy on all**, i.e., that he may have mercy on every race of men: *but you have mercy upon all* (Wis 17:24). This does not extend to the demons in accord with the error of Origen, nor even to men individually, but according to every race of men [i.e., all Jews and gentiles]. For the distribution is made according to races of individuals, and not according to individuals of races. But God wills all to be saved by his mercy, so that they might be humbled by this and ascribe their salvation not to themselves but to God. *[D]estruction is your own, O Israel: your help is only in me* (Hos 13:9). **That every mouth may be stopped, and all the world may be subject to God** (Rom 3:19).[52]

THE DISCUSSION OF POSSIBLE WORLDS IS TOO AMBIGUOUS

Another potential objection is that the ontological status of possible worlds is ambiguous and needs to be clarified.

---

51. Thomas Aquinas, *Commentary on the Letter of Saint Paul to the Romans* (trans. F. R. Larcher; ed. J. Mortensen and E. Alarcon; vol. 37 of The Latin/English Edition of the Works of St. Thomas Aquinas; Lander, WY: The Aquinas Institute for the Study of Sacred Doctrine, 2012), 259.

52. Aquinas, *Commentary on the Letter of Saint Paul to the Romans*, 317–18, boldface and italics original.

Response. I simply do not believe that such a clarification is necessary. My point is that, as long as the world could have been different than it actually is, the argument is sound. Since most analyses of possible worlds I am aware of grant this intuition,[53] I think we are on safe ground to offer the argument without giving such an analysis.

That said, I think I would be remiss if I did not offer at least a taste of my own version of possible-worlds semantics; so, rather than wade through the various options proposed in the philosophical literature, I will simply state my own position.

I uphold a Thomistic metaphysic, which has as its core concept the real distinction between essence and existence[54] within contingent reality. That is to say, within every contingent thing—i.e., whatever is changing, finite, and dependent on another for its existence—there is a real distinction between *what it is* (essence) and *the fact that it is* (existence). To put it another way, every contingent thing is composed of actuality and potentiality—i.e., every created thing actually exists, but has the potential to be other than what it is. For example, I exist; but I have the potential to be other than what I am (e.g., taller, shorter, fatter, thinner, smarter, dumber, etc.). Creation, then, is the act of God whereby he grants existence to a particular essence in his mind. As we read in the creation story, "Let Us make man in Our image, according to Our likeness" (Gen 1:26). God has an idea in his mind (i.e., the essence of a divine image bearer called "man" or "human") and brings that essence into existence. Hence there is a real distinction between essence and existence in humans, along with every other created reality.

God, however, is quite different and distinct from the created realm precisely because, in him, there is no distinction between essence and existence. He is pure actuality with no potentiality. He is his own act of existing; or, in other words, his essence is to exist. As such, there is no potential in

---

53. For a helpful interaction with those who reject this intuition (e.g., J. L. Mackie and Larry Powers), see Stalnaker, *Ways a World Might Be*, 26–39.

54. Kerr rightly points out that *esse* (often translated "being" or "existence") is best left untranslated since the term is somewhat richer than bare "existence." That said, for non-specialists and/or those unfamiliar with Thomas's work, it may be helpful to read *esse* simply as "existence." See Gaven Kerr, *Aquinas's Way to God: The Proof in* De Ente et Essentia (Oxford: Oxford University Press, 2015), 9.

God for change, growth, movement, or even nonexistence. Hence, God is immutable, unmoved, uncaused, and necessarily existent. This metaphysical language of the Thomist is captured quite nicely in YHWH's revelation to Moses as the Great I AM: "I AM WHO I AM ... . Thus you [Moses] shall say to the sons of Israel, 'I AM has sent me to you'" (Exod 3:14).[55] God is the one who simply is. He needs no cause, inspiration, motivation, movement, or anything else from anything or anyone outside of himself. What is the definitional name of God? *Qui est*.

What, then, is a possible world according to Thomism? One thing is for sure, on the Thomistic analysis, *possibility* can *never* be more basic than *actuality*. Indeed, the One who is pure act is the foundation for whatever else is possible. As Kerr explains:

> For Aquinas, possibility is not grounded in some ontologically independent entities, but (i) in the mind of God or (ii) in the potencies of actually existing entities; in both cases possibility is founded upon actuality. Consequently, Aquinas is not prepared to admit that possibility is more basic than actuality, with the actual world being just one of the so many possible worlds; rather possibility is derivable from actuality, whether that be God's understanding of the imitability of His essence or in the potencies that an actual being displays.[56]

As we have already noted, Thomas makes the distinction between God's necessary and free knowledge. Thus, for him, the ontological status for a possible world is that no possible world exists anywhere except the divine mind until God decides to select it and bring it into being via his creative decree.

---

55. See Kerr, *Aquinas's Way to God*, 166–72. We are aware that the Hebrew construction of Exod 3:14 uses the qal imperfect, which some insist should be translated in the future tense (i.e., "I will be who I will be"). However, the present tense is grammatically possible, and even more probable precisely because of the theophany accompanying YHWH's word to Moses. Indeed, a burning yet unconsumed bush is a clear picture of divine aseity! See Umberto Cassuto, *A Commentary on the Book of Exodus* (trans. Israel Abrahams; Jerusalem: Magnes, 1967), 37–38; *The Holy Bible: The Net Bible® (The New English Translation™)* (Biblical Studies Press, 2001), 143–44n12.

56. Kerr, *Aquinas's Way to God*, 89.

THOMISM RAISES TOO MANY
PROBLEMS FOR THIS ARGUMENT
TO UNCONDITIONAL ELECTION

This objection raises an interesting dilemma: if God *could* have chosen otherwise than he actually did, then the conclusion "God is contingent" would seem to be entailed for anyone's theology. But, if one claims that God *could not* have chosen otherwise, then we no longer seem to be talking about "the classical tradition," since such theologians as Duns Scotus and Thomas Aquinas insist that God *could* have done differently.

Response. Fortunately, Thomas Aquinas answered this dilemma roughly eight hundred years ago. First, could God have chosen otherwise than he in fact did? Thomas's answer is in the affirmative. For God alone is able to create from nothing, therefore, "anything that can be brought into being only by creative causality must necessarily be produced by Him."[57] Indeed, "whatever does not imply a contradiction is subject to the divine power."[58] Thomas continues:

> Now, there are many entities which do not exist in the realm of created things, but which, if they did so exist, would imply no contradiction; particular obvious examples are the number, quantities, and distances of the stars and of other bodies, wherein, if the order of things were different, no contradiction would be implied. Thus, numerous entities, non-existent in the order of reality, are subject to the divine power. Now, whoever does some of the things that he can do, leaving others undone, acts by choice of his will, not by necessity of his nature. Therefore, God acts by His will, not by necessity of His nature.[59]

Second, how can God create without himself undergoing change? Indeed, whenever a cause produces its effect, the cause must change intrinsically.

---

57. Thomas Aquinas, *Summa Contra Gentiles* 2.23.2. All quotations of the *SCG* (book 2) are taken from Thomas Aquinas, *Summa Contra Gentiles—Book Two: Creation* (trans. James F. Anderson; Notre Dame, IN: University of Notre Dame Press, 1975).

58. Aquinas, *SCG* 2.23.3.

59. Aquinas, *SCG* 2.23.3.

For example, if I choose to make a chair, I must undergo various chang-es—e.g., the movement from not wanting a chair to wanting one; the move-ment from not deciding to actually make my own chair to deciding to make a chair; the movement from not producing the chair to producing one; and so on. In short, creation involves change *in* the agent doing the creating. But a changing being is, by definition, a contingent being—i.e., one that is composed of actuality and potentiality. Therefore, the God of Thomism cannot be pure act, but is necessarily contingent.

Fortunately, Thomas also anticipated this objection. The basic problem with this challenge is that it commits a category mistake, insisting that all causal agents must begin their creative activity, thereby moving themselves into action. But God transcends time, and hence he never begins to create. Indeed, God creates from eternity. In the words of Aquinas:

> God need not be moved either essentially or accidentally if His effects begin to exist anew. ... For the newness of an effect can indi-cate change on the agent's part inasmuch as it does manifest new-ness of action; a new action cannot possibly be in the agent unless the latter is in some way moved, at least from inaction to action. But the newness of an effect produced by God does not demonstrate newness of action in Him, since His action is His essence. ... Neither, therefore, can newness of effect prove change in God.[60]

However, if God's action of creation is eternal, then the effect itself must also be eternal. And so, even if there is nothing internally contradictory in the Thomistic conception of God, clearly Aquinas's view contradicts the biblical doctrine of *creatio ex nihilo*.

Of course, Thomas anticipates this objection as well, noting that, while God's act of creation is eternal, the effect itself (i.e., the creation) is tem-poral. For, while God could have freely chosen to create an eternally exist-ing universe, we learn through revelation that God creates the cosmos out of nothing. How does an eternal cause produce a temporal effect? By his freedom of choice to produce one kind of effect instead of another. God

---

60. Aquinas, *SCG* 2.35.2.

eternally wills that a temporal finite universe exists, and even ordains the order in which events fall out in the flow of time.[61]

SUMMARY AND CONCLUSION

This chapter has laid the groundwork for my philosophical case for sovereign election. I have offered an argument from minimalistic theism to unconditional election, and I have shown that most (if not all) objections against the syllogism are not very strong. But there is one way of escape that we have not explored. And so we will examine this very important way out of our argument in the next chapter.

---

61. Aquinas, SCG 2.35.3–9. For a thorough analysis of the Thomistic doctrine of creation, see Reginald Garrigou-Lagrange, *The Trinity and God the Creator: A Commentary on St. Thomas' Theological Summa*, Ia, q. 27–119 (trans. Frederic C. Eckhoff; St. Louis: B. Herder, 1952), 337–455. Notice, then, that God never changes *intrinsically*, but does change *extrinsically*. That is, his essence is absolutely immutable and independent, yet there is a change in the way God relates to his creatures. As a father remains the same height while his son grows to be taller than him—thus, relationally changing from "taller than" to "shorter than" his son—thereby changing merely *extrinsically* with respect to his son, but not *intrinsically* (while the son changes *both* intrinsically *and* extrinsically), so also God changes merely extrinsically with respect to creation, while creation changes both extrinsically (with respect to God) and intrinsically. As Thomas wants to say, the creation is really related to God, but God is not really related to creation (ST Ia.13.7).

In fact, while other types of theists may not stress this point, it is precisely because Thomism upholds the simplicity of God that all of the distinctions made about him in this chapter must be understood *analogically* rather than *univocally*. Indeed, Thomists will admit only a virtual, as opposed to a real, distinction between God's attributes, and even more so between God's natural and free knowledge. In reality, God does not have to wait for his own decree to comprehend what is to occur in this world-ensemble. He just eternally knows the content of this world, and even knows that it is the actual world (instead of merely a possible world). However, we must also say that he was absolutely free in creating this world and not another, that he had genuine options "before" creating this world, and that our world-ensemble is contingent upon God. There is something about God that makes all of these affirmations true. And so we are justified in affirming a virtual distinction between his natural and free knowledge. For more on this issue, see Reginald Garrigou-Lagrange, *The One God: A Commentary on the First Part of St. Thomas' Theological Summa* (trans. Dom. Bede Rose; St. Louis, MO: B. Herder Book Company, 146, 170).

5

ARMINIANISM, CONDITIONAL
ELECTION, AND THE
SCIENTIA MEDIA

> *That kind of God's knowledge which is called "practical," "of simple
> intelligence," and "natural or necessary," is the cause of all things through
> the mode of prescribing and directing, to which is added the action of the Will
> and Power; (Psalm civ, 24;) although that "middle" kind of knowledge must
> intervene in things which depend on the liberty of a created will.*
> —James Arminius, "Disputation 4.XLV"

> *From these follows a FOURTH DECREE concerning the salvation of these
> particular persons, and the damnation of those: This rests or depends on
> the prescience or foresight of God, by which he foreknew, from all eternity
> [quinam] what men would, through such administration, believe by the aid of
> preventing or preceding grace, and would persevere by the aid of subsequent or
> following grace; and who would not believe and persevere.*
> —James Arminius, "On the Decrees of God" (XV.4)

In the Protestant tradition, one school of thought that has stood against
the doctrine of unconditional election is Arminianism. As our opening
quotations show, Arminius and his followers argue that the divine election unto salvation is based on what God foreknows a creature would do
with the supernatural and prevenient grace given to the sinner—a grace
given to aid a person, corrupted as he is by original sin, in coming to faith.
Those who would make good use of that grace, God elects unto salvation;
those who would not, God reprobates. One will also notice that Arminius
believed that, while natural knowledge comprehends everything God can

do via his sovereign power, the *scientia naturalis* does not have any sway over the rational creature, endowed as he is with free will. Indeed, the divine knowledge that comprehends what a creature would do under various circumstances is neither natural nor free knowledge but is instead somewhere in the *middle*.

The doctrine of middle knowledge, then, is an attempt to reconcile traditional theism with conditional election. Arminian theologians and philosophers who have embraced this option include scholars such as Paul Copan,[1] John Laing,[2] and William Lane Craig.[3] These thinkers agree that an omnipotent and omniscient deity creates the universe from nothing— thereby affirming explicitly, *and by their own admission*, that God foreordains everything that comes to pass via the divine creative decree. And they even admit that a world in which every person freely believes divine truth, and is thereby saved, is a logical possibility. However, while a world in which everyone is freely saved is possible, such a state of affairs is not feasible.

The distinction between that which is *possible* and that which is *feasible* is based on our common sense intuitions. Indeed, we use this sort of distinction all of the time in day-to-day discourse. For example, it is logically possible that I, Travis Campbell (who is in his forties, mind you), will become an NBA basketball star within the next two years. After all, there may be some latent skill I am not (yet) aware of, and so it is possible that I could call up my old student Andre Young (former point guard for the Clemson Tigers), who agrees to coach me in basketball, thereby turning me into a star. It is *possible*. *But it is not feasible!* As the saying goes, it's just not in the cards for me, and this is why, despite its logical possibility, I am under no delusions of grandeur of becoming an NBA star.

Of course, while most of us agree that certain logical possibilities are not feasible for human beings, what could possibly make something infeasible for God? The answer is, according to these Arminian thinkers, human

---

1. See Paul Copan, *"That's Just Your Interpretation": Responding to Skeptics Who Challenge Your Faith* (Grand Rapids: Baker, 2001), 74–89.

2. John D. Laing, *Middle Knowledge: Human Freedom in Divine Sovereignty* (Grand Rapids: Kregel, 2018).

3. See, e.g., William Lane Craig, *The Only Wise God: The Compatibility of Divine Foreknowledge and Human Freedom* (Grand Rapids: Baker, 1987).

free will. Indeed, while a world in which everyone is freely saved is a logical *possibility*, human freedom may very well render such worlds *infeasible*. For example, it may be that there is a logically possible world wherein both Adolf Hitler and Dietrich Bonheoffer are freely saved; however, such a world may not be feasible, for it may be the case that Hitler's unbelief created the context for Bonheoffer's belief or perseverance in the faith. We can imagine a number of scenarios whereby the unbelief of a person led to the faith of another (and vice versa)—e.g., think of the (late) atheist Christopher Hitchens and his Christian brother, Peter. It may be, for example, that the states of affairs wherein Peter Hitchens has faith are precisely those states of affairs wherein Christopher does not, and vice versa. Of course, according to these Arminians, in any given scenario the choices of human creatures are their own—they could have, in all of these circumstances, done otherwise—and God always has the power to override the free wills of human beings and drag them kicking and screaming into heaven. But God will not do that—for God wants an eternal love relationship with his creatures; and since forced faith is neither free nor loving, God will never override the free will of a person so as to effectually draw her to faith.

Thus, God not only knows what *could* happen (*natural knowledge*) and what *will* happen (*free knowledge*), he also knows what *would* happen were various states of affairs to obtain. His knowledge of what *would* happen is not his natural knowledge, since that comprehends necessary truths and those that are merely possible, nor is it his free knowledge, since that comprehends the actual, which obtains through the decree; hence, the knowledge of what *would* happen is called by these thinkers "middle knowledge"—since it comprehends every contingent, feasible world (and thus is not reduced to mere possibilities—*natural knowledge*) and comes before the divine creative decree (and thus is not reduced to actualities—*free knowledge*). Hence these Arminians posit *three* logical moments in the life of God (instead of two); i.e., natural knowledge of what *could* be (moment 1), middle knowledge of what *would* be (moment 2), and free knowledge of what *will* be (moment 3).

The most famous advocate of the doctrine of middle knowledge was Luis de Molina (d. 1600), a Jesuit Counter-Reformer who sought to give an answer to Reformational theology by reconciling the doctrine of human libertarian free will with divine omniprescience and meticulous providence.[4] His solution, middle knowledge, was brought into Protestant theology via the work of Arminius not long before his death in 1609.[5] Because

---

4. Luis de Molina, *Liberi Arbitrii cum Gratiae Donis, Divina Praescientia, Providentia, Praedestinatione et Reprobatione Concordia*. This famous work of Molina's, most commonly known as *The Concordia*, has been partially translated by Freddoso. See Luis de Molina, *On Divine Foreknowledge (Part IV of the* Concordia) (trans. Alfred J. Freddoso; Ithaca, NY: Cornell University Press, 1988). For a full biography of Molina's life, as well as a lucid exposition of his theology (including his doctrine of middle knowledge), see Kirk R. MacGregor, *Luis de Molina: The Life and Theology of the Founder of Middle Knowledge* (Grand Rapids: Zondervan, 2015). See also William Lane Craig, *The Problem of Divine Foreknowledge and Future Contingents from Aristotle to Suarez* (Brill's Studies in Intellectual History 7; New York: E. J. Brill, 1988), 169–206. Beyond the works already cited, the best works among modern analytical philosophers offering the pros and cons of Molinism include William Lane Craig, *Divine Foreknowledge and Human Freedom: The Coherence of Theism; Omniscience* (Brill's Studies in Intellectual History 19; New York: E. J. Brill, 1991); Thomas Flint, *Divine Providence: The Molinist Account* (Ithaca, NY: Cornell University Press, 1998); Ken Perszyk, ed., *Molinism: The Contemporary Debate* (Oxford: Oxford University Press, 2011); and Eef Dekker, *Middle Knowledge* (Leuven: Peeters, 2000). For an historical overview and analysis of middle knowledge from a Reformed perspective, see Sze Sze Chiew, *Middle Knowledge and Biblical Interpretation: Luis de Molina, Herman Bavinck, and William Lane Craig* (Contributions to Philosophical Theology 13; Frankfurt am Main: Peter Lang, 2016).

5. See James Arminius, "On the Understanding of God," in *Disputations on Some of the Principle Subjects of the Christian Religion* (1828; repr., vol. 2 of *The Works of James Arminius*, trans. James Nichols and William Nichols; Grand Rapids: Baker, 1986), 123–24. For Arminius's discussion of conditional election, which was quoted in my introduction, see Arminius, *Disputations on Some of the Principle Subjects*, 719. MacGregor offers strong evidence that Arminius's doctrine of middle knowledge differs significantly from Molina's, so much so that it is doubtful that Arminius ever read Molina at all—much less his doctrine of the *scientia media*. A similar reading of Arminius is endorsed by Roger E. Olsen, *Arminian Theology: Myths and Realities* (Downers Grove, IL: InterVarsity Press, 2006), 196. In short, while Molina's views provided a philosophical foundation for Arminius's theology, Molina himself would have probably rejected both the theology proper and soteriology of Arminius. See MacGregor, *Luis de Molina*, 245–48. If MacGregor's analysis is correct, Reformed theologians will need to recant their common assertion that Molinism is little more than the Catholic or Jesuit version of Arminianism. Indeed, if MacGregor is correct, then such a recantation will need to begin with me! See Travis James Campbell, "Middle Knowledge: A Reformed Critique," *Westminster Theological Journal* 68, no. 1 (Spring 2006): 14–15.

This all becomes quite confusing when we realize that Arminians such as Craig, though probably possessing a far better grasp of Molina's perspective than Arminius ever did, use Molina's views to defend an Arminian understanding of redemption. Hence, *philosophically* Craig is a Molinist, while *theologically* he is a Wesleyan Arminian—see William Lane Craig, "Middle Knowledge: A Calvinist-Arminian Rapprochement?," in *The Grace of God and the Will of Man* (ed. Clark H. Pinnock; Minneapolis: Bethany, 1989), 141–64. On the other hand, a thinker such as MacGregor, as much as a Baptist is able to do so, is Molinist through and through (i.e., philosophically *and* theologically—though, perhaps, *not* anthropologically); see MacGregor, *Luis de Molina*, 133–57; MacGregor, *A Molinist-Anabaptist Systematic Theology* (Lanham, MD: University Press of America, 2007), 31–33, 63–86. Thus, to avoid this confusion

Arminius's theology is largely misunderstood, and since (as a result) there are so many versions of Arminianism out there, many Christian philosophers advocating middle knowledge today, even those who are evangelical Protestants, call themselves "Molinists." But, truth be told, the current revival of Molinism today is little more than a renaissance of classical Arminianism (but see n. 5 below).

Some modern Arminians who endorse a doctrine of middle knowledge believe that the deity has utilized his *scientia media* to so order a feasible world in which the maximum number of people are saved via their own free will; and, as far as at least one of these thinkers is concerned, those who are lost are those for whom there is no feasible world wherein they would freely choose the gospel.[6] Craig says, "It is up to God whether or not we find ourselves in a world in which we are predestined unto salvation; but it is up to us whether or not we are predestined in the world in which we find ourselves."[7]

HOW DOES THE MOLINIST AVOID ORIGENISM?

In the previous chapter we looked at several versions of theism that are often offered as ways out of our argument for unconditional election. One was offered by Origen, who insisted that humans do not act because God foreknows their actions; rather, God foreknows their actions because they act. For example, take the following proposition:

(1) God believed eighty years ago that Paul would mow his lawn in 2020.[8]

I will, throughout this work, attempt to limit the use of the word "Molinism" to refer to a particular philosophical theology that utilizes a doctrine of middle knowledge; and I will attempt to limit the use of the word "Arminianism" to refer to a particular brand of Protestant theology and soteriology that endorses the doctrine of conditional election. That said, and given the confusion just noted, I hope the reader will forgive me if these labels become fluid from time to time.

6. William Lane Craig, "'No Other Name': A Middle Knowledge Perspective on the Exclusivity of Salvation through Christ," *F&P* 6 (April 1989): 181–2.

7. Craig, "'No Other Name,'" 179.

8. This is an updating of Plantinga's example, which had Paul mowing his lawn in 1999. See Alvin Plantinga, "On Ockham's Way Out," in *The Concept of God* (Oxford Readings in Philosophy; Oxford: Oxford University Press, 1987), 189.

Origen argued that Paul did not mow his lawn because God believed he would do so; rather, God believed he would do so because Paul chooses to mow his lawn in 2020. However, we saw two problems with this solution. First, it entails backwards causation, which (to say the least) is counter-intuitive. Second, it entails fatalism; for no effect can exist without its cause—and, the effect having already obtained (God believes eighty years ago), the cause *must* occur (Paul would mow his lawn in 2020).

Molinists generally follow William of Ockham (1285-1349)[9] in his distinction between propositions that are strictly about the past and those that, though spoken in the present or past tense, are tied to the future.[10] Modern proponents of Ockhamism use the nomenclature of *hard facts versus soft facts* to express this distinction. To use Plantinga's examples,[11] take the proposition,

(2) Socrates is seated.

This statement (2) is strictly about the present; and, if it is now true, then

(3) Socrates was seated

will be true from now on. Indeed, (3) is, *per our assumptions*, a hard fact about the past, and so it is what we call "accidentally necessary." By this we mean that, before the event obtains—before Socrates sits down—it was not necessary for it to occur—i.e., Socrates could freely sit or stand. But once the event occurs—i.e., once Socrates sits down—it becomes necessary in the sense that not even God can make it the case that Socrates never sat down. "In the same way, in 1995 BC God could have brought it about that Abraham did not exist in 1995 BC; now that is no longer within his power. As [Jonathan] Edwards says, it's too late for that."[12]

---

9. Indeed, some argue that Molinism stands or falls with Ockhamism (see Laing, *Middle Knowledge*, 154-56). Or, at the very least, Molinism gets a lot of mileage from Ockham's presuppositions, albeit with significant modifications (see Craig, *Aristotle to Suarez*, 184-88).

10. William Ockham, *Predestination, God's Foreknowledge, and Future Contingents* (2nd ed.; trans. Marilyn McCord Adams and Norman Kretzmann; Indianapolis: Hackett, 1983), 46-47.

11. Plantinga, "On Ockham's Way Out," 181.

12. Plantinga, "On Ockham's Way Out," 180.

But then, consider this proposition:

(4) In 400 BC, Socrates correctly believes that Plato will vindicate his legacy.

Assuming for a moment that Socrates believed this at that time, then at the time it was believed it is *present as to its wording*, but *actually about the future*. In other words, (4) is a soft fact in 400 BC, though it became a hard fact after Plato wrote his famous dialogues. It seems intuitively obvious to many that all soft facts can, in principle, be changed. For example, Plato can, in the years following 399 BC (up until his death), falsify Socrates's belief. Hard facts, on the other hand, cannot be so falsified.

Now, with the *soft-fact/hard-fact* distinction in place, let us return to our initial proposition, but add a twist:

(1)′ Eighty years ago it was true that Paul would *not* mow his lawn in 2020.[13]

"Even if true," (1)′ "is not accidentally necessary,"[14] for it is not strictly about the past—i.e., it is not a hard fact but a soft one. And, since it is a soft fact, "it is clearly possible that Paul have the power," in 2020, "to mow his lawn; but if he were to do so, then [1]′ would have been false."[15] And, what is true of (1)′ is also true of

(1) God believed eighty years ago that Paul would mow his lawn in 2020.

That is to say, God is essentially omniscient and, hence, if Paul chooses to mow his lawn in 2020, then God knows that. On the other hand, had Paul not chosen to mow his lawn in 2020 (i.e., if [1]′ is true), then God *would* have known *that*.

Thus, contrary to Origen, it's not so much that Paul retroactively causes God to have the knowledge he does. Rather, Paul is able to act in such a

---

13. Again, Plantinga's example, my year ("On Ockham's Way Out," 188).
14. Plantinga, "On Ockham's Way Out," 188.
15. Plantinga, "On Ockham's Way Out," 188–89.

way that, were he to act differently than God believes he will, God's foreknowledge would be different than it in fact is. Hence, the creature does
not have *causal* power over the past; but he does have *counterfactual* power
over the past. The free agent is able to act in such a way that, if he had contradicted what God currently foreknows, then God would have foreknown
that (instead of what he actually foreknows). Notice the word "would"
in the previous sentence; and remember that, according to the Molinist,
God possesses a middle knowledge of what people *would* do in all feasible
circumstances wherein they make their choices. Thus, middle knowledge
comprehends counterfactual truths.

What is a counterfactual? A counterfactual is a subjunctive conditional
that presupposes the falsity of the antecedent. For example, "If the sun
had not risen this morning, I would not be typing these words." Also, "If
Judas had been born one year earlier, he would not have betrayed Christ."
Counterfactuals, then, are "iffy history." They describe what would have
happened had other circumstances obtained. Caesar could have chosen to
not have crossed the Rubicon. However, he actually did cross the Rubicon.
What circumstances would need to obtain to ensure that Caesar would
freely choose to refrain from making his crossing? It's easy to think of a
plausible example—e.g., "Had Caesar's army been devastated by disease
one week before his fateful decision, he would have freely chosen to refrain
from crossing the Rubicon."

Reformed theologians, along with their Thomistic friends, have long
acknowledged that counterfactual propositions can be true. In fact, it seems
obvious that many *are* true—e.g., "If the sun had not risen this morning, I
would not be typing these words"; "Had one Vienna art school approved of
Adolf Hitler's application for admittance, he would have freely chosen to
attend that academy." Indeed, all one needs in order to verify this point is a
fertile imagination, combined with the commonsense intuition that certain
events would have been very different had an alternative state of affairs
obtained. To offer one more example, "Had Booth failed in his attempt to
assassinate Lincoln, Reconstruction would have gone along much more
smoothly for the South." In fact, Scripture itself is replete with examples
of true counterfactual propositions—e.g., "None of the rulers of this age

understood this; for if they had, they would not have crucified the Lord of glory" (1 Cor 2:8 NRSV).[16]

The difference between the Reformed Thomist and the Molinist is that the former insists on counterfactual propositions being true *only posterior* to the divine creative decree. Before the decree, all contingent truths are merely logical possibilities inhering in the divine *natural* knowledge. Molinists, on the other hand, insist that counterfactual propositions can be true *prior* to the divine decree, being comprehended by the divine *middle* knowledge.[17] God comprehends, via his *scientia media*, true counterfactual propositions describing not merely what each person *could* do in any situation, but what each person *would* do in each situation. God then decrees this actual world to come into being, thereby weakly actualizing all free choices by strongly actualizing the precise circumstances wherein free agents strongly actualize the very decisions God *knows* they *would* make *via* his *middle* knowledge and *will* make *via* his *free* knowledge.

The distinction between *strong* and *weak* actualization was first introduced by Plantinga.[18] Thomas Flint gives a helpful example illustrating the distinction:[19] Henry II (1133–1189), frustrated as he was at Thomas Beckett, asked, "Who will rid me of this priest?" At this point four knights obliged him and stabbed Beckett to death in Westminster Abbey. Henry strongly actualized his question, since he directly caused the words to come out of his mouth, while he weakly actualized the murder of Beckett, since he didn't actually cause the murder, but merely set up the circumstances to ensure its actualization. Similarly, the Molinist believes that God never strongly actualizes the free choices of his creatures. Rather, he weakly actualizes them insofar as he is the one who, via his creative decree, sets up the circumstances wherein all free decisions are made. But this raises a serious question—i.e., if God is the one who is able to set up all circumstances wherein human choices are made, why didn't he choose to weakly actualize only and all good choices by selecting precisely those circumstances

---

16. See William Lane Craig, "Middle Knowledge, Truth-Makers, and the 'Grounding Objection,'" *F&P* 18 (July 2001): 338–39. For an analysis of 1 Cor 2:8, along with other biblical texts, see Laing, *Middle Knowledge*, 283–304.

17. But see page 304n5 below.

18. Alvin Plantinga, *The Nature of Necessity* (Oxford: Clarendon, 1974), 172–74.

19. See Flint, *Divine Providence*, 110–11.

wherein all creatures would shun evil and do good? Take, for example, Adam and Eve. Surely there are circumstances in which Adam would have freely rejected Eve's offer of the forbidden fruit! Perhaps it is the case that, had Adam been married to a different woman, he would have freely refrained from sinning. Or, perhaps, had Eve been married to a different man, she would have been less tempted to eat the fruit and thus would have freely refrained from doing so. Or, perhaps, had other humans been chosen to take the role of the first parents, they would have passed the test.

Plantinga anticipates our challenge by introducing the concept of "transworld depravity."[20] Transworld depravity is the property of sinning at least once in every feasible world in which one finds oneself. For example, it may be the case that God surveyed every feasible world and discovered that every potential person would sin if they were placed in the same paradisiacal circumstances as Adam and Eve. It may even be the case that every potential person would eventually sin no matter what circumstances obtain.

It is not only possible that everyone sins, regardless of what circumstances obtain, but also that there are some people who, regardless of the potential circumstances, would never believe the gospel if it were offered to them. In other words, in every feasible world in which such persons exist, they refuse to believe and be saved. So they not only suffer from transworld depravity (as all free creatures do), but they also suffer from something worse—namely, "transworld damnation."[21] For Craig, every unsaved person in our world is such that there is no feasible world wherein he repents. In Craig's own words, "God has actualized a world containing an optimal balance between saved and unsaved, and those who are unsaved suffer from transworld damnation."[22]

Why would God strongly actualize the existence of persons who suffer from transworld damnation, thereby weakly actualizing their decision to damn themselves? Could not God instead use his middle knowledge to cut out, as it were, the transworldly damned, leaving behind only the transworldly depraved who freely accept the gospel and are saved? But

---

20. Plantinga, *Nature of Necessity*, 184–89.
21. This idea was first introduced by Craig, "'No Other Name,'" 181–84.
22. Craig, "'No Other Name,'" 184.

things might not be so easy. Remember again the example of the Hitchens brothers. It may be that growing up with a skeptical brother is precisely what led Peter to seek Christ and be saved. It may be that in every feasible world wherein Christopher is out of the equation, Peter rejects the gospel.

But it does seem a little unfair, does it not, to think that God would bring a transworldly damned person into existence just for the purpose of helping another person come to faith? What about the transworldly damned person? What rights does he have in this equation? These questions, however, fail to understand how the Molinist system works. For even if there is no feasible world wherein certain persons are freely saved, there are plenty of *logically possible* worlds wherein they are redeemed. In fact, all circumstances in which the damned find themselves are freedom preserving, and so their damnation is really of their own doing. At the end of the day, every damned person will look back on many opportunities in which, though he heard the gospel and felt the call of God in his heart, he nevertheless shunned the grace of God and freely chose to reject him.

But does it not seem strange that, of the (virtually) infinite world-ensembles God contemplates, he cannot think of at least one wherein everyone is freely saved? Yes it does! This is why Molinists tend to reject the presupposition underlying the question. As Craig notes, all things being equal, God does prefer a world wherein all are saved over and against a world wherein only some are. However, it is not at all clear that God prefers just any world wherein all are saved over and against any world wherein only some are saved. For, perhaps, every feasible world wherein all are saved consists of only a handful of people! Craig writes:

> Is it not at least possible that such a world is less preferable to God than a world in which great multitudes come to experience His salvation and a few are damned because they freely reject Christ? Not only does this seem to me possibly true, but I think it probably is true. Why should the joy and blessedness of those who would receive God's grace and love be prevented on account of those who would freely spurn it? An omnibenevolent God might want as many creatures as possible to share salvation; but given certain true counterfactuals of creaturely freedom, God, in order to have a multitude

in heaven, might have to accept a number in hell. Hence, contrary to [the presupposition that God necessarily prefers *any* world wherein all are saved and none are damned to a world in which some are saved and some are damned] the [Molinistic] theist might well hold that ... God prefers certain worlds in which some persons fail to receive Christ and are damned to certain worlds in which all receive Christ and are saved.[23]

HOW DOES MIDDLE KNOWLEDGE RECONCILE DIVINE OMNISCIENCE WITH CONDITIONAL ELECTION?

While it is true that God foreordains whatever comes to pass, he is able to do so without sacrificing genuine human freedom because he possesses middle knowledge. With his *scientia media* God is able to strongly actualize precisely those freedom-preserving circumstances wherein every free creature will make his respective choice. Since every person suffers from transworld depravity, it is simply not feasible for God to create a world wherein everyone only does what is right; and because the very circumstances wherein one depraved person freely embraces the gospel are precisely those wherein another freely rejects it, a world wherein everyone is freely saved is also not feasible for God.[24] God desires everyone to meet the condition(s) for salvation, but it is infeasible for him to bring such a world into being; therefore, God does the next best thing by bringing into existence a world wherein the maximum number of people meet the condition(s) for salvation, and those who meet the condition(s) are elected to receive salvation in time. Hence, God's election of a person for salvation is conditional. However, as Laing notes, "it must be emphasized that the conditions upon which election is based are not good works or merit, but rather saving faith effected by the movement of the Holy Spirit upon the individual."[25] God foresees a person having faith in Christ and elects him or her accordingly. As Laing writes:

---

23. Craig, "'No Other Name,'" 182–83.

24. Unless, of course, God makes a world containing only a handful of people.

25. Laing, *Middle Knowledge*, 175.

In point of fact, when Arminians say that God elects based on foreseen faith, what most really mean is that God elects based on the
counterfactuals of creaturely freedom that refer to individual faith
responses persons would have if placed in the right circumstances,
and then God predestines them by ensuring they will find themselves in those circumstances where they will believe. This approach
allows for an explanation of why all persons do not get saved, even
if it is God's desire that they do so.[26]

In foreordaining all that comes to pass, God is in no way strongly actualizing the choices of creatures in the world he ordains; rather, he is only
strongly actualizing the world itself (along with all of the circumstances
contained therein); but he is weakly actualizing creaturely choices, as
he knows with certainty what they would do in the states of affairs he is
strongly actualizing. Thus, God never strongly actualizes a person's choice
to reject the gospel any more than he strongly actualizes another person's
faith. Hence, God is able to sincerely desire everyone's salvation, even
though he has ordained a world wherein all are not saved.

AN EVALUATION OF ARMINIANISM

I am impressed with the erudition that goes into this understanding of
the divine election. In fact, once one grants a few Arminian presuppositions—e.g., conditional election, divine omniprescience, the divine creative
decree, and so on—something like middle knowledge is difficult to avoid.
Three examples illustrate this point. First, consider the work of the late
R. B. Thieme Jr., pastor-teacher of Berachah Church in Houston.[27] Thieme
explicitly rejects Arminianism, telling us that "Arminius and his followers
distort the sovereignty of God. ... They claim that man's volition is beyond
God's control, that man can cause things that are not in the divine decrees.
This is totally false; nothing can be certain until God decrees it to be cer-
tain."[28] Indeed, "We can see where Arminianism departs from orthodoxy; it

---

26. Laing, *Middle Knowledge*, 175.

27. See Robert B. Thieme Jr., *The Integrity of God* (2nd ed.; Houston: R. B. Thieme, Jr. Bible
Ministries, 1987).

28. Thieme, *Integrity of God*, 265.

holds falsely that events can occur without being decreed by God to occur."[29] This is roughly stated, but his point seems to be that God cannot know contingent truths unless he decrees them; before the decree, contingencies are mere possibilities in the divine mind. If we are correct here, then Thieme sounds quite Reformed. He even goes so far as to tell us that the divine omniscience precedes "the decree, then [comes] foreknowledge. The decree is based on omniscience; foreknowledge is based on the decree."[30]

Despite his critique of Arminius and his followers, Thieme clearly favors Arminius's view of election, writing:

> God elected or chose believers in the sense, first, that He *knew* ahead of time that, if given free will, they would freely choose to believe in Christ; second, that He *decreed* that such an act of faith would actually occur; third, that He *agreed* not only that their positive volition to the Gospel would occur at a certain point in time but also that all the blessings of salvation plus certain unique blessings would be their eternal possessions.[31]

Notice the implicit adherence to middle knowledge in this paragraph—i.e., God knew that, if particular persons are given free will, they *would* freely choose to believe in Christ. Earlier in his discussion of the divine decrees, Thieme elaborates on God's ability to discern the (potential) choices of free agents: "God knows what would have been involved in every case where a man's decision might have been different from what it was." For example, "Imagine that you are confronted by twenty possible courses of action and must choose one. Even though God knew which way you would choose to go and decreed only that one to become reality, He knows all the repercussions of each alternative."[32] So, *according to Thieme*, God decrees that course of action he knows would obtain via free will if a person were given various options. He elects unto salvation those whom he knows would choose him.

---

29. Thieme, *Integrity of God*, 265.

30. Thieme, *Integrity of God*, 265. This seems to be Thieme's version of classical Reformed theology—i.e., natural knowledge, then the decree, then free knowledge.

31. Thieme, *Integrity of God*, 268, italics original. Compare this quotation with those of Arminius that opened this chapter!

32. Thieme, *Integrity of God*, 262.

So, Thieme believes that nothing is certain until God decrees it to be so, and yet he also believes that, prior to his decree, God knows with certainty what a person would do if placed in a particular state of affairs. *Thieme's viewpoint, then, is little more than an incoherent version of Arminianism!*

Second, consider the work of Norman Geisler, who has written a refutation of what he calls "extreme Calvinism." Extreme Calvinism partly consists of the idea that God unconditionally elects persons unto salvation. For Geisler, this extreme view should be replaced with his own moderate Calvinist view of "unconditional election"—i.e., "Unconditional election, for moderate Calvinists, is unconditional from the standpoint of the Giver, even though there is one condition for the receiver—faith."[33] Of course, this statement is muddled, for it *just is* the Arminian doctrine of conditional election. Indeed, Geisler is here confusing God's unconditional *offer* of salvation (which is to everyone) with election itself—which, he claims, is conditional.

Geisler also adores Thomas Aquinas, saying, "As for myself, I gladly confess that the highest compliment that could be paid to me as a Christian philosopher, apologist, and theologian is to call me, 'Thomistic.'"[34] Strange, since everyone knows that Thomas embraced the Augustinian (Calvinist) doctrine of unconditional election.[35] On this score, at least, Thomas is one of Geisler's extreme Calvinists, whom he should therefore shun. It is also perplexing to see Geisler, on the one hand, offer a standard Thomistic refutation of middle knowledge,[36] only to turn around and affirm one of the basic presuppositions Molinists champion. Indeed, while refuting a standard argument against divine foreknowledge,[37] Geisler says, "If we had chosen otherwise, then an all-knowing, eternal God would have known for certain it would be *that* way."[38] In other words, we have counterfactual power over God's knowledge. No Molinist has ever said it any better! For

---

33. Norman L. Geisler, *Chosen but Free: A Balanced View of God's Sovereignty and Free Will* (3rd ed.; Minneapolis: Bethany, 2010), 149n24.

34. Norman L. Geisler, *Thomas Aquinas: An Evangelical Appraisal* (Grand Rapids: Baker, 1991), 14.

35. See, e.g., Thomas Aquinas, *ST* Ia.23.5.

36. Geisler, *Chosen but Free*, 149n24.

37. I.e., (1) What is infallibly foreknown cannot be otherwise; (2) What is free can be otherwise; (3) Therefore, what is infallibly foreknown cannot be free. See Geisler, *Chosen but Free*, 117n16.

38. Geisler, *Chosen but Free*, 117n16, italics original.

these and many other reasons, as one reads through Geisler's tome, one cannot help but agree with Pinnock when he says, "Geisler is an Arminian."[39] Not only so, but Geisler's Arminianism is incoherent without a doctrine of middle knowledge.

A third example of a thinker who finds a difficult time avoiding Molinism is Jerry Walls. Of our three examples, Walls is the only one who is explicitly Wesleyan Arminian in his soteriology.[40] However, he wonders whether middle knowledge is able to reconcile divine sovereignty and human freedom as cleanly as Molinists seem to think; and he is even more dubious of the Molinist claim that middle knowledge is able to reconcile God's universal love with his choice to make a world in which he knew particular persons would choose to reject the gospel. Walls asks us to consider the example of two profligate men, both of whom are familiar with Christianity. At a certain point in time, both are involved in an automobile accident, in which one survives and the other dies. The survivor eventually embraces the gospel and is saved. "Suppose God knows the first [i.e., the deceased] would also have become a saint if he had lived."[41] If Molina is right, such is a genuine possibility, in which case Molinism is as bad (or almost as bad) as Calvinism. Walls argues:

> Given God's desire to save all persons, a decisive negative response only makes sense in light of optimal grace. That is to say, a negative response to God is decisive only if one persists in rejecting God in the most favorable of circumstances. Only then is it clear that one had rejected God in a settled way with full understanding.
>
> Thus, in our case above of the two profligate men, I am inclined to say the one killed had not decisively rejected God. Although his initial response to grace was negative, he would have become a

---

39. Clark Pinnock, "Clark Pinnock's Response [to Geisler]," in *Predestination & Free Will: Four Views of Divine Sovereignty & Human Freedom* (ed. David Basinger and Randall Basinger; Downers Grove, IL: InterVarsity Press, 1986), 95. For a full expose of the many inconsistencies in Geisler's soteriology, see James R. White, *The Potter's Freedom: A Defense of the Reformation and a Rebuttal to Norman Geisler's* Chosen But Free (2nd ed.; Merrick, NY: Calvary, 2009).

40. See Jerry L. Walls and Joseph R. Dongell, *Why I Am Not a Calvinist* (Downers Grove, IL: InterVarsity Press, 2004).

41. Jerry L. Walls, "Is Molinism as Bad as Calvinism?," *F&P* 7, no. 1 (January 1990): 91.

saintly person had he lived longer. This suggests that his initial negative reaction to God was not really a settled response. If God knows this, it may be the case that God will give him the grace at the moment of death to begin to become what he would have become if he had not died. Further spiritual growth could occur after death.[42]

Walls avoids using the label "Molinist" to describe his view, as we have seen, due to the fact that Molina had difficulty reconciling divine sovereignty with divine love. Craig would say that Molinism has all the resources necessary to answer the problems raised by Walls. For example, Craig's own doctrine of transworld damnation entails that there is no feasible world wherein a person who dies would have believed the gospel had he lived longer. If that had been the case, God would have so providentially ordered the world in such a way that that individual would live longer and so believe. Of course, Walls is not very attracted to Craig's doctrine, finding it "extremely implausible. This account [of transworld damnation] could not be disproved, of course, even if offered as a sober proposal about what is actually the case, but it is exceedingly hard to entertain seriously the notion that all the persons who lived and died in countries the gospel did not reach for centuries would have rejected it if they had heard it."[43] Yet, on *this* point, Walls is not unlike many Molinists, who also reject transworld damnation. Also, Walls's soteriology simply does not make sense without the *scientia media*, as he admits:

> When libertarian freedom is consistently maintained, it will be recognized that God's ability to bring about certain states of affairs is contingent upon the choices of free creatures. In view of this, perhaps God cannot create a world in which everyone is saved, as the universalist supposes. Nor is it the case if some are lost, it follows that God is unwilling to save them. For God could be willing to save

---

42. Walls, "Is Molinism as Bad as Calvinism?," 93. In other words, Walls leans heavily in favor of postmortem salvation, wherein those who die without sufficient grace to believe are evangelized in the hereafter and so are given, as it were, a "second chance" at faith. He develops this notion further in Jerry L. Walls, *Hell: The Logic of Damnation* (Notre Dame, IN: University of Notre Dame Press, 1992), 83–103.

43. Walls, *Hell*, 97.

everyone, but unable to do so, while remaining properly omnipotent. It could be that he loves everyone and enables all of them to receive grace and be saved. If so, everyone would have a genuine opportunity to be saved. However, some might choose to continue in evil and be forever separated from God's love. It is the essence of the doctrine of hell that this possibility is realized in our world.[44]

How is it that there are some who might choose evil no matter how much grace is given to them? How is it that God is unable to realize a world wherein all are redeemed? How can God's choices be contingent on the free will of the creature? None of these assertions makes sense without middle knowledge. Indeed, Walls is not a Molinist *only in the sense that he does not accept all of Molina's ideas*.[45] Also, he does not embrace the label "Molinist." That said, even he admits that in formulating his views he is "assuming a broadly Molinist conception of absolute foreknowledge, which is compatible with some being eternally damned."[46]

What our three examples demonstrate, then, is that it is virtually impossible to adhere to (at least) a minimalistic theism and consistently maintain a conditional view of election unless one embraces something like a doctrine of middle knowledge. Indeed, all three of our examples (Thieme, Geisler, and Walls) uphold a conditional view of election while explicitly distancing themselves from Molinism to one degree or another, only to end up embracing the core of this perspective.

A CRITIQUE OF ARMINIANISM

Having shown how middle knowledge plays a fundamental role in the development of any plausible doctrine of conditional election, there are three points I would like to make by way of critiquing Arminianism: (1) the feasibility/possibility distinction is highly implausible when it is applied to God; (2) the Arminian doctrine of conditional election compromises the orthodox doctrine of *sola gratia*; and (3) the Arminian doctrine of conditional election is incoherent.

---

44. Walls, *Hell*, 81.

45. For that matter, neither does any self-proclaimed Molinist I am aware of.

46. Walls, *Hell*, 103.

THE FEASIBILITY/POSSIBILITY DISTINCTION IS HIGHLY IMPLAUSIBLE WHEN IT IS APPLIED TO GOD

Indeed, while we have already noted how commonsensical it is to affirm this distinction while talking about human beings, the idea that there are some worlds that are not feasible for *God* seems to border on blasphemy. Are we really to believe that God, with all of his resources, cannot envision a world ensemble consisting of billions on billions of people wherein every person is saved?

In answer to our rhetorical question, a critic could raise the following objection: this statement—i.e., "the idea that there are some worlds that are not feasible for God seems to border on blasphemy"—is a serious charge that warrants some argument. For one could imagine a possible world where the only creaturely actions are acts of abominable evil, a world where everything that happens is horrendously evil. Why would we consider this feasible for a God who is necessarily good? Doesn't it also "border on blasphemy" to allow those worlds as feasible for God?

But this line of argumentation is muddled, since it confuses feasibility and possibility with *narrow possibility* and *broad possibility*. As we noted in the previous chapter, narrowly construed, it is logically possible for evil to prevail over the good; however, broadly construed—i.e., when we take into account the existence of a necessarily good and sovereign God—it is impossible for evil to prevail. If the critic wants to insist that a world wherein evil prevails is not feasible for God, that is fine. But it is one thing for there to be infeasible worlds *with respect to God's nature*; it's another thing entirely for the creature to act in such a way that even God himself cannot instantiate the world he wants. God himself determines what is feasible for him, not the creature!

Even more disturbing is Craig's doctrine of transworld damnation. On this model, God brings a person into the world who would never believe in Christ, regardless of the circumstances that would feasibly obtain. This logically entails that there are persons who are such that not even God can conceive of a world wherein it's feasible for them to freely believe. And yet he brings them into existence anyway! Why does he do this? Because, as we have seen, the unbelief of some is what creates the context for the belief of others. Hence, the reason the transworldly damned exist is to create states of affairs for others to embrace Christ as Savior. But how is this not sheer utilitarianism, wherein the transworldly damned are not ends in themselves but rather nothing more than tools God uses to draw others to himself?[47]

We are aware of the irony of this critique brought against the Arminian who embraces transworld damnation. Craig's purpose in articulating such a doctrine seems to be to ensure that recalcitrant unbelief is in no way controlled by God. However, whatever horrors the Arminian fears in Calvinism, something even more horrific is implied by transworld damnation. For the transworldly damned are destined to disbelieve by something outside God's control. Yet they are ordained to disbelieve via the divine creative decree! When they come into existence, many find themselves in a context wherein they don't even hear the gospel. For why send the gospel to them if they would not believe upon hearing it? In short, there are people on this earth who are literally unredeemable. How is this good news to the unbelieving world?

The reader should refer to our brief defense of original sin in appendix 1. There I quote Chesterton, who noted that what is often music to our ears at first hearing becomes absolutely terrifying after further reflection and experience; and what may seem horrible at first becomes wonderful and sublime when put into practice. I think this insight applies equally well to Arminianism versus Calvinism. At first glance the Arminian promises many wonderful things, including a God who is universally loving, who does not interfere with our freedom, and who makes everyone savable. But further reflection and experience brings us face to face with a God who cannot, *in principle*, save many, or even render them *truly* savable. And so a transworldly damned person is not truly free, but finds herself in irredeemable bondage (John 8:34). According to this schema, she simply cannot be freed! Even God cannot touch her! In contrast, Calvinism offers truths that are, upon first hearing, difficult to accept—e.g., we are bound

---

47. Of course, I have no problem with the notion that God uses human beings to accomplish certain ends (which can include the salvation of others). But I do have a problem with the notion that there are humans who are *reduced* to such a status, indicating that the purpose for their existence is *merely* to serve such an end and then go to hell. In short, the doctrine of transworld damnation tends to dehumanize more than a few humans.

to sin, we cannot in any way save ourselves, God alone ordains whatsoever comes to pass, and there is no world rendered infeasible for him by the creature. But upon reflection and experience we come to realize that these truths are what make the gospel a true gospel. For here, in the Reformed faith, we encounter a God mighty to save, so much so that even the most recalcitrant sinner, regardless of his circumstances, is accessible to his Creator-Redeemer. The Arminian who believes in transworld damnation places many a sinner in the hands of impersonal, infeasible worlds that guarantee his recalcitrant unbelief; the Calvinist places all sinners in the hands of a holy and just God who guarantees us all that he will do what is good or just for everyone (Gen 18:25; Deut 32:4; Isa 61:11; Ps 111:7). As Van Til wrote so many years ago in a hypothetical dialogue with an unbeliever:

> It ought to be pretty plain now what sort of God I believe in. It is God the All-Conditioner. It is the God who created all things, who by His providence conditioned my youth, making me believe in Him, and who in my later life by His grace still makes me want to believe in Him. It is the God who also controlled your youth and so far has apparently not given you His grace that you might believe in Him.
>
> You may reply to this: "Then what's the use of arguing and reasoning with me?" Well, there is a great deal of use in it. You see, *if you are really a creature of God, you are always accessible to Him.* When Lazarus was in the tomb he was still accessible to Christ who called him back to life. It is this on which true preachers depend. The prodigal thought he had clean escaped from the father's influence. In reality the father controlled the "far country" to which the prodigal had gone.[48]

Scripture itself seems to mitigate, if not utterly demolish, the notion that all reprobates in the actual world suffer from transworld damnation: "Woe to you, Chorazin! Woe to you, Bethsaida! For if the deeds of power done in you had been done in Tyre and Sidon, they would have repented long ago in sackcloth and ashes" (Matt 11:21 NRSV). On this text the Molinist has a

---

48. Cornelius Van Til, "Why I Believe in God," in Greg L. Bahnsen, *Van Til's Apologetic: Readings and Analysis* (Phillipsburg, NJ: Presbyterian & Reformed, 1998), 139, italics added.

choice: either interpret it as extreme hyperbole on Jesus' part,[49] having no bearing on the issue of counterfactuals;[50] or agree with the prima facie reading of the text. If the latter, then the doctrine of transworld damnation is false. If the former, then the Molinist has lost a helpful proof-text establishing the fact that counterfactuals have truth-values. Also, what nonarbitrary standard can the Molinist offer in adjudicating what is mere hyperbole and what is factual? Without such a standard, other texts (e.g., 1 Cor 2:8) may very well be written off as hyperbolic as well, leaving Molinism with absolutely no biblical foundation.[51]

If, as Matthew 11:21 suggests, there are feasible worlds wherein the factually damned are counterfactually saved, why is God unable to actualize a world wherein all are saved? Here is a feasible world: God actualizes a world with trillions of people, wherein billions freely choose to be saved, while billions on billions more do not; to those who freely choose to be saved, God not only brings them into heaven, but he gives them special rewards for using their freedom wisely; and to those who reject divine love, God just overrides their free wills and saves them anyway. To be sure, those forced into the kingdom may very well have a lower status than those who entered freely, but at least they're saved. *That is a perfectly feasible world!* Would it not be better to have everyone debating the justice of it all in heaven than having billions suffering in hell?

Arminians commonly answer that God will never violate another person's free will in order to save him, for to do so contradicts the very notion of love and freedom. But I am not sure why this is the case. If someone I love is about to use his freedom to harm himself, would it really be loving for me to "respect his free will" so much that I am not willing to literally do everything possible to save him from harm? Most people would no doubt call me unloving toward someone if I could have saved him but, for the

---

49. This is the option Craig embraces (see *Only Wise God*, 137n1).

50. This is Laing's position, who states that, at a minimum, "this passage [i.e., Matt 11:21–24] cannot establish the truth of counterfactuals of creaturely freedom" (*Middle Knowledge*, 286).

51. See MacGregor, *Luis de Molina*, 148. Elsewhere MacGregor writes: "Admittedly realizing its [i.e., Matt 11:21–24] *prima facie* significance, proponents of transworld damnation who believe in biblical infallibility are forced to interpret the text in ways other than grammatico-historical" (*Molinist-Anabaptist Systematic Theology*, 68–69). See also Chiew, *Middle Knowledge and Biblical Interpretation*, 132–35; 198–204.

sake of his freedom, I refrained. How is this not loving free will more than people? How is this not the love of a metaphysical property more than the love of a person who has it?

ARMINIAN CONDITIONAL ELECTION COMPROMISES THE ORTHODOX DOCTRINE OF SOLA GRATIA

As we noted in our second chapter, the proposition that humans are saved solely by divine grace is a bedrock nonnegotiable truth every Christian embraces. Grace alone is a sine qua non of Christianity, so much so that a self-conscious denial of this truth is proof enough that one is not really a Christian (regardless of any other profession one gives). Fortunately, Arminians join the chorus of the orthodox in affirming *sola gratia*. Hence my point is not that Arminians deny salvation exclusively by divine grace. Rather, my point is that the doctrine of *conditional election is inconsistent* with *sola gratia*, so much so that the charge of incoherence can be laid at the Arminians' feet. To be consistent, the Arminian must either abandon conditional election or forsake *sola gratia*. She cannot consistently have both.

To illustrate our point, we turn to the recent work of John Laing. After explaining quite clearly that he eschews human merit in the acquisition of salvation,[52] Laing, as we have already seen, informs us that, "when Arminians say that God elects based on foreseen faith, what most really mean is that God elects based on the counterfactuals of creaturely freedom that refer to individual faith responses persons would have if placed in the right circumstances."[53] To illustrate his own position concerning effective grace, Laing lays out two examples:

The Molinist can maintain that prior to creating, God saw:

If I give a certain amount of grace to John to enable him to believe in me, he will believe;

and

---

52. Laing, *Middle Knowledge*, 175.
53. Laing, *Middle Knowledge*, 175.

> If I give a certain amount of grace to Martin to enable him
> to believe in me, he will not believe.
>
> In this case, God uses this information to decide which world
> to actualize, and indeed give John grace so he can believe (and thus
> effecting John's faith), and to not give Martin grace so he can believe
> (thus preserving God's sovereignty over salvation without causing
> Martin's unbelief or preventing Martin from believing) and with-
> out it being the case that God withheld the grace that would have
> enabled Martin to believe. In this case, the grace given to John is
> efficacious because it will get the result for which it was intended.
> Martin was not given grace to enable him to believe because, even
> if he were, he would not believe.
>
> The important point to note here is that under this model,
> the efficaciousness of God's grace is not dependent upon human
> response as if the human response "activates" God's grace, or trans-
> forms it from general/common grace to efficacious/effectual. God
> gives efficacious grace to John, and John believes. Similarly, this
> model does not claim that unbelievers are given grace that is meant
> to be efficacious, but because of their unbelief, it is made ineffec-
> tual, as if efficaciousness is "up in the air" until the human either
> believes (making it efficacious) or does not believe (making it inef-
> fectual). Such a reading is a misinterpretation of the proper logical
> order of things.[54]

This, among all the Arminian treatises we have read, is the most valiant
effort given to show that salvation is wholly of grace. Notice that Laing dis-
tances himself from those who want to ground the efficacy of divine grace
in the human will. Such is a common Arminian move, which renders salvation a joint effort between the Creator-Redeemer and the creature-sinner. Curiously, Laing eschews the common Arminian belief that God gives
grace to all, at least to those he knows will not believe. This would imply
that, on Laing's view, God is not really making an effort to save literally

---

54. Laing, *Middle Knowledge*, 177.

everyone, since he refuses to give redemptive grace to the reprobate. Can Laing consistently believe that God truly desires the salvation of everyone, as he does elsewhere,[55] if he also thinks God withholds grace? I don't think so, for if God truly desires a person's salvation, then God is not going to withhold grace even if he knows that person will spurn it.

Also, if Martin would not receive grace if it were offered to him, would this not imply that he suffers from transworld damnation? This leads us back to our earlier questions: Why place Martin in those circumstances? Where is the biblical evidence for transworld damnation?

More importantly, what is it about John that moves him to freely receive grace, while Martin freely rejects it? This question is sobering and speaks to the heart of the issue in the debates between the Augustinians, Thomists, and Reformed (on the one hand) and the Molinists,[56] Arminians, and Wesleyans (on the other hand). Every orthodox believer agrees with some version of prevenient grace—i.e., a movement of the Holy Spirit on/with the soul that strengthens the will, weakened as it is by sin, in such a way that one is able to believe in Christ. The question concerns whether this prevenient grace is *extrinsically* or *intrinsically* effectual. In other words, does human free will cooperate in such a way with the Spirit of God that divine grace *becomes* effectual at the point of faith (i.e., synergism)? Or is the grace of the Holy Spirit *alone* sufficient *in and of itself* to move the human soul "sweetly and suavely" so that it beholds Christ for the beautiful Savior he is and certainly, albeit freely, comes to Christ and receives him through faith (i.e., monergism)? If the former, then grace is merely extrinsically effectual, and it is the sinner, not God, who distinguishes one person from another; and so it is the sinner who is able to boast, even if ever so slightly, that he had something to do with his own salvation. If grace is intrinsically efficacious, then the Spirit himself effectually moves the sinner to embrace the Savior; and thus salvation is truly *sola gratia*. In short, conditional election opens one to the charge of salvation by merit. For if faith is not *wholly* a work of grace in the soul of the sinner, then it becomes a joint effort between God and man. In short, if faith is not *wholly* a gift of grace, then it is (at least partially) a work of humanity. Laing feels

---

55. Laing, *Middle Knowledge*, 176.

56. Molinists agree with Arminians concerning prevenient grace.

the pinch precisely at this point, which is why he words his doctrine the way he does. It is just counterfactually true that, if John were to be given grace, then he would believe. Nothing more is said, for to do so would tip the scales either in the direction of monergism or synergism. But even if we were to grant Laing's perspective, salvation still remains synergistic, and *sola gratia* is compromised. John can still boast in something other than the Lord. For John is able to say that he has distinguished himself from Martin. Martin just didn't have what it takes to receive grace. If he did, then the above counterfactual describing his unbelief would be false. So, on the schema of conditional election, every believer, like John, can now conclude that he is better in some way than the unbeliever—i.e., he's more intelligent, discerning, spiritual, or righteous, or possesses what the French call a sort of *je ne sais quoi* lacking in those who would refuse divine grace—for he is the one who made good use of his own free will, along with divine prevenient grace, while the unbeliever did not.[57]

Since no Christian can consistently boast in anyone except God for her own salvation (Eph 2:8-9; 1 Cor 1:30-31), Molinists and Wesleyan Arminians try to maintain a doctrine of *sola gratia* via their insistence that God has given prevenient grace to them, and that *this*, ultimately, is why they believe. But this only postpones the problem, for why does one person respond positively to prevenient grace while another does not? Again, on this model there *is* room for human boasting. As Garrigou-Lagrange notes, the Molinist doctrine of prevenient grace

> is a vain subterfuge, for ... this choice itself, an act strictly meritorious, establishing the most profound separation between the bad and the good; indeed, it is the ultimate actuality of our liberty while on earth. ... In fact, for the Molinists themselves, it is something so precious that not even God can touch it; but in that case the thing which is most precious in the role of salvation is withdrawn from the causality of God. It should be evident that, just as all being depends on [the] first being, all good on the first good, so

---

57. See R. C. Sproul, *Chosen by God* (Wheaton, IL: Tyndale House, 1986), 124-25.

all free determination toward good depends upon the supreme, free determination of God.[58]

Similar to Laing, Molinist Kenneth Keathley is persuaded that, if the divine effectual calling is synergistic, then the believer has something to boast about over and against the nonbeliever.[59] His way out is to affirm the monergistic nature of grace, along with its *resistibility*. To illustrate his point, Keathley asks us to consider a patient being delivered to the hospital by an ambulance. He has done nothing to get healed; he's just along for the ride. Hence, he does absolutely nothing to heal himself—the credit belongs wholly to those who stabilize him and eventually operate on him. Yet, technically, the patient can resist the kindness of the EMTs taking him to the hospital—and they are legally obligated to let him go if he insists that they do so. Theirs is to heal, and if the patient is healed it is wholly from them and not from him; his is only to resist. In a similar manner, God, contrary to Laing's model, gives converting grace to literally everyone—and so if a person believes, one can say that it is wholly from the Holy Spirit's grace; but if a person resists, it's all on him.[60]

Keathley's model of divine grace is a hair's breadth away from the Thomistic understanding of sufficient grace, as Keathley acknowledges.[61] The problem with Keathley's proposal is that it positively denies the implicit answer to Paul's question, "Who distinguishes you from another?" (1 Cor 4:7).[62] Paul's answer is that *God* is the one who makes the distinction

---

58. Reginald Garrigou-Lagrange, *Grace: Commentary on the Summa Theologica of St. Thomas, I^{a}II^{ae}, q. 109-114* (trans. Dominican Nuns of Corpus Christi Monastery in Menlo Park, CA; St. Louis: B. Herder, 1952), 248.

59. Kenneth Keathley, *Salvation and Sovereignty: A Molinist Approach* (Nashville: Broadman & Holman, 2010), 102-3.

60. Keathley, *Salvation and Sovereignty*, 104-8.

61. Though he does not cite Thomas Aquinas on this score but Terrence Tiessen, *Who Can Be Saved?* (Downers Grove, IL: InterVarsity Press, 2004), 230-58, 493-97. See Keathley, *Salvation and Sovereignty*, 105n12.

62. "For who maketh thee to differ *from another*? and what has thou that thou didst not receive? now, if thou didst receive *it*, why dost thou glory, as if thou hast not received *it*?" (1 Cor 4:7 KJV; see also NIV, ESV, NRSV); Greek: τίς γάρ σε διακρίνει; τί δὲ ἔχεις ὃ οὐκ ἔλαβες; εἰ δὲ καὶ ἔλαβες, τί καυχᾶσαι ὡς μὴ λαβών. The KJV, NIV, ESV, and NRSV are to be preferred over the NASB—i.e., "For who regards you as superior ..." In the words of Fee, "The exact intent of the first question, however, is not immediately transparent. The difficulty lies with the meaning of the verb *diakrinei* ('discern, distinguish'), which is probably something of a wordplay on

between saved and lost. Unfortunately, Keathley does not interact with this passage at all in his otherwise excellent study. Also, this proposal never really overcomes the problem that originally pinched Keathley, for the choice of nonresistance is still a choice and, hence, the believer still has something to boast about—that is, *Why did you resist and not me?* Surely there is something in me that moved me to accept God's gift, while something in you moved you to resist it! To his credit, Keathley has an answer to this counterargument—i.e., on his model, monergistic grace is fully sufficient to save, and so the only thing a person can do to damn herself is resist grace; but resistance is a sin of omission, and "omissions are not efficient causes. ... Such omissions [are] 'quasi-causal' because they control events but do not cause events."[63] However, it need not always be the case that omissions are noncausal (or even "quasi-causal"). To offer a few examples: omitting to pay one's taxes will eventually cause the government to pursue legal action against you; if a woman does not tell a potential sex partner she has an STD, and even remains wholly passive, albeit consensual, in the sex act, such will nevertheless cause the man to contract the same disease. In any case, the Bible never portrays resistance to God's gracious overtures as mere sins of omission; for all sin is resistance to grace (Rom 6:14; 14:23), and all sinners engage in activities that actually cause genuinely bad things to happen in this world (see Mark 7:14-23; Acts 7:51-8:1; Rom 1:18-28; 2:1-3:18).

---

the *anakrinō* ('examine') and *krinō* ('judge') of vv. 3-5. It is common to see it as referring to the Corinthians' being 'puffed up' against one another within the community. Thus: 'Who makes you different from anyone else?' (NIV). The implication is that there are no grounds for anyone's exalting himself/herself over another, since any differences are ultimately attributable to God." As he goes on to say, "The alternative is to see the question as directly related to v. 6 and their pride vis-à-vis Paul. In this case the question would mean, 'Who distinguishes *you*?' On what possible grounds do you boast in this manner? The implication is that their boasting in wisdom, which allows them to 'examine' Paul, is strictly self-proclaimed. ... If the first question marks the Corinthian conceit as *presumptuous*, the second marks it as *ungrateful*—and is singularly devastating: 'What do you have that you did not receive?' This is an invitation to experience one of those rare, unguarded moments of total honesty, where in the presence of the eternal God one recognizes that everything—absolutely everything—that one 'has' is a gift. All is of grace; nothing is deserved, nothing earned. Those who so experience grace also live from a posture of unbounded gratitude. Those ... who think of themselves as especially gifted with the Spirit and wisdom, thereby enabling them to judge another, reflect a total misunderstanding of grace, and quite miss the 'humility of God' expressed in the crucified One." See Gordon D. Fee, *The First Epistle to the Corinthians* (NICNT; Grand Rapids: Eerdmans, 1987), 170-71, italics original.

63. Keathley, *Salvation and Sovereignty*, 105n11.

The choice to resist God's grace is a bad one that is condemned in Scripture (Isa 5:1–6:13; Acts 7:51). So why does the believer not make the bad choice to resist divine mercy? If he is the deciding factor, it must be because he is better than the unbeliever in some way.

Objections. Leighton Flowers has recently attempted a critique of this argument with four criticisms. Here I will answer two of them.[64] First, *a person's choice does not merit salvation just because it is his choice*.[65] Another way of making this point, which we often hear from Arminians, is that the Bible nowhere states that faith is a meritorious work. Here I agree. The fact that a person makes a choice, in and of itself, does not prove that he has merited the thing chosen. But herein lies the rub! Under what circumstances can one truly say that one's choices are nonmeritorious? If I choose to buy a car with money that I earned, then I have good reason in taking pride in what I have accomplished (i.e., I myself earned the money to purchase the car). On the other hand, if I am given the car, then I have no reason to take pride in my choice to drive the car. In a similar way, if faith comes *from* me as the deciding factor in my salvation, then I have good reason to take pride in what I have accomplished (i.e., I myself made a choice that resulted in my salvation). On the other hand, if faith comes *to* me as a gift from God, then I have no reason to take pride in my choice to believe in Christ. Faith is indeed *not* a meritorious work whereby we earn God's favor; however, if faith were not a gift of God's grace it would be a meritorious work whereby we earn God's favor; and this is precisely why Scripture teaches that faith is a gift from God (John 6:44; Eph 2:8–9; Phil 1:29). In short, faith is not a work; therefore, it must be a gift.

Rejoinder. At this point the Arminian will double down on his insistence that his choice to believe did not merit salvation, for just as I cannot boast in my choice to drive a car given to me, I cannot boast in my choice to believe in Christ precisely because it was prevenient grace that enabled me to believe in the first place.

---

64. I only answer his last two objections because in the first two he presupposes that all Calvinists are compatibilists, which, as we have seen, is not true. See Leighton Flowers, *The Potter's Promise: A Biblical Defense of Traditional Soteriology* (N.p.: Trinity Academic Press, 2017), 155–59. See chapter 2 above.

65. Flowers, *Potter's Promise*, 161–65.

However, this kind of response only brings us full circle back to our critique of the Wesleyan Arminian doctrine of prevenient grace. Again, this view of grace only postpones the problem, since we are still left wondering why one sinner made good use of the prevenient grace given while another did not. The answer is that one makes good use of the grace given either because of the extra grace given to her that was not given to another or because of something within her. If the former, then Augustinian prevenient grace is true; if the latter, then there is something about one sinner that is better than another, and thus the redeemed sinner can boast (at least partly) in herself for her salvation.

Second, *a similar charge of boasting can be laid at the feet of the Calvinist.* According to Flowers it is Calvinism, not Arminianism, that gives a sinner room to boast in his salvation. For it makes little sense for one to boast in an ability that he shares with everyone else. Indeed, if everyone were given the ability to sing equally well, would it not be a little strange to find someone boasting in his ability to sing? On the other hand, if I were given the ability to sing while others were not, then I have reason to boast in the favor shown to me by God. Similarly, the Arminian submits that it is strange to think that I can boast in the exercise of my faith, since God has given that same ability to all; and yet it seems particularly arrogant to embrace Calvinism, for on this model a sinner can take pride in the favor shown to him by God.[66]

Response. Flowers's argument actually gives us further reason to embrace Calvinism. Going back to his illustration, imagine that everyone is given the ability to sing equally well, and everyone actually makes good use of this gift by singing whenever he or she can. Surely no one in this circumstance would ever boast, for everyone is making good use of the gift they have received. But now imagine everyone given the gift of a beautiful singing voice, but only some are willing to use it. In this case, those who choose to sing have room to boast in the fact that they have the courage, wherewithal, stamina, and so on to use the precious gift that others refuse to share. Similarly, the Arminian believes the same kind of grace is given to all, but only some make good use of this gift. This is a recipe for boasting!

---

66. Flowers, *Potter's Promise*, 159–61.

We need to recall that, according to the Reformed doctrine of election, no basis is found in the creature as an explanation for why God chooses an individual to be saved. God looks on the mass of humanity, all involved in one common ruin—i.e., each person making the terrible choice to spurn God's law; each choosing to condemn herself through her own sin—and chooses one evil person over another. The one chosen was just as worthy of condemnation as the one passed over. God did not choose his elect ones because they were more intelligent, or more beautiful, or more pious, or more moral than those passed over (1 Cor 1:26–31; Deut 7:6–7). As Martin Luther once famously said, the only things we contribute to our salvation are sin and resistance. Election is all of grace. Hence, the redeemed have absolutely no right to boast in anyone except the gracious God who redeems them out of sheer mercy.

It is true, of course, that many persons in our world are given wonderful gifts in the form of natural talent, money, good looks, and so on; and the rest of the world looks in wonder at these people as they often squander their gifts by showing a complete lack of humility due to the favor bestowed on them. What is true of the world in general is even more true of many card-carrying Calvinists of our day. We should all be concerned at the fact that some of the most prideful, and even mean-spirited, people of our day are Calvinists. As one Presbyterian pastor remarked in my presence, it is somewhat ironic that so many Reformed Christians take pride in being totally depraved!

What all of this illustrates is that some people are better than their worldview, while others fail to live up to what logically follows from their own core beliefs. More than a few Arminians are kind and humble servants of Christ, but that is due to the fact that they are better than their own soteriology. More than a few Calvinists are mean and prideful, but that is due to the fact that they are sinners and are far worse than their theology. The solution to these circumstances is for Arminians to become more consistent by embracing a Reformed soteriology, and for Calvinists to examine themselves to make sure they have really thought through the implications of what they say they believe.

There is yet another reason to think the Arminian doctrine of conditional election entails a denial of *sola gratia*—namely, *according to Arminius*

and his followers, faith is not the only condition one must meet in order to be elect.
As we read in the opening statements of this chapter, Arminius himself
clearly taught that election unto salvation is based on God's foreknowledge of who would believe *and persevere* in the faith until the end of their
lives. Eighteenth-century Arminian theologian van Limborch concurs with
Arminius at this point, saying: "Namely by virtue of that Decree whereby
he had determin'd to bestow Salvation on the Believers and Obedient; to
which Decree is annex'd the Design of bringing all the Faithful in time to
Salvation."[67] A few pages later, while answering the charge that his view
of predestination cannot be reconciled with human freedom and liberty,
"either of attaining Salvation by the Assistance of the Divine Grace, or of
incurring the Guilt of Damnation by a wilful Disobedience," van Limborch
writes:

> These two things are not inconsistent: Because the Divine Prescience
> not only presupposes that Salvation may be obtain'd by Faith and
> Obedience, and Men be damn'd for their Infidelity and Impenitence;
> but also, since Salvation may be attain'd, it presupposes that it may
> be acquir'd or not acquir'd by our own Virtue or Vice. For the Divine
> Prescience not only presupposes a thing future, but even the very
> manner also wherein it shall come to pass.[68]

It seems that Arminius and van Limborch have taken their presuppositions
to their logical conclusion. For if the sinner has the final say in whether
he is elect or not, then it logically follows that he can freely choose to fall
away from the faith and perish. As is often said, if you can choose to get
in, you can choose to get out! Modern Arminians are torn at precisely this
point, with some maintaining the classical Arminian view that it is possible

---

67. Philipp van Limborch, *A Compleat System, or Body of Divinity, Both Speculative and
Practical, Founded on Scripture and Reason: Volume One* (trans. William Jones; London, 1702;
repr., London: Forgotten Books, 2015), 343. Van Limborch's statement here would seem to imply
middle knowledge, though he never explicitly endorses it in his passing acknowledgement
of the doctrine (see van Limborch, *Compleat System*, 66).

68. Van Limborch, *Compleat System*, 345–46.

for a true believer to apostatize and perish,[69] while others take a different route and insist that apostasy is not damnable.[70] However, the latter perspective flies in the face of those biblical texts that offer a warning to those who fall away—namely, their very souls are at risk (see Heb 6:1–8; 10:26–31; Jas 5:19–20; 2 Pet 2:20). Indeed, this perspective is traditionally called "antinomianism," which literally means "against the law." Antinomianism entails that sanctification is not a necessary result of justification. The church has virtually unanimously seen antinomianism as a heresy.

But what of the classical Arminian perspective that it is possible for one to lose one's salvation?[71] Again, we think this logically follows from basic Arminian presuppositions. Of course, what this means is that, in order for one to be elect, as Arminius and van Limborch explicitly state, one must meet not only the condition of faith but also of perseverance. However, while it may be debatable whether self-generated faith is a work (and I have argued that it is), it should be obvious that *perseverance in the faith* is indeed a work. So, if faith *and* perseverance are the grounds for being elected by God for salvation, then we must conclude that we are (at least partially) saved by works and not by grace alone (Rom 11:6).

THE ARMINIAN DOCTRINE OF
CONDITIONAL ELECTION IS INCOHERENT

Not only is conditional election inconsistent with *sola gratia*, but it does not even seem consistent with itself. There are two reasons for this. First, *it is difficult to understand how conditional election is even a form of election.* For notice that, on this scheme, God looks down the corridor of time and sees certain persons choosing God (or Christ) as Savior; he then elects

---

69. See William Lane Craig, "'Lest Anyone Should Fall': A Middle Knowledge Perspective on Perseverance and Apostolic Warnings," *International Journal for Philosophy of Religion* 29 (1991): 65–74.

70. See Laing, *Middle Knowledge*, 185, where he writes: "So an Arminian analysis predicated on middle knowledge can also affirm perseverance, but with one difference: it can account for the situations in which persons are reborn, but fall away from the faith and die in their sins. It will still maintain that those individuals are ultimately saved, but it has an explanation for how persons may have been pulled away by sin."

71. To be sure, Arminius was somewhat ambiguous as to whether a true believer could apostatize. Van Limborch, on the other hand, explicitly denies the absolute perseverance of the saints (see van Limborch, *Compleat System*, lx).

them for salvation. But this is not one person (God) choosing another (a sinner) for a specific reason or purpose, but creatures choosing salvation for themselves. This is not divine election but human election, with God standing on the sidelines as the eternal "recognizer of human choices." As at least one Arminian scholar has noted, a motive for embracing corporate election is that it "has the distinct advantage of construing election as a divine decision and not the pale notion of God's ratifying our choices as in the standard Arminian interpretation. If election is understood as a corporate category, then it would be God's unconditional decision and be potentially universal as regards all individuals."[72] In this light, note the insights of John Girardeau, who gives several good reasons for thinking that the doctrine of conditional election is incoherent:

1. *It fails to make God the sole author of our salvation.* "For while it represents God as providing the means by which the sinner may be saved, it makes the sinner by his free will determine himself to the saving use of those means. It is, therefore, really the sinner who elects God, and not God who elects the sinner. His election of God as a Saviour conditions God's election of him as saved."[73]

2. *It denies individual election.* "For it affirms the election only of a condition upon which individuals may be saved, if they will to comply with it." Indeed, individuals are not elected to meet the condition of faith, since they may or may not meet that condition. "To say that if they do they are elected to salvation, is to affirm a hypothetical and contingent election, which is no election at all. It is a contradiction in terms."[74]

3. *It denies the efficacy of divine love.* For it "makes the love of God secure the salvation of none of his children. It only secures for them a possible and contingent salvation. It is therefore less than the love of

---

72. Clark H. Pinnock, "From Augustine to Arminius: A Pilgrimage in Theology," in Pinnock, *The Grace of God and the Will of Man* (Minneapolis: Bethany, 1989), 20. We have answered various exegetical arguments for an exclusively corporate view of election in chapter 3.

73. John L. Girardeau, *Calvinism and Evangelical Arminianism Compared as to Election, Reprobation, Justification, and Related Doctrines* (1890; repr., Harrisonburg, VA: Sprinkle, 1984), 127.

74. Girardeau, *Calvinism and Evangelical Arminianism*, 127.

earthly parents to their children, for they would save their children if they could. To say that God cannot save all his children would be heresy deepening into blasphemy."[75]

4. *It renders election superfluous.* "For it denies that election is in order to faith and holiness and affirms that it is conditioned upon persever-ance in them to the end—that is, the end of life and the attainment of heaven. It follows necessarily that when the sinner is foreknown to get to heaven he is elected to get there. Where is the use of such election? One is obliged to apply to it Occam's razor—the law of par-simony, that causes are not needlessly to be multiplied for a given effect. If, through the assistance of grace and the free determina-tions of his own will, a man has persevered in holy obedience to the end and has attained to heavenly happiness, why should a cause be invoked to ensure the result which without it has been secured? It is inconceivable that God would elect men *to be* saved in consequence of his foreknowing that they *are* saved; or that he would have elected *to save* men who, he foreknew, would by the assistance of grace *save themselves*. God does nothing in vain; but this doctrine represents him as doing a vain thing."[76]

Second, *the doctrine of middle knowledge entails the doctrine of uncondi-tional election.* I earlier pointed out that, if one wants to maintain a minimal commitment to theism and creation out of nothing, but also accept a con-ditional view of election, middle knowledge seems to be the best (*if not the only*) game in town. I even surveyed three scholars who, though formally eschewing middle knowledge (or aspects of it), end up embracing it as they articulate their own views concerning conditional election. Yet, at the end of the day, the only hope for Arminianism ends up being the seeds of its own destruction; for if there is a *scientia media* then God elects unconditionally.

On the doctrine of middle knowledge, God ponders those counterfac-tual truths feasible for him to actualize and then instantiates them in real-ity. Such counterfactuals include those persons who would or would not

---

75. Girardeau, *Calvinism and Evangelical Arminianism*, 130. In other words, if Arminianism is true, then God does not love us!

76. Girardeau, *Calvinism and Evangelical Arminianism*, 130–31, italics original.

believe if given prevenient grace. Unless one is to embrace the strange and unfounded doctrine of transworld damnation, many (if not all) persons who find themselves in a world where they do not believe would have believed had they been placed in another world. They did not choose to be born in a world wherein they are condemned, and God could have placed them in a world wherein they choose to be saved. The same can be said of the elect. Those who find themselves in a world wherein they believe may very well have been placed in a world wherein they do not believe. Thus, we are right back to our conclusion established in chapter 3. That is, even if election is based on foreseen faith, the foresight itself is based on God's free decision to actualize this world and not another. Interestingly, even Molina agrees with us on this score. As MacGregor points out:

> However, we must not therefore think that predestination, for Molina, depends on human free choice. For every elect person, God could have just as easily chosen another feasible world in which the same individual would have freely rejected his saving grace or not existed at all. Likewise, for every reprobate person, God could have just as easily chosen another feasible world in which the same individual would have freely embraced his salvation or not existed at all. Molina insisted that no reason can be given concerning why God selected one feasible world over a host of others except for his sovereign will. Since this predestinary choice is in no way predicated on how any person in that world would respond to his grace, Molina's doctrine of predestination champions the doctrine of unconditional election. This is the clear teaching of Romans 9 ... and 2 Timothy 2:20. Hence, Craig observes, "Molina held that God's choosing to create certain persons has nothing to do with how they would respond to His grace; He simply chooses the world order He wants to, and no rationale for this choice is to be sought other than the divine will itself. In this sense, predestination is for Molina wholly gratuitous, the result of the divine will, and in no way based on the merits or demerits of creatures."[77] Thus God's choosing to

---

77. Craig, *Aristotle to Suarez*, 204. This is an interesting statement on Craig's part and leads me to recant a point made in my earlier essay on middle knowledge. In that work I

elect or reprobate certain individuals by creating a world in which they would or would not attain to salvation rather than another world where they would freely do the opposite or not even exist has nothing to do with their freely chosen belief or unbelief; God simply, in his absolute sovereignty, selects the world he wants.[78]

---

wrote the following: "According to Molina, God's election of certain persons unto salvation is based on his foresight of human merit. In other words, Molina promoted salvation by works" (Campbell, "Middle Knowledge: A Reformed Critique," 13). In the footnote I stated the following: "Craig himself would agree with this, writing: 'If one adopts the view that our good works merit salvation, then Molinism would, indeed, seem to lead to works-righteousness on the part of man, since it is not God who does the works, but we ourselves, at God's instigation. On the Thomist view, the works are viewed as works of God to which He causally determines us, and therefore salvation by human works does not result. But then it is difficult to see either how man is genuinely free with regard to such works or how the merit wrought by such works can be attributed to man rather than to God. The conclusion follows, then, that the Molinist who wishes to remain a Molinist ought to reject the Catholic doctrine of justification in favor of a Protestant understanding of salvation as a wholly unmerited and freely accorded gift of God's grace' (DFHF, 272). It is interesting to note that the Roman Catholic Church has not officially declared which view, Thomism or Molinism, is the ortho-dox understanding of grace. But as the Council of Orange decreed, and as Thomas Aquinas confirmed, we are made members 'of Christ through grace alone' (ST IIIa.62.1; cf. Eph 2:8–9; Rom 11:6). Cf. Ludwig Ott, The Fundamentals of Catholic Dogma (4th ed.; trans. Patrick Lynch; ed. James Canon Bastible; Rockford, Ill.: Tan Books & Publishers, 1974), 42–43). Note also how close some Catholics come to affirming, with Molina, election according to human merit (thus showing the plausible historical [if not logical] connection between rejecting sola fide and rejecting sola gratia [cf. Rom 3:28; 4:1–5; 5:1]); cf. Robert A. Sungenis, Not By Faith Alone: The Biblical Evidence for the Catholic Doctrine of Justification (Santa Barbara, Calif.: Queenship Publishing, 1997), 670. Thus, Craig seems right to say that, in order to preserve the orthodox doctrine of sola gratia, 'a Christian would therefore seem compelled to choose either Thomism or Protestantism' (DFHF, 332 n. 51)." See Campbell, "Middle Knowledge: A Reformed Critique," 13n45. DFHF = Divine Foreknowledge and Human Freedom.

While I stand by my conviction that anyone who self-consciously denies that salvation is wholly and exclusively by God's grace cannot be a Christian, and while I still affirm that an historical (if not logical) connection exists between a denial of sola fide and a denial of sola gratia, I gladly admit my mistake in asserting that Molina is a non-Christian because he affirmed salvation by works. MacGregor has demonstrated to my satisfaction that Molina affirmed that election for salvation is wholly gratuitous on God's part, and so human merit contributes nothing to one's redemption. In fact, I am perplexed by the stark contrast between what I read of Molina's doctrine of election in Craig's Divine Foreknowledge and Human Freedom and his Aristotle to Suarez. For if, as Craig notes, Molina's doctrine of predestination is wholly gratuitous, then he cannot be correct when he tells us that Molinist predestination leads one to affirm works-righteousness. Yet, once one leaves the issue of election and enters into a discussion of prevenient grace, one does find a serious inconsistency in the thought of Molina (as we have seen). For while Molina did believe in unconditional election, he also affirmed a merely extrinsic effectual grace that takes away with one hand what is given by another.

78. MacGregor, Luis de Molina, 150–51.

Not only Molina, but quite a few thinkers have integrated the doctrine of the *scientia media* with Augustine's account of sovereign grace. Francis Suarez, for example, was an early seventeenth-century Jesuit who upheld a libertarian view of the will, middle knowledge, unconditional election, and effectual calling. Those who belong to his school of thought often call their viewpoint *congruism*. In our day, thinkers such as John Frame, John Feinberg, Bruce Ware, and Terrence Tiessen all embrace a Calvinistic version of middle knowledge.[79] Hence, even if Molina himself had embraced conditional election, I would see no reason to follow him on this score. But when we take cognizance of the fact that even he, the "Father of Middle Knowledge," embraced sovereign election, we can only wonder why so many who embrace his *scientia media* would want to contradict him on this most important point. Thus, I think it is wise to conclude our critique of Arminianism with the insights of yet another Molinist:

> God's omniscient foreknowledge is the Achilles' heel for most Arminian presentations of election. If God has exhaustive fore-knowledge of all future events, then conditional election does not really remove the unconditional nature of God's decisions. If God knows that a certain man will freely accept the gospel while that man's brother freely will not, and yet God decides to create both of them anyway, then this is a mysterious, sovereign, and unconditional determination on the part of God.[80]

SUMMARY AND CONCLUSION

In chapter 4 I set forth an argument that moved from explicitly Pelagian presuppositions to the doctrine of unconditional election—i.e., if there is an omnipotent and omniscient deity who creates the universe from nothing, then the doctrine of unconditional election is true; and there is such a deity; *ergo*, the doctrine of unconditional election is true. Here, in chapter 5, we have explored what is perhaps the most common way Arminians try to

---

79. For an exploration of these alternatives, see Campbell, "Middle Knowledge: A Reformed Critique," 12–13.

80. Keathley, *Salvation and Sovereignty*, 154.

escape our conclusion—namely, the doctrine of middle knowledge. For on this model of the divine omniscience, the Arminian may be able to state that God elects those individuals unto salvation who, if they were offered salvation and given the prevenient grace, would freely place their faith in Christ. In other words, God middle-knows what every creature would do in whatever feasible circumstances he finds himself. Those who *would* trust the Savior, *if* given the opportunity to do so, God (on that basis) elects unto salvation; and those who *would* reject the Savior, *if* given the opportunity to do so, God reprobates unto damnation.

We saw several good reasons to think the Arminian doctrine of conditional election is false. First, I do not see any good reason to think the free will of a creature could ever render any world infeasible for God. Second, there are good reasons to think conditional election, along with its attendant doctrine of prevenient grace, compromises the orthodox doctrine of *sola gratia*. Third, there is good reason to think that conditional election is incoherent; and, even if God does possess a *scientia media*, unconditional election is virtually undeniable.

Of course, those of us in the Reformed tradition have traditionally closed ranks with our Dominican friends in our opposition to the doctrine of middle knowledge. For the Reformed Thomist, the *scientia media* compromises the biblical doctrine of God so much that we think it should be abandoned altogether. When this is done, unconditional election becomes even more plausible. For those interested, there is an appendix explaining why I reject Molina's doctrine (appendix 2).

However, while I have set forth a strong case in favor of unconditional election, there is still one last arrow remaining in the Arminian's quiver— i.e., if unconditional election is true, then God is not all loving. But God really does love everyone. In fact, God truly desires the salvation of every soul. Therefore, the doctrine of unconditional election must be false. This is indeed a formidable consideration, which is why I feel compelled to answer it over the next two chapters.

6

THE ULTIMATE ARMINIAN REMONSTRANCE

When we say that God is sovereign in the exercise of His love,
we mean that He loves whom he chooses. God does not love everybody.
—Arthur Pink, The Sovereignty of God

Indeed, I think a better image of the Calvinist view of the love of God
would be Christ with one arm extended in love, but with his other arm
behind his back, with his fingers "secretly" crossed. Calvinism simply cannot
make coherent sense of God's love for all persons and it would be better to
forthrightly admit that, than to maintain a posture of love for all
that is utterly hollow when carefully examined.
—Jerry Walls, Does God Love Everyone?

Historically, the most important Arminian argument for conditional election,[1] which also serves as a critique of Calvinian unconditional election, is that the Reformed view contradicts the clear biblical teaching concerning God's desire for everyone's salvation. Indeed, in chapter 4, we noted that, even on a minimalistic theism, *there is some sense* in which God does not will the salvation of all. This implies that God does not love everyone (at least savingly). Calvinists such as Pink admit this, saying, "God does not love everybody."[2] Arminians such as Walls insist that this is precisely why one should reject the Augustinian view of election.

---

1. I.e., God's choice of who will be saved is based on or conditioned by the creature's response to the divine offer of salvation. This is in direct contradiction to unconditional election.

2. Arthur W. Pink, *The Sovereignty of God* (3rd ed.; Pensacola, FL: Chapel Library, 1999), 17, quoted in Jerry L. Walls, *Does God Love Everyone? The Heart of What's Wrong with Calvinism* (Eugene, OR: Cascade Books, 2016), 3.

Indeed, Arminians argue that this Calvinistic notion clearly contradicts the Scriptures, which teach a universal salvific will on the part of God. Thus the following contra-Calvinian argument:

(A) If God genuinely desires every person to be saved, then the doctrine of unconditional election cannot be true.

(B) God genuinely desires every person to be saved.

∴ (C) The doctrine of unconditional election cannot be true.

From the conclusion established by this argument, the Arminian theologian will, no doubt, want to reason as follows—unconditional election is false; however, it cannot be denied that the Bible speaks about God choosing (or electing) persons for salvation (see Rom 8:29; Eph 1:4; 2 Thess 2:13; 2 Tim 2:10); therefore, divine election must be conditional rather than unconditional. That is to say, the reason why God chooses a person unto salvation is because that person freely chose to believe in Christ, and the reason God does not choose a person unto salvation is because that person freely chose to reject Christ. In short, election is *conditioned on* or *based on* foreseen faith. It is not, as Calvinists believe, grounded in the divine will— wholly apart from any human activity.

GOD GENUINELY DESIRES EVERY PERSON TO BE SAVED

(B) God genuinely desires every person to be saved. I think it is best to start with an analysis of this minor premise, an exercise that will occupy our attention for this entire chapter. Does God genuinely desire the salvation of everyone? Arminians answer in the affirmative and back up their response with several biblical passages (e.g., see Ezek 18:23, 32; 33:11; 1 Tim 2:1-4; 2 Pet 3:9). If even (only) one of these texts tells us of God's genuine desire for everyone's salvation, then this premise has been established. Let us consider, then, what is perhaps the best example among the texts cited: "The Lord is not slow about His promise, as some count slowness, but is patient toward you, not wishing for any to perish, but for all to come to repentance" (2 Pet 3:9). This verse seems clear enough—God does not want anyone to perish, and so he wants everyone to come to repentance and, thus, be saved.

Hence, throughout his book on election Geisler often appeals to this verse, saying that the "biblical God is infinitely loving, that is, omnibenevolent. He wills the good of all creation (Acts 14:17; 17:25), and He desires the salvation of all souls (Ezek. 18:23, 30–32; Hos. 11:1–5, 8–9; John 3:16; 1 Tim. 2:4; 2 Peter 3:9)."[3]

A CALVINIST OBJECTION

Of course, many Calvinists have pointed out that the major issue in interpreting this text is establishing the antecedent of "any"—as in, "not wanting *any* to perish." In the words of R. C. Sproul:

> What is the antecedent of any? It is clearly *us*.[4] Does *us* refer to all of us humans? Or does it refer to us Christians, the people of God? Peter is fond of speaking of the elect as a special group of people. I think what he is saying here is that God does not will that any of us (the elect) perish. If that is his meaning, then the text [of 2 Pet 3:9] ... would be one more strong passage in favour of [Augustinian] predestination.[5]

James Boice concurs, writing:

> 2 Peter 3:9 ... is not talking about the salvation of all men and women, but only of the elect. The issue [in the context of the passage] is the delay of Christ's return, and Peter is explaining that God has delayed it, not out of indifference to us and what we may be suffering, but because he wants to bring to repentance all whom he has determined in advance will be gathered in. If Christ should come now, there would be generations of yet unborn people, containing generations of Christians yet to come, who would not be in heaven.

---

3. Norman L. Geisler, *Chosen but Free: A Balanced View of God's Sovereignty and Free Will* (3rd ed.; Minneapolis: Bethany, 2010), 165.

4. Technically, the antecedent of the word "any" in 2 Pet 3:9 is "you." But Sproul's question remains valid. Is God not wanting any *of you* to perish? Well, what does he mean by "you"? Is God not wanting any *of you humans* to perish? Or is God not wanting any *of you readers of my epistle* to perish? Or is God not wanting any *of you elect persons, chosen unto salvation,* to perish?

5. R. C. Sproul, *Chosen by God* (Wheaton, IL: Tyndale House, 1986), 197.

Therefore, "The Lord is not slow in keeping his promise, as some understand slowness. He is patient with you, not wanting [any of his elect ones] to perish, but everyone to come to repentance." This is how John Owen understood the text. He wrote:

> Who are these of whom the apostle speaks, to whom he writes? Such as had received "great and precious promises," chap. 1:4, whom he calls "beloved" (chap. 3:1); whom he opposeth to the "scoffers" of the "last days," verse 3; to whom the Lord hath respect in the disposal of these days; who are said to be "elect" (Matt. 24:22). Now, truly, to argue that because God would have none of those to perish, but all of them to come to repentance, therefore he hath the same will and mind towards all and everyone in the world (even those to whom he never makes known his will, nor ever calls to repentance, if they never once hear of his way of salvation), comes not much short of extreme madness and folly.[6]

This reading of the text is accepted by a good number of other Calvinistic scholars and writers, including Gordon Clark[7] and James White.[8] White gives one of the more impressive contemporary arguments for this interpretation one can find, noting that the overall context of the epistle establishes the identity of "any" and "all" in 2 Peter 3:9. In the tradition of Owen, White says that the letter is written to those who have "received a faith of the same kind as ours" (2 Pet 1:1), indicating that believers (not unbelievers) are the recipients of the epistle. Also, in the immediate context of the third chapter of the epistle, Peter contrasts those who scoff at the coming of Christ with those who look for the coming of a new heavens and a new

---

6. James Montgomery Boice and Philip Graham Ryken, *The Doctrines of Grace: Rediscovering the Evangelical Gospel* (Wheaton, IL: Crossway, 2002), 127, quoting John Owen, *The Death of Death in the Death of Christ: A Treatise of the Redemption and Reconciliation That Is in the Blood of Christ* (vol. 10 of *The Works of John Owen*, ed. William H. Goold; London: Banner of Truth, 1967), 348.

7. Gordon H. Clark, *Predestination* (Phillipsburg, NJ: Presbyterian & Reformed, 1987), 140–44.

8. James R. White, *The Potter's Freedom: A Defense of the Reformation and a Rebuttal to Norman Geisler's Chosen but Free* (2nd ed.; Merrick, NY: Calvary, 2009), 145–50.

earth (3:13), indicating that the "any" and "all" of 3:9 is "you" (i.e., the recipients of the letter, who eagerly await the return of the Lord, in contrast to those who scoff at such an idea).[9] White concludes: "There is no reason to expand the context of the passage into a universal proclamation of a desire on God's part that every single person come to repentance. Instead, it is clearly His plan and His will that *all the elect* come to repentance, and they most assuredly will do so."[10]

A REFORMED RESPONSE

I have the utmost respect for this common interpretation among Calvinists, along with the Reformed scholars who endorse it, for it has much to commend it. Indeed, the strongest argument in its favor is that the antecedent of "any" is "you"—presumably, the recipients of Peter's second letter. There are two ways to interpret "you" in this context. First, one could follow the common Calvinistic exegesis of the text and agree that the "you" here refers to the elect. But, on that assumption, we have good reason to think God's desire is that everyone, elect *and* reprobate, come to repentance. In other words, the reason God is patient toward the elect is the same reason he is patient toward everyone—i.e., he does not want anyone (elect or nonelect) to perish but desires the salvation of all. Similarly, one could see Peter's promise as an a fortiori argument—to wit, since God is patient toward literally everyone, how much more should you trust in his patience toward you, his own people? At the very least, these insights suggest that, even if the common Reformed interpretation of the passage is correct, it in no way mitigates the Arminian conviction that God wants literally everyone to be saved.[11]

A second approach, which is my own understanding of the passage, is to insist that the "you" is *not* limited to the elect, but literally refers to *anyone who comes across the epistle*. Indeed, why would Peter emphasize that he doesn't want the elect to perish? That would be redundant, to say the least! Also, if the immediate antecedent of "any" is "you," and "you"

9. White, *Potter's Freedom*, 146–57.

10. White, *Potter's Freedom*, 147–48, italics original.

11. I am grateful to Dr. Paul Owen for giving me these insights (via personal correspondence).

refers only to the original recipients of the letter, then the promise of this text—i.e., *the delay of the second advent is due to God's desire to bring all to repentance*—cannot be extended to our generation, since the letter is, after all, only for the *immediate* recipients of the epistle.

To limit the "any" of 3:9 to "the elect" is to read one's theology into the text, for nowhere in the immediate context of this passage does Peter refer to his readers as "elect" or "chosen."[12] To limit the "any" and/or "all" of 2 Peter 3:9 to "believers" would entail that God wants all believers to come to repentance, which is redundant (to say the least). So it would seem that the "any" and "all" refer to all unbelievers, including the "scoffers" mentioned in 3:3. The fact that "the beloved" and "the scoffers and false teachers" are constantly contrasted throughout the epistle is not a refutation of this doctrine, since all of us know of scoffers who have come to repentance (see Mark 15:32; Luke 23:39-43). In this light, the *NET Bible* has given insightful commentary to this text:

> *He does not wish for any to perish.* This verse has been a battleground between Arminians and Calvinists. The former [i.e., Arminians] argue that God wants all people to be saved, but by inability or restriction of his own sovereignty does not interfere with peoples' wills. Some of the latter [i.e., Calvinists] argue ... the "any" here means "any of you" and that all the elect will repent before the return of Christ, because this is God's will. Both of these positions have problems. The "any" in this context means "any of you." (This can be seen by the dependent participle which gives the reason why the Lord is patient "toward you.") There are hints throughout this

---

12. To be sure, some may want to appeal to 2 Pet 3:1: "This is now, beloved, the second letter I am writing to you in which I am stirring up your sincere mind by way of reminder." Presumably, the other letter Peter is referring to is 1 Peter, which begins as follows: "Peter, an apostle of Jesus Christ, to those who reside as aliens, scattered throughout Pontus, Galatia, Cappadocia, Asia, and Bithynia, who are chosen, according to the foreknowledge of God the Father" (1 Pet 1:1-2a). Interestingly, Peter refers to this first epistle in the immediate context of 2 Pet 3:9, and, so the argument goes, he's limiting the "you" to the elect alone after all. But this line of reasoning is far from conclusive, since it is not uncommon for preachers to refer to their congregations as "brothers and sisters in Christ" or "elect believers," even though they well know that theirs is usually a mixed audience. And so, while 1 Pet 1:1-2 illustrates for us that election is indeed all of grace, it cannot be appealed to in support of the kind of inference many Calvinists are trying to secure.

letter that the readership may be mixed, including both true believers and others who are "sitting on the fence" as it were. But to make the equation of this readership with the elect is unlikely. This would seem to require, in its historical context, that all of these readers would be saved. But not all who attend church know the Lord or will know the Lord. Simon the Magician, whom Peter had confronted in Acts 8, is a case in point. This is evident in contemporary churches when a pastor addresses the congregation as "brothers, sisters, saints, etc.," yet concludes the message with an evangelistic appeal. When an apostle or pastor addresses a group as "Christian" he does not necessarily think that every individual in the congregation is truly a Christian [or necessarily will become a Christian]. Thus, the literary context seems to be against the Arminian view, while the historical context seems to be against (one representation of) the Calvinist view.[13]

I find the last sentence of this quotation somewhat ambiguous. What does the editor mean by "the Arminian view"? If by this phrase he is referring merely to the standard Arminian interpretation of 2 Peter 3:9, then he seems to be mistaken. For all the standard Arminian interpretation of this text is saying is that God wants everyone to be saved, for he is not willing that anyone perish. We cannot restrict the "any" and "all" to the original believing/elect readership of this letter, as the above quotation suggests, for (1) it would (as we have seen) entail that only those who first heard the letter are the recipients of the promise; (2) since "the new heavens and new earth" were not established in the first century, limiting the "any" to the original readership would seem to entail that the scoffers now have a good argument against the faith;[14] and (3) the Word of God is for *all* generations,

---

13. *The Holy Bible: The Net Bible®* (*The New English Translation™*) (Biblical Studies Press, 2001), 2273n4, italics original.

14. In other words, if the Lord is no longer delaying his second coming because of his patience in not willing that any perish—but for all to come to repentance—then the question once again arises; namely, *Why is God still delaying his coming?* On the other hand, if the Lord's reason for his delay of the second coming remains the same, then he continues to delay so that even people in our generation will have a chance to repent. But if his promise also applies to our generation, then the "any of you" in 3:9 applies to *anyone* (first century and beyond) who comes across Peter's epistle. It is quite safe to assume that reprobate people have, from time

and so the promises that are given to the body of Christ in the first century belong to all of us (see Luke 1:48; John 17:20; Heb 1:1; 11:40; 2 Pet 3:13).[15]

Thus, I see 2 Peter 3:9 as a reference to any church that receives, reads, or hears Peter's letter—originally, to those who first heard the letter (2 Pet 1:1) and subsequently to anyone in the churches who longs for and/or inquires about Christ's return (2 Pet 3:8-13), which would include every generation of church attendees since the first century. Interestingly, this letter was not written to just one local body of believers, but to all who have received a common faith—i.e., a common body of beliefs (2 Pet 1:1; but see 3:1-2)—and this, of course, would apply to all churches (past, present, and future) that have received the deposit of doctrine given to us by the apostles.[16] And since, as the editor(s) of the *NET Bible* point(s) out, all local churches are mixed with believers and unbelievers and/or elect and reprobate, we are being told here that anyone who can hear Peter's message is to know that God wants all to be saved.

To state my point another way, Peter is wanting as wide a readership as possible, implying that anyone who receives this letter is to know that the reason the Lord tarries is that he is patient, not wanting *anyone* to perish but for all people to come to repentance. Or, in the words of (Calvinist) New Testament scholar Thomas Schreiner, "A thousand years are like one day to Him, and in any case, the interval before Christ's coming gives people opportunity to repent."[17] Schreiner's interpretation implies that the delay of the Lord is so that people in general, *not just the elect*, have an opportunity to repent. Calvinist Samuel Storms concurs more explicitly when he insists that 2 Peter 3.9 is "universal in scope, encompassing every person, both elect and non-elect."[18] While John Piper is open to the interpretation

---

to time, read the second Petrine letter; therefore, we must conclude that God is not willing that anyone, including any reprobate person, perish.

15. Consider 2 Pet 3:13—if the "we" in that verse cannot be applied to all generations beyond those who first received the epistle, then we who are now living are not waiting for a new heavens and a new earth, which is absurd!

16. See J. N. D. Kelley, *A Commentary on the Epistles of Peter and of Jude* (Peabody, MA: Hendrickson, 1969), 296.

17. Thomas R. Schreiner, "Notes on 2 Peter," in *The Apologetics Study Bible* (ed. Ted Cabal et al.; Nashville: Holman Bible, 2007), 1860.

18. Samuel Storms, *Chosen for Life: The Case for Divine Election* (Wheaton, IL: Crossway, 2007), 197.

of scholars such as Owen, Sproul, and White, he nevertheless states, "as a hearty believer in unconditional, individual election I rejoice to affirm that God does not delight in the perishing of the impenitent, and that he has compassion on all people."[19] Not only so, but even John Calvin agrees with this interpretation of 2 Peter 3:9, writing:

> So wonderful is his love towards mankind, that he would have them all to be saved, and is of his own self prepared to bestow salvation on the lost. But the order is to be noticed, that God is ready to receive all to repentance, so that none may perish; for in these words the way and manner of obtaining salvation is pointed out. Every one of us, therefore, who is desirous of salvation, must learn to enter in by this way.[20]

---

19. John Piper, "Are There Two Wills in God? Divine Election and God's Desire for All to Be Saved," in *The Grace of God, The Bondage of the Will* (ed. Thomas R. Schreiner and Bruce A. Ware; Grand Rapids: Baker, 1995), 1:108.

20. John Calvin, *Commentaries on the Second Epistle of Peter* (in *Commentaries on the Catholic Epistles*; Calvin's Commentaries 22; trans. John Owen; Grand Rapids: Baker, n.d.), 421. It is sometimes suggested that "Calvin the exegete" never met "Calvin the theologian," since his doctrines of election and effectual calling are presented in such harsh ways in his *Institutes*, while in his commentaries—as illustrated here in his exegesis of 2 Pet 3:9—his views appear to be open, gracious, and less severe; see Kenneth Keathley, *Salvation and Sovereignty: A Molinist Approach* (Nashville: B&H Academic, 2010), 53. While I grant that Calvin often presents his doctrine rather provocatively, he nevertheless affirms God's universal salvific will even in his *Institutes*. For example, while commenting on 2 Pet 3:9, along with other texts that speak of God's desire to save "all," Calvin writes: "But why does he say 'all'? It is that the consciences of the godly may rest more secure, when they understand there is no difference among sinners provided faith be present. On the other hand, the wicked cannot claim they lack a sanctuary to which they may hie themselves from the bondage of sin, inasmuch as they, out of their own ungratefulness, reject it when offered. Therefore, since God's mercy is offered to both sorts of men [i.e., godly and wicked; elect and reprobate] through the gospel, it is faith—the illumination of God—that distinguishes between pious and impious, so that the former feel the working of the gospel, while the latter derive no profit from it." John Calvin, *Institutes of the Christian Religion* (ed. John T. McNeill; trans. Ford Lewis Battles; Library of Christian Classics 22; Philadelphia: Westminster, 1960), 3.24.17. In any case, Reformed Christians have options within their own tradition—e.g., Bullinger, who expressed his concerns to Calvin that the Genevan Reformer did not adequately preclude God from being the author of sin, insisted "that God 'is a lover of man (*philanthropos*) who, because of his mercy, 'wants all men to be saved' (*vult omnes homines salvos facere*)." Quoted in Cornelius P. Venema, *Heinrich Bullinger and the Doctrine of Predestination: Author of "The Other Reformed Tradition"?* (Grand Rapids: Baker, 2002), 59.

So it is settled. Calvinists *can* agree with the common Arminian interpreta-tion of 2 Peter 3:9, for God really does want everyone to be saved. In saying this I am not, of course, calling everyone else who holds to a different inter-pretation hyper-Calvinists. I am simply saying that there is no need for a Calvinist to deny the prima facie reading of this verse. In short, *God desires every human being to be saved.*

Of course, if by "Arminian view," the editor(s) of the *NET Bible* mean(s) the standard Arminian *inference* from 2 Peter 3:9, I agree. The standard Arminian inference from 2 Peter 3:9 is that, since God wants all to be saved, he has chosen to limit his sovereignty by not interfering with human free will, thereby ensuring that election is conditioned on faith and proving that the doctrine of unconditional election is false. Since this inference of the Arminians pertains to premise (A) of the argument, we will hold off our discussion of this issue until the next chapter.

Besides some of the other texts we have cited (e.g., Ezek 18:23, 30–32), there are more than a few biblical passages which portray God's posture toward all of his creatures as "the open hands of acceptance and not rejec-tion." Think, for example, of YHWH's desire that all the people fear him (Deut 5:29), and of his disappointment that Israel has grown stubborn and will not obey his law (Ps 81:13). We learn in the New Testament that God the Father demonstrates his love for all by giving everyone, *just and unjust,* rain, sunshine, and all things necessary for life (Matt 5:44–48; Acts 14:16–17; 17:24–28). This love of God is no mere manifestation of a general good-ness, but is a salvific love of the world, to whom the Father has given the Son, so that anyone who believes will have eternal life (John 3:16). Carson, a Calvinist New Testament scholar, offers comments on this passage that are worth noting: "I know that some try to take κόσμος ('world') here to refer to the elect. But that really will not do. All the evidence of the usage of the word in John's Gospel is against the suggestion." After surveying the evidence, he concludes: "On this axis, God's love for the world cannot be collapsed into his love for the elect."[21] So God holds everyone account-able for the saving gifts given to them (Rom 2:1–4), and since he is the good Lord and Sustainer of all creatures, "God is now declaring to men that all

---

21. D. A. Carson, *The Difficult Doctrine of the Love of God* (Wheaton, IL: Crossway, 2000), 17.

everywhere should repent" (Acts 17:30), and all on the earth are to look to him and be saved (Isa 45:21–22).

THE GREAT HYPER-CALVINIST
AND SKEPTICAL REJOINDER

To be sure, there are a few theologians within the Reformed camp, along with many skeptical readers of the Bible, who will not concede our premise that God genuinely desires the redemption of all. Their contention is precisely the opposite—namely, the God of the Bible does *not* desire the redemption of everyone. This presupposition is secured via two lines of evidence. First, the God of the Bible is clearly the author of evil, proving that he does not love everyone. Second, the supralapsarian understanding of the divine decree is the most plausible view of the divine unconditional election, and this entails that God neither loves the reprobate nor desires their salvation. I respond that, when all of the evidence is brought together, these two lines of argumentation are simply unbiblical and unsound.

GOD IS THE AUTHOR OF EVIL

Both skeptics and hyper-Calvinists are agreed that the biblical God is the author of evil—or, in other words, God creates evil. From there they draw different conclusions. The hyper-Calvinist will glory in the absolute sovereignty of the one who made all things, including evil.[22] The skeptic will

---

22. In the words of R. C. Sproul Jr.: "But wait a minute. Isn't there an obvious argument against this line of reasoning? Isn't it impossible for God to do evil? Of course it's impossible for God to do evil. He can't sin. This objection, however, is off the mark. I am not accusing God of sinning; I am suggesting that he created sin. There is a difference. We must define our terms. The Westminster Confession of Faith [sic] defines sin as 'any lack of conformity to or transgression of the law of God' [*Westminster Shorter Catechism* Q. 14]. Where, I must ask, does the law of God forbid the creation of evil? I would suggest that it just isn't there. Someone might object that of course it isn't there, because man hasn't the power to create sin. And I would rest my case." Still later he says, "It all hinges on the fall, on the changing of Eve's (and Adam's) inclination from good to bad, an event which was, on the one hand, a terrible tragedy but, on the other, the means by which God might be glorified." Hence Sproul Jr.'s celebration: "We ought to be jumping up and down for the sublime wisdom of his [God's] plan. It is an incredible plan. He creates a world. He stamps his image upon two of his creatures. He declares them to be good. He then changes their inclination, either directly or indirectly, such that they fall into sin." Amazingly, Sproul Jr. glories in a god who inclines human beings to sin so that he can exercise his wrath on many and his mercy on some (*Almighty over All: Understanding the Sovereignty of God* [Grand Rapids: Baker, 1999], 54, 59, 58). This is not the

conclude that such a god is not worthy of one's trust. Here is the argument in a nutshell:

(A) If God is the author of evil, then God does not savingly love everyone.

(B) God is the author of evil.

∴ (C) God does not savingly love everyone.

(A) IF GOD IS THE AUTHOR OF EVIL, THEN GOD DOES NOT SAVINGLY LOVE EVERYONE

There are several good reasons to believe that this premise is closed under entailment and hence is necessarily true: First, if God created evil, then he himself must be evil—for effects, to one degree or another, reflect their causes. An evil effect, then, must come from an evil cause. The hyper-Calvinist cannot save the absolute holiness of God at this point by saying that God is both good and evil, for then we would only need to change our point ever so slightly and say that God created evil with an evil motive. For the assertion, "a good motive moved God to *do* evil," is a contradiction in terms.[23] Nor can the hyper-Calvinist hide behind mystery here, as if to say that it is a complete mystery how the holy God of Scripture caused evil to come into existence without himself being evil. For while mysteries are tolerable in the Christian worldview, contradictions are not, and a *purely* holy God

---

God of Scripture. *This is Satan!* Indeed, where Sproul Sr. would say no, "Sproul Jr. has taken the plunge" (Keathley, *Salvation and Sovereignty*, 83).

23. To those who would point out that they know people who, out of ignorance, do evil with good motives, I agree. The difference, however, between God and humans is that God is all-knowing; therefore, if he does evil, he never does it out of ignorance! Sproul Jr. all but admits this. He explains that, "like man, God always acts according to his strongest inclination. What is different is that with God all things are equal in the sense that his choices are never limited." In the next paragraph he states: "It is because of this similarity (God always acting according to his strongest inclination) and this difference (God always getting exactly what he wants) that we can know that whatever comes to pass must be what God most wished to come to pass, his strongest inclination" (*Almighty over All*, 54). Still later he asserts: "God ... cannot do what he does not want to do and cannot want what is against his nature," and such an assertion does not constitute real limitations in God (*Almighty over All*, 134). Thus, putting all of Sproul Jr.'s presuppositions together: (1) God created sin and evil; (2) God, like humans, always acts according to his strongest inclination; (3) God's desires can never be obstructed; (4) God can never desire what is contrary to his nature; (5) God desired to create sin and evil (from 1–4); therefore, (6) God possesses an evil nature. Technically, (7) should be construed as (7)′ *evil is not contrary to God's nature*. But, in the end, this is a distinction without a difference.

who creates evil *is* a contradiction in terms. Indeed, if God is the creator of evil, then he is evil. And if he is evil, then skepticism follows—that is, God, even if he exists, is not worthy of our trust. Clark Pinnock was right to say the following:

> Far be it for the Calvinists to deny God the glory in causing everything! It should be clear to the reader why the number of strict Calvinists is relatively small. It involves one in agonizing difficulties of the first order. It makes God some kind of terrorist who goes around handing out torture and disaster and even willing [or causing] people to do things the Bible says God hates. ... One need not wonder why people become atheists when faced with such a theology. A God like that has a great deal for which to answer.[24]

Or, in the words of Keathley, if one is willing to embrace this sort of hard (or even mechanical) determinism, then one might as well get it over with and become an atheist.[25] Indeed, if this God does exist, and if he wants us to know the truth about him (1 Tim 2:4), then it would appear that, once

---

24. "Clark Pinnock's Response," in *Predestination and Free Will: Four Views of Divine Sovereignty and Human Freedom* (ed. David Basinger and Randall Basinger; Downers Grove, IL: InterVarsity Press, 1986), 58.

25. Keathley: "Why do most Christian philosophers advocate some type of libertarianism? Perhaps one reason is because they spend a great deal of time and effort engaging with non-Christian philosophers. Non-Christian philosophers generally accept causal determinism instead of agent causation because determinism can be explained in purely physical terms. Enlightenment philosophers argued for 'LaPlace's Demon,' the hypothesis that, if a sufficient intellect knew the precise location and momentum of every atom in the universe, then it could use Newton's laws to reveal the entire course of cosmic events, past and future. Early determinists held to mechanical determinism while recent determinists argue for biological determinism. At this point determinists often protest that this criticism amounts to guilt by association and that it is unfair to group them together with materialistic determinists. Yet the logic of causal determinism is a stubborn thing. If God causes all things, then He does so either directly or by secondary causation. If He does so directly, then God is the sole cause of all events and secondary causation is an illusion. ... Like a cartoon in which one character hits another toon with a tomato, it appears that the characters are causing the actions, but this is an illusion occurring only in the observer's mind. The animator draws one frame after another; the missile leaves the hand and frame-by-frame moves toward the head. It may seem that Bugs Bunny splattered Elmer Fudd with the tomato, but the real causal agent was the animator" (Keathley, *Salvation and Sovereignty*, 95–96). What, then, is the difference between believing in such a god—i.e., one who causes a person to commit murder—and believing merely in physical forces that mechanistically determine our behavior? The difference is that the latter allows one to sleep better at night, since hell is now one less thing to worry about!

we learn he created evil, we cannot help but distrust him. Can the human mind truly trust in a god who inclines his heart toward evil? Indeed, the moment one concludes that God wants us to know that he is the author of evil, one loses trust in this deity—proving that the deity does not really care whether any of us achieves salvation.

Second, if God is the author of evil, then God desires for people to sin as such—in which case God does not want everyone to be saved from sin. For it makes little sense to think God wants any of us to be saved if he wants any of us to sin. Indeed, if God is the author of sin, it is hard to imagine that he loves *anyone*—let alone *everyone*. A believer can take little comfort in the promises concerning God's love for him once he learns that God inclines human hearts toward evil. For all he knows, his current faith only represents a sliver of time whereby God is ripening him up for the day of slaughter.

(B) GOD IS THE AUTHOR OF EVIL

Given the virtual undeniability of the first premise, we are obligated to either give up our belief in the biblical God or reject this second proposition. I opt for the latter. My warrant for rejecting (B) is found in philosophico-theological considerations, along with the explicit testimony of holy writ.

IS GOD GOOD?

The word "good" is so basic and intuitive to all of us that it is difficult to define. A standard dictionary gives the following definitions:

> a general term for approval or commendation **1** a) suitable to a purpose; effective; efficient ... b) producing favorable results; beneficial; salutary ... **2** fertile [*good soil*] **3** fresh; unspoiled; uncontaminated [*good eggs*] **4** valid; genuine; real ... **8** enjoyable, desirable, pleasant, happy, etc. [*a good life*] ... **10** thorough; complete ... **12** adequate; ample; sufficient ... **13** morally sound or excellent; specif .... c) kind, benevolent, generous, sympathetic; etc.[26]

---

26. *Webster's New World College Dictionary* (4th ed.; Cleveland: Wiley, 2002), 611.

Most of these terms adequately describe the God of classical theism. Indeed, God is consistently described in the classical theistic tradition as the efficient cause of the universe who gives good gifts (or favor) toward humanity. He is wholly sufficient unto himself, morally pure, and to be desired for his own sake. He is wholly joyful in who he is and in all that he does. Perhaps the most important ontological definition of good given above is "goodness is that which is uncontaminated." The metaphysical attribute corresponding to this notion is the Reformed-Thomist doctrine of the divine nature as pure act. God is pure actuality with no potentiality. Indeed, he who has no potential has no contamination in his being. Perhaps the most important ethical definition of good given above is "goodness is that which is kind, benevolent, and generous." The moral attribute corresponding to this notion is the common Christian doctrine of the divine nature as self-giving love. For "God proves his love for us in that while we still were sinners Christ died for us" (Rom 5:8 NRSV; see John 3:16).[27]

Biblically speaking, we know that God is good from the explicit testimony of Scripture. For example, "Be perfect, therefore, as your heavenly Father is perfect" (Matt 5:48 NRSV). The context here indicates that it is a moral perfection Jesus is referring to—for our actions are to reflect the perfection of God. This injunction is an echo of the Torah: "You shall be holy, for I the LORD your God am holy" (Lev 19:2 NRSV). As Jesus teaches us elsewhere, God himself is the source of all goodness, for no "one is good but God alone" (Mark 10:18 NRSV).

IS GOD ALL-GOOD?

That is to say, how do we know that God is *wholly* good and morally pure? Why not say that God, like us, consists of both good and evil? Our philosophico-theological answer is grounded in two sources—namely, a standard dictionary and Augustinian-Thomistic theology. Consider the following definition(s) of evil: "**1** a) morally bad or wrong; wicked; depraved b) resulting from or based on conduct regarded as immoral ... **3** offensive

---

27. For a philosophical defense of these (and other) classical attributes from a Thomistic point of view, see Edward Feser, *Five Proofs of God* (San Francisco: Ignatius Press, 2017), 169–248. From a Reformed perspective, see James E. Dolezal, *All That Is in God: Evangelical Theology and the Challenge of Classical Christian Theism* (Grand Rapids: Reformation Heritage Books, 2017).

or disgusting [*an evil odor*] **4** threatening or bringing misfortune; unlucky; disastrous; unfortunate."[28] Notice that the term "evil" carries with it the connotation of "being depraved," and when we look up *that* term we encounter words such as "corrupt," "contamination," "deterioration," "perverted," and "debased" (which means "that which is lacking in quality, value, or dignity").[29] Since these are the terms still generally associated with the word "evil," Augustine is hardly to be blamed when he tells us "that evil is that which falls away from essence and tends to nonexistence" (*On the Morals of the Manicheans* 2.2).[30] Indeed, evil is not to be defined in a positive way, but is rather a negative term denoting the loss of goodness: "For evil has no positive nature; but the loss of good has received the name 'evil'" (*On the City of God* 11.9). Concerning those who define evil as "corruption," Augustine writes: "Undeniably this is a general definition of evil; for corruption implies opposition to nature; and also hurt. But corruption exists not by itself, but in some substance which it corrupts; for corruption itself is not a substance" (*On the Morals of the Manicheans* 5.7).

Evil, then, is neither a thing nor a substance. Rather, it is the *corruption* or *contamination* or even *privation* of a thing or a substance. To give just one example, consider a blind person. Notice that what is evil about this person is not the person herself; nor is her eye, as such, evil. What is evil, then? The evil is found in what the blind eye *lacks*—namely, the ability to see. Evil, in this instance, is the corruption or privation of eyesight within the eye. Blindness is not a thing (i.e., it is not something positive) but a privation of a thing (i.e., a lack of something in the eye).

CLARIFICATION

As a point of clarity, we must qualify ourselves a bit and say that evil, by definition, is not so much a negation of good, but it is a privation of a good *that is owed (all things being equal)*. For example: the eye is for seeing; therefore, every eye ought to see; so when we notice a blind eye, we note that the eye itself is not evil, but its privation is evil. On the other hand, seeing is

---

28. *Webster's New World College Dictionary*, 493.

29. *Webster's New World College Dictionary*, 372, 388.

30. All of the quotations of Augustine in this paragraph are taken from Norman L. Geisler, ed., *What Augustine Says* (1982; repr., Eugene, OR: Wipf & Stock, 2003), 188–89.

a good; but a rock is not meant to see; therefore, the negation of the good that is sight with respect to a rock is not an evil, but merely the absence of some good. Thus, a contingent thing (e.g., a rock) that lacks some good (e.g., sight) is not an evil; however, a circumstance whereby a contingent being (e.g., a human person) is deprived of a good *that is, all things being equal, owed* (e.g., sight for his eye, which was meant to see), precisely because the person cannot be/do what he was meant to be/do, is an evil circumstance.

In light of our definition of evil, God must be absolutely good and morally pure, with no evil whatsoever in his being. Indeed, he who is pure actuality can have no corruption or contamination or privation in his nature; and he who is morally pure is one whose will never moves via any defect whatsoever. Indeed, we have already seen Jesus affirm the idea that God alone is good. Elsewhere we learn that righteousness and justice are the foundation of God's rule (Ps 89:14) and that he is too pure to even look upon iniquity (Hab 1:13), for "God is light and in him there is no darkness at all" (1 John 1:5 NRSV). Thus, God is omnibenevolent.

ARGUMENTS THAT GOD CANNOT BE THE CAUSE OF EVIL OR THE CREATOR OF SIN

In light of the foregoing I am in a position to demonstrate my firm conviction that God cannot be the cause of evil and/or creator of sin. Indeed, there are two strong arguments that warrant this point of view. First, we may offer the following philosophico-theological argument: God is pure actuality, with no potentiality whatsoever; God is due all praise and glory for his metaphysical and moral perfection (i.e., God is "owed" all goodness or joy or blessedness due to his inherent righteousness); evil is a privation of a good that is owed; there are at least two necessary preconditions for God being able to cause evil—i.e., (1) evil must reside in his nature which, in turn, contaminates his will, and (2) evil must be a substance that God brings into existence; but (1) is impossible since God is pure act, and in his will there is no defect or contamination, and (2) is also impossible, since evil is not a substance but a privation of a substance, and hence it is not a thing that God could possibly bring into existence;[31] therefore, God is not the author of evil.

---

31. This refutes a common atheistic argument from evil to God's nonexistence: God is the creator of all things (outside himself); and evil is a thing; therefore, God is the creator of

Second, besides the texts we have already quoted or cited, there is one passage of Scripture in particular that explicitly denies God's involvement in the creation of sin and evil:

> Blessed is anyone who endures temptation. Such a one has stood the test and will receive the crown of life that the Lord has promised to those who love him. No one, when tempted, should say, "I am being tempted by God"; for God cannot be tempted by evil and he himself tempts no one. But one is tempted by one's own desire, being lured and enticed by it;[32] then, when that desire has conceived, it gives birth to sin, and that sin, when it is fully grown, gives birth to death. Do not be deceived, my beloved.
>
> Every generous act of giving, with every perfect gift, is from above, coming down from the Father of lights, with whom there is no variation or shadow due to change. (Jas 1:12–17 NRSV)

Notice that those who endure temptation are enduring a test that has come on them. The overall context of this chapter suggests that God is the one who is allowing or permitting the test to take place. For James there is a difference between a *test* and a *temptation*. God permits us to be tested in order to draw out of us a firm and living faith: "You know that the testing of your faith produces endurance: and let endurance have its full effect, so that you may be mature and complete, lacking in nothing" (Jas 1:3–4 NRSV). In the classroom, a teacher allows students to sit next to one another while taking an exam; and so the test is the set of math problems to be solved by

---

evil. *On the contrary*, God is the creator of all things (outside himself); but evil is not a thing (it is a privation of a thing); therefore, God did not create evil.

32. Notice that it is the *creature's own desire* to sin that entices one to sin. James here is ruling out God's involvement in our inclination to sin. In short, this assertion by James directly contradicts the heretical assertion of Sproul Jr.: God "changes their inclination, either directly or indirectly, such that they fall into sin" (*Almighty over All*, 58). As Calvin notes: "The meaning [of v. 13] is, that man in vain evades, who attempts to cast blame of his vices on God, because every evil proceeds from no other fountain than from the wicked lust of man. And the fact really is, that we are not otherwise led astray, except that every one has his own inclination as his leader and impeller. But that God tempts no one, he proves by this, because he is not tempted with evils. For it is the devil who allures us to sin, and for this reason, because he wholly burns with the mad lust of sinning. But God does not desire what is evil: he is not, therefore, the author of doing evil in us" (Calvin, *Commentaries on the Catholic Epistles*, 289).

the student, while the temptation may exist within the heart of the student to look on her peer's paper. The teacher is the cause of the test; the temptation is caused by the student. Similarly, in life God may allow a married man to go on a business trip. While on the business trip the traveler may stay in a hotel that happens to be close to a strip club. God is permitting this test to take place. More bluntly, God is indeed the cause of the circumstances in which this married man finds himself. He is giving the man a test. But God is not the cause of any temptation the man may be having to be unfaithful to his wife. That temptation arises from the man alone, in his heart (the seat of desire), and if he gives in to it he alone is responsible for his sin. "For you are not a God who delights in wickedness; evil will not sojourn with you" (Ps 5:4 NRSV; see also v. 8). As James goes on to say, God's unchanging nature renders him invincibly good. Sin comes wholly from the creature. Only good comes from God. In the words of Calvin:

> This [passage from James] is an argument from what is opposite; for as God is the author of all good, it is absurd to suppose him to be the author of evil. To do good is what properly belongs to him, and according to his nature; and from him all good things come to us. Then, whatever evil he [i.e., a man] does, is not agreeable to his [i.e., God's] nature. But as it sometimes happens, that he who quits himself well through life, yet in some things fails, he meets this doubt by denying that God is mutable like men. But if God is in all things and always like himself, it hence follows that well-doing is his perpetual work.[33]

John Owen, the editor of Calvin's *Commentary on the Epistle of James*, concurs: God "never varies in his dealings with men, and shews [sic] no symptom of any change, being the author and giver of all good, and the author of no evil, that is, of no sin."[34]

---

33. Calvin, *Commentaries on the Catholic Epistles*, 291.
34. Calvin, *Commentaries on the Catholic Epistles*, 291–92n1.

HOW DO WE KNOW THAT
EVIL IS A PRIVATION?

The preceding argument hinges on our definition of evil as "a privation of the good," which is inspired by a respectable theological tradition and confirmed by a standard dictionary. But why, really, should anyone think it is true? Consider the following argument:

1. Good and evil are contradictions, being opposed to one another.
2. Being is a positive term.
3. Good and being are convertible terms.
4. Evil is nothing positive, but a negation and/or a privation.

Premise (1) is grounded in intuition, for the most basic understanding of good and evil is that they are opposites. Premise (2) is self-evident, for something is not nothing; hence, being is not to be defined or understood negatively, but positively. Premise (3) tells us that "good" and "being" are convertible in the sense that every being *as such* is good, and every good *as such* is being. To be or to have existence is an intrinsic good—or, as our standard dictionary has already noted, that which is good is that which is "genuine, valid, and real." The very fact that every living thing naturally seeks to preserve its own being or existence is an indication that whatever exists, insofar as it exists, is good. But then the conclusion (4) is established—for if evil is opposed to good, and if good is being, then evil is opposed to being and, thus, that which is evil is nothing positive but a privation of the good. In the words of Garrigou-Lagrange: "Good is everything that is desirable. But every nature desires to preserve its being and its perfection. Therefore all being and every perfection is something good, and therefore, too, evil is not some being or some positive nature, but is either the negation or the privation of good."[35]

---

35. Reginald Garrigou-Lagrange, *The Trinity and God the Creator: A Commentary on St. Thomas' Theological Summa, Ia, q. 27–119* (trans. Frederic C. Eckhoff; St. Louis: B. Herder, 1952), 462.

BUT ISN'T PAIN SOMETHING POSITIVE?

People who deny this definition of evil often point out the horrible effects evil has on the world. These effects are positive in the sense that really bad events or things occur in our lives. It would appear, then, that this definition of evil does not take into account the terrible pain people often feel during evil times. In short, defining evil as a privation seems too abstract. This definition does not seem to capture what is really going on in our experience. A toothache, for example, is a sore that *positively* hurts. Evil, then, is not a privation but something positive.

Response. Thomas Aquinas was aware of this kind of objection and offered the following reply:

> Just as two things are requisite for pleasure; namely, conjunction with good and perception of this conjunction; so also two things are requisite for pain; namely, conjunction with some evil (which is in so far evil as it deprives one of some good),[36] and perception of this conjunction. Now whatever is conjoined, if it have not the aspect of good or evil in regard to the being to which it is conjoined, cannot cause pleasure or pain. Whence it is evident that something under the aspect of good or evil is the object of pleasure or pain. But good and evil, as such, are objects of the appetite. Consequently, it is clear that pleasure and pain belong to the appetite.[37]

Therefore, in the words of one of Thomas's greatest interpreters,

> Pain and pleasure are contraries, and as pleasure is connected to some good act easily exercised, such as the grace of youth, so pain is connected with some act more or less impeded, or some immoderate act which produces fatigue. Hence pain is not something privative,

---

36. The translation here should be more lucid, as in, "which is evil insofar as it deprives of some good."

37. Thomas Aquinas, *Summa Theologica* (trans. Fathers of the English Dominican Province; Allen, TX: Thomas More, 1948), Ia.IIae.35.1.

but it is connected with privation and arises from the perception of the union with some evil.[38]

ISAIAH REJECTS THIS DEFINITION OF EVIL

As it is written, "Woe to them that call evil good, and good evil; that put darkness for light, and light for darkness; that put bitter for sweet, and sweet for bitter!" (Isa 5:20 KJV). This objection arises from the fact that, if Augustine and Thomas are correct, then good is the subject of evil—that is, evil, since it is a privation of the good, in some sense resides *in* the good or *on* that which is good and, thus, is in some sense caused by the good. For only that which has being can be the cause of anything; and evil must come from some cause, since every event (including an evil act) needs a cause; but evil is not a being but a privation of a being and hence a privation of the good; therefore, evil must be caused by good (or being).

Response. My definition is in perfect accord with Isaiah, for I have clearly distinguished good and evil. Good is not evil, and evil is not good. Good is positive, since it is being, and is to be desired for its own sake. Evil is negative, since it is a privation of being (or good), and so is to be avoided. Our definitions, far from denying what Isaiah teaches, presuppose the very distinction advocated by the prophet.

HOWEVER, JESUS DENIES THAT
GOOD CAN CAUSE EVIL

Evidence for this fact is found in the following words of the Master: "Every good tree bears good fruit, but the bad tree bears bad fruit. A good tree cannot bear bad fruit, nor can a bad tree bear good fruit" (Matt 7:17–18 NRSV). This contradicts our earlier point that good is the source or cause of evil.

Response. Jesus is not trying to comment on the origin and metaphysics of evil; rather, he is giving a standard whereby we should judge all teachers (7:15–16). Look at their lives and their doctrine! If they are faithful to God, they will bring forth good deeds grounded in true doctrine. If they are false

---

38. Garrigou-Lagrange, *Trinity and God the Creator* , 464.

prophets, such will bear out in their teaching and in their behavior.[39] Jesus' words in no way contradict Augustine's definition of evil!

An important point we will develop in the following chapter is that in one sense this objection, based as it is in Jesus' words, is correct. Good and/or being never causes evil; for being is always an efficient cause of its effects. But evil cannot be the effect of an efficient cause. Indeed, only *deficient* causes can bring about evil. So a blind man falls down the stairs and breaks his leg. The efficient cause of his walking down the stairs is his effective use of his legs. However, the movement of his legs did not cause him to fall; rather, that was caused by his deficient perception due to blindness, which is itself a privation of sight. Afterwards, the blind man walks with a limp. The movement of his leg is the effect of his mind efficiently moving his body to action; but his limp is the result of his *deficient* motor skills, which are themselves the result of his fall.

GOD MUST THEREFORE BE THE CAUSE OF EVIL!

This seems to follow from everything we have said so far. For if evil is caused by good, then God—the Supreme Good—must be the ultimate cause of evil.

Response. This objection does not take into account the distinction between efficient and deficient causes. Also, once we rule out the impossible, whatever remains, however improbable, must be the truth. We have demonstrated that it is impossible for the one who is pure act to cause evil, since pure actuality has no defect or privation in either his being or his will. Therefore, God cannot be the cause of evil, either ultimately or proximately.[40]

---

39. See John Nolland, *The Gospel of Matthew: A Commentary on the Greek Text* (New International Greek Testament Commentary; Grand Rapids: Eerdmans, 2005), 337-38.

40. At this juncture many critics of our position will appeal to Isa 45:7 as proof that God is the creator of evil. For a full exploration of this issue, see appendix 3.

WHERE DOES EVIL COME FROM?

Once we rule out the impossible, whatever remains, however improbable, must be the truth. It is impossible for God, who is pure actuality with no potentiality, to cause evil. Therefore, the only realm in which evil and sin can first appear is in a realm where there is at least some potential. The entire created realm is metaphysically contingent—meaning that it is composed of actuality and *potentiality*. Thus the created universe is the only realm wherein evil *could* originate, since it is the only actuality with a potential for evil. Now, the created realm is made up of creatures, some of which are and some of which are not free agents. But evil cannot originate in those creatures that are not free agents, for contingent beings who move sans the power of free choice are not the cause of their own movement—hence, they move in accordance with another cause (e.g., the laws of physics and biology, or even God himself; if the former, then evil arose in a creature mechanically caused to produce evil by laws put in place by the Creator [similar to a domino effect]; and if the latter, then God moved the hapless creature to do evil; either way, God is the cause of evil, which is impossible). Therefore, evil arose wholly from within one or more creaturely free agents who freely chose to misuse their freedom and perform an evil act.[41]

WHY DOES GOD ALLOW EVIL?

If God is all-powerful he can make a world without evil; and if he is all-knowing he knows how to make a world without evil; and if he is all-good he wants to make a world without evil; but evils occur in this world; therefore, God either does not exist or lacks at least one of the aforementioned properties. I agree that God could have created a universe containing creaturely free agents who only and always freely choose the good and constantly shun evil.[42] So how can such a God exist?

Response. There are two stages in answering this challenge. To the skeptic who denies the existence of the theistic God, I point out that it is at least logically possible that an all-knowing God has a good and sufficient reason

---

41. For an exposition and defense of classical Christianity's understanding of the very first fall, see appendix 4.

42. In other words, I reject the notion that some worlds are infeasible for God and that all free creatures possess the property of transworld depravity (discussed throughout chapter 5).

for allowing evils to occur. For those who believe the theistic God exists, I offer an exposition of what that reason is in the following chapter.[43] For now, I simply note that, even if I am wrong in my answer and am forced to admit that I have absolutely no idea as to why God created a world knowing evils will occur, such would not disprove the existence of God. Indeed, the mere *possibility* that God has a good reason for allowing evil to obtain renders God and evil compossible.[44]

SUPRALAPSARIANISM

Hyper-Calvinists offer yet another consideration to mitigate the common Christian belief that God savingly loves every single human—namely, that a supralapsarian order of the divine decree entails that God does not desire the salvation of every person.

WHAT IS SUPRALAPSARIANISM?

Generally speaking, Calvinists of all stripes share at least three presuppositions in common: first, God foreordains everything that comes to pass; second, the divine decree, precisely because it flows from the eternal God who is absolutely one (simple), is itself one eternal decree; third, while the decree is one, a study of the logical order of the decree is pertinent to understanding how God relates to his creatures, for the human mind cannot comprehend the simple decree any more than it can comprehend the divine omniscience; hence, an exploration into the logical order of the decree is indispensable for apprehending divine revelation.

Beyond these basic agreements, Calvinists generally split into two camps regarding the ordering of the decree—i.e., supralapsarians and infralapsarians. A *lapsarian* is someone who believes that humans have *lapsed* or *fallen into sin*.[45] A *supralapsarian* is someone who believes that,

---

43. In other words, there is a distinction to be made between a *defense* of God in light of the problem of evil and a *theodicy*. The former is merely a demonstration that the logical argument from evil to God's nonexistence is unsound. The latter is more ambitious, attempting to show exactly why God allows evil to obtain in this world. As one can see, success in offering a defense does not hinge on a successful theodicy. For more on how to defend the theistic concept of God in light of the problem of evil, see chapter 2 above.

44. For more on this, see chapter 2 above.

45. For a vindication of this claim, see appendix 1.

in the ordering of the divine plan of redemption, the decree of election and reprobation precedes the decree of the creation and the fall. Hyper-Calvinism is often identified with supralapsarianism.[46] *Infralapsarians* (aka *sublapsarians*) believe that, in the divine counsel concerning humanity's salvation, the decrees to create humans and then permit their fall into sin preceded the decree of election and reprobation. Those who embrace infralapsarianism are often called moderate Calvinists. It is generally noted that the supralapsarian follows the more logical order, proceeding "on the assumption that in planning the rational mind passes from the end to the means in a retrograde movement, so that what is first in design is last in accomplishment."[47] Hence the common supralapsarian order of the divine decree:

1. The election of some human beings unto salvation in Christ, and the reprobation of other human beings unto damnation in Adam
2. The creation of the universe out of nothing, which contains both types of humans
3. The ordination to permit the fall of humanity into sin
4. The redemption of the elect via the work of Christ—most notably his atoning death and resurrection
5. The application of the benefits of Christ's redemptive work to the elect via the ministry of the Holy Spirit[48]

As one can see, if this (or something like it) is the true logical order of the divine decree, then it is extremely difficult to reconcile the divine plan of redemption with the doctrine of God's saving love for all humankind. This is for at least two reasons: First, given the symmetrical relationship between election and reprobation, the divine choice of the blessed and damned

---

46. Which, to be sure, is not entirely accurate. Supralapsarianism is a necessary but insufficient condition for hyper-Calvinism, and yet few are ever one without being the other. Other elements of hyper-Calvinism include the affirmation that God creates evil, the denial of human freedom, and the rejection of aggressive evangelism for the lost.

47. Louis Berkhof, *Systematic Theology* (rev. and enl. ed.; Grand Rapids: Eerdmans, 1996), 119.

48. This ordering is almost exactly like that of supralapsarian theologian Robert L. Reymond, *A New Systematic Theology of the Christian Faith* (2nd ed.; Nashville: Thomas Nelson, 1998), 488.

is equally ultimate, and hence God never looks at the reprobate as those he may want to save. They are always, in his mind, objects of his wrath. Second, precisely because election and reprobation are equally ultimate in the divine mind, it stands to reason that God pursues the one to the same degree he pursues the other. Hence, it makes little sense that those who are damned were ever the objects of God's love and affection.

The following represents the common infralapsarian order of the divine decree:

1. The creation of the universe out of nothing, which includes every human
2. The ordination to permit the fall of humanity into sin
3. The election of some human sinners unto salvation in Christ, and the reprobation of other human sinners unto damnation in Adam
4. The redemption of the elect via the work of Christ—most notably his atoning death and resurrection
5. The application of the benefits of Christ's redemptive work to the elect via the ministry of the Holy Spirit[49]

On this ordering of the divine decree, it is at least *possible* that God savingly loves everyone. And this for at least two reasons: First, since the decree to create precedes the decree to permit the fall, which in turn precedes the decree to elect and reprobate, every human being serves a purpose that is broader than his/her redemption or damnation—for the first thought of humanity in the divine mind is as his *creation as such, not* as an object for either special blessing or wrath. Second, since the divine reprobation concerns humans as sinners, it can *possibly* be said that God reprobates humans only in the sense that he *allows* them to resist his gracious over-tures—not in the sense that he actively works in history so as to ensure their damnation. In short, by offering an historical ordering of the decree, sublapsarianism *at least allows for the idea* that reprobation and subsequent damnation occur via God's permission rather than his promotion.

---

49. Reymond, *New Systematic Theology*, 480; see also Berkhof, *Systematic Theology*, 120.

WHERE DOES THE EVIDENCE
POINT—SUPRA- OR INFRA-?

I will offer my own understanding of the divine decree, at least broadly speaking, closer to the end of our study. There I will make the case that, instead of a *decretal* ordering of the divine plan, we should actually think more in terms of an *ordering of the divine omniscience*.[50] Hence, on my view, neither supralapsarianism nor infralapsarianism fully captures the biblical understanding of the divine decree. That said, I think the infralapsarians have a better grasp of the divine plan of redemption, and hence, while I am not sublapsarian, I think their perspective at least points us in the right direction.

REASONS FOR INFRALAPSARIANISM

There are at least five good reasons to think something like the *spirit* of infralapsarianism is promoted in Scripture: First, in contrast to supra-lapsarianism, infralapsarianism appreciates the asymmetry between election and reprobation—i.e., the basis for one (grace) is not the basis for the other (justice). The elect are so *wholly* by God's mercy; the reprobate are so *wholly* because of God's justice. In other words, election is *unconditional* in the sense that God's choice of who will be saved is *not* based on anything a person does (e.g., faith, works, perseverance, etc.), but is instead "according to the purpose of his will, to the praise of his glorious grace" (Eph 1:5–6 ESV), while reprobation is *conditional* in the sense that those who are not chosen are condemned *wholly* on the basis of their disobedience to God's moral law (sin) and their recalcitrant unbelief.[51] Supralapsarianism, by

---

50. Perhaps the greatest contribution to the entire discussion on predestination since the Reformation has been the observation that we should shift our thinking from "an order of decree" to "an order of knowledge." I only know of one scholar who has *explicitly* made this distinction (though perhaps one might suggest that it was implicit in the work of Molina [among others] all along). That theologian is Kenneth Keathley—see, for example, his *Salvation and Sovereignty*, 150. Unless there are other theologians explicitly saying the same thing who have gone unnoticed (at least by me), Keathley deserves high praise for this contribution. For it is rare for anyone in the modern world to offer anything new to this discussion, which has occupied the minds of so many throughout church history.

51. Robert Dabney writes: "But it is urged, with an affected over-refinement, the sin of the non-elect cannot be the ground of God's preterition [i.e., *the divine determination to pass over some humans and leave them in their sin*], because all Adam's seed being viewed as equally depraved, had this been the ground, all would have been passed by." In other words, divine reprobation has to be grounded in something more than just human sin, and hence

placing the decree of election and reprobation *first* in the logical order, embraces the equal ultimacy of double predestination, wherein God pursues the redemption of his chosen in the same way and to the same degree he pursues the damnation of the reprobate. So, on this schema, the reprobate are condemned, not as an act of justice, but by a wholly arbitrary decision on God's part. Hence the doctrine of symmetry subverts the goodness and justice of God.

Second, there are numerous scriptural texts that, when placed side by side, illustrate quite beautifully the asymmetry of the divine predestination. For example:

The Lord is not slow about his promise, as some think of slowness, but is patient with you, not wanting any to perish, but all to come to repentance. (2 Pet 3:9 NRSV)

---

it must also be grounded in God's sovereign will, lest we embrace a *conditional* decree and hence Arminianism. This is the supralapsarian's nose under the camel's tent; for with this one admission (which many infralapsarians concede), the hyper-Calvinist drives home the point that God must really desire some to be damned in the same way he desires some to be saved and, if *that* is the case, it is just a short step from there to affirm the decree of election/ reprobation as first in the order of God's plan (see, e.g., Reymond, *New Systematic Theology,* 481–84). Hence Dabney's retort: "I reply, yes; if this had been the only consideration, *pro* or *con,* present in God's mind. The ill-desert of all was in itself a sufficient ground for God to pass by all. But when His sovereign wisdom suggested some reason, unconnected with the relative desert or ill-desert of sinners, which was a good and sufficient ground for God's choosing a part; this only left the same original ground, ill-desert operating on His mind as to the remainder. It is perfectly true that God's sovereignty concerns itself with the preterition as well as the election; for the separate reason which grounded the latter is sovereign. But with what propriety can it be said that this secret sovereign reason is the ground of his preterition, when the very point of the case was that it was a reason which did not apply to the non-elect, but only to the elect? As to the elect, it overruled the ground for their preterition, which would otherwise have been found, in their common ill-desert. As to the non-elect, it did not apply, and thus left the original ground, their ill-deserts, in full force. If all sinning men had been subjects of a decree of preterition, nobody would have questioned, but that God's ground for passing them by was simply their ill-desert. Now, then, if a secret, sovereign motive, counterpoising that presented by the ill-desert, led to the election of some; how does this alter the ground for God's preterition of the rest? Three traitors are justly condemned to death for capital crimes confessed. The king ascertains that two of them are sons of a noble citizen, who had died for the commonwealth; and the supreme judge is moved by this consideration to spare the lives of these men. For what is the third criminal hung? No one has any doubt in answering: 'For his treason.' The original cause of death remains in operation against him, because no contravening fact existed in this case." Robert L. Dabney, *Systematic Theology* (2nd ed., 1878; repr., Carlisle, PA: Banner of Truth Trust, 1996), 240–41. Hence the supralapsarian has given me no good reason to deny my firm conviction that reprobation is conditional, while election is unconditional.

So it [election] depends not on human will or exertion, but on God
who shows mercy. (Rom 9:16 NRSV)

Notice, then, that Scripture affirms two truths—i.e., God unconditionally
elects some sinners unto salvation, and God truly desires the salvation of
every human sinner. At this point one has only two choices. One can insist
that the Bible is contradicting itself (i.e., since one biblical author believes
in universal divine benevolence, while another believes in particular election) or one can hold the texts in tension. The problem with the former
stance is that we sometimes discover the *very same human author* adhering
to both conditional reprobation and sovereign grace. Note in this regard
the words of Luke:

> Then both Paul and Barnabas spoke out boldly, saying, "It was nec-
> essary that the word of God should be spoken first to you. Since *you*
> *reject it and judge yourselves to be unworthy of eternal life*, we are now
> turning to the Gentiles. For so the Lord has commanded us, saying,
> "'I have set you to be a light for the Gentiles,
> so that you may bring salvation to the ends of the earth'"
> [Isa 49:6].
> When the Gentiles heard this, they were glad and praised the
> word of the Lord; and *as many as had been destined for eternal life*
> *became believers*. (Acts 13:48 NRSV)[52]

Notice that in the space of just three verses we have an illustration of the
asymmetrical relationship between election (i.e., the divine ordination of
some to salvation) and reprobation (i.e., the divine permission of the recalcitrant unbelief of some). The vast majority of Jews Paul and Barnabas had
been preaching to in Antioch rejected the gospel message; and, as we just
read, by rejecting the apostolic message they judged or rendered themselves unworthy of eternal life. The rejection, then, was not so much God's
rejection of them as it was their rejection of him. On the other hand, there
were many gentiles who believed the gospel message. Why did they believe?

---

52. For an exegesis of this text, see chapter 3.

Because they had been destined to do so by God. It would appear, then, that the only way to understand these verses is to insist that election is unconditional while reprobation is conditional.

Third, Romans 9:16–23 suggests that infralapsarianism is closer to the truth:

> So it depends not on human will or exertion, but on God who shows mercy. For the scripture says to Pharaoh, "I have raised you up for the very purpose of showing my power in you, so that my name may be proclaimed in all the earth" [Exod 9:16]. So then he has mercy on whomever he chooses, and he hardens the heart of whomever he chooses.
>
> You will say to me then, "Why does he still find fault? For who can resist his will?" But who indeed are you, a human being, to argue with God? Will what is molded say to the one who molds it, "Why have you made me like this?" [Isa 29:16]. Has the potter no right over the clay, to make out of the same lump one object for special use and another for ordinary use? What if God, desiring to show his wrath and to make known his power, has endured with much patience the objects of wrath that are made for destruction; and what if he has done so in order to make known the riches of his glory for the objects of mercy, which he has prepared beforehand for glory. (NRSV)

Note several features of this passage: First, unconditional election is affirmed, for election is not according to human choice or effort, but it is wholly of God's mercy. This is why we read of God showing mercy to whomever he pleases and hardening whomever he pleases. Second, Paul raises the very questions the Arminian raises to the Calvinist—"How is any of this fair? How can God judge us when he is the one who sets it all up? How can anyone resist God's will?" How does Paul answer this (possibly) imaginary interlocutor? "No, you don't understand, God gives equal opportunity for all to be saved! He's pulling for you, Satan is pulling against you, and you break the tie! For his choice is fairly based on your foreseen faith or lack thereof!" No, we do not see such an answer! Instead Paul says, "Who are you to argue with God?"

A third point we need to make about this text is that Paul actually answers the questions of his interlocutor. He does so with his "potter and clay" analogy. As we noted in the above quotation, Paul clearly quotes Isaiah, who rhetorically asks whether the thing made has the right to question its maker. This inquiry solicits a negative answer and confirms Paul's prior reprimand against anyone who would question God. Then, interestingly, he answers the objector's question by saying, "Has the potter no right over the clay, to make out of the same lump one object for honorable use and another for ordinary use?" (9:21). This question solicits a positive answer. Surely God does have that right! But notice that, according to Paul, it is from *one single lump* that he prepares one vessel for honorable and another for common use—hence, it is from the same corporate humanity that God elects some and reprobates others (9:22-23). The question we need to ask is, What is the state of the humanity from which the Lord distinguishes the elect from the reprobate?

There are at least three good reasons to think that, according to Paul, at the point of selection and preterition, humanity is considered as fallen into one corporate and sinful ruin: (1) the context indicates that those who are fallen are the ones who are called—e.g., "And in the very place where it was said to them, 'You are not my people,' there they shall be called children of the living God" [Hos 2:23], "If the Lord of hosts had not left survivors to us, we would have fared like Sodom and been made like Gomorrah" [Isa 1:9] (9:26, 29 NRSV)—and the strong conceptual ties here between election and calling[53] indicate the decree of election occurs posterior to the decree of the fall; (2) in verses 22-23 we learn that God "has endured with much patience the objects of wrath that are made for destruction; ... in order to make known the riches of his glory for the objects of mercy, which he has prepared beforehand for glory" (NRSV). Curiously, these two clauses contain two intriguing verbs—i.e., κατηρτισμένα (as in, "*made* for destruction") and προητοίμασεν (as in, "he *pre-prepared* for glory")—with the former being passive and the latter being active. Why this change in voice within one

---

53. Notice that, in the text itself, God is saying, e.g., "Those who are not my people will be called my people." This is not calling per se, but the *choice* to call out a people who will belong to God—which *just* is election. And since it is *sinners* ("not my people," whose destiny is destruction [i.e., Sodom and Gomorrah]) who are chosen for the calling, the decree to elect is logically *posterior* to the decree to allow the fall.

sentence, in the space of two clauses? It is certainly reasonable to think that Paul accomplishes two objectives via this change: first and foremost, he ensures that God is the one who places the reprobate and the elect in their respective conditions; second, he is hinting toward an asymmetry that exists between reprobation and election, for while the former is not caused by God (hence the passive voice) the latter is wholly from his mercy (hence the active voice).[54] Notice also that election is according to mercy and grace (see 9:15-16; 11:5-6). But grace presupposes sin, never neutrality, much less goodness (Rom 4:4-5; 11:6; Eph 2:1-9); therefore, the decree to elect is posterior to the decree to permit the fall. Finally, (3) we have the imagery of the potter and the clay, which, though clearly rooted in Isaiah 29 (which Paul explicitly quotes), also harks back to the days of Jeremiah, where the prophet, while visiting the home of a potter, rhetorically asks: "Can I not do with you, O house of Israel, just as this potter has done? says the LORD. Just like the clay in the potter's hand, so are you in my hand, O house of Israel" (Jer 18:6 NRSV). Indeed, few there are who deny that Paul is thinking of this passage from Jeremiah while he composes his own text.[55] When we delve further into Jeremiah's prophecy, it becomes clear that the clay YHWH is dealing with is that which has done evil, not good. Hence, YHWH says, "Turn now, all of you from your evil way, and amend your ways and your doings" (18:11b NRSV). Jeremiah rhetorically asks, "Is evil a recompense for good?" Of course it is not! However, if supralapsarianism is true, then YHWH has brought evil on those who, in principle, do not deserve it. Therefore, supralapsarianism is not true.

Fourth, supralapsarianism, as we have seen, insists that the decree of election precedes the decree of the fall. We have also seen that this viewpoint entails a symmetry between election and reprobation, wherein God pursues the damnation of the latter to the same degree and in the same way he pursues the salvation of the former. This further entails that God, precisely because he desires the curse of the reprobate *in the same way* he desires the blessing of the elect, actually desires the fall to take place.

---

54. For more on this, see John Piper, *The Justification of God: An Exegetical and Theological Study of Romans 9:1-23* (2nd ed.; Grand Rapids: Baker, 1993), 213-14. See also Charles Hodge, *Commentary on Romans* (rev. ed., 1864; repr., Carlisle, PA: Banner of Truth Trust, 1986), 321; and Thomas R. Schreiner, *Romans* (BECNT; Grand Rapids: Baker, 1998), 513-23.

55. See, e.g., Piper, *Justification of God*, 197; Schreiner, *Romans*, 516; Hodge, *Romans*, 319.

The fall becomes a necessary means for the destiny of the reprobate to be achieved. Sproul Jr. puts it more boldly than any hyper-Calvinist I have ever read: "It was his [God's] desire to make his wrath known. He needed, then, something on which to be wrathful. He needed to have sinful creatures. He wanted to make his mercy known. He needed, then, something that deserved wrath on which he could show mercy instead."[56] In short, God is wrathful, and so needs sin in order to display his wrath.[57] This makes God the author of sin, as we have already noted. It also entails that God in no way desires the salvation of every person. But we have already shown that God can in no way be the author or creator of evil; and 2 Peter 3:9 demonstrates conclusively that God truly desires every person to achieve salvation. Therefore, supralapsarianism is false.

Fifth, for those of us who love and adore the Reformed tradition, we proudly note that the classical creeds and confessions of the Reformed faith are all infralapsarian in spirit—even if not in letter. As we have already noted, there is a better way to construe the ordering of the divine plan of redemption—which I articulate at the end of this study. But that way is an infralapsarian way, wherein God presupposes the fall while expressing his love via his choice of certain sinners unto salvation. It is clear that the creeds and confessions express this fundamental point quite explicitly—i.e., in election and reprobation, the fall is presupposed. Hence the following quotations from two Reformed creeds:

> We believe that all the posterity of Adam, *being thus fallen into perdition and ruin by the sin of our first parents*, God then did manifest himself such as He is; that is to say, merciful and just: merciful, since He delivers and preserves *from this perdition* all whom He, in His eternal and unchangeable counsel, of mere goodness hath elected in

---

56. Sproul Jr., *Almighty over All*, 57.

57. I was as astonished at Sproul's words as Keathley: "Maybe my reading list is not as well-rounded as it should be, but this is the first time I've ever heard of an evangelical theologian claiming that God needs sin" (*Salvation and Sovereignty*, 84). Indeed, a common mistake Calvinists make is believing that wrath is an attribute of God. But wrath is not a divine attribute, *justice is!* Wrath is a just *action* or *punishment* against sinners who deserve it. Because wrath is not a divine attribute, there is no sense in which God *needs* to punish people. A more biblical perspective is to say that God's end game is the expression of his goodness as grace—a point we develop in the next chapter.

Christ Jesus our Lord, without any respect to works; just, in *leaving others in the fall and perdition wherein they have involved themselves.* (Belgic Confession, Article 16)

Election is the unchangeable purpose of God, whereby, before the foundation of the world, He hath out of mere grace, according to the sovereign good pleasure of His own will, chosen, from the whole human race, *which had fallen through their own fault from their primitive state of rectitude into sin and destruction,* a certain number of persons to redemption in Christ, whom He from eternity appointed the Mediator and Head of the elect, and the foundation for salvation. (Canons of Dort, Article 15)[58]

OBJECTIONS FROM A SUPRALAPSARIAN POSITION

OBJECTION 1

There is another way to construe the supralapsarian position, wherein the doctrine of equal ultimacy is exonerated from many of the charges that have been brought against it. Reymond, for example, believes that a truly consistent supralapsarianism may be articulated as follows:

(1) The election of some sinful human beings unto salvation in Christ, and the reprobation of the rest of sinful humankind in order to make known the riches of God's gracious mercy to the elect
(2) The creation of the universe out of nothing, which contains both types of humans
(3) The ordination to permit the fall of humanity into sin
(4) The redemption of the elect via the work of Christ—most notably his atoning death and resurrection

---

58. See Joel R. Beeke and Sinclair B. Ferguson, eds., *Reformed Confessions Harmonized* (Grand Rapids: Baker, 1999), 28–36.

(5) The application of the benefits of Christ's redemptive work to the elect via the ministry of the Holy Spirit[59]

As Reymond notes: "This revision of the more common scheme addresses the infralapsarian objection that supralapsarianism depicts God as discriminating among men viewed simply as men and not among men viewed as sinners."[60]

Response. First, this does not seem to be a consistent solution to the sublapsarian critique of supralapsarianism. For, as Bruce Ware points out, already implicit in this first decree is the creation of humankind and the permission of their fall into sin.[61]

Second, either the reprobate deserve their reprobation or they do not. If they do, it is because they have sinned. If they do not, but are reprobate anyway, then God is unjust. Reymond himself has given an ambiguous answer to this dilemma. On the one hand, he tells us that the reprobate are so because of sin.[62] On the other hand, he tells us that Paul's famous metaphor of the potter and the clay favors supralapsarianism. Why? Because, if "the lump" from which the honorable and dishonorable vessels are made represented sinful humanity, then the potter would only need to make one kind of vessel (i.e., the honorable one), since "the lump" would already be sinful and thereby deserving dishonor.[63] This would suggest, says Reymond,

---

59. Reymond, *New Systematic Theology*, 489. See also Robert L. Reymond, "A Consistent Supralapsarian Perspective on Election," in *Perspectives on Election: Five Views* (ed. Chad Owen Brand; Nashville: Broadman & Holman, 2006), 178.

60. Reymond, *New Systematic Theology*, 489.

61. Bruce Ware, "Responses to Robert Reymond," in *Perspectives on Election*, 198–99. Ware also notes a curious quotation of Reymond's, which destroys his very articulate and careful defense of supralapsarianism: "And the biblically informed Christian is also aware, while it is true that God's determination to pass by the rest of mankind (this 'passing by' theologians designate 'preterition' from the Latin *praeteritio*) is grounded solely in the unsearchable counsel of his own will, that his determination to ordain those whom he passed by to dishonor and wrath (condemnation) took into account the condition which alone deserves his wrath—the fact of their sin" (Reymond, "Consistent Supralapsarianism," 154; see Ware, "Responses," 199n2). So which is it? Either the reprobate are so because they deserve it or because they do not deserve it. If they deserve it it's because they have sinned, in which case reprobation logically follows the decree to permit the fall. If they have not sinned then they don't deserve their reprobation. And if they are reprobate anyway, then God is unjust!

62. Reymond, *New Systematic Theology*, 489; idem, "Consistent Supralapsarianism," 185. He surely wants to say this in light of his wording "the first decree" the way he does.

63. Reymond, "Consistent Supralapsarianism," 176.

"that the lump has no particular character beforehand—good or bad—which would necessarily determine the potter toward a given vessel's creation for one kind of use or the other."[64] Here we meet one of the most disturbing aspects of Reymond's doctrine of election, for not only has he pressed a metaphor way beyond its intended limits,[65] he fails to connect the illustration with what Paul says just a few verses later (e.g., the passive and active verbs concerning reprobation and election respectively). Even worse, on Reymond's reading of the metaphor, the lump of humankind possesses a neutral character in abstraction; but then God actively molds

---

64. Reymond, "Consistent Supralapsarianism," 176.

65. Of course, if Reymond insists on pressing the metaphor, we are happy to oblige him. Let us leave the potter analogy for a moment and move into the classical artistic realm, traveling to the academy in Florence and into Michelangelo's "Great Room." As you enter the room you notice that on either side are more than a few unfinished sculptures, which seem to portray men tearing themselves out of the rock from which they came. In the center of the "Great Room" stands *David*, which, as "a work of art ... has few equals in the world. Michelangelo took a piece of marble so flawed that no one thought it could be used, and out of it he carved this overwhelming statue." Francis A. Schaeffer, *How Should We Then Live?* (vol. 5 of *The Complete Works of Francis A. Schaeffer*; 2nd ed.; Wheaton, IL: Crossway, 1985), 114. It is reasonable to interpret Michelangelo's point in this arrangement of the statues as follows: the incomplete statues represent man carving himself out of the rock and setting forth his own destiny; and the destiny of man is *David*, the ideal man, who, though coming from mean origins, has sculpted himself into a vision of perfection.

But if the reader will indulge us for a moment, we can actually baptize Michelangelo's arrangement into the Reformed worldview. Imagine an artist who from a single, flawed piece of marble begins breaking the huge rock into different, albeit large, pieces and sculpting each of them. Each piece of marble is equally flawed and hence equally hard to work with. Yet, for the artist's own designs and own plans, the artist stops working on every piece of marble save only one—from which emerges a beautiful statue of the male form.

Now we may return to the potter and his clay. From the same dirty, brittle, flawed lump of clay, the potter forms various vessels—each equally difficult to work with. Eventually, after enduring with much patience these lumps of clay, whose forms and textures resist his artistic skills, the potter decides to stop working with many of them and concentrates on a select number. In the end, many of the pottery works, though not without some value, exist only for common use—while those selected for completion have been refined for honorable use at banquets and parties.

Hopefully the reader can see the relevancy of this analogy. Indeed, when we connect it with, say, the rebels of Jeremiah's prophecy (see Jer 18:1–12), we see a major dissimilarity between the inanimate piece of clay a potter works with and the animate image bearers, made of dust, who contend against God. God, while calling on all people everywhere to repent, and even giving them sufficient grace to believe, endures with much patience these sinful jars of clay who constantly resist his gracious overtures (see Rom 2:4; Acts 7:51). Eventually he passes many of these jars over and turns to a selected number, who are molded into the kind of people he wants them to be. Thus, contrary to Reymond, Paul's analogy of the potter and the clay perfectly fits a kind of infralapsarian scheme, wherein election/reprobation presuppose humanity's fall into sin.

some of that lump into humans who are destined to inherit his blessing, all the while actively molding others to become the heirs of his wrath through sin. In thus pursuing the damnation of the reprobate in the same way he pursues the salvation of the elect, Reymond effectively makes God the author and/or creator of sin.

OBJECTION 2

Infralapsarians insist that supralapsarianism is flawed, since the latter thinks reprobation is applied to humanity as an abstraction (or, at least, to humans as unfallen). But what happens when the infralapsarian considers the fall of angels?

Why did God allow many angels to sin while keeping others from falling? Reymond writes:

> Apparently, for reasons sufficient to himself, God simply by decree granted the grace of perseverance in holiness to some angels and denied it to the others. If God did so relative to the destiny of angels, did he not do so, to use the infralapsarian's word, "arbitrarily"? And if he did so, is there any reason he should not have done so regarding the destiny of humans?[66]

Response. The reason why God might allow any of his creatures to fall into sin, thereby bringing evil into the world, is explored in the following chapter. For now, I make two basic points. First, as incorporeal spirits, the angels do not share the same kind of corporate solidarity humans do. Indeed, the most plausible view of angels is that each is a manifestation of his own species.[67] Thus, when the angels fell into sin and became the demons, each did so of his own free agency. The same goes for those angels who remained true. Each did so of his own freedom of choice. Indeed, it makes no sense to say that any demon is fallen "in Satan." Nor does it make any sense to say that Michael the Archangel is redeemed "in Christ." Angels are saved by works, and demons are damned by their own sin. On the other hand, Reformed theology traditionally teaches that all humans are fallen in Adam, and, that being presupposed, God chooses some humans for salvation and

---

66. Reymond, "Consistent Supralapsarianism," 170.
67. Aquinas, *ST* Ia.50.4.

then chooses to pass over others and permit them to remain in their fallen condition. The burden of proof is on the critic of this theology to show its inconsistency.

Second, Reymond may remind us that Michael's perseverance, along with Satan's sin, are both the working out of the divine decree. Hence, God could have just as easily decreed for Satan to persevere and for Michael to fall. True. But on our traditional scheme, this universe having been decreed to exist, no angel is elected unto salvation or reprobated unto damnation in anything like a supralapsarian manner precisely because *there is no redemption of any of the angels after their fall*.[68] In the end, I find this sort of objection more curious than cogent.[69]

OBJECTION 3

The Bible teaches that God hates certain persons and even deceives them into believing lies in order to punish them.

Concerning the divine hatred, there are, indeed, no less than sixteen places in Scripture where we are told quite explicitly that the "boastful will not stand before your eyes; you hate all evildoers" (Ps 5:5 NRSV), and the "LORD tests the righteous and the wicked, and his soul hates the lover of violence" (Ps 11:5 NRSV).[70]

Concerning the divine deception, we once again encounter numerous texts where God actually sends evil spirits to lead people astray: "For this reason God sends them a powerful delusion, leading them to believe what is false" (2 Thess 2:11 NRSV). Indeed, "If a prophet is deceived and speaks a word, I, the LORD, have deceived that prophet, and I will stretch out my hand against him, and will destroy him from the midst of my people Israel" (Ezek 14:9 NRSV).[71] Indeed, Paul clearly teaches that Pharaoh's heart was

---

68. Ware, "Responses," 199.

69. Besides Reymond, I know of only one other theologian who thinks the election of angels approximates the supralapsarian scheme—Berkhof, *Systematic Theology*, 121.

70. See Lev 20:23; 26:30; Deut 32:19; Pss 53:5; 73:20; 78:59; 106:40; Prov 6:16–19; 22:14; Lam 2:6; Hos 9:15; Zech 11:8; Mal 1:3; Rom 9:13. The KJV usually translates these texts using the word "hate," indicating that the object of divine hate is specific persons or entire groups of people. Where "hate" is not used, "abhor," "reject," or some such equivalent is given to denote God's denouncement of those under judgment. The same is true of the NRSV.

71. See 1 Kings 22:20–23; Jer 4:10; 20:7, 10; Matt 13:10–17; Mark 4:10–12; Luke 8:9–10. Yet, Jeremiah's statement—i.e., "Ah, Lord GOD, how utterly you have deceived this people and

hardened (Rom 9:17–18), indicating that there is at least one who is not savingly loved.

The implication of these texts is clear. If God actually hates people, hardens them, and even sends lying spirits to deceive them so as to ensure their recalcitrant unbelief, then we must conclude that God does not savingly love everyone, and hence he pursues the damnation of the reprobate in the same way he pursues the salvation of the elect. Indeed, returning to the potter analogy discussed in Isaiah, Jeremiah, and Paul (among other places), Reymond writes: "Proverbs 16:4, in my opinion, aptly expresses the intention of the metaphor: 'The Lord has made everything for his own purpose, even the wicked for the day of evil.'"[72]

Response. Concerning God's hatred of certain persons, we affirm with full conviction that God really does love every single human being he has made in his image; and, *as persons*, no human being is actually hated by God. As one Jewish tradition argues: "For you love all things that exist, and detest none of the things that you have made, for you would not have made anything if you had hated it" (Wisdom 11:25 NRSV). This is an intriguing argument, which we can reduce to a simple question—i.e., why would God create anything he hates? As Scripture itself tells us: "For God so loved the world that he gave is only Son, so that everyone who believes in him may not perish but may have eternal life. Indeed, God did not send the Son into the world to condemn the world, but in order that the world might be

---

Jerusalem, saying, 'It shall be well with you,' even while the sword is at the throat" (4:10 NRSV; see also 20:7, 10)—will have to be ruled out as suggesting deceit on *God's* part. Indeed, we must "see in such an utterance not so much a considered judgment, but the spontaneous reaction of a man who felt deeply about the tragedies of life, whether his own or those of others." See J. A. Thompson, *The Book of Jeremiah* (NICOT; Grand Rapids: Eerdmans, 1980), 222. There were two messages being articulated in Jeremiah's day—i.e., Jeremiah spoke of an impending judgment, while the other "prophets" all predicted good times ahead for the people of Judah. "Jeremiah stood in a dilemma. The prophets of the day spoke of peace. Jeremiah saw judgment unfolding, either before his inner eyes in a vision or with a deeper understanding of the Babylonians than they had at the time. What he saw he declared. Perhaps his declaration may have been hindered for a time as he hoped that the danger might pass as it had in the days of Hezekiah. But his inner heart told him otherwise. Anything else was false. And if Yahweh had given the word to his contemporary prophets, it was a 'lying word' that he had given (cf. 1 K. 22:19–23)." Indeed, "To prophesy falsely was 'an appalling and horrible thing' (5:30). And even if he dismissed the popular prophets by saying that they prophesied by Baal (2:8), he may have felt that they were as much under God's control as were the prophets of Ahab when faced with Micaiah (1 K. 22)" (Thompson, *Jeremiah*, 223).

72. Reymond, "Consistent Supralapsarianism," 175.

saved through him" (John 3:16-17 NRSV).[73] Notice also the following passage: "Those who say, 'I love God,' and hate their brothers or sisters, are liars; for those who do not love a brother or sister whom they have seen, cannot love God whom they have not seen" (1 John 4:20 NRSV). True, in context, John is speaking about a Christian's love for fellow Christians; yet in his Gospel he illustrates how Christ loved unbelievers (e.g., John 4:7-42). Jesus' idea of loving one's neighbor is to love literally *anyone* who comes across our path (Luke 10:29-37; see Lev 19:18). Thus, consider the following argument: (1) we emulate God only insofar as we love (1 John 4:7-12; 16-17); (2) when we hate anyone, the love of God is not in us (1 John 4:20-21; see 1:5-2:6); (3) but a God who hates specific persons while commanding us to love everyone we encounter is a God who wants us to be more loving than he is (*which is absurd*; 1 John 4:8, 10, 16); therefore, (4) God loves everyone and hates no one.[74]

Consider also the following argument of Thomas Aquinas: (1) to love something *just is* to will and/or accomplish some good in that thing; (2) existence, as we have already seen, is a positive good; (3) God causes the existence of all things other than himself; (4) so God causes whatever is good in all things other than himself; therefore, (5) God loves all things other than himself.[75]

What, then, do we do with texts like the fifth and eleventh Psalms, which explicitly speak of a hatred that God has toward some persons? Aquinas answers in the following way:

> Nothing prevents one and the same thing being loved under one aspect, while it is hated under another. God loves sinners in so far as they are existing natures; for they have existence, and have it

---

73. If the purpose of the Son's coming is *not* to condemn, but to save the world, he must love all. "The 'world' in the Fourth Gospel is sometimes identical with 'the Jews' (15:18-16:2), but refers to the Samaritans in the following narrative section (4:42). Jesus as a 'light to the world' (8:12) may be Isaiah's 'light to the nations' (Isa 42:6; 49:6; cf. 60:3), so in Johannine theology God's love for the 'world' represents his love for humanity. This remains a love for potential believers that is qualified by wrath toward those who refuse to respond to his gracious gift (3:36)." See Craig S. Keener, *The Gospel of John: A Commentary* (Peabody, MA: Hendrickson, 2003), 1:569.

74. Keener, *Gospel of John*, 1:569.

75. Aquinas, *ST* Ia.20.2.

from Him. In so far as they are sinners, they have not existence at all, but fall short of it [since the sin or evil in them is a privation of the good or nature]; and this in them is not from God. Hence, under this aspect, they are hated by Him.[76]

That most of us have heard of love-hate relationships may illustrate Thomas's point. Indeed, hatred and love are not contradictory ideas, and so God can love and hate every sinner at the same time as long as he does it in different ways. In light of what we have established so far, I maintain that God loves all people insofar as he creates them, sustains them, and genuinely desires their salvation; and yet he hates them insofar as he allows many to perish—"They are like a dream when one awakens; on awaking you despise their phantoms" (Ps 73:20 NRSV). Or still another way to word our point is to say that God hates the *sinner* but loves the *person*.[77] At the end of the day, however, I think it is truly appropriate to say, with most modern Christians, that God loves the sinner and hates the sin. As Thomist philosopher Peter Kreeft says,

God practices what He preaches to us: love the sinner and hate the sin. God loves even the being He created in the devil, but not the lack of being in the devil's sin. St. Thomas is not saying that sinners have no existence, but that they lack the fullness of existence that comes from loving the good. Vice and virtue have an ontological dimension as well as a moral one; we diminish our being when we sin and augment it by the virtues.[78]

---

76. Aquinas, *ST* Ia.20.2.

77. I am grateful to Dr. Todd Mangum, professor of theology at Missio Seminary in Philadelphia (formerly Biblical Seminary in Hatfield, PA) for sharing this insight with me.

78. Peter Kreeft, *Summa of the* Summa (San Francisco: Ignatius Press, 1990), 166n160. Carson believes that the phrase "love the sinner, hate the sin" should be abandoned (Carson, *Difficult Doctrine*, 69). However, he does not interact with any Thomistic qualification that may lend credit to the statement. Again, God loves all persons insofar as they are persons, but hates them insofar as they are sinful. *In this sense,* God loves the sinner and hates his sin. While the idea of a love-hate relationship between God and humans is not contradictory, there would be a contradiction in the Bible if we had texts saying that God does *not love* certain people, for while love and hate need not be contradictions, love and nonlove most definitely are. There is one text that comes very close to saying that God does *not love* certain people: "Every evil of theirs began at Gilgal; there I came to hate them. Because of the wickedness of

Those passages of Scripture that speak of God's deception of people are few and far between, and yet we understand how some may easily draw false inferences from these texts. One will notice that, in every instance wherein YHWH is portrayed as a deceiver, his "deception" is actually a judgment on those who have spurned the message of his true prophets.[79] Prophet Micaiah has a vision of a wicked spirit YHWH orders/allows to deceive the prophets who offer a good message to King Ahab, who hates Micaiah for his pessimism (1 Kgs 22:13–28). This vision comes on the heels of two important texts describing Ahab's character—i.e., his allegiance to Baal (1 Kgs 16:29–34) and his participation in the murder of Naboth (1 Kgs 21:1–16). Also, we should not miss the obvious irony in this story. Indeed, YHWH may have allowed the deception to take place, but *he is also the one who warns Ahab of the deception!* Thus, even though Ahab has been placed under YHWH's curse, having been handed over to his own passions and unbelief, the Lord's posture toward the king is that of a gracious deity who will accept the repentance of even him, the most wicked of kings (see 1 Kgs 21:17–29). Hence, there is nothing even seemingly immoral about God's "act of deception" here.

Jesus surprisingly tells his disciples that he speaks in parables in order to confound those who are not his followers. In other words, the parables are a means whereby God deceives people (Matt 13:10–17; Mark 4:10–12; Luke 8:9–10). However, when we broaden the context we learn that the parables are not serving their deceptive purpose until *after* the enemies of

---

their deeds I will drive them out of my house. I will love them no more; all their officials are rebels" (Hos 9:15 NRSV). This is the fate northern Israel is to soon face, due to her rebellion against YHWH. But, when we read further on, things are not so simple, since the Lord has loved Israel since she was a child (11:1), and though he called her to come to him she resisted his grace and chased after other gods (11:2); however, though the people of God are bent on turning against him (11:7), "My heart recoils within me; my compassion grows warm and tender. I will not execute my fierce anger; I will not again destroy Ephraim [or northern Israel]; for I am God and no mortal, the Holy One in your midst, and I will not come in wrath" (11:8b–9 NRSV), and hence YHWH will draw his people back to himself from all corners of the world (11:10–11). It is precisely because YHWH is the Holy One of Israel, and no mortal, that his love for her is never fickle or changing—even though her deeds are such that they *deserve* a mere fickle sentimentality from God. They deserve to be loved no more; and yet, despite their sin God remains loving and gracious toward them. Hence, when YHWH says he will love Israel no more, this seems to express what *Israel deserves* more than *what God will do or is doing.*

79. The exception to this point is found in Jeremiah, where we witness not so much the deceit of YHWH as the inner turmoil of the "Weeping Prophet" (see page 209–210n71 above).

Christ commit the blasphemy of the Holy Spirit (Matt 12:22–32; Mark 3:22–30); or, as in the case with Luke's Gospel, a recalcitrant unbelief establishes itself in the heart of the religious leaders (Luke 7:30; see also 11:14–23).

Paul is clearly saying that the delusion sent by the Lord is a punishment directed at those who have set their hearts against God and his holy law (2 Thess 2:1–12). Indeed, what Paul says about the generation of the future, Isaiah says about many in his own day:

> Go now, write it before them on a tablet,
>   and inscribe it in a book,
> so that it may be for the time to come
>   as a witness forever.
> For they are a rebellious people,
>   faithless children,
> children who will not hear
>   the instruction of the LORD;
> who say to the seers, "Do not see";
>   and to the prophets, "Do not prophesy to us what is right;
> speak to us smooth things,
>   prophesy illusions,
> leave the way, turn aside from the path,
>   let us hear no more about the Holy One of Israel."
>   (Isa 30:8–11 NRSV)

Hence, when God sends a delusion by allowing an evil spirit or an evil person to prophesy lies to the people, he is only giving them what they want to hear. As Block notes in his comments on Ezekiel 14:9, in all of the texts we have considered,

> in each case, Yahweh answers insincerity with insincerity. Unrepentant kings and unrepentant people, who seek confirmation of their perverse ways, and who clamor for reassurances of well-being, do not deserve a straight answer. ... By giving the people

lying prophets, who proclaim to the people exactly what they want to hear, Yahweh ensures the people's judgment.[80]

Indeed, from the beginning of his agreement with Israel God warns that confusion and frustration will be his punishment for breaking his covenantal law (see Deut 28:15-20; 32:1-43). So the Lord warns that disobedience will result in his sovereign ordinance that false prophets will come and deceive the people. God is not inspiring their deceptive words (Deut 18:21-22; Num 23:19; 1 Sam 15.29), but he is, as we saw in the case of Micaiah, allowing them to be deceived by another spirit.[81] It would be one thing if God went around lying to people. Liars do not tell the truth about their lies (unless they are caught). And, if God were a liar, who could ever catch him in his deception? But God is not portrayed in Scripture as going from place to place and lying to people. Rather, he warns of deception that will come if the people spurn his word and disobey his laws. He even warns people whenever an act of deception has taken place (see 1 Kgs 22:20-23). This once again raises an important question: If I tell you that I am going to deceive you, have I really deceived you?

A similar interpretation should accompany those texts saying that God hardened Pharaoh's heart. Indeed, while YHWH does initially prophesy that he will harden the king's heart, as the events in the story play out we

---

80. Daniel I. Block, *The Book of Ezekiel: Chapters 1-24* (NICOT; Grand Rapids: Eerdmans, 1997), 434-35.

81. In other words, all events in time are caused by God in the sense that he decrees them to take place. This is plausibly why a text such as Ezek 14:9 is worded in the way it is. YHWH is conveying the fact that even the false prophets are ultimately under his control. But, left unchecked, one can easily conclude that all events occur because God mechanically moves them in a particular direction, much like one moves one's food to one's mouth, or someone moves the stick to strike a ball to move another ball into the table pocket. However, Reformed theologians have always insisted that there is an asymmetry in the divine decree, wherein many events do indeed occur because God actually (mechanically) causes them to occur, while many others happen because he sovereignly *permits* them to happen. In short, all events are under God's sovereign control, and yet what God controls is not always what he either causes or approves. This seems to be the best way to interpret events that seem to have both God and Satan as their cause—i.e., God is sovereignly *permitting* Satan to act, sometimes as a punishment for sin and sometimes as a test of the righteous (2 Sam 24:1; 1 Chr 21:1; see also Job 1:6-12; 2:1-7; 2 Thess 2:9-12). Thus, when YHWH warns that he is the one deceiving the prophet (Ezek 14:9), we are not to interpret this as God actually breathing lies into the souls of people, but rather in the way it plays out in the days of Micaiah, i.e., God allows an evil spirit—*one who actively volunteers to do so*—to go out and spread lies among the false prophets (1 Kgs 22:20-23).

read that it was Pharaoh who actually did the hardening.[82] This indicates that the hardening was actually a divine judgment against the king for his sin and disbelief. Paul speaks elsewhere of God giving recalcitrant sinners over to a depraved mind and will in response to their rebellion (Rom 1:24–32), which in turn renders them even more rebellious. God does not make them rebels; however, it is his prerogative to stop wrestling with the human sinner and allow him to go his own way. Hence, divine hardening is divine judgment due to prior sin; and it does not consist of God mechanically moving the heart to become callous to divine truth, but is simply the divine permission for one to continue in rebellion, no longer impeded by God's gracious conviction of the rebel's conscience. As Aquinas writes: "God is not said to harden anyone directly, as though he causes their malice, but indirectly, inasmuch as man makes an occasion of sin out of things God does within or outside the man; and this God himself permits. Hence, he is not said to harden as though by inserting malice, but by not affording grace."[83] Thus it is not altogether unreasonable to think that God once displayed a sincerely loving and saving grace toward Pharaoh that made it genuinely possible for him to freely embrace YHWH as the true and living God. However, divine mercy having been spurned by the Egyptian king,

---

82.   See Exod 4:21; 7:3, 13–14, 22; 8:15, 19, 32; 9:12, 34–35; 10:1, 20, 27; 11:10; 14:4, 8, 17. Some may object to this interpretation, noting that a passive verb is used as we read about the first "hardening"—i.e., "Yet Pharaoh's heart was hardened" (Exod 7:13), suggesting that it was God who hardened the king's heart, not the king himself; however, things are not so simple, for in the very next verse YHWH says to Moses, "Pharaoh's heart is stubborn [alternative reading is 'hard']; he refuses to let the people go." Notice here that the refusal, which *just is* another term for hardening, is of Pharaoh's own doing. Still later we read, "But Pharaoh hardened his heart this time also, and he did not let the people go" (Exod 8:32), which indicates that the prior cases of hardening were of Pharaoh himself as well. Why, then, the passive voice ("and his heart was hardened"), and why does YHWH say he will harden Pharaoh's heart? YHWH says he will harden Pharaoh's heart as a judgment of his sin, which included his attempt to murder all of the firstborn sons of Israel (Exod 1:8–22); and the verbs initially appear in the passive voice to indicate that God really was involved in this insofar as it was a fulfillment of his decree. But this does not indicate a mechanical movement on God's part whereby he infuses a recalcitrant heart into Pharaoh; rather, the hardening is God's act whereby he hands a person over to his own sins, who in turn is responsible for them. For a slightly different interpretation, which nevertheless preserves the responsibility of Pharaoh in these matters, see Umberto Cassuto, *A Commentary on the Book of Exodus* (trans. Israel Abrahams; Jerusalem: Magnes, 1967), 55–57.

83.   Thomas Aquinas, *Commentary on the Letter of Saint Paul to the Romans* (trans. F. R. Larcher; ed. J. Mortensen and E. Alarcon; vol. 37 of The Latin/English Edition of the Works of St. Thomas Aquinas; Lander, WY: The Aquinas Institute for the Study of Sacred Doctrine, 2012), 262.

YHWH withdrew his grace, thereby giving him over to an obstinate and rebellious heart wholly generated out of the monarch's own soul.

Proverbs 16:4, at first glance, does indeed suggest that God made wicked people or, at the very least, made people for the purpose of becoming evil. However, this would contradict other clear Scriptures that teach just the opposite—e.g., "Only see this: I have discovered that God made people upright,[84] but they pursued many schemes" (Eccl 7:29 HCSB); "So God created humankind in his image, in the image of God he created them; male and female he created them. ... God saw everything that he had made and, indeed, it was very good" (Gen 1:27, 31 NRSV). Also, such an interpretation would suggest that God is the author of sin, which we have already shown to be impossible.

Yet, there is another interpretation that presents itself, and even harmonizes with everything we have established so far—i.e., כֹּל פָּעַל יְהוָה לַמַּעֲנֵהוּ וְגַם-רָשָׁע לְיוֹם רָעָה can be translated as follows: "The LORD works out[85] everything for its own answer[86]—even the wicked for the day of disaster" (Prov 16:4 NET). It would not be terribly inappropriate to translate the text as, "The LORD works out an answer for everything—even the wicked for a calamitous day." In any case, the text is not suggesting that God makes wicked people as such. Instead, what we learn here is that "God ensures that everyone's actions and the consequences of those actions correspond—certainly the wicked for the day of calamity. In God's order there is just retribution for every act."[87] Indeed, we have already seen that the wicked who manifest their sinfulness in horrendous deeds and recalcitrant unbelief will receive exactly what they want—*a godless existence.*

OBJECTION 4

Supralapsarianism is more rational. In the words of Reymond:

---

84. NRSV = "straightforward"; KJV = "upright"; NASB = "upright"; ESV = "upright"; NET = "upright."

85. "The Hebrew verb translated 'works' (פָּעַל, pāʻal) means 'to work out; to bring about; to accomplish.' It is used of God's sovereign control of life (e.g., Num 23:23; Isa 26:12)" (*NET Bible*, 1103n12). See also BDB, 821.

86. While the *NET Bible* translates לַמַּעֲנֵהוּ as "ends," the editors go on to explain that the "term has been taken to mean either 'for his purpose' or 'for its answer.' The Hebrew word is מַעֲנֶה ('answer') and not לְמַעַן ('purpose')" (*NET Bible*, 1103n13). See also BDB, 775.

87. *NET Bible*, 1103n13.

The infralapsarian scheme, by espousing the historical order of the decrees, reverses the manner in which the rational mind plans an action. The infralapsarian scheme moves from means (if, indeed, the earlier decrees can be regarded as means at all, disconnected as they are in purpose from the later decrees) to the end, whereas "in planning the rational mind passes from the end to the means in a retrograde movement, so that what is first in design is last in accomplishment,"[88] and, conversely, what is last in design is first in accomplishment.[89]

Response. There are two basic problems with this claim. First, the only way this kind of objection can have any teeth to it is if we abandon the doctrine of analogy and embrace univocism. For only then will we want to insist that God plans things out in the same logical order or way we humans do. It is, indeed, no surprise to us that Reymond gives a fairly long-winded defense of univocal God-talk in his oft-celebrated tome on theology.[90]

Second, note the words of the prophet Isaiah:

> To whom will you liken me and make me equal,
>   and compare me, as though we were alike? (46:5 NRSV)[91]

> Remember this and consider,
>   recall it to mind, you transgressors,
>   remember the former things of old;
> for I am God, and there is no other;
>   I am God, and there is no one like me,
> declaring the end from the beginning
>   and from ancient times things not yet done,
> saying, "My purpose shall stand,
>   and I will fulfill my intention,"

---

88. Quoting Berkhof, *Systematic Theology*, 119.

89. Reymond, "Consistent Supralapsarianism," 174.

90. Reymond, *New Systematic Theology*, 95–110.

91. When we combine this text, which speaks of God being *unlike* us, with other passages of Scripture, which speak of God being *like* us (see Gen 1:26–27; 2 Pet 1:4), we have biblical warrant for embracing the *analogia entis* between God and creation (see Kreeft, *Summa of the* Summa, 123–33).

calling a bird of prey from the east,
    the man for my purpose from a far country.
I have spoken, and I will bring it to pass;
    I have planned, and I will do it. (46:8–11 NRSV)

Notice, first of all, that God is not like us; therefore, we should not be too quick to believe that the order of the divine plan should be modeled after *our* mode of rationality. Indeed, I have already noted that I am neither supra- nor infralapsarian, for I think it is more proper to speak of an ordering of the divine omniscience than an order of the divine decrees. Isaiah's words here at least point us in that direction, for if YHWH knows "the end *from* the beginning," then the historical order *just is* the logical order. Indeed, our DVD analogy becomes pertinent at precisely this point. For when a person watches a DVD, she does not start at the end, even though that is obviously where the story is heading. She starts from the beginning and moves to the end. Similarly, the divine mind, which is simple and thus one with its knowledge, comprehends the entire world-ensemble of the actual universe in an eternal act of intuition. So it only makes sense that, analogously speaking, there would be a one-to-one correspondence between the way the divine mind conceives of this world and the way events fall out in time. This model seems far more comprehensive in its scale and hence more worthy of the God we worship.

SUMMARY AND CONCLUSION

We began our chapter by looking at an argument that, if sound, refutes the Reformed doctrine of unconditional election—namely, if God genuinely desires every person to be saved, then the doctrine of unconditional election cannot be true; but God genuinely desires every person to be saved; therefore, the doctrine of unconditional election cannot be true. This chapter was dedicated to a rigorous defense of the second premise of the argument. Based on texts such as 2 Peter 3:9, we can know for sure that the God of the Bible genuinely desires the salvation of every single human being.

Amazingly, there are those in the visible church who wish to do away with a universal divine benevolence and insist that God creates people for the purpose of destroying them in hell. Two basic contentions are sometimes given in favor of this perspective. First, there are those who believe the God of the Bible creates evil. Second, there are those who believe that, in the ordering of the divine decree, election and reprobation precede the decree of the creation and humanity's subsequent fall into sin. I carefully answered these contentions, noting that it is impossible for God to be the creator of evil and that the proffered ordering of the divine decree entails a host of difficulties for any Christian who desires to be faithful to Scripture and sound reason.

Having given a thorough defense of the second premise of the argument, what shall I say about the first premise? Is it closed under entailment? If it is, then what we accomplished in chapters 3–5 has been refuted. If it is not, then it is at least possible to reconcile universal benevolence and sovereign election. It is to such a reconciliation that we turn in our next chapter.

Excursus. Before we close this chapter, however, I think it is imperative that I offer the following warning to the reader, which illustrates why we need to take the doctrine of the hyper-Calvinist seriously. There is a danger in our doctrine of the universal love of God for all humankind—namely, *it can be easily abused.* This is most manifest in our culture, where God's love is just taken as a matter of course. It is often taken for granted, which is why so many in our day seem complacent when we tell them that they are loved by God. It is almost as if people think it's God's job to love them, and so they grow comfortable in their sin and refuse to seek the Savior with all their hearts. This is utter foolishness! We need to always remember that, while Scripture clearly reveals the universal, saving love of God, such love is not so much an emanation of his essence as it is an act of his free choice. To be sure, the essence of God is love (1 John 4:16), and so his love toward us would be, as it were, an emanation if we were intrinsically good. But we are not good. We have all sinned (1 John 1:8; Rom 3:23), and so we deserve the everlasting punishment of God (Rom 6:23; John 3:18). His love for us, then, is an act of free grace![92] As such, it should never be taken for granted!

---

92. This is the major difference between the Reformed and their Arminian, and even universalistic, friends. For the latter, God's love is not a choice but an emanation of his

7

A RAPPROCHEMENT BETWEEN UNCONDITIONAL ELECTION AND UNIVERSAL REDEMPTIVE LOVE

Calvin speaks much about God's justice and mercy, but little of His love.
Furthermore, he always limits God's mercy and love to the elect.
Indeed, how could it be said that God is merciful and loving toward
those whom He has predestined to eternal torment?
—*Dave Hunt*, What Love Is This?

Christ opens up the first cause, and, as it were, the source of our salvation,
and he does so, that no doubt may remain; for our minds cannot find repose,
until we arrive at the unmerited love of God. … Both points are distinctly
stated to us: namely, that faith in Christ brings life to all, and that Christ
brought life, because the Heavenly Father loves the human race,
and wishes that they should not perish.

essence, which is why it goes to everyone equally. See Walls, *Does God Love Everyone?*, 3–8; 75–78; and Thomas B. Talbott, "Universal Reconciliation and the Inclusive Nature of Election," in *Perspectives on Election*, 208–14. However, one can only wonder (contra Arminians) why divine love fails to actually accomplish the salvation of everyone; and one also wonders (contra universalists) why divine love emanates out to those who sinfully spurn God's love over and over again. As Warfield notes, divine love is tempered by divine righteousness; and so, while God's love naturally emanates to everyone, it does not do so once sin unnaturally taints the human nature. Thus, "to plead that his love has suffered an eclipse because he does not do all that he has the bare power to do, is in effect to deny to him a moral nature." Indeed, in light of human sin and rebellion, God no longer loves immanently but freely. So, rather than insisting that God saves all he can, we say that "God in his love saves as many of the guilty race of man as he can get the consent of his whole nature to save. Being God and all that God is, he will not permit even his ineffable love to betray him into any action which is not right. And it is therefore that we praise him and trust him and love him. For he is not part God, a God here and there, with some but not all the attributes which belong to true God: he is God altogether, God through and through, all that God is and all that God ought to be." See Benjamin B. Warfield, *The Plan of Salvation* (1915; repr., Eugene, OR: Wipf & Stock, 2000), 74.

... And he has employed the universal term whosoever, both to invite
all indiscriminately to partake of life, and to cut off every excuse from
unbelievers. Such is also the import of the term World, which he formerly used;
for though nothing will be found in the world that is worthy of the favour
of God, yet he shows himself to be reconciled to the whole world, when he
invites all men without exception to the faith of Christ.
—John Calvin, Commentary on John

Prior to either regeneration or faith, the Holy Spirit does convict the lost
sufficiently so that those who reject God's grace are wholly to blame for their
lost condition, and effectively in the elect, so that those who are saved must
acknowledge that their faith is wholly a gift of God.
—J. Oliver Buswell, Systematic Theology

In the previous chapter I offered a defense of the second premise of the following argument:

   (A) If God genuinely desires every person to be saved, then the doctrine of unconditional election cannot be true.

   (B) God genuinely desires every person to be saved.

∴ (C) The doctrine of unconditional election cannot be true.

So, having defended (B), we turn to the major premise—(A) *If God genuinely desires every person to be saved, then the doctrine of unconditional election cannot be true.* Indeed, we have seen a good number of Calvinists (including Calvin himself) accept (B). Thus, in order for the Arminian or conditional view of election to follow through, (A) must be established by demonstrating that the proposition is closed under entailment (i.e., the antecedent *logically necessitates* the consequent).

Unfortunately, most Arminian scholars we are familiar with just take it for granted that God's sincere desire for universal salvation negates the doctrine of unconditional election. Robert Shank, for example, tells us that "God 'desires all men to be saved and to come to a knowledge of the truth' (1 Tim. 2:4 RSV). That some men are lost reflects the fact that salvation, offered to all by the grace of God, is not unconditional."[1] Elsewhere in his book Shank says, "No 'hidden purpose' of arbitrary unconditional reprobation of the mass of mankind exists to impugn the sincerity and infinite compassion with which God addresses himself to all the sons of men."[2] Notice that Shank just assumes that *all* Calvinists believe reprobation is unconditional. However, as we saw in chapter 6, this assumption just isn't true! Geisler draws the following inference from 1 Timothy 2:4 and 2 Peter 3:9 in a rather tortured statement: "In short, it is God's ultimate and sovereign will that we have free will to resist His will that all be saved."[3] Again, no line of reasoning is offered to support this bare claim.

Fortunately, there are Arminian scholars who have offered an actual argument to secure the point that sovereign election is incompatible with universal love. One such scholar is Jerry Walls, who argues as follows:

1. God truly loves all persons.
2. Not all persons will be saved.
3. Truly to love someone is to desire their well-being and to promote their true flourishing as much as you properly can.
4. The well-being and true flourishing of all persons is to be found in a right relationship with God, a saving relationship in which we love and obey him.
5. God could give all persons "irresistible grace" and thereby determine all persons to freely accept a right relationship with himself and be saved.
6. Therefore, all persons will be saved.[4]

Clearly this argument entails a contradiction, since the conclusion contradicts (2). So, which premise should we give up? The universalist insists we should reject (2); however, we have already cited numerous biblical texts

---

1. Robert Shank, *Elect in the Son: A Study of the Doctrine of Election* (Minneapolis: Bethany, 1989), 124.

2. Shank, *Elect in the Son*, 97.

3. Norman L. Geisler, *Chosen but Free: A Balanced View of God's Sovereignty and Free Will* (3rd ed.; Minneapolis: Bethany, 2010), 103.

4. Jerry L. Walls, *Does God Love Everyone? The Heart of What Is Wrong with Calvinism* (Eugene, OR: Cascade Books, 2016), 30.

indicating that some will be damned. As Walls notes, for the Arminian, (5) is the premise we ought to give up. Of course, he also insists that God's grace is a necessary condition for faith; however, the grace given by God to the sinner is resistible.[5] For Walls the choice is clear: those who believe in unconditional election must give up (1)—i.e., the universal love of God.

Tu quoque, Arminius! There are several responses we can give to the Arminian line of reasoning reconstructed in the previous paragraph. In the words of Owen:

> And here, methinks, they place God in a most unhappy condition, by affirming that they are often damned whom he would have to be saved, though he desires their salvation with a most vehement desire and natural affection,—such, I think, as crows have to the good of their young ones: for that there are in him such desires as are never fulfilled, because not regulated by wisdom and justice, they plainly affirm; for although by his infinite power, perhaps, he might accomplish them, yet it would not become him so to do.
>
> Now, let any good-natured man, who hath been a little troubled for poor Jupiter in Homer, mourning for the death of his son Sarpedon, which he could not prevent, or hath been grieved for the sorrow of a distressed father, not able to remove the wickedness and inevitable ruin of an only son, drop one tear for the restrained condition of the God of heaven, who, when he would have all and every man in the world to come to heaven, to escape the torments of hell, and that with a serious purpose and intention that it shall be so, a vehement affection and fervent natural desire that it should be so, yet, being not in himself alone able to save one, must be forced to lose his desire, lay down his affection, change his purpose, and see the greatest part of them to perish everlastingly, yea, *notwithstanding that he had provided a sufficient means for them all to escape, with a purpose and intention that they should do so.*[6]

---

5. Walls, *Does God Love Everyone?*, 31–33.

6. John Owen, *A Display of Arminianism* (vol. 10 of *The Works of John Owen*; ed. John Goold; Carlisle, PA: Banner of Truth Trust, 1967), 50–51, italics original.

Recall Walls's third premise: "Truly to love someone is to desire their well-being and to promote their true flourishing as much as you properly can." Walls assumes that it would be improper to override the free will of a sinner so as to compel him to come to heaven.[7] However, we analyzed this presupposition in chapter 5 and found it wanting. Indeed, there are times when it is entirely proper to override the free will of someone; so if God desires anyone's salvation, no creaturely obstacle could or should stand in his way.

One should remember my exegesis of Scripture in chapters 3 and 6, wherein I demonstrate that the Bible really does teach two seemingly contradictory, truths—i.e., God unconditionally elects and universally loves. Recall also Spurgeon's insights from the prologue. There Spurgeon insisted on affirming whatever the Bible teaches, even if we have no idea as to how to reconcile its assertions. For a Christian committed to the truth of Scripture, it's better to contradict oneself than the word of God!

The reader should appreciate that Spurgeon's intuition is not wholly irrational. For there are good reasons to think Scripture is inspired by God.[8] If we are right about *that*, then we are being perfectly reasonable in believing that God is able to reconcile those biblical truths that are seemingly contradictory.

To be sure, we need to be extremely careful when accepting apparent contradictions as true. More than a few Christians have gone so far as to say that God operates with a totally different set of logical principles than we do, and before long they are affirming propositions that, when brought together, formally break the laws of logic. We need to always keep in mind that God is never illogical, though he is often supralogical; and so as long as

---

7. Walls, *Does God Love Everyone?*, 31–33.

8. See Norman L. Geisler, *Christian Apologetics* (2nd ed.; Grand Rapids: Baker, 2013); Benjamin B. Warfield, *The Inspiration and Authority of the Bible* (ed. Samuel G. Craig; Phillipsburg, NJ: Presbyterian & Reformed, 1948); Josh McDowell and Sean McDowell, *Evidence That Demands a Verdict: Life Changing Truth for a Skeptical World* (4th ed.; Nashville: Thomas Nelson, 2017); Michael J. Kruger, *Canon Revisited: Establishing the Order and Authority of the New Testament Books* (Wheaton, IL: Crossway, 2012); Roger Beckwith, *The Old Testament Canon of the New Testament Church* (Grand Rapids: Eerdmans, 1985); R. C. Sproul, *Explaining Inerrancy* (Orlando: Ligonier Ministries, 1996); Norman L. Geisler, ed., *Inerrancy* (Grand Rapids: Zondervan, 1980); Jason Lisle, *Keeping Faith in an Age of Reason: Refuting Alleged Contradictions in the Bible* (Green Forest, AR: Master Books, 2017); and Gleason L. Archer Jr., *Encyclopedia of Bible Difficulties* (Grand Rapids: Zondervan, 1982).

we have good reasons to think we are not affirming a formal contradiction with respect to God, then we are justified in accepting the mystery—*assuming, of course, that there is evidence for the propositions in question.*

Beyond the fact that the Bible says so, are there good reasons to think sovereign election and universal love constitute a mystery rather than a contradiction? I think so. For consider, first of all, Hugh Ross's insight that physics has proven the existence of no fewer than six dimensions in our universe beyond the four we experience (i.e., length, width, height, and time).[9] To get perspective on this, one may recall the book most geometry students are introduced to, wherein the characters all exist in a world with only two dimensions.[10] If I possess length and width, but have no height, then I will often confront ideas that, though seemingly contradictory to me, are easily resolved with an extra dimension. A circle and a square cannot be combined with each other in a two-dimensional plane; however, if one adds the dimension of height, one can combine the two figures into a cone.[11] When we take note of the fact that we are living in a universe in which the God who created it has access to dimensions that we cannot even imagine and even have difficulty conceiving, then it should become apparent to us that many of the paradoxes of Scripture (e.g., divine sovereignty/human freedom; divine unity/divine plurality; one person/two natures, etc.) can, at least in principle, be resolved on a higher plane. So, as long as no formal contradiction exists in our interpretation of Scripture, we are justified in believing in the mystery.

Of course, Walls, at this point, will insist that our current situation does not apply, since he has offered a formal argument demonstrating the logical incompatibility between sovereign election and universal love. Indeed, the problems facing his system do not automatically entail that we can do better! Hence we must face Walls's argument directly and demonstrate that it is unsound.

---

9. See Hugh Ross, *Beyond the Cosmos: The Transdimensionality of God* (Covina, CA: Reasons to Believe, 2017), 39.

10. See Edwin A. Abbott, *Flatland: A Romance of Many Dimensions* (1884; repr., ed. Philip Smith; Mineola, NY: Dover, 1992).

11. Obviously, we are not irrationally asserting that square circles can exist; we are simply pointing out that extra dimensions allow one to combine two ideas (or figures, as the case may be) in ways otherwise impossible.

Walls believes that, in order to maintain a doctrine of unconditional election (or irresistible grace), one ought to deny (1) God's universal love. I disagree. For consider premise "(3) Truly to love someone is to desire their well-being and to promote their true flourishing as much as you properly can." While I agree with this premise, I see an ambiguity in the phrase "as much as you properly can." As we have seen, those who oppose unconditional election locate this propriety in a (purportedly) divine principle to never overrule human freedom regarding salvation. Hence, propriety is ultimately located in the creature, whose free will is so sacred that not even God can touch it. But this brings us back once again to all of the problems I raised against Arminianism in chapter 5.

Calvinists locate propriety in the divine essence itself, insisting, as Warfield does, that God saves as many persons as his nature allows.[12] This indicates, as I demonstrated in chapters 2, 3, and 6, that it is logically possible for God to have morally sufficient reasons for creating a good world that becomes evil. And, as I have pointed out many times in this work, if creatures of their own free will become sinful, God is now free to love them in any way he sees fit. These presuppositions, in turn, allow for the following reconstruction of Walls's argument, which demonstrates a logical compatibility between sovereign election and universal love:

1.' God has a morally good and sufficient reason for creating a good world that becomes evil.

2.' God has a morally good and sufficient reason for creating a world wherein only some are saved.

3.' It is not the case that all persons will be saved.

4.' Truly to love someone is to desire their well-being and to promote their true flourishing as much as you properly can.

5.' The well-being and true flourishing of all persons is to be found in a right relationship with God, a saving relationship in which we love and obey him.

6.' No person deserves divine love of any kind, as it is defined in (3) & (4).

---

12. Benjamin B. Warfield, *The Plan of Salvation* (1915; repr., Eugene, OR: Wipf & Stock, 2000), 74.

7.′ God freely chooses to love all persons, in accordance with (3) & (4), as much as is properly consistent with his nature.

8. God could give *any* person "irresistible grace," whereby he effectually calls each and every person out of the darkness and into the light, thereby freeing him or her to place his or her trust in Christ.

9. It is not proper for God to give irresistible grace to every single person.

10. Therefore, universal love is not incompatible with sovereign grace.

The premises that will probably receive the heaviest assault are (8) and (9), presumably because it's contradictory to say that God gives grace to all but not to all. But notice that we intentionally changed the wording of (8), approximating Walls's (5) — i.e., "God could give all persons 'irresistible grace' and thereby determine all persons to freely accept a right relationship with himself and be saved." However, to say that God can give grace to any (our eighth premise) is not the same thing as saying that he can give grace to all (Walls's fifth). He can give to any in the sense that nothing in the creation prevents him from saving any creature; for as we argued in chapter 5, no creature-sinner is inaccessible to his Creator. He cannot give grace to all creatures only in the sense that there is something in his nature that prevents him from doing so. As Warfield says, "God in his love saves as many of the guilty race of man as he can get the consent of his whole nature to save."[13]

To be sure, the Arminian will want to know what it is about God's nature that makes it improper for him to give irresistible grace to all. However, as the theist is often just as perplexed as the atheist is as to why God allows evil to exist, but also wonders why her ignorance of God's reason for allowing evil proves the unreality of God, so also the Calvinist may be at a total loss as to what it is about the divine nature that precludes a universal distribution of irresistible grace; and yet this sad state of affairs in no way renders unconditional election and universal love logically incompatible.

What I have established, then, is an adequate *defense* of Calvinistic theism in light of the soteriological problem of evil. For as long as unconditional

---

13. Warfield, *Plan of Salvation*, 74.

election and universal love are possible, one is acting rationally in believing these two biblical doctrines even if one is unable to explain why exactly God has created a world wherein only some are saved. However, as I noted in the chapter 2, the goal of this work is to set forth an actual *theodicy*, not only for the problem of evil, but even the *soteriological* problem of evil. That said, even if this theodicy fails, this defense remains intact.

The following is my analysis of two theodicies in light of the soteriological problem of evil. The first is Molinism. The second is Reformed Thomism. While both schools of thought are consistent (at least, once one grants a handful of their basic presuppositions), the many problems we have already explored in Molinism (and more besides) render Reformed Thomism the more plausible view.

THE MOLINIST SOLUTION

We should recall from the fifth chapter that a common move Arminians make in order to preserve meticulous providence, libertarian freedom, divine prescience, God's universal salvific will, and conditional election is to embrace *middle knowledge*. However, the "father of middle knowledge" himself affirmed unconditional election. Indeed, the doctrine of the *scientia media* seems to entail an unconditional, rather than a conditional, view of God's salvific choice. We should also recall that Molina himself stressed God's desire to save everyone; and so it is not at all obvious that God's sovereign election and universal redemptive will are incompatible.

How does Molina reconcile universal salvific love with unconditional election? On Molinism, God surveys every feasible state of affairs and chooses that world-ensemble wherein the maximum number of people are saved. But we need to remember a few qualifications. First, it is perfectly rational to think that God had alternatives in making his choice. That is to say, there is more than one feasible world containing that maximum number of saved individuals. Indeed, there is quite possibly an infinite number of such worlds. The difference lies in the actual people who are freely saved in each feasible world that God middle-knows—e.g., in middle-world 1, Hitler, Mao, Judas, and Stalin all freely receive Christ as their Redeemer, while Calvin, Oliphint, Edgar, and Tipton freely reject him; in middle-world 2, Hitler, Mao, Judas, and Stalin freely reject Christ, while

Calvin, Oliphint, Edgar, and Tipton freely receive him as Savior; in middle-world 3, none of the people mentioned in middle-worlds 1 and 2 exist; and so on. All of these feasible worlds are made up of freedom-preserving circumstances that in no way constrain people to make the choices they make. Also, the circumstances include God's prevenient grace, which makes it genuinely possible for each individual to freely choose Christ. So, in each and every hypothetical world, God does manifest his sincere desire that all are saved. Yet, in choosing which world will become actual, God in no way takes into account the faith and/or works of anyone. He just chooses which world will obtain. "Thus God's choosing to elect or reprobate certain individuals by creating a world in which they would or would not attain to salvation rather than another world where they would freely do the opposite or not even exist has nothing to do with their freely chosen belief or unbelief; God simply, in his absolute sovereignty, selects the world he wants."[14] Herein lies the reconciliation between unconditional election and universal salvific love—that is, God's *direct* selection of a feasible world, wherein some freely choose a universally offered salvation and others reject it, *just is* an act of unconditional election; for in selecting such a world God does not take into account the actions of any person in that world and so, in an *indirect* manner, he unconditionally elects specific persons to be saved; and yet at the very same time, God is all the while providing prevenient grace to everyone, which is a sincere act of the God who would have all to be saved. In every feasible world, God desires the redemption of all and relishes the reprobation of none. As MacGregor goes on to say:

> At this juncture it must be emphasized that God is not guilty of foisting a divine sting operation on the reprobate, as the circumstances in the world he chooses to actualize (as well as every other feasible world) are freedom preserving and do nothing to cause either the reprobate to spurn prevenient grace or the elect to embrace it. Hence no one could legitimately complain before the throne of God, "Since I rejected you because of my unfortunate life circumstances, my condemnation is unfair." In this case, God would reply, "While

---

14. Kirk R. MacGregor, *Luis de Molina: The Life and Theology of the Founder of Middle Knowledge* (Grand Rapids: Zondervan, 2015), 151.

you freely chose to reject me in a world where you experienced various circumstances, those circumstances were irrelevant to your choice; you could have just as easily chosen to accept me under those same circumstances. So your condemnation is entirely fair as well as self-incurred." Consistently with his justice, then, God does not "set up" anyone for damnation in choosing to create a certain feasible world, as no feasible world is salvifically unfair.[15]

Thus we should recall the Molinist's dictum: "It is up to God whether or not we find ourselves in a world in which we are predestined unto salvation; but it is up to us whether or not we are predestined in the world in which we find ourselves."[16] Hence universal love and sovereign election are logically compatible.

A CALVINIAN REMONSTRANCE

Is Molinism fair? On the surface, it would appear so. The great Counter-Reformer has created a system that seems to bring all of the elements of the biblical view of election and salvation together beautifully and without strain. This is an impressive vision that, technically speaking, combines a doctrine of unconditional election with a universal divine desire for all to be saved.

However, once we dig a little deeper, there are significant problems in this view of election that are independent of the critique we have already lodged against the doctrine of middle knowledge in the fifth chapter.[17] First, notice that, on Molinism, God *directly* selects a feasible world to obtain, thereby *indirectly* electing persons unto salvation. But this seems contrary to Scripture, which portrays God as directly electing *persons* unto salvation, not *feasible worlds* containing those persons. Indeed, time and again we see the Lord placing his electing love on specific persons and/or groups of people, thereby ordaining them to eternal life. For example, in the famous text "I have loved Jacob, but I have hated Esau," notice that it is *persons* God is

---

15. MacGregor, *Luis de Molina*, 151.

16. William Lane Craig, "'No Other Name': A Middle Knowledge Perspective on the Exclusivity of Salvation through Christ," *F&P* 6 (April 1989): 179.

17. See appendix 2.

choosing, *not circumstances*; and this is confirmed a few verses later, where God proclaims, "I will have mercy on whom I have mercy, and I will have compassion on whom I have compassion," showing that the mercy of election is given to *specific creatures*, and not *selected circumstances*; and still later, God's decision to harden Pharaoh's heart clearly exemplifies the fact that reprobation concerns *free agents* and not merely *feasible worlds* (Rom 9:13, 15, 17–18; see Exod 9:16; 33:19). Indeed, as we demonstrated throughout chapter 3, the Scriptures are replete with assertions and allusions to the intimate nature of the divine electing love.

Secondly, despite MacGregor's insistence to the contrary, Molinism entails that God is setting up the reprobate to fail. Indeed, even when we grant that God in no way takes the actions of his creatures into account when choosing a feasible world to become actual, he undoubtedly does so with the full knowledge that, in choosing such a world, particular individuals are going to be damned. Just as a detective may set up a sting operation so as to ensure that a drug dealer is caught red-handed, God has set up a series of circumstances that ensure the damnation of the reprobate. Just as the judge at the trial can rightly say that the drug dealer could have acted differently, *for the sake of argument we will grant that*,[18] possibly, God can say that the reprobate could have believed differently. But none of this undermines the fact that, just as in any sting operation where a criminal is set up to fail, God has set up the failure of the reprobate by not creating a feasible world wherein they trust the Savior. Moreover, we *may* say that the detective acted justly toward the criminal and, similarly, we *may* (for the sake of argument)[19] say that God does the same toward the reprobate; and yet, just as we would never say that the officer acted *lovingly* toward the criminal, so also we should never say that, in creating this feasible world and not another, God acts lovingly toward the reprobate. Making and/or manipulating circumstances, even those that are "freedom preserving," so as to ensure an outcome may testify to one's wisdom, justice, insight, and sovereignty, but it says nothing favorable about one's love. Indeed, it positively denies it.

---

18. Why I only grant this for the sake of argument is made clear in my third point.
19. Why I only grant this for the sake of argument is made clear in my fourth point.

Third, I wonder whether the circumstances in which the reprobate is placed are truly freedom preserving. Indeed, the subjunctive conditionals God contemplates before creating the universe are, in the nature of the case, necessary truths whose truth-values are not at all determined by the free will of the creatures.[20] We say these must be necessary truths because, according to Molinism, in *every* hypothetical circumstance wherein "*p* finds himself in *c*, *p* would do *a* rather than ~*a*." To be sure, there are some feasible worlds where *p* does not find himself in *c*. In fact, there are numerous feasible worlds wherein *p* does not even exist. That said, in every feasible world wherein *p* finds himself in *c*, he chooses to perform *a* rather than ~*a*. Since every feasible world is also a logically possible one, we can also say that, in every logically possible world wherein *p* finds himself in *c*, it is true to say that he performs *a*. Necessary truths are such because they obtain in every logically possible state of affairs—e.g., the laws of logic are necessarily true, since there is no world wherein contradictions (for example) exist. These truths God naturally knows, prior to his decree. Contingent propositions are either those wherein the truth-value of a contradiction is yet to be determined (e.g., the divine natural knowledge that "*p* while in *c* does *a*" and "*p* while in *c* does ~*a*" are equally possible), or those that are dependent on some prior event or action or cause (e.g., the divine free knowledge that "*p* will do *a*," based on the divine creative decree). Notice that the subjunctive conditionals contemplated by the divine middle knowledge have truth-values and so are not mere possibilities being contemplated

---

20. See Campbell, "Middle Knowledge: A Reformed Critique," 7. This may seem to contradict the earlier criticism I gave of middle knowledge in appendix 2—namely, that the *scientia media* compromises the aseity of God insofar as it maintains that the creature, not the Creator, determines the content of the divine mind (i.e., God's middle knowledge). But this criticism, which we (again) maintain is most significant, simply takes the Molinist doctrine at face value. Indeed, the Molinist himself, at least when we unpack his own statements, tells us quite explicitly that the creature possesses counterfactual power over the content of the divine cognition. The criticism we are offering here—i.e., that the subjunctive conditionals making up the content of the *scientia media* are necessary rather than contingent truths—is a far more direct contradiction of what the Molinist doctrine actually teaches or wishes to convey. Indeed, the contingency of these subjunctive conditionals is the sine qua non of the creature having counterfactual power over their respective truth values. If this particular critique of Molina's doctrine is sound, then neither God nor the creature determines the truth values of these hypothetical states of affairs, in which case we are getting a severe dose of fatalism and/or determinism of the circumstances. Thus, these criticisms actually complement each other, for one demonstrates that Molinism compromises the biblical view of God, while the other shows how it compromises the biblical view of human freedom.

by the divine natural knowledge; nor are they true only posterior to the divine creative decree. Thus they are not contingent in any meaningful sense whatsoever. Since there are only two modalities—necessary and contingent—the subjunctive conditionals making up the divine middle knowledge are necessary truths that cannot *not* obtain in any hypothetical world describing their respective circumstances. "Therefore, between the two propositions, 'A will be, A will not be,' the necessity of one of them, at the very moment when I am uttering it, excludes the possibility of the other: 'From all eternity is the flow of imperishable truth.'"[21] Of course, if it is necessarily true that Judas, being placed in precisely those states of affairs described in the Gospels, would betray Christ, then his action could not have been otherwise, which *just is* a denial of human freedom.[22]

Finally, Molina's doctrine renders God unjust. I understand how this critique may sound when it reaches Molinists' ears, for one of their main motives in articulating the doctrine of middle knowledge is to ensure the goodness of God. Yet, just as their doctrine, despite all intentions to the contrary, compromises human free will, divine sovereignty, and divine aseity, so also does the *scientia media* compromise the justice of God. Notice that, on Molina's doctrine of unconditional election, God directly selects a world wherein his creatures will live, thereby unconditionally, albeit indirectly, electing certain persons to obtain salvation through the good use of their free wills. Notice, then, that God is indirectly choosing

---

21. Reginald Garrigou-Lagrange, *God: His Existence and Nature (A Thomistic Solution to Certain Agnostic Antinomies)* (5th ed.; trans. Dom Bede Rose; St. Louis: B. Herder, 1945), 2:84. We should recall that Molina and his disciples want to affirm the aseity of God. But this current critique I am offering exacerbates the problems inherent in middle knowledge. For, on the one hand, middle knowledge posits an infinite number of worlds containing subjunctive conditionals that are out of God's control, and yet contingent, and yet have nothing grounding their truth. But, on the other hand, Molina posits a divine cognition, including middle knowledge, that is wholly *a se*. Note, in response, the insights of the father of neo-Thomism: "In vain some Molinists seek to avoid this difficulty [of middle knowledge destroying human freedom via a determinism of the circumstances] by saying that God knows the truth of conditionally future things not in themselves but in His own essence, which contains eminently all truth." However, "It is clear that a contingent truth cannot be determined in the divine essence previous to any divine decree. [For] It would be present there *on the same grounds* as absolutely necessary truth, and hence would be a necessary truth" (Garrigou-Lagrange, *God: His Existence and Nature*, 2:84, italics original). This also raises problems against the doctrine of transworld damnation. Indeed, if there is no feasible world wherein, say, Judas believes the gospel, *then his unbelief is necessary* and hence he is not free.

22. For more on this, see Campbell, "Middle Knowledge: A Reformed Critique," 7–9.

creatures *qua creatures* (i.e., *not as sinners*) to find themselves in a world wherein they are either elect or reprobate. By extending election to world-ensembles rather than merely to creatures living inside a particular world, the Molinist is suggesting that God is choosing one good person over another good person to be saved. For it is the *essence* of Judas *as such* that God causes to exist in this world; and it is the *essence* of Peter *as such* that God causes to exist in this world. In and of themselves, *as mere creatures*, neither Judas nor Peter are evil or sinful—and thus, in and of themselves, *as mere creatures*, neither Judas nor Peter deserves damnation. Yet, by making this world and not another, God has ensured the damnation of Judas while also ensuring the salvation of Peter. God could have just as easily created a world containing circumstances wherein Peter is damned and Judas is saved; but by a sheer act of unmitigated and arbitrary sovereignty, the good essence of Judas Iscariot was placed in this world, thereby ensuring his damnation. This is supralapsarianism with a vengeance! The Molinist has outdone the hyper-Calvinist![23] However, since everyone intuitively knows that it is unjust for a judge to ensure the punishment of a good person, it is unjust for God to ensure the damnation of the essence, *considered as such*, of anyone. *Molinism, then, falls prey to the same critique we offered against Pelagianism in chapter 4!*

To be sure, Molinists feel justified in affirming their own brand of unconditional election, for they think they can find the very same teaching in Paul. Speaking of Jacob and Esau before their births, Paul tells us that "even before they had been born or had done anything good or bad (so that God's purpose of election might continue, not by works but by his call) she [Rebecca] was told, 'The elder shall serve the younger'" (Rom 9:11–12 NRSV). To state the inference from this passage given to us by MacGregor, "Thus God's choosing to elect or reprobate certain individuals by creating a world in which they would or would not attain to salvation rather than another world where they would freely do the opposite or not even exist has nothing to do with their freely chosen belief or unbelief; God simply, in his absolute sovereignty, selects the world he wants."[24] Notice again that, for

---

23. Especially those who place the decree of the election/reprobation of *sinners* as first in the logical order!

24. MacGregor, *Luis de Molina*, 151.

the Molinist, *it is worlds God is selecting* and *not* people; and notice again that, by suggesting that the divine election concerns world-ensembles rather than the intimate choice of specific persons within a particular world, God is indirectly choosing one good person over another. Yet, when we read Romans 9:11–12, we do not see anything about the selection of feasible worlds; rather, God is (again) choosing a person to be saved from within the specific circumstances in which she finds herself. Indeed, the promise is not stated in abstraction, but is concretely given while the twins are wrestling in the womb. So when Paul speaks of election preceding the births (*and, by extension, the merits*) of those he chooses, he is simply asserting that the grace of election does not take human works into account. All talk of feasible worlds, subjunctive conditionals, and the like is wholly foreign to Paul's intended meaning.

SUMMARY AND CONCLUSION

Molinism offers us a system that, if true, adequately reconciles sovereign election with universal benevolence. However, we have seen more than a few problems with Molinism throughout this work. In appendix 2 we see that the *scientia media* lacks biblical support and even compromises the biblical doctrines of the divine aseity and sovereignty. Here I have noted four basic problems with Molinism's doctrine of unconditional election: (1) it is unbiblical insofar as it contradicts the many scriptural examples of election being an intimate, covenantal, affair between God and his chosen people; (2) it is unloving insofar as it postulates a divine sting operation on the part of God; (3) it is contrary to human freedom insofar as the counterfactuals known by God via his middle knowledge are necessary rather than contingent truths; and (4) it is unjust insofar as God is portrayed as one who elects one good essence over another. Hence Molinism does not offer a plausible reconciliation of election and benevolence.

However, even if the Molinistic view of unconditional election is unacceptable, such does not mean that the Reformed tradition can do any better. How does the Calvinist articulate a doctrine of divine unconditional election that is consistent with itself and biblical revelation, while at the same time is also consistent with the divine desire that all come to repentance?

A REFORMED THOMIST RECONCILIATION

While the mystery of predestination cannot be fully comprehended by the human mind, there are good and helpful distinctions we can use to show that the universal divine benevolence and the particular divine predilection are, despite initial appearances to the contrary, noncontradictory. Indeed, such distinctions even go quite a distance in explaining how God is justified in his decision to unconditionally elect some even though he genuinely desires the salvation of everyone. How is it that texts such as Romans 9:16 (i.e., election is not based on the person who believes or works but on the God of mercy) and 2 Peter 3:9 (i.e., God desires every person to be saved) are noncontradictory? How can God at the same time desire the salvation of all and yet unconditionally choose some for salvation? The law of noncontradiction tells us that two contradictory propositions cannot both be true at the same time and in the same sense. Our contention is that God's desire for all to be saved and his desire that only some be saved are both true at the same time—or, to be more precise, they are both true in the now of the divine eternity—*but not in the same sense.* In other words, there is an equivocal use of the word "desire" being employed here, and so it is important to distinguish between desires or wills in God. Thus, to demonstrate this dual sense of the words "will" and "desire," when these terms are predicated of God, I will explain one way[25] in which the will of God is distinguished, offer several good reasons to think this distinction is both biblically and philosophico-theologically sound, and also give helpful illustrations of my main point.

One way the divine will can be distinguished is to note the difference between God's antecedent *will and his* consequent *will.*[26] If this distinction is even

---

25. Calvinism, of course, is not committed to merely one way of reconciling sovereign election and universal benevolence. Reformed theologians should welcome as many ways as possible, for the more ways there are to reconcile these truths, the greater is our confidence that our doctrine is coherent. To this end, I heartily recommend the solution offered by Guillaume Bignon, who offers a cogent defense of the distinction between God's decretive and preceptive wills. See Bignon, *Excusing Sinners and Blaming God*, 202–28.

26. While many Reformed theologians in history reject the antecedent/consequent distinction, it is clear that what most are arguing against is the *Arminian* version of the doctrine, not necessarily the teaching per se. Reformed theologians who seem to have rejected *all* versions of the antecedent/consequent distinction include John Owen, *Death of Death in the Death of Christ* (in vol. 10 of *Works*), 322–23; Carl Truman, "Puritan Theology as Historical Event: A Linguistic Approach to the Ecumenical Context," in *Reformation and Scholasticism: An*

possible, then we have even more reason to think that premise (A) of the Arminian argument from universal benevolence to conditional election does not follow through; and, if it is both reasonable and true (as I contend), it points us to a true justification and rationale for God's choice to permit evil to obtain, as well as allow some sinners to perish.

An exposition of the distinction between God's antecedent will and his consequent will. The term "antecedent" in this context means "prior to an event." The word "consequent" means "following as an effect or result" or "something posterior to an event or fact." Thus it is possible to distinguish the will of God as follows:

a/c *Antecedently* (i.e., before any fact, event, state of affairs, etc.), God desires that every human being gets saved;[27] *consequently* (i.e., after the fact, event, state of affairs, etc., in question), God wills that only the elect are saved.

To be sure, there is more than one way to interpret this proposition. Indeed, the Arminians also make a distinction between the antecedent and consequent will of God, stating that

---

Ecumenical Enterprise (ed. Willem J. van Asselt and Eef Dekker; Grand Rapids: Baker Academic, 2001), 269–73. The same *may perhaps* be said of Francis Turretin, *First through Tenth Topics* (vol. 1 of *Institutes of Elenctic Theology*; ed. James T. Dennison Jr.; trans. George Musgrave Giger; Phillipsburg, NJ: Presbyterian & Reformed, 1992), 226–31. One example of a Reformed theologian who makes a clear distinction between the Arminian/Lutheran version(s) of the antecedent/consequent distinction versus the Reformed/Augustinian version of the same, and even appears to accept the latter over the former, is Charles Hodge, *Systematic Theology* (Grand Rapids: Eerdmans, n.d.), 1:404. Buswell, as we have seen, advocates a distinction between sufficient and efficient grace, which actually presupposes the distinction between the antecedent and consequent will of God. See J. Oliver Buswell, *A Systematic Theology of the Christian Religion* (Grand Rapids: Zondervan, n.d.), 2:163. Edwards applies the sufficient/ efficient distinction to the fall. See Jonathan Edwards, "Entry 436," in *The "Miscellanies" (Entry Nos. a–z, aa–zz, 1–500)* (vol. 13 of *The Works of Jonathan Edwards*; ed. Thomas A. Schafer; New Haven, CT: Yale University Press), 485.

27. Notice that the Molinist cannot say this consistently; for, antecedently, the God of Molinism selects a world that (indirectly) ensures the damnation of many, and hence (logically speaking) he antecedently does not desire the salvation of everyone. Also, it would be a contradiction in terms to assert that God, consequently, savingly loves everyone, for then we would have a scenario wherein the simple will of God goes unfulfilled (which is impossible).

a/c' *Antecedently* (i.e., before taking human sin and unbelief into account), God desires everyone to be saved; *consequently* (i.e., after taking human faith [on the one hand] and human resistance [on the other hand] into account), God wills only elected believers (i.e., those elected because of their faith) to be saved.

We agree with the Arminian that a distinction between one's antecedent will and one's consequent will is reasonable and can even be seen in day-to-day discourse. For example, one can imagine that, going into trial, and antecedent to or before the evidence for a man's guilt is given, a judge desires that the accused man go free (since it is his natural disposition to assume a person is innocent until proven otherwise, he desires that all people are innocent and thus deserve freedom); but when the trial nears its end, and (so) consequent to or after the evidence for the man's guilt is given, the judge desires that the accused man is convicted and thus does not go free (since he is a just judge and will by no means acquit the guilty). So the Arminian may reason that God is like that judge—for, antecedent to considerations of a person's sin and/or faith, it is God's intense desire that everyone is saved; but consequent to considerations of a person's sin and/or faith (or lack thereof), it is God's desire that a person is saved or lost—depending on whether she has faith.

However, there are two problems with this version of the distinction. First, it is not clear that an Arminian (especially if he embraces middle knowledge) can consistently maintain that God antecedently loves everyone (see n. 27 above). Second, God's antecedent will is fulfilled only if human beings cooperate with it; and the consequent will is dependent on foreseen faith—which, we have seen, are not plausible premises.

The Reformed Thomist, however, can make use of the antecedent/consequent distinction without compromising the gratuity of election. As Thomas Aquinas explains:

> According to Damascene ... [the things God wills that are not fulfilled, e.g., his desire that every person is saved,] are [to be] understood of the antecedent will of God; not of the consequent will. This distinction must not be taken as applying

to the divine will itself, in which there is nothing antecedent nor consequent [since, after all, it is simple in and of itself], but to the things willed [i.e., effects]. To understand this we must consider that everything, in so far as it is good, is willed by God. A thing taken in its primary sense, and absolutely considered, may be good or evil, and yet when some additional circumstances are taken into account, by a consequent consideration may be changed into the contrary. Thus that a man should live is good; and that a man should be killed is evil, absolutely considered. But if in a particular case we add that a man is a murderer or dangerous to society, to kill him is a good; that he live is an evil. Hence it may be said of a just judge, that antecedently he wills all men to live; but consequently wills the murderer to be hanged. In the same way God antecedently wills all men to be saved, but consequently wills some to be damned, as His justice exacts. Nor do we will simply, what we will antecedently, but rather we will it in a qualified manner; for the will is directed to things as they are in themselves, and in themselves they exist under particular qualifications. Hence we will a thing simply inasmuch as we will it when all particular circumstances are considered; and this is what is meant by willing consequently. Thus it may be said that a just judge wills simply the hanging of a murderer, but in a qualified manner he would will him to live, to wit, inasmuch as he is a man. Such a qualified will may be called a willingness rather than an absolute will. Thus it is clear that whatever God simply wills takes place; although what He wills antecedently may not take place.[28]

Or, in the words of Garrigou-Lagrange: "Antecedently God wills a thing according as it is good in itself, for example, that all men be saved, that all His commands be ever fulfilled." In other words, the antecedent will of God is a wish or desire that something is so, but it is not a purpose or a decree

---

28. Thomas Aquinas, *Summa Theologica* (trans. Fathers of the English Dominican Province; Allen, TX: Thomas More, 1948), Ia.19.7.

that it *will* be so. God's antecedent will or desire considers human beings as his *creatures*, but does not take into account all that they have chosen (whether good or evil) in their particular circumstances. As he goes on to say, "at the same time [i.e., consequently] He permits to some extent the opposite evil for the sake of a greater good."[29] That is, the consequent will of God is directed toward human beings, warts and all, in the particular circumstances in which they reside; it takes into account the choices (both good and evil) that humans have made. Via his consequent will, God chooses to permit a particular person to either resist his will, commit sin, or choose not to have faith, or he gives a particular person intrinsically efficacious grace—thereby ensuring his conversion.

God's antecedent will, then, is his benevolence (i.e., good [*bene*] will [*volo/velle*]) directed toward all people. Love, by definition, is to will the good of another. Hence, *to will the good* of every person is *to love* every person. God's antecedent will is his love for all, manifested in a sincere desire that all of his creatures have an eternal love relationship with him. This is the will of God that all of us resist throughout our lives. All of us sin against this will, resist it, and suppress the grace manifested through it in unrighteousness. It is partly because of our reaction to God's antecedent will that the Great Being is wholly (morally) free to do with us as he wills. The consequent will, then, takes into account the creatures' sin and resistance to his gracious overtures. So Thomists commonly note that, just as a sea merchant may antecedently will to retain his merchandise, but when caught in a storm with his life in danger he consequently wills to throw his merchandise overboard; so also God may antecedently will the salvation of all, but for the sake of a greater good, he may consequently permit many to perish.

The key in all of this is the principle of "the greater good." I believe God antecedently wills that all the fruits of the earth become ripe, and yet for the sake of a greater good, he consequently wills to permit this to not happen in some cases; God antecedently wills that Adam and the woman not fall, but for the sake of a greater good, he consequently wills to permit

29. Reginald Garrigou-Lagrange, *Grace: Commentary on the Summa Theologica of St. Thomas*, I*II*, q. 109–114 (trans. Dominican Nuns of Corpus Christi Monastery in Menlo Park, CA; St. Louis: B. Herder, 1952), 184.

their fall into sin; and God antecedently wills for everyone in the human race to achieve salvation, but in light of their fall into sin, and for the sake of a greater good, he consequently wills to permit some to remain in their sinful condition while electing others unto salvation. What is the greater good that motivates God to *not* accomplish all that he antecedently wills? Both Calvinists and Thomists answer that the greater good has to be God himself—*the summum bonum or the highest good*—along with the glory he displays in particular election (whereby he manifests the goodness that is grace and mercy), as well as the honor he receives in reprobation (whereby he manifests the goodness that is justice).[30] Hence, the words of Warfield: "God in his love saves as many of the guilty race of man as he can get the consent of his whole nature to save."[31]

However, if God himself is the greater good that motivates him to not accomplish all that he antecedently wills, am I not suggesting here that God is a moral monster? No! But isn't it immoral for God to place his own glory over the needs of the creature? No! Isn't it immoral for God to love himself more than he loves any creature? No! In fact, it would be immoral for God to do anything less than love himself more than any creature. It would be unethical for him to rank his own glory as less than or even equal to anything else. For the absolutely holy and righteous Being is our *summum bonum*, the greatest conceivable Being and, since he is of infinite intrinsic value, he deserves the highest honor and praise and love conceivable—both *from the creature* and *from himself*. In the words of Wayne Grudem:

> Reformed theologians say that God deems his own glory more important than saving everyone, and that (according to Rom. 9) God's glory is also furthered by the fact that some are not saved. Arminian theologians also say that something else is more important to God than the salvation of all people, namely, the preservation of man's free will. So in a Reformed system God's highest value is his own glory, and

---

30. This answers the question raised earlier with respect to Walls's argument against unconditional election; that is, there is something about God's nature that renders it improper for him to grant saving grace to everyone.

31. Warfield, *Plan of Salvation*, 74.

in an Arminian system God's highest value is the free will of man. These are two distinctly different conceptions of the nature of God, and it seems that the Reformed position has much more explicit biblical support than the Arminian position does on this question.[32]

But how, exactly, is God glorified in a world wherein only some are saved? Paul suggests an answer in Romans 9:21, where he insists on God's right to make from the same lump of clay one vessel for honorable use (the elect) and another for common use (the reprobate). He then asks: "What if God, although willing to demonstrate His wrath and to make His power known, endured with patience vessels of wrath prepared for destruction? And *He did so* to make known the riches of His glory upon vessels of mercy, which He prepared beforehand for glory, *even* us, whom He also called, not from among Jews only, but also from among Gentiles" (Rom 9:22–24). Paul suggests here that the reason the world exists is that God wants a reality, distinct from himself, that reflects all of his attributes in all their varied splendor. The more his creation reflects his essence, the more he takes pleasure in it and is thereby glorified.[33]

Many Calvinists, at precisely this point, say that God needs to express his wrath on something and thus plans everything out the way he does so that this need can be met. This very strange doctrine has raised the ire of Arminians, who rightly question the sanity of it all.[34] The presupposition such Calvinists apparently have is that wrath is an attribute of God.[35] However, wrath is not an attribute but an activity; i.e., it is the *act of*

---

32. Wayne Grudem, *Systematic Theology: An Introduction to Biblical Doctrine* (Grand Rapids: Zondervan, 1995), 684.

33. For a full exploration of this perspective, see Jonathan Edwards, *Concerning the End for Which God Created the World* (part I of *Two Dissertations*; vol. 8 of *The Works of Jonathan Edwards*; New Haven, CT: Yale University Press, 1989); and John Piper, *God's Passion for His Glory: Living the Vision of Jonathan Edwards (With the Complete Text of* The End for Which God Created the World*)* (Wheaton, IL: Crossway, 1998).

34. See Walls, *Does God Love Everyone?*, 48–51.

35. In what is perhaps the most famous modern work on the attributes of God, J. I. Packer writes, "And wrath, the Bible tells us, is an attribute of God." See *Knowing God* (Downers Grove, IL: InterVarsity Press, 1993), 148. This is a most unfortunate error in an otherwise excellent study of the divine essence. Indeed, as one reads through his chapter on divine wrath, it becomes clear that Packer is confusing the term "attribute" with "activity." For example, "The

God whereby he rationally and justly punishes those who sin against him. Wrath is not an attribute, but eternity, for example, is. So what is it that God wishes to display? His attributes. What are his attributes? Goodness is one of them. So, for example, God wants to create a world wherein his goodness is displayed in all its varied splendor as much as is possible in a finite creation. One aspect of the divine goodness is justice, and another is mercy. However, God cannot display his mercy in a world wherein everything and everyone is good. For those who are good have earned their blessings, in which case God *justly* gives them their due. But in a world wherein there is evil, God is able to display his justice and mercy in all their variety—to those who are good, he justly blesses; to those who are evil, he justly condemns; to those who repent, he kindly shows mercy. Wrath, then, is *not* the endgame for God. *Grace is!*

But if God allows evil to obtain for the sake of grace, is he not thereby morally culpable for the evil he allows? He brought a world into being knowing that evils would happen. How does this fact not accentuate the problem of evil? For God knew that particular evils would occur before he

---

wrath of God in Romans denotes God's resolute action in punishing sin" (*Knowing God*, 154). But clearly there is a distinction to be made between God's unchanging attributes and his changing activities. The former describe qualities that are true of God's nature, which inhere wholly, simply, and eternally in YHWH. The latter describe the effects that flow out of the one eternal decree and are temporal, diverse, discreet, quantitative, and varied. So the same author who tells us that God is the same today, yesterday, and forever (unchanging essence) also tells us that God has revealed himself in many portions and in many ways (changing effects)—see Heb 1:1-3; 13:8. Thus, the divine eternity is an attribute, while creation is an activity; goodness is an attribute, while blessing is an activity; knowledge is an attribute, while planning is an activity. If we fail to make a distinction between what God *is* and what God *does*, we end up confusing the creature with the Creator and, possibly worse, making God the author of evil.

The issue as to whether wrath is an attribute or an activity is a case in point. If wrath is an attribute, then God has been wrathful from eternity and hence *must* manifest his wrath somehow. For it makes as little sense for him to be a God of wrath with no one to punish as for him to be a God of love with no one to bless. Hence God *had* to create this world and allow it to fall into sin so that he could punish sinners. Sin and evil, then, are *necessities* that God had to bring about in order for him to manifest his anger. In short, evil and sin cannot not exist, and God, being their author, was moved by his wrathful nature to ensure their coming into existence. Not only so, but we are now forced to embrace a sort of eschatological pessimism, wherein good shall never wholly triumph over evil. All of this, of course, compromises the goodness of God, along with his freedom in deciding to create in the first place! Not only so, but it contradicts the biblical eschatology of optimism, wherein God assures us that good will ultimately prevail over evil (Isa 2:1-4; 9:1-7; 11:1-10; 65:17-25; Mic 4:1-5; 1 Cor 15:1-58; Rev 21:1-27). In short, conceiving of wrath as an attribute of God, rather than an activity, undermines both theism and biblical authority.

even created the world and yet went on creating anyway! It is precisely at this point when we should remember the law of double effect. To illustrate this law: a pregnant woman who has cancer undergoes chemotherapy, not to kill her unborn child but to preserve her life, and hence she is not morally culpable for the child's death (i.e., she is not in any way guilty of murder)—even though the child's certain demise is an unintended, albeit foreknown, consequence of her actions. Similarly, God brings a world into being knowing it would contain much evil and sin, not because he intended those evils and sins to occur, but in order to manifest his attributes in all their splendor. Hence he is not morally culpable for the evils that obtain— i.e., he is not guilty of their coming to pass—for their certain occurrence is an unintended, albeit foreknown, consequence of his creation of this world-ensemble.

To be sure, God's own intrinsic right to glorify himself in redeeming some and not others should not be construed as the *only* justification for the divine decision to create a world wherein evil obtains and many are damned. Indeed, given the infinite nature of the divine wisdom (Ps 147:5), who are we to limit God to only one reason and/or means for justifying what he does!

I think there are at least two more considerations that render the divine decision to make a world wherein sin and damnation obtain is justifiable. But, before I offer these reasons, we need to take into account the clear difference between a *quantitative* good and a *qualitative* good. A quantitative good is one that is distributed to a large number of people—e.g., *quantitatively*, it is good that everyone's stomach is filled with food, even if that food is unhealthy (for it is better to eat an unhealthy meal, such as a bowl of worms, than to starve to death). A qualitative good is one that is desired for its own sake and has intrinsic value in and of itself—e.g., *qualitatively*, a healthy meal, consisting of fresh fruits and vegetables and proteins eaten by a few, is better than an unhealthy meal consumed by all. Indeed, no one desires an unhealthy meal as such. A person only partakes of an unhealthy meal, such as the worms just mentioned, in times of desperation.

Now it seems to me that there are qualitative goods that simply cannot obtain in a world lacking any evils whatsoever, as well as one wherein everyone freely chooses not to sin. For example, while humans bear the divine image, rendering them intrinsically valuable, no human is of infinite worth since no human is unlimited. However, the act of God whereby he incarnates himself as one of us does no less than ensure that the human nature as such is of infinite value, since it has been united to the divine essence. To be sure, there are theologians in the Christian tradition who have insisted that Christ would have become incarnate had humans remained unfallen. I see no need to enter that debate here! Our point is that, apart from human sin, a divine incarnation as human flesh is an infinitely qualitative good; but if the human race falls into sin, resulting in their condemnation, and so faces the genuine possibility of being damned, then yet another infinitely qualitative good becomes a reality in our world— namely, an act of incarnation *that is redemptive* in character. Thus, had God not allowed humans to fall into sin, the infinitely qualitative good of *redemptive* incarnation would have never obtained. Yet, a world wherein the *genuine* possibility of damnation obtains *just is* a world wherein some, at least, actually experience damnation.[36]

Other qualitative, albeit finite, goods that could never have obtained in a world without evil and sin and suffering are the various virtues one obtains via these factors. If there is no evil, then the virtue of the *courage* it takes to fight it would have never obtained. If there were no sin, then the virtue of *perseverance* would have never been developed in the human soul. If there were no suffering, then the virtue of *patience* could never be manifested.[37] Also, for these to be actual virtues of the person possessing

---

36. At this point the reader may be tempted to specify this general principle—as if to say, the reason God permits *this* particular person, as opposed to another, to remain in his sins is because he wants a world wherein the genuine possibility of damnation obtains. But we need to remember that we are talking about why God chose one *kind* of world to exist rather than another; when one gets to specifics—i.e., God's predilection of one individual over another— we are now firmly in the realm of mystery. In the words of Garrigou-Lagrange, "The solution of this problem, that God permits evil only for some greater good, is at once clear and obscure; it is clear in the abstract and in general but obscure in the concrete and in particular, because only in heaven shall we see this greater good because of which God permits evil." Reginald Garrigou-Lagrange, *The Trinity and God the Creator: A Commentary on St. Thomas' Theological Summa, Ia, q. 27–119* (trans. Frederic C. Eckhoff; St. Louis: B. Herder, 1952), 502.

37. Once again, I think it is inappropriate to take these general principles and apply them to any specific instance of suffering or evil. It would be the height of presumption, let alone the lack of empathy accompanying it, to say to a person currently going through a trial and/ or suffering in some way, "The reason God is allowing this to happen is to give you the virtue of patience." Again, I am speaking about the type of world God has chosen to create, not the specific plans he has for each individual in that world.

them, they have to be the result of genuine choices the person has made. Hence the qualitative, albeit finite, good of *human free agency that resists evil* can only exist in a world containing evil and suffering. Such a world, in the nature of the case, must therefore possess the genuine possibilities of destruction, anarchy, tyranny, sin, despair, and so on.[38]

Hence, in order to do justice to both God's desire to save all, as well as his unconditional choice of some, I first and foremost presuppose an absolutely sovereign God who is wholly *a se*. Second, I affirm that, for several justifiable reasons (mostly known only to himself, some partially revealed to us), God decrees this universe to obtain and not another—a good world that becomes evil, possessing within it the genuine possibilities of destruction, death, and damnation for many. Thus we cannot affirm a/c′, but rather

> a/c″ *Antecedently*, God desires everyone to be saved, thereby giving every human being a sufficient grace that renders it genuinely possible for them to believe; however, God chooses to glorify himself in a world in which evil exists and only some are saved instead of a world in which there is no evil and/or all are saved—for only in a world wherein genuine evils occur, including the evil of the recalcitrant rejection of divine truth, can otherwise unobtainable

---

38. One will notice that I am appealing to what are traditionally known as the "soul-making theodicy" and the "freewill theodicy." The difference between what I am advocating and what most other advocates of the freewill theodicy assert is that (1) I believe God could have created a world wherein everyone freely does not sin, and (2) I think God could have created a world wherein everyone freely chooses God's plan of salvation. As we have seen, these are two premises Arminians, and even Molinists, reject. Where I agree with Arminians and Molinists on this score is that certain qualitative goods—e.g., redemptive incarnation, patience, courage, creaturely freedom, etc.—cannot obtain apart from a world containing the kinds of evils we experience on a day-to-day basis. And, as far as the issue of freedom is concerned, it should be clear that I believe quite strongly that human beings possess the power of free choice, even after the fall. If we were not free agents, God would be unjust in holding us accountable for our sins. My concern with open-view theists, Molinists, and classical Arminians is not so much their definition of freedom—though my own views concerning the freedom of the will are still being refined—but their affirmation of human autonomy insofar as they insist that there are possibilities, or at least feasibilities, beyond God's control. For, as we have seen multiple times, these perspectives suggest that human beings in some sense are able to act independently of God, which is unbiblical in the extreme. While I disagree with their Arminianism/Molinism, I find the insights found in the following works extremely helpful in dealing with the intellectual problem of evil: Douglas R. Geivett, *Evil and the Evidence for God: The Challenge of John Hick's Theodicy* (Philadelphia: Temple University Press, 1993); Alvin Plantinga, *God, Freedom, and Evil* (Grand Rapids: Eerdmans, 1974).

goods obtain (e.g., redemptive incarnation, justice, patience, freedom, courage, etc.); *consequently*, God effectually wills that certain sinful persons, his elect, be saved by giving them an intrinsically efficacious grace that moves them to believe, while also permissively willing other sinners, the reprobate, to damn themselves via their resistance to sufficient grace.

An important point we should make is that, on this understanding of the divine will, the God of Reformed Thomism does no less for the reprobate than the God of Arminianism. According to the Arminian, God gives sufficient (or, better still, *extrinsically* efficacious) grace to everyone;[39] the same can be said of the Reformed Thomist. Again, we are contending that God does no less for the reprobate than Arminians assert. However, according to the followers of Augustine, Thomas, Calvin, Bullinger, and others, God does provide effectual (or, better still, *intrinsically* efficacious) grace to the elect alone. He gives a grace to some that he does not give to others; or, better still, he sovereignly brings his sufficient grace to full fruition in some (thereby making it effectual), while allowing others to fall short of the end for which that grace is given. Thus God's antecedent will makes it actually possible for all human beings to be saved—*if they would but answer the call to faith*—by providing extrinsically efficacious grace to everyone (elect and reprobate); however, in light of the resistance to his sufficient grace by every single human being (Christ excepted), God's consequent will permits the reprobate to resist the external call of the gospel, while also intrinsically and efficaciously—"sweetly and suavely"—moving the elect to *freely* trust in Christ.

Two broad lines of evidence support the distinction between God's antecedent will (manifested in sufficient grace) and his consequent will (manifested in permissive preterition and [intrinsically] efficient grace). First, the Bible offers evidence for this distinction. Second, there is one good philosophico-theological argument for the distinction.

---

39. An exception here would be Laing, who denies that God gives grace to the reprobate, seemingly rendering God unloving toward many persons. See John D. Laing, *Middle Knowledge: Human Freedom in Divine Sovereignty* (Grand Rapids: Kregel, 2017), 117.

BIBLICAL ARGUMENTS FOR THE
DISTINCTION BETWEEN THE ANTECEDENT
WILL AND THE CONSEQUENT WILL

It is indeed difficult to read 2 Peter 3:9 and not come to the conclusion that God really does desire the salvation of every human being; but it is equally difficult to read Romans 9 and not conclude that God wills that only his elect are saved. The antecedent/consequent distinction seems to reconcile these texts quite nicely. Another passage of Scripture that apparently affirms God's universal desire for everyone's salvation is 1 Timothy 2:4. But what happens when we place this verse alongside a similarly worded passage in its twin epistle? Here are the two texts:

> This is right and is acceptable in the sight of God our Savior, who desires everyone to be saved and to come to the knowledge of the truth. (1 Tim 2:3–4 NRSV)[40]

> And the Lord's servant must not be quarrelsome but kindly to everyone, an apt teacher, patient, correcting opponents with gentleness. God may perhaps grant that they will repent and come to know the truth. (2 Tim 2:24–26 NRSV)

---

40. The common interpretation of this verse among Christians in general is disputed by many formidable exegetes in the Reformed camp. More than a few take the verse to be saying that God simply desires all *kinds* of people to be saved, not that God genuinely desires the salvation of *everyone*. Aquinas himself leaned in favor of this view. See, e.g., *ST* Ia.19.7; *Commentaries on St. Paul's Epistles to Timothy, Titus, and Philemon* (trans. Chrysostom Baer; South Bend, IN: St. Augustine's Press, 2007), 25. I will not engage in a lengthy response to this common Calvinistic interpretation. However, I point the reader to Spurgeon's comments on this text in the prologue. Also consider the words of Machen: "It has been suggested that the phrase 'all men' in this verse in 1 Timothy means 'all sorts of men,' and that the verse is directed against those who limited salvation to the Jews as distinguished from the Gentiles or to the wise as distinguished from the unwise. There is perhaps something to be said for such a view because of the context in which the verse occurs. But I am rather inclined to think that the phrase 'all men' is to be taken more strictly, and that the verse means that God takes pleasure in the salvation of the saved, and does not take pleasure in the punishment of those who are lost, so that so far as His pleasure in the thing directly accomplished is concerned He wishes that all men shall be saved." J. Gresham Machen, *The Christian View of Man* (1937; repr., Carlisle, PA: Banner of Truth Trust, 1965), 72. Interestingly, Machen affirms this interpretation in a chapter where he defends the Reformed doctrine of unconditional election.

To the very same student, Timothy, Paul is insisting, on the one hand, that God desires everyone to come to a knowledge of the truth, and yet, on the other hand, God may *perhaps* grant certain unbelievers the gift of repentance that leads to a knowledge of the truth. Notice here that Paul is not absolutely convinced that certain persons will be given the grace that leads to salvation. But why would God be unwilling to grant certain persons the grace that leads to a knowledge of the truth if he desires all people to come to a knowledge of the truth? I think the best answer to this question is that, while God *antecedently* desires everyone to be saved and to come to a knowledge of the truth, *for the greater good of his own glorification (among other reasons)*, God *consequently* wills to *not* grant the gift of faith to some while also giving it to others.

I think there are numerous biblical texts that indicate that God's disposition toward all human beings is the posture of open hands inviting everyone to receive his salvation. But God's desire is no *mere* wish. His goodness moves him to freely give grace to all people, rendering them genuinely able to come to Christ in faith. Hence his antecedent will that all are saved is not an abstract feeling that never touches the hearts of people; rather, it manifests itself in a sufficient grace that enables all to believe. For example, Paul is inspired to wish himself damned for the sake of many who are perishing (Rom 9:3); many are called, though few are chosen (Matt 22:14), indicating that more are invited than receive; Jesus is willing to tell a clearly unredeemed scribe in his day that he is not far from the kingdom of heaven (Mark 12:28-34);[41] Jesus mourns over Jerusalem, expressing his desire that all receive him, despite their resistance (Matt 22:37);

---

41. This is just one example in Scripture where we confront an individual who, on the one hand, does not believe and yet, on the other hand, is not a nonbeliever either (see, e.g., John 2:23–3:2; Acts 10:1–48; 17:24–27). We need a category for such a person—and, it would seem, the best word(s) to use is "wayfarer" or "seeker." But, of course, we are confronted with a problem, for Scripture clearly states: "There is no one who is righteous, not even one; there is no one who has understanding, there is no one who seeks God" (Rom 3:10–11 NRSV; see Pss 14:1–4; 53:1–3). Presumably, Paul is suggesting that *absolutely no one* seeks after God, unless of course they have trusted the Savior (Rom 3:21–28; 5:1; 9:25–33), and (of course) no one can trust the Savior apart from grace (John 6:44; Acts 16:14; Eph 2:8–9; Phil 1:29). But how is it that we have people who are clearly nonbelieving and yet also seeking? The answer must be that, *in and of themselves*, they would have never sought after God; but God has given them grace that moves them to seek after him. Yet, even after receiving such grace there is no guarantee that they will repent (2 Tim 2:20–26). The doctrine of sufficient grace brings all of this together beautifully and without strain.

Stephen laments that the religious leaders of his day continually resist the Holy Spirit (Acts 17:51); Paul says that the kindness of God ought to lead all to repentance (Rom 2:4) and that God's grace has appeared to all people (Titus 2:11). The first four texts clearly point to a divine will that all are saved (Rom 10:2), while the last three texts suggest a grace given to all that is so sufficient that everyone ought to believe because of it, though it can be (and often is) resisted by many if not all. Indeed, Paul also teaches us that his labor in the gospel is motivated by the fact that "we have our hope set on the living God, who is the Savior of all people, especially of those who believe" (1 Tim 4:10 NRSV). Nothing in the immediate context in any way suggests that Paul is limiting the "all" to "all types of people," or some such notion. Thus Millard Erickson, who is himself a Calvinist, comments on this verse as follows: "Apparently the Savior has done something for all persons, though it is less in degree than what he has done for those who believe."[42] But to do something for all persons, in this context, means that God has done something *savingly* for all persons; and this *just is* the essence of the doctrine of sufficient grace.

We could go on, but consider finally the famous text in Isaiah: [YHWH speaking] "What more was there to do for my vineyard that I have not done in it? When I expected it to yield grapes, why did it yield wild grapes?" (Isa 5:4 NRSV). Notice that the text does not say that there was nothing more that God *could* have done; rather, there is nothing more that he *needed to do* in order to expect people to bear fruit.[43] The text is not saying that God expected people to bear fruit, as if to say that he foresaw them bearing fruit and yet they falsified his prediction. Such an interpretation would violently contradict what Isaiah says elsewhere (Isa 40:13-14; 41:21-24; 44:24-28; 45:1; 46:8-11). Indeed, the expectation here is not one of foresight but one of command. God has given Israel abundant gifts of grace that render

---

42. Millard J. Erickson, *Christian Theology* (2nd ed.; Grand Rapids: Baker, 1998), 851.

43. This subtle point is lost on Jerry Walls and John Wesley (whom Walls cites), who both adhere to a common translation of Isa 5.4: "What more could I have done for you which I have not done." See Walls, *Does God Love Everyone?*, 70. This could lead one to think that God has already done all he can for people and so must watch in horror as they spurn his good graces, though such is not a necessary inference from this rendering. However, the NRSV offers the better rendition, which allows for the idea that God has done all he *needed* to do, but not necessarily all he *could* do. For a vindication of the NRSV's rendering, see Edward J. Young, *The Book of Isaiah*, vol. 1, *Chapters 1-18* (Grand Rapids: Eerdmans), 199n4.

them ready and able to produce fruit (Isa 5:1-2), but they have resisted his will and produced wild grapes instead. "I [YHWH] was ready to be sought out by those who did not ask, to be found by those who did not seek me. I said, 'Here I am, here I am,' to a nation that did not call on my name. I held out my hands all day long to a rebellious people" (Isa 65:1-2a NRSV). God is clearly calling, moving, and saying to recalcitrant sinners, "We entreat you on behalf of Christ, be reconciled to God" (2 Cor 5:20 NRSV), which makes little sense if God does not desire everyone's salvation or doesn't give grace to all (see Rom 10:21; Isa 45:22).

Equally certain is the fact that, while God's will (*in one sense of the term*) can be resisted, his will (*in another sense of the term*) *cannot* be resisted; for Paul himself rhetorically asks, *who can resist the will of God*, to which the obvious answer is, *no one* (Rom 9:19). Jesus explicitly says that all whom the Father gives to Christ will come to him in faith, and the one who does so will not be cast out by God, since no one can believe in Christ unless he is drawn by the Father (John 6:37, 44). Indeed, no one can enter the kingdom of heaven unless he is born from above, a birth that is not the result of the human will, but of God's Spirit (John 3:3; see also 1:12-13; Jas 1:18; 1 Pet 1:23). Faith, then, is a gift of God's grace (Acts 16:14; 1 Cor 1:30; Eph 2:8-9; Phil 1:29), "for it is God who is at work in you, enabling you both to will and to work for his good pleasure" (Phil 2:13 NRSV). Hence God is the one who distinguishes the elect from the reprobate (1 Cor 4:7; Rom 9:13). Indeed, while God has done something savingly for all persons, he has done even more for those who believe (1 Tim 4:10). So we have biblical warrant in affirming God's consequent will that always accomplishes its purpose in (intrinsically) efficaciously drawing sinners to saving faith (Acts 13:48; 16:14), as well as permitting other sinners to remain in their sin and unbelief (Acts 13:46; 1 Pet 2:8; Jude 4).

A PHILOSOPHICO-THEOLOGICAL ARGUMENT FOR THE ANTECEDENT/ CONSEQUENT DISTINCTION

My argument can be formulated in two stages. In stage one I demonstrate the reality of the antecedent will; in stage two I argue for the consequent will.

STAGE ONE: THE ARGUMENT FROM GOD'S GOODNESS TO HIS ANTECEDENT WILL

God is good, holy, and just. As such, he will never impose demands on the creature that the creature cannot accomplish. In the words of Augustine, "God does not command the impossible."[44] Now, the Scriptures teach that every human creature is totally depraved or full of sin and therefore unable to fulfill God's will (e.g., see Rom 3:9–18; 8:7–8; 1 Cor 2:14). Hence, love is not an emanation of the divine essence, but an act of grace freely chosen by God. Indeed, though nothing in the sinner obligates God to give the creature-sinner grace, there is something in God that moves him to be gracious to the sinful creature—namely, his righteous desire to produce good in his image-bearers as such. Hence, by his free grace and love he makes it genuinely possible for the creature to do his will, which includes coming to God in Christ through faith. Thus, God antecedently desires the salvation of every one of his human creatures, manifesting this desire via an extrinsically effectual grace that is given to each and every one of them that thereby makes it genuinely possible for each sinner to trust in Christ as he is offered in the gospel.

---

44. The entire quotation is as follows: "What he [Pelagius] says, however, is true enough, 'that God is as good as just, and made man such that he was quite able to live without the evil of sin, if only he had been willing.' For who does not know that man was made whole and faultless, and endowed with a free will and a free ability to lead a holy life? Our present inquiry, however, is about the man who 'the thieves' left half dead on the road, and who, being disabled and pierced through with heavy wounds, is not so able to mount up to the heights of righteousness as he was able to descend therefrom; who, moreover, if he is now in 'the inn,' is in the process of cure. God therefore does not command impossibilities; but in His command He counsels you both to do what you can for yourself, and to ask His aid in what you cannot do. Now, we should see whence comes the possibility, and whence the impossibility. This man [Pelagius] says: 'That proceeds not from a man's will which he can do by nature.' I say: A man is not righteous by his will if he can be by nature. He will, however, be able to accomplish by remedial aid what he is rendered incapable of doing by his [own] flaw." Augustine, On Nature and Grace 50, in Augustin: Anti-Pelagian Writings (vol. 5 of Nicene and Post-Nicene Fathers; ed. Philip Schaff; trans. Peter Holmes and Robert Ernest Wallis; rev. trans. Benjamin B. Warfield; Peabody, MA: Hendrickson, 1994), 138. Notice two important points here: First, when Augustine says that "God does not command impossibilities," he is clearly speaking of divine commands given to human beings in their fallen state and prior to their conversion. Second, and contrary to Pelagius, human nature, because it is fallen, is incapable of obeying the divine commands; however, God's grace renders our own obedience actually possible. All of this, of course, suggests an implicit endorsement of universal sufficient grace by Augustine. All fallen sinners, apart from grace, cannot comply with any divine command. But God will never command the impossible; therefore, God makes everyone genuinely able to obey him via his sufficient or extrinsically efficacious grace.

However, the antecedent will of God is not *intrinsically* efficacious, for it considers the human person merely as a creature, regardless of his circumstances and standing before God. But no good can be realized apart from its accompanying circumstances[45]—e.g., the good of health can only be realized in the context of a good diet, lack of disease, exercise, and so on; the good of childbirth can only be realized in the context of sexual intercourse and normal prenatal care. So a thing considered in its primary and absolute sense may be good, and yet with an accompanying circumstance may very well be turned into its opposite. For example, it is good for a judge to will the life of a person; but if that person proves to be a murderer, it is good for a judge to will his death. Hence, just because God antecedently wills that all of his human creatures, *as divine image-bearers*, are saved, we have no reason to think that such a desire on his part will actually effect their salvation; and, given their sin and resistance (*which is wholly from the creature-sinner, not God*) to his grace (which is *extrinsically* efficacious), it is good (or morally justifiable) for God to permit the continual resistance of some in such a state and, thus, to allow them to perish. Indeed, as contingent creatures humans have the potential to become corrupted or defective in some way; and so, "God can permit sin on account of a higher good and He is not bound always to preserve in goodness what is itself defective, for it is reasonable that a thing which is in itself deficient should sometimes evince a defection."[46]

STAGE TWO: THE ARGUMENT FROM PURE ACTUALITY TO THE CONSEQUENT WILL

Evil, by definition, is a lack of goodness that is owed. Evil is the privation of the good. God, because he is pure actuality (thereby possessing no potentiality in his being), cannot be lacking in anything—let alone goodness. Therefore, there can be no evil in his nature, nor can he will evil (for such a will would be lacking a good and proper end), nor can he induce his creatures to commit evil acts (or sins), nor can he be the author of sin and evil.

---

45. On Molinism, God indirectly elects persons by placing them in their respective circumstances; and so the good of election is accomplished apart from such states of affairs, thereby nullifying this commonsense intuition.

46. Garrigou-Lagrange, *Grace*, 224.

To be sure, he can permit evil to occur; and because of his omnipotence, God is always able to bring a greater good from the evil he allows—e.g., redemptive incarnation, the patience of the martyr, the courage of the soldier, and so on.

Because God cannot be the source or origin of corruption, evil must have its origin within the created realm—for creation, because it exists, is actual; but because it need not exist, is potential—i.e., the created realm is contingent, being a mixture of actuality and potentiality. In other words, evil can arise only where there is the potential for evil; but there is no potential (at all) in God (*actus purus*); hence, he can in no way be the source of evil; thus, evil has its ultimate and proximate origin in the only other realm there is (i.e., creation), for it is the only reality that has potential and thus the potential for evil. Any evil that obtains, therefore, must come wholly from the created order; and hence any sin committed (whether it be the disobedience of a divine command or the resistance to divine grace) must come wholly from the creature. God can *permit* evil and sin without impunity, but he can in no way *cause* it—metaphysically, because he is *actus purus*; morally, because he is the *summum bonum*.

Since God is, by definition, *the Good*, as well as the Source of everything that obtains in the universe (evil excepted), and since he is the Creator and Sustainer of the universe (out of nothing), any good found in the creature must have its ultimate origin in God himself. Now, the motive of God's bestowal of goodness to his creatures is his desire that they benefit from his benevolence—which, by definition, is love. In other words, "since God's love is the cause of goodness in things ..., no one thing would be better than another, if God did not will greater good for one than for another."[47] Or, "no one would be better than another were he not more loved and helped by God. This is the equivalent of St. Paul's: 'For who distinguisheth thee? Or what hast thou that thou hast not received?' [1 Cor 4:7]."[48] This is the principle of predilection—the act of God whereby he shows favor toward some that he does not show toward others. This entails, of course, that the reason some creature-sinners receive the good of eternal life, while others do not, is that God loves them more—i.e., he bestows his electing

---

47. Aquinas, *ST* Ia.20.3.
48. Garrigou-Lagrange, *Grace*, 435.

love and intrinsically effectual grace on them and passes over others. Hence he loves Jacob and hates Esau (Rom 9:13)—not in the sense that he looks on the latter with a vitriolic feeling of unmitigated anger, but in the sense that he loves him less than Jacob and/or gives mercy to one that he does not to give to the other.[49] In short, God savingly loves all sufficiently, but only some efficiently. Herein we find the reconciliation between sovereign grace and universal benevolence.

A final consideration in favor of the antecedent-consequent/ sufficient-efficient distinction is chiefly directed at Reformed Christians who are wary of this viewpoint—inspired as it is by Thomas Aquinas. That some of the best thinkers in the Reformed tradition often make a distinction regarding Christ's particular atonement—i.e., it is sufficient for all, efficacious only for the elect—should indicate that the Calvinist has a strong precedent within his own faith tradition for precisely this way of thinking. For clearly the atonement is the ultimate act of saving grace (Rom 5:8); hence its being sufficient for all and effectual for the chosen *just* is a distinction between God's sufficient grace and his efficient grace. But the sufficient-efficient distinction presupposes the antecedent-consequent will in God; and so, once a Reformed Christian embraces the former (as she does regarding the atonement),[50] consistency demands that she embrace the latter as well.

---

49. "This passage, as well as the one quoted in ver. 12, and just referred to, relates to the descendants of Jacob and Esau, and to the individuals themselves; the favour shown to the posterity of the one, and withheld from that of the other, being founded on the distinction originally made between the two brothers. The meaning therefore is, that God preferred one to the other, or chose one instead of the other. As this is the idea meant to be expressed, it is evident that in this case the word *hate* means to *love less, to regard and treat with less favour.*" Charles Hodge, *Commentary on Romans* (rev. ed., 1864; repr., Carlisle, PA: Banner of Truth Trust, 1986), 311–12. A slightly different approach is taken by Moo: "'Love' and 'hate' are not here, then, emotions that God feels but actions that he carries out. In an apparent paradox that troubles Paul (cf. 9:14 and 19 following) as well as many Christians, God loves 'the whole world' at the same time he withholds his love in action, or election, from some." Douglas J. Moo, *The Epistle to the Romans* (Grand Rapids: Eerdmans, 1996), 587. But see as well the more qualified comments in John Murray, *The Epistle to the Romans* (Grand Rapids: Eerdmans, 1968), 1:23–24.

50. John Owen wrote the magisterial work defending limited atonement that is widely considered to be greatest defense of the doctrine in history. He clearly upheld the distinction between the atonement's sufficiency and efficiency. In his own words: "It was, then, the purpose and intention of God that his Son should offer a sacrifice of infinite worth, value, and dignity, sufficient in itself for the redeeming of all and every man, if it had pleased the Lord to employ it to that purpose; yea, and of other worlds also, if the Lord should freely make them, and would redeem them. Sufficient we say, then, was the sacrifice of Christ

I am aware of four objections that have been thrown at this anteced-
ent-consequent/sufficient-efficient distinction that are worth answering.
The first two can be found in the literature, while the last two were given
in personal correspondence.

OBJECTION 1: REFORMED THOMISM
ENTAILS THAT GOD CAUSES PEOPLE TO SIN

Of course, I explored this objection in some detail here and in chapter 6, but
it may be helpful to offer several points that approach this issue from yet
another perspective. First, just as God cannot be the cause of evil in general,
he cannot be the cause of any particular evil or sin. Biblically, this fact is
established by texts such as James 1:12–18 (as we have seen). Philosophico-
theologically, we know that God cannot directly cause sin; for a precondition of being an agent who directly causes sin is to possess a defection in
one's nature, but God, who is *actus purus*, has no defect, therefore he cannot
directly cause sin.[51] Also, in the words of Garrigou-Lagrange, "God cannot
be the indirect cause of sin. To be the indirect cause of sin is to refrain

---

for the redemption of the whole world, and for the expiation of all the sins of every man in
the world." A few lines later he says that the atonement "was in itself of infinite value and
sufficiency to *have been made a price* to have bought and purchased all and every man in the
world." He goes on to say, "Hence may appear what is to be thought of that old distinction
of the schoolmen, embraced and used by divers protestant divines, though by others again
rejected,—namely, 'That Christ died for all in respect of the sufficiency of the ransom he paid,
but not in respect of the efficacy of its application;' or, 'The blood of Christ was a sufficient
price for the sins of all the world;'—which last expression is corrected by some, and thus
asserted, 'That the blood of Christ was sufficient to have been made a price for all;' which is
most true, as was before declared." Owen then draws an inference from this distinction: "If
there were a thousand worlds, the gospel of Christ might, upon this ground, be preached to
them all, there being enough in Christ for the salvation of them all, if so be they will derive
virtue from him by touching him in faith; the only way to draw refreshment from this fountain
of salvation." Owen, *The Death of Death in the Death of Christ* (1852; repr., Carlisle, PA: Banner
of Truth Trust, 1967), 183–85, italics original. What does Owen mean when he says "if it had
pleased the Lord to employ it to that purpose"? Presumably, it means that, *had God wanted*
the atonement to be sufficient for all, then it would have been. But he then goes on to say the
atonement was sufficient to redeem "every man in the world." So, which is it? Is the atonement
hypothetically sufficient or *actually* sufficient? I would like to believe that he affirms the latter
and that his former statement was a slip of the pen—though some of the other statements
given above draw me into doubt. In any case, I (at least) affirm that, if a reprobate person
were (*per the impossible*) to place his faith in Christ, the Lord would not have to come down
and die a second death for him. Indeed, the atonement is actually sufficient to save any and
all persons, including those whom God has not elected; but the intention or design or efficacy
of the atonement is for the elect alone.

51. Garrigou-Lagrange, *Trinity and God the Creator*, 504.

from preventing it when we can and should prevent it. But according to His wisdom and justice God is not bound to prevent the sins which He permits. Therefore, when God does not provide the help to avoid sin, He is not the indirect cause of sin."[52] Proof of the minor premise is provided by Aquinas:

> [There is a difference between a person] who has care of a particular thing, and one whose providence is universal, because a particular provider excludes all defects from what is subject to his care as far as he can [e.g., a good house servant will try his best to make sure everything in the house is clean and in order]; whereas, one who provides universally allows some little defect to remain, lest the good of the whole should be hindered [e.g., the master of the house may allow the servant to work into his old age, despite the many mistakes his servant makes, out of loyalty to the service given in the past, and also to allow the servant to continue on with a daily purpose, the care of his own family, etc.]. Hence, corruption and defects in natural things are said to be contrary to some particular nature; yet they are in keeping with the plan of universal nature; inasmuch as the defect in one thing yields to the good of another, or even to the universal good: for the corruption of one is the generation of another, and through this it is that a species is kept in existence. Since God, then, provides universally for all being, it belongs to His providence to permit certain defects in particular effects, that the perfect good of the universe may not be hindered, for if all evil were prevented, much good would be absent from the universe. A lion would cease to live, if there were no slaying of animals; and there would be no patience of martyrs if there were no tyrannical persecution.[53]

---

52. Garrigou-Lagrange, *Trinity and God the Creator*, 507.
53. Aquinas, *ST* Ia.22.2; see Garrigou-Lagrange, *Trinity and God the Creator*, 507–8.

OBJECTION 2: THE GOD OF REFORMED
THOMISM IS A UTILITARIAN DEITY

Kirk MacGregor argues against the notion that God permits evils to occur for the sake of some greater good, insisting that this idea is nothing less than the utilitarian notion that we should always act for the greatest good for the greatest number of people. On *utilitarianism* (aka *consequentialism*), the results of one's behavior determine whether one's activity is moral or immoral. A common critique of utilitarianism is that it entails that the end justifies the means—that is, if the torture of a child somehow led to a utopia, I would be morally justified in torturing the child. Indeed, this kind of reasoning was not born in the eighteenth century via the brain of Jeremy Bentham but has always been with us and has always been condemned in Scripture (see Gen 4:18–24; Rom 3:8). Hence, according to MacGregor, we must admit that there are gratuitous evils in this world.[54]

Response. First, as the locus of objective moral values, God has no (intrinsic) moral duties toward human beings, as even some Molinists say.[55] *As a principle*, we have duties to him; he has no duties toward us.[56] Second, utilitarianism teaches us that a moral principle's value resides in its utility in producing nonmoral values.[57] However, God's purpose in the permission of evil is to achieve *moral*, rather than *nonmoral*, values as

---

54. See Kirk MacGregor, *A Molinist-Anabaptist Systematic Theology* (Lanham, MD: University Press of America, 2007), 110–13.

55. See J. P. Moreland and William Lane Craig, *Philosophical Foundations for a Christian Worldview* (2nd ed.; Downers Grove, IL: InterVarsity Press, 2017), 536–37.

56. *Qualification:* God is morally obligated to fulfill all of his covenants, including those made with a creature (see Gen 15:1–21).

57. "The essence of **utilitarianism** can be stated in this way: *the rightness or wrongness of an act or moral rule is solely a matter of the nonmoral good produced directly or indirectly in the consequences of that act or rule.* … In clarifying the notion of **nonmoral** value (sometimes called **goodness**), a utilitarian can correctly point out that a number of things can have intrinsic value without that value being moral. In this context, **moral value**, sometimes called **rightness**, refers to moral rules (do not steal) or individual moral actions (an act of stealing) or kinds of actions (for example, stealing-type actions in general). Examples of nonmoral intrinsic value (things with intrinsic value apart from moral rules and actions) are these: health, beautiful art, friendship, mathematical knowledge. … If something has intrinsic value—for example, joy—then it is valuable in and of itself, it is an end in itself, and it is good and worthy of being desired for its own sake" (Moreland and Craig, *Philosophical Foundations*, 449, emphasis original). Classically speaking, I should always act in a way so as to produce the greatest good for the greatest number—where the good produced is nonmoral (e.g., I promote truth telling in order to contribute to a peaceful society built on trust).

ends. Also, utilitarianism entails that it is morally permissible to thwart a moral duty in order to achieve a greater good. For example, all things being equal, the doctor should protect the life of the innocent; however, so as to avoid the terrible consequence of back-alley abortions and denying a woman her intrinsic right to choose what to do with her own body, (so the argument goes) the doctor may justifiably induce an abortion. Yet, as the *summum bonum*, God has no duties toward us. For example, it is false to say that, *all things being equal, God has a duty to preserve the first human pair in their unfallen state, and yet for a greater good he allows them to fall.* This proposition is false, since God thwarts no duties in drawing a good out of evil *precisely because he has no duties.* Hence MacGregor's argument commits a category mistake.

Second, and interestingly enough, Aquinas raised and answered a form of MacGregor's objection way back in the thirteenth century:

> Some have said that although God does not will evil, yet He wills that evil should be or be done, because, although evil is not a good, yet it is good that evil should be or be done. This they said because things evil in themselves are ordered to some good end; and this order they thought was expressed in the words *that evil should be or be done.* This, however, is not correct; since evil is not of itself ordered to good, but accidentally. For it is beside the intention of the sinner, that any good should follow from his sin; as it was beside the intention of tyrants that the patience of the martyrs should shine forth from all their persecutions. It cannot therefore be said that such an ordering to good is implied in the statement that it is a good thing that evil should be or be done, since nothing is judged of by that which appertains to it accidentally, but by that which belongs to it essentially.[58]

Thus, Aquinas concludes, "God therefore neither wills evil to be done, nor wills it not to be done, but wills to permit evil to be done; and this is a good."[59]

---

58. Aquinas, *ST* Ia.19.9, italics original.
59. Aquinas, *ST* Ia.19.9.

Scripture supports Thomas's contention. Indeed, at the end of the book of Genesis, Joseph famously says to his brothers—after they had sold him into slavery, and after he had been afflicted by a dark providence—"You [my brothers] meant evil against me, *but* God meant it for good in order to bring about this present result, to preserve many people alive" (Gen 50:20). Notice here that *one and the same act* was intended to take place by both God and Joseph's brothers; however, the brothers had evil intentions in the act, while God's intentions were good. Thomas's explanation of this phenomenon appears unassailable, for how are we to understand the notion that God wills an evil without causing it? Answer: *God permits evil for the sake of a greater good.* A few more texts are worth mentioning in this regard. For example, note the words of Christ himself in response to a question from his disciples:

> As He passed by, He saw a man blind from birth. And His disciples asked Him, "Rabbi, who sinned, this man or his parents, that he would be born blind?" Jesus answered, "*It was* neither *that* this man sinned, nor his parents; but *it was* so that the works of God might be displayed in him. We must work the works of Him who sent Me as long as it is day; night is coming when no one can work. While I am in the world, I am the Light of the world." (John 9:1-5)

Blindness is evil, for eyes were meant to see, and yet a blind eye is one that lacks sight. Notice that Jesus locates the cause of this evil in neither the particular sins of the blind man, nor in those of his parents. This reminds us of the words of Chesterton, who, when speaking of original sin, tells us that the seemingly terrifying doctrine allows us all to pity the beggar and distrust the king. Indeed, this man was born into a fallen world and suffered a horrible consequence of living in this reality. But Jesus also adds that this condition was allowed by God so that his works would be displayed in the poor man. God has allowed a horrible evil to obtain so that he may draw from it a greater good! Also, the greatest evil ever perpetrated was the crucifixion of the divine Son; but the Scriptures teach us that God actually foreordained this evil deed from all eternity, perpetrated as it was by sinful people, so as to draw from it our glorious redemption (see Acts 2:23; 4:27-28; 20:28; 2 Cor 5:21; Rev 13:8).

HOW EXACTLY IS GOD NOT A UTILITARIAN?

The answer, again, is that there is nothing about evil per se that is good—for evil is a privation of the good. Hence the sinner does not wish a good to come from his evil act—e.g., the tyrant does not intend the patience of the martyr while persecuting the faithful; the adulterer does not intend the good of childbirth while pursuing his lust for another woman. Indeed, whatever goods may follow from an evil act, they are in no way essentially or necessarily related to the evil pursued. This is why many evil deeds do *not* result in an *immediate* good—e.g., martyrs are known to fall into despair; sexual immorality does not always produce a child; criminals are not immediately caught; and cancers often go uncured.[60] If there were something intrinsically good about evil (i.e., if good and evil were essentially bound together), then God may be called a utilitarian; just as, for example, there is a perceived link between the tyrant's killing of heretics and the establishment of social justice (i.e., *the end* [social justice] *justifies the means* [killing heretics]), which renders the tyrant a consequentialist.

If evil were somehow intrinsically and/or essentially connected with good, then in pursuing such a good one would be pursuing evil. For example, a tyrant may feel that social justice is achieved by slaying heretics, for in bringing the heretics to trial and execution he thinks he will bring order into his realm or society. So it is for the sake of social justice that the tyrant pursues the death of the heretics. But to kill a person for adhering to her own conscience is a form of murder; therefore, in pursuing a perceived good the tyrant performs an evil act. We know there is no intrinsic connection between murder and justice, for *murder is the subversion of justice.* But the tyrant believes in the intrinsic connection just the same.

As we saw in the previous chapter, hyper-Calvinists believe in a utilitarian deity who does evil that good may come. Those whom we analyzed believe God actually creates evil for the sake of a greater good. He creates

---

60. For this reason many argue as follows: Nothing good can come of this evil, therefore God was not justified in allowing it. Or, this horrible event has no foreseeable purpose, therefore there is no God. The flaw in this line of reasoning is that it fails to appreciate the fact that God is able to draw a good from *any* event that *may* not come to fruition for *many years.* Where a contingent being can only see a necessarily bad consequence of an evil event—e.g., the evil of cancer results in the death of a young woman—God is able to draw from that event an unforeseeable good in no way *essentially* related to it—e.g., the patience and fortitude produced in the daughter, and the reception of Christ, years later, by her Buddhist father.

the wicked (evil) so that he can punish sinners (good) and ensure the eternal contrast between them and those saved by his glorious grace (good). Of course, anyone who creates evil *is* evil. Thus, hyper-Calvinists have proven the existence of Satan, not the existence of God. For, in reality, the God of hyper-Calvinism creates (one kind of) evil for the sake of (another kind of) evil—e.g., he commits the *evil of guilt* so as ensure the *evil of punishment.*

What if God himself believed that the only way a particular good could be achieved would be to *allow* a specific evil to exist? Then we would have on our hands the ultimate utilitarian deity—one who allows evil so that good may come. Ironically, that is exactly what we find in MacGregor's own work! MacGregor follows Leibniz, who famously said that, because he is perfect, God must create the best of all possible worlds; but whatever is not God is by definition not perfect and, since no conceivable creatable thing, such as the universe, is God, it is not perfect; but an imperfection is an evil; therefore, in making the world, God makes evil.[61] In MacGregor's own words: "Such immediately solves the problem of natural evil; it is logically necessary to the universe, and God simply has to put up with it if he chooses to create a universe at all. ... Hence, it is logically impossible for God to have created a universe with less natural (and moral) evil than this one without lessening the balance obtaining in this universe between saved and lost."[62] It is here that I am reminded of a few lines from Voltaire's satire of Leibniz:

> Candide answered:—" ... a wise man, who has since had the misfortune to be hanged, taught me that everything was marvelously well arranged. Troubles are just the shadows in a beautiful picture."

> "—Your hanged philosopher was joking," said Martin; "the shadows are horrible ugly blots."

> "—It is human beings who make the blots," said Candide, "and they can't do otherwise."

---

61. This perspective is fleshed out in G. W. F. Leibniz's *Theodicy.*
62. MacGregor, *Molinist-Anabaptist Systematic Theology,* 115.

"—Then it isn't their fault," said Martin.[63]

TU QUOQUE *REFORMED THOMIST*

Insights drawn from *Candide* inevitably lead to even more specific objections to my position on this matter. For example, some have objected (in personal correspondence):

> You say there is no intrinsic connection between the evil permitted and the good obtained, but this whole discussion started with the statement that the reason God brought this world into existence, knowing all along that it would become evil, is so that he could draw from it goods otherwise unattainable. How is *that* not postulating an intrinsic connection between good and evil?

Response. My answer is that evil (in general) is a *necessary* precondition for certain goods otherwise unattainable, but it is not a *sufficient* condition for the attainment of those goods. For example, God is free to permit the human race to fall into sin and then choose to never redeem them. In such a case, many of the otherwise unattainable goods we have mentioned would have never come into fruition, which proves there is no intrinsic connection between the sin allowed and the redemption obtained. Indeed, while God clearly wants these goods to obtain in the world, so that he can manifest his goodness in all its varied splendor, reality would have moved along just as smoothly had God *not* wanted it that way and thus simply allowed the race to fall and be subsequently punished via his retributive justice. God is free to create any kind of world he wants. So, while our theodicy *justifies* the divine decision, it doesn't *dictate* it to him—as if God's *only* moral and free choice were to make a world that displayed his attributes in all their varied splendor. Also, this objection assumes that God can draw good from evil in abstraction (i.e., God decides to make a world-*ensemble* that becomes evil so as to draw good from it; therefore good is essentially related to evil). But no good can be realized apart from its particular circumstances. So a necessary condition for the good of redemption is a *particular* sin resulting

---

63. Voltaire, *Candide or Optimism* (2nd ed.; trans. and ed. Robert M. Adams; New York: W. W. Norton, 1991), 51.

in the fall of the human race. Proof that sin is insufficient for redemption is found in the fact that many sinners are never saved. Hence there is no intrinsic connection between any particular evil (e.g., sin) and a specific good drawn from it (e.g., a saved soul).

HOWEVER, THOMISM TRUMPS MODERATE CALVINISM

This leads us inevitably to Garrigou-Lagrange's critique of Reformed theology, where he cites the Canons of Trent as a correct assessment and condemnation of Calvinism: "Whosoever shall say that it is not in the power of man to make his ways evil, but that God produces bad works as well as good, not permissively only, but properly and of himself, so that the treachery of Judas is no less his proper work than the calling of Paul, let him be anathema."[64]

Response. Calvin himself answers this canon by approvingly quoting Augustine:

> [Augustine says,] "God worketh in the hearts of men to incline their wills as he pleaseth, whether to good, of his mercy, or to evil, according to their deservings [sic], and that by his judgment, sometimes open, sometimes hidden, but always just;" for he immediately adds the qualification, that "the malice is not his." (*De Verb. Dom. Serm.* 63.) In like manner he had said a little before, "He does not command the wicked by ordering, in which case obedience would be laudable, but by his secret and just judgment he bends their will, *already bad by their own depravity,* to this misdeed or that." [*De Gr. et Lib. Arb.* c. 21] For there is nothing here but what the Scriptures teach almost in the same words when they speak of inclining and turning, hardening and doing.[65]

Garrigou-Lagrange says virtually the same thing: "As the universal provider, God moves only that will to sin which is in itself evilly disposed and

---

64. *Canon VI*; see Garrigou-Lagrange, *Trinity and God the Creator*, 504.

65. John Calvin, *Acts of the Council of Trent with the Antidote*; https://www.monergism.com/thethresh-old/sdg/calvin_trentantidote.html (accessed September 12, 2016), italics added.

which thus disposed needs to be moved"[66] To illustrate: A father holds a toddler's hand so as to make him walk and hence may be called the cause of the child's movement. To be sure, the movement of the child is 100 percent from the father and 100 percent from the child, even though the father puts far less energy in causing the child's movement than the child does in walking. But the father is not the cause of the child's stumbling over the pebbles lying on the ground. No, the stumbling is *wholly* from the child's defective motor skills. In a more intimate and mysterious manner, God, via his decree, is an internal cause of the movement of the human will—for God not only moves our free wills into action, he is himself the very cause of the freedom of our acts;[67] but he is not the cause of the sin in those actions, which rather results from our defective natures. As Garrigou-Lagrange himself states:

> It is not necessary for us to be masters of the divine decree or of the divine motion, *if this latter causes in us and with us the free mode of our act.* Divine causality contains our own causality eminently, and God is more intimate to us than we are to ourselves. We should not conceive His motion as a *constraint* exerted externally by a created agent; it is entirely the interior causality of Him who creates and preserves us in being. The mystery in this case is not greater than that of creation, and is but a result of it. A person whom we love makes us *will freely* what he desires. Why could not God do so in a nobler, more certain, and very intimate manner that belongs to Him alone?[68]

Thus, Thomas notes, "Accordingly God is the cause of the act of sin: and yet He is not the cause of sin, because He does not cause the act to have a defect ... even as the defect of limping is reduced to a crooked leg as its cause, but not to the motive power, which nevertheless causes whatever there is of movement in the limping."[69]

---

66. Garrigou-Lagrange, *Trinity and God the Creator*, 509.
67. See Aquinas, *ST* Ia.83.1.
68. Garrigou-Lagrange, *God: His Existence and Nature*, 2:363, italics original.
69. Aquinas, *ST* Ia-IIae.79.2.

Biblically, we have clear examples of God causing people to commit acts of sin, only to later punish those people for committing those very same sins (see Judg 14:1-20; 2 Sam 24:1, 10, 25; 1 Kgs 22:18-40). The only way to reconcile this paradox[70] is to say that *God is the cause of the act* of sin, but *not the sin* in the act. "Thus when God is said to have sent a lying spirit to deceive Ahab (1 K. 22:22), it is not of him approving, but permitting and efficaciously ordaining it for the punishment of the wicked king."[71]

Philosophically, we have the following argument: All contingent events require an efficient cause; the movement of the human will is a contingent event; therefore, the movement of the human will requires an efficient cause; nothing contingent can be the ultimate cause of its movement, nor can there be an infinite regress of contingent causes; therefore, the ultimate cause of the movement of the human will must be the first uncaused Cause; however, sin is a defect; but pure act has no defects; therefore, while *actus purus* causes the human will to move, he cannot cause whatever is defective in its movement; thus, the defects of sin are wholly caused by the human will.[72]

Historically, the Reformed tradition (in general) and the Presbyterian Church (in particular) have endorsed this doctrine. The Westminster Confession of Faith states:

> The almighty power, unsearchable wisdom, and infinite goodness
> of God so far manifest themselves in his providence that it extend-
> eth itself even to the first fall, and all other sins of angels and men,
> and that not by a bare permission, but such as hath joined with it
> a most wise and powerful bounding, and otherwise ordering and
> governing of them, in a manifold dispensation, to his own holy ends;
> yet so as *the sinfulness thereof proceedeth only from the creature*, and

---

70. I.e., if God is the one who moves us to sin, then he is the cause of sin; and if he holds us responsible for our sins, then it follows that he is not the cause of sin. If he were the cause of sin, then he would be immoral for moving us to perform evil deeds, and doubly so for punishing us for doing what he compelled us to do. God would then not be all-good. God would not be God.

71. Turretin, *First through Tenth Topics*, 525.

72. See Aquinas, *ST* Ia-IIae.79.1-2.

not from God; so, being most holy and righteous, neither is nor can be the author or approver of sin. (5.4, italics added)

Or, as Turretin says,

So this [argument] does not hold good—the human will is the cause of sin; God is the cause of the human will; therefore he is the cause of sin—for when the created will sins, it turns aside and fails [or falls] from the order of the first cause. And God who is the cause of the will per se, cannot be called the cause of the evil action, which is from the will not simply in the genus of being (as it is from God), but from the will failing as to the law in the genus of morals.[73]

Rejoinder. If God is the cause of the act of sin, then he is the cause of sin. As one Reformed Christian once stated: "The intellectual razor one must use to slice the difference between act and sin is too fine for the tastes of many."[74] Indeed, a classic critique of Thomism, precisely at this point, is that the "cause of anything is also the cause of that which essentially belongs to it."[75] However, some acts are essentially tied to the evils conjoined to them. For example, a particular human chooses to hate God. Notice that, in this instance, there is no real difference between the act of will and the hatred itself; and so there is no distinction to be made in this case between the act and the sin inhering in it. In short, if God is always the cause of the human act, then he is at least sometimes the cause of the sin (e.g., hatred) inhering in the act. This makes God the author of sin, at least on some occasions.

Response. In the words of Garrigou-Lagrange, "Thomists commonly point out that nothing is more clearly delimited than the causality of a potency or power, which is so completely concerned with its object that it touches on nothing else, no matter how closely anything else may be

---

73. Turretin, *First through Tenth Topics*, 525. Commenting on his doctrine that God causes the human will to move, but not the human will to sin, Turretin states: "For it is known that the Thomists and Dominicans agree here with us" (Turretin, *First through Tenth Topics*, 530). In short, Turretin was, on this issue at least, a Reformed Thomist!

74. Campbell, "The Beautiful Mind," 238.

75. Garrigou-Lagrange, *Trinity and God the Creator*, 510.

conjoined to its object."[76] He offers an apple as an example: One and the same apple can have three essential characteristics intimately tied to it—color, taste, and smell. A tongue touches the apple, which causes it to sense a particular taste; and yet the same sense of taste can discern neither the color nor the odor of the apple, despite their being intimately conjoined to it and hence to one another. Similarly, there is an act and the malice that motivated it. While still tied together, they are far less so than the color, taste, and smell of an apple; for an act is something positive, while sinful malice (e.g., the hatred of God), being negative, pertains to a different order of causality. Whatever lacks any defect can have nothing to do with a malicious motive, and so no sin can ever be the proper object of the divine will or power, regardless of how intimately the sinful motive and its action are conjoined. Indeed, "every agent acts in a manner at least analogically similar to itself," but "between God and the malice of guilt there is not even an analogical similarity. Hence, even if God willed to be the cause of sin, He could not, just as a man who willed to see sound could not."[77]

I have on occasion appealed to the law of double effect to illustrate the overall point, using a pregnant woman taking chemotherapy as an example. Her intention to save her life is a good one, but her decision results in the death of her child, which is bad. Even though her decision directly causes the death of the child, it is still a good decision precisely because of the intention behind it. Similarly, God chooses to bring into existence a good world that becomes evil in order to draw from it greater goods otherwise unattainable. Because he intends this for good, he is not guilty of the evil that results from his decision. Two challenges often arise at this point. First, if his purpose in allowing evil was to bring about a greater good, then his decision to make this world caused evil to obtain, which makes him the cause of evil. Indeed, the difference between God and the pregnant woman is that she lacks omnipotence (and so cannot help her situation) while God is all-powerful. Yet it is precisely at this point that the analogy between the woman and God becomes remote—for she *does cause* the death of her child (albeit without impunity), while God *never causes* the evils he allows; and the bad result of her choice is both inevitable and essentially tied to

---

76. Garrigou-Lagrange, *Trinity and God the Creator*, 510.

77. Garrigou-Lagrange, *Trinity and God the Creator*, 510.

the good pursued, while the good God intends and the evil he allows are never essentially related to each other.[78]

A second challenge often raised against our perspective is that God is able to prevent people from sinning and/or condemning themselves; therefore, he is obligated to do so. Sometimes the following proof for this proposition is offered: If a positive entails a positive, then one causes the other; and if a negative entails a negative, then one causes the other. For example, the sunrise positively causes light, and its not rising negatively causes darkness. Similarly, God's effectual grace causes us to freely believe in him; and so his choice to not give efficient grace to some causes them to sinfully reject him. By not giving saving grace to all, God causes many to commit the sin of rejecting him. Thus, to avoid being sin's cause, God is morally obligated to give efficient grace to all. However, the Thomist answer to this line of reasoning is sound: if we are dealing with one and only one cause, the argument holds; but when we are dealing with two causes, one indefective and the other defective, the argument becomes invalid. The sin of unbelief is occasioned by God's choice not to give effective grace *and* the human choice to resist sufficient grace. Notice there are two factors in this equation—i.e., the choice not to give grace and the choice to resist grace. A teacher chooses, for the sake of a greater good, not to give a detailed study guide for the upcoming test—one that would ensure that every student will pass; and yet she does give every student sufficient information in her lectures and assigned readings that make it genuinely possible for them to do well. The student who refuses the sufficient information offered cannot reasonably claim that the teacher caused him to fail because she chose not to give him a more detailed study guide. Similarly, no one can reasonably charge God with their own sin of resistance simply because he chooses not to give that individual efficient grace, especially since God does give him sufficient grace.[79]

---

78. Garrigou-Lagrange, *Trinity and God the Creator*, 503–19.

79. Garrigou-Lagrange, *Trinity and God the Creator*, 503–19. We should stress here that God is never obligated to give any kind of grace to anyone, whether it be sufficient or efficient. Thus, if God had chosen not to give any kind of grace to anyone, no one would be justified in calling his decision evil. Thus, that God gives sufficient grace *does not* justify his decision to not give efficient grace. He needs no justification for not giving grace. On the other hand, the fact of sufficient grace does make the creature-sinner's charge of unfairness all the more irrational.

OBJECTION 3: SUFFICIENT GRACE
IS A MERE FORMALITY

It looks like the Reformed Thomist is just trying to have her cake and eat it too. You see these contradictory texts in Scripture, whereby God wills the salvation of all on the one hand and does not will the redemption of all on the other, and so you concoct an ad hoc distinction so as to save face. But what is sufficient grace, really? It is nothing. For of itself it accomplishes nothing genuinely good for the sinner. It's just a term we give to a wish God has that he never intends to fulfill, which is just incoherent.

Response. This is a caricature of the doctrine, for sufficient grace accomplishes a great deal. Indeed, sufficient grace is expressed in those biblical texts where God wrestles with those who resist him, endures with great patience persons who oppose him, and aids those who cannot believe. Were it not for sufficient grace, there would be no seeker, no wayfarer, no mere theist, nor anyone who assents to basic Christian truths.

The Reformation famously noted three aspects of faith that are necessary for our justification before God—i.e., knowledge, assent, and trust. By "knowledge" I mean that one must first hear and understand at least the very minimal or basic truths of the gospel—e.g., that Jesus Christ, the Messiah of Israel and unique Son of God, died in the place of human sinners, was buried, rose again from the dead, and appeared to his earliest followers (1 Cor 15:3–5; Rom 10:9-10). By "assent" I mean that one must acknowledge and/or accept as true the basic gospel message. By "trust" I mean that one must wholly rely on the person of Christ, as he is given to us in the gospel, as our one and only Savior.[80]

Now, as we have noted throughout this study, all humans are born in sin, being as it were dead in our trespasses and evil deeds. Apart from grace none of us would so much as understand the contents of the gospel at all. So we should not be surprised when we run into persons who, when discussing spiritual matters, look at us like a deer caught in the headlights, as if they just don't get it. For they are spiritually dead and so cannot of themselves

---

80. For a modern defense of this understanding of faith, see Kim Riddlebarger, "What Is Faith?," in *Christ the Lord: The Reformation and Lordship Salvation* (ed. Michael Horton; Grand Rapids: Baker, 1992), 81–105; and J. Gresham Machen, *What Is Faith?* (1925; repr., Carlisle, PA: Banner of Truth Trust, 1991).

even begin to understand spiritual matters (1 Cor 2:14). However, we often do find people who, though they have never given their lives to Christ, seem to have a clear understanding of the content of the gospel (Mark 12:32–34). We attribute this understanding to sufficient grace, for without it they would never understand; with it, they understand the gospel even if they do not assent to it.

Many who know and understand the contents of the gospel have no interest in assenting to it. However, there are atheists who have admitted they have a difficult time rejecting the evidence for God's existence[81] or who have become theists because of that evidence;[82] or who, though Jewish or Muslim, nevertheless assent to the proposition that Jesus rose from the dead.[83] In other words, in wrestling with such people, God via his sufficient grace is able to use various means (e.g., church worship, charity, apologetic arguments, etc.) to bring them to a mental assent to these basic truths.[84] Without this sufficient grace, they would have never so much as

---

81. See Robert Jastrow, *God and the Astronomers* (2nd ed.; New York: W. W. Norton, 1992).

82. See Mortimer J. Adler, *How to Think about God: A Guide for the 20th-Century Pagan* (New York: Macmillan, 1979). For Adler's own conversion story from "pagan theism" to Christianity, see his "A Philosopher's Religious Faith," in *Philosophers Who Believe: The Spiritual Journeys of 11 Leading Thinkers* (ed. Kelly James Clark; Downers Grove, IL: InterVarsity Press, 1993), 201–21. Feser was an atheist before being convinced that the classical proofs for the existence of God are sound. See Edward Feser, *The Last Superstition: A Refutation of the New Atheism* (South Bend, IN: St. Augustine's Press, 2008); Feser, *Five Proofs of God* (San Francisco: Ignatius Press, 2017).

83. For the person who has already embraced the reality of God, the evidence for the resurrection has proven itself to be quite compelling. For two examples of how the evidence for the resurrection has convinced the "not-already-convinced," see Pinchas Lapide, *The Resurrection of Jesus: A Jewish Perspective* (1982; repr., trans. Wilhelm C. Linss; Eugene, OR: Wipf & Stock, n.d.); and Nabeel Qureshi, *Seeking Allah, Finding Jesus: A Devout Muslim Encounters Christianity* (Grand Rapids: Zondervan, 2014). Both of these men, who have now passed on to their reward, indicate their extreme skepticism at the beginning of their research, wherein both, without becoming Christians, came to believe that Jesus had risen. To our knowledge Lapide never came to faith in Christ, even after accepting the resurrection (e.g., see Lapide, *Resurrection of Jesus*, 130); Qureshi, while resisting for some time after assenting to the reality of the resurrection (see *Seeking Allah, Finding Jesus*, 167–68), eventually came to faith (see *Seeking Allah, Finding Jesus*, 280–83). Their testimonies illustrate our point that there is an important difference between assent and trust; and, while no one converts *because* of the evidence, few there are who convert without it.

84. Ross, who was an atheist before God changed his mind via the evidence, spent several weeks as a non-Christian who was convinced of Christianity's truth. He had "assent" but not "saving faith." He eventually trusted in Christ as his Savior and has spent the past fifty-four years evangelizing unbelievers by using scientific evidence that corroborates the reality of God and the reliability of the Bible. The story of his conversion, along with accounts of his numerous evangelistic encounters, wherein *many* people have become believers through

listened to sermons or apologetical arguments, and much less would they assent to God's existence or Christ's resurrection; with it, they assent to basic Christian truths even if they do not rely on Christ.[85]

Of course, there are many in the church who call themselves Christians, who assent to all of the essential truths of Christianity (and more besides), but have never really trusted in or relied on the person of Christ as their Savior. They affirm so strongly that it's often difficult to distinguish their mental affirmation from actual trust. To all appearances they look like Christians precisely because their mental assent is sincere. Indeed, many of these persons become missionaries, pastors, apologists, and theologians. However, they are not actually justified before the divine tribunal (Matt 7:21-23). Why? Is it because God is moving them into unbelief? No, for God always maintains the posture of the open hands of acceptance,

---

apologetics, can be found in Hugh Ross and Kathy Ross, *Always Be Ready: A Call to Adventurous Faith* (Covina, CA: Reasons to Believe, 2018).

85.   Thus Sproul Sr. notes that the evidence for the inspiration of Scripture is, in itself, sufficient to produce a mental assent to the truth claims of biblical theism, but not wholehearted trust (reliance on) Christ and/or the Bible as the Word of God. See R. C. Sproul, "The Internal Testimony of the Holy Spirit," in *Inerrancy*, 348. But if the evidence is sufficient to bring all to an acknowledgment of the truth, why doesn't everyone assent (at least, sans *trust*) to God's revelation upon hearing the evidence? The answer is that humans resist the evidence or indications (*indicia*) concerning the truthfulness of Christian theism. The evidence is sufficient to convince, but not to convict; it is adequate for proving, but not for persuading. It takes the Spirit of God to do *that* (1 Cor 2:6-16). In fact, *everyone* would resist the *indicia* were it not for the grace of God working on human hearts. Thus, elsewhere Sproul cites renowned Dutch Reformed theologian Gisbertus Voetius (1589-1676), who acknowledges that unconverted persons "may be convinced theoretically of the 'truth of the Gospel and of other dogmas of the faith.' This he [Voetius] considers possible 'only by a general assistance or a kind of general grace of the illuminating and convincing Spirit.'" See R. C. Sproul et al., *Classical Apologetics* (Grand Rapids: Zondervan, 1984), 297. So, while shying away from the term, it is clear that some in the Reformed tradition advocate something virtually identical to the Thomistic doctrine of sufficient grace. This also seems true of those who, to my knowledge (despite my concerted efforts to find out), have never explicitly endorsed Reformed theology (see Archer, *Bible Difficulties*, 390-95; Lisle, *Keeping the Faith*, 102-3). I see a parallel between the adequate (objective) evidences for the truthfulness of Christian theism, along with the sufficient grace necessary for a (subjective) mental acknowledgment of it, and the (objective) self-attesting Scriptures, along with the efficient grace necessary for the sinner's (subjective) acquiescence of her whole mind, heart, and will to the Word of God. Indeed, as Sproul goes on to emphasize, the internal witness of the Holy Spirit is not a new revelation, given as a supplement to the Bible; rather, it is the work of the Spirit wherein he convicts the human soul of his own sin, along with the truthfulness of the gospel (John 16:8-11). After conversion, the Spirit's testimony remains the primary anchor for the believer's assurance that her faith is true and that she belongs to God's adopted family (Rom 8:12-17; 1 John 5:7-9). See Sproul, "Internal Testimony," 348-49.

even after giving people over to their sins. He truly and sincerely desires their redemption. Indeed, the reason these individuals are not saved is that they have not wholly relied on Christ as Savior; and the reason they have not truly trusted the Savior is that they are resisting God's sufficient grace (Acts 7:51).

Therefore, sufficient grace is no mere formality. Through it God accomplishes much, including bringing many people to a mental assent to the truths of the gospel. All of this serves as God's way of preparing people to come to genuine saving faith. Also, if such persons would just trust the Savior, they would attain a right standing before God.

OBJECTION 4: SUFFICIENT GRACE IS A DIVINE TRICK

Since sufficient grace is not actually effective to save, it turns out to be nothing more than a cosmic trick to butter people up for the fires of hell. The real grace is effectual grace, which only the elect receive. So in the end God does not really, savingly love the reprobate.

Response. I disagree with this sentiment, precisely because I side with Thomas's doctrine of prevenient grace—that is, sufficient and effectual grace are actually the same kind of grace, given to all, albeit brought into full flower for the elect alone. Indeed, love is no mere emotional sentiment; it is a verb. God makes good his claim to love all by giving everyone a grace that is sufficient to save them. Grace is an expression of God's love, whereby he makes all totally depraved persons genuinely able to believe. Any resistance to that grace comes wholly from the creature; it never comes from God. Efficient grace is offered to the creature via sufficient grace. So, in a sense the objection is accurate, at least insofar as it claims that only the effectual grace is real. True. Since all are given sufficient grace, *in which is offered* efficient grace, God is genuinely gracious to everyone.

Garrigou-Lagrange explains both the differences and similarities between sufficient and efficient grace in the following:

> Furthermore, this very resistance to sufficient grace is an evil which would not occur, here and now, without the divine permission, and nonresistance itself is a good which would not come about here and

now except for [the] divine consequent will. Therefore, there is a real difference between sufficient grace, to which is attached the divine permission of sin and by reason of which the fulfillment of the commandments is really possible, and efficacious grace, on the other hand, which is a greater help whence follows not only the real possibility of observing the commandments, but their effective fulfillment.

Moreover, in sufficient grace, efficacious grace is offered to us, as the fruit is in the flower; but if resistance is made on account of our defectibility, then we deserve not to receive efficacious grace.[86]

God gives sufficient grace to everyone, thereby making it genuinely possible for all to be saved. But everyone, to one degree or another (including many who assent to much of his truth), resists the divine call on their life; therefore, God the Holy Spirit is free to either draw the sinner to rely on Christ, thereby rendering his sufficient grace *intrinsically* efficacious, or leave the sinner in his resistant state, thereby rendering his sufficient grace merely *extrinsically* efficacious. Thus Garrigou-Lagrange says,

It is apparent that the ultimate bases of the distinction between grace efficacious in itself and sufficient grace, as well as between [the] consequent divine will and [the] antecedent will, is to be found in these two principles: "Nothing happens which God has not either willed efficaciously if it is good, or permitted if it is an evil"; and "God never commands the impossible, but renders the fulfillment of His commands really possible when He imposes them and to the extent to which He imposes them and to which they can be known."

If the true meaning of each of the terms of these two principles is well weighed, especially the opposition that exists between "efficaciously willed" and "permitted," it can be seen that there is a real difference between efficacious grace, the result of the intrinsically efficacious [or consequent] will of God, and merely sufficient grace, the result of His antecedent will accompanied by the divine

---

86. Garrigou-Lagrange, *Grace*, 184–85.

permission of sin. In the first case, God confers the free, salutary action. In the second, He gives the real power to act, but not to act efficaciously.[87]

In all of this we need to remember that, in giving sufficient grace to every single person, God does no less for the reprobate than the Arminian says he does. Indeed, one could argue that he does more—for we have seen an Arminian or two denying that God gives grace to those he knows will not believe; and middle knowledge traps the reprobates in infeasible worlds, often rendering them literally unredeemable. For the Reformed Thomist, no one is beyond saving (Mark 10:27). None are beyond his reach (Isa 59:1; Num 11:23), and so all are accessible to him (Isa 65:24; Jer 32:17); thus, his saving grace is given to everyone (1 Tim 4:10; Titus 2:11). God via his sufficient grace makes it genuinely possible for every person to believe the gospel; therefore, if they do resist his grace to the end, the fault lies with them and not God. Destruction is our fault alone; our hope can only be found in God our Savior (Hos 13:9).

Turretin, while opposing the distinction between sufficient and efficient grace, does qualify his opposition by saying "that it may be evident in which sense it [i.e., the sufficient/efficient grace distinction] is proposed by our opponents and rejected by us, as in a sound sense can be admitted by us."[88] How is the distinction between sufficient and efficient grace admitted by Turretin? He writes, "Still we do not deny that in a certain sense the division can be admitted if a sufficiency, not absolute and simple is meant, but a relative sufficiency both with knowledge of the truth and temporary faith (Heb. 1:26; Lk. 8:13) and for conviction and inexcusability (*anapologian*, Jn. 15:22). But for conversion, we recognize no sufficient grace which is not equally efficacious."[89] One can only wonder why, if Turretin concedes this distinction, he rejects that between the divine antecedent and consequent wills.

---

87. Garrigou-Lagrange, *Grace*, 441.

88. Francis Turretin, *Eleventh through Seventeenth Topics* (vol. 2 of *Institutes of Elenctic Theology*; ed. James T. Dennison Jr.; trans. George Musgrave Giger; Phillipsburg, NJ: Presbyterian & Reformed, 1994), 510.

89. Turretin, *Eleventh through Seventeenth Topics*, 511.

In any case, herein lies the subtle distinction between Thomists and many Reformed on this particular issue. That is, on the one hand, the Thomist wants to say that, from the divine point of view, the giving of both sufficient and efficacious grace is one and the same act whereby the ability to believe is given to everyone, since efficacious grace is offered in sufficient grace in the same way the fruit is offered in the flower; and yet human resistance to this grace allows God to *either permit the sinner to continue resisting divine grace*, thereby remaining in her sins, *or bring this grace to its ultimate fruition or end*—namely, the conversion of the sinner. To explain how this *could* be so, imagine a father who desires to take his twin sons, who are six years old, fishing: both resist his will as he grabs each by the hand (i.e., one on his left, one on his right), and while he is walking toward the woods, to the trail that leads to the river, both sons are pulling back and insisting that he let them go; the father speaks to both of them with kind words, explaining how much fun they will have while fishing; they continue to resist; eventually, he lets go of the hand of one son, but continues to hold on to the other, whereby his son eventually complies with his father's will, no longer resists, and holds onto his father's hand freely while he is walked to the river. Notice that the actions of the father, regarding his sons, are indistinguishable up until the time one is released. It is the same movement, the same act. This act is accompanied with the exact same intention—i.e., the father genuinely wants both of his sons to fish with him. Also, both sons are equally resistant, even up until the time the father releases one of them (thereby allowing him to pout in the yard). So his choice of one son over the other had nothing to do with the notion that one freely assented to the offer while the other resisted. Both were equally resistant and rebellious at the moment of "release." The second son, who ends up going fishing, was eventually fully compliant, not because his father gave him a different kind of grace, but because the father decided to carry the exact same grace given to both to its proper end—i.e., a fun day of fishing—while also permitting the other boy to stay behind.

On the other hand, many Reformed theologians want to say that sufficient and efficient grace are two different kinds of grace—i.e., one that enlightens sinners and renders them inexcusable, and one that actually moves the human will to embrace the gospel; the former, relatively sufficient grace, is sometimes identified with "common grace," while the latter is intrinsically effectual grace.[90] That said, it would appear that the results of both soteriologies are the same. The Reformed, like the Thomist, can admit a sufficient grace given to all that is distinguished from intrinsically efficacious grace. It is *relatively* sufficient and/or *extrinsically* effectual in the sense that, like a beggar who is offered food that can nourish his body, if the sinner would but partake of the gift of salvation being offered to him, his soul would be saved. The beggar's refusal to eat does not take away from the efficacy of the food, much less the sincerity of the offer. Similarly, the sinner's resistance to relatively sufficient grace does not take away from its efficacy, much less the sincerity of God in offering it; much less does it obligate God to give more sufficient graces than he has already given; and even more so is God *not* obligated to give that *intrinsically* effectual grace to ensure his free response of faith.

I think it is in better keeping with the Bible, which speaks of a genuine desire on God's part for everyone's salvation, to follow Thomas on this score; for if God really does desire the salvation of all, then it would seem that efficient saving grace would be offered to everyone *in* sufficient permissive grace. So, just as I would encourage my Thomistic friends to rethink their stance on justification and turn to the Reformation, whereby an unobscured gospel is offered to the sinner, I would ask my Reformed friends to give Thomas's view of sufficient and efficient grace a second glance; for in here we can see a true reconciliation of sovereign grace and unbounded love.

SUMMARY AND CONCLUSION

In chapter 3 of this work I offered exegetical evidence for the doctrine of unconditional election. In chapter 4 of this work I offered the following argument: if an omnipotent and omniscient deity creates the cosmos from nothing, then unconditional election is a true doctrine; there is such a deity who absolutely creates; therefore, unconditional election is true. I also explored several ways of avoiding this argument, finding them wanting. In chapter 5 I examined the doctrine of middle knowledge, concluding that it,

---

90. Turretin, *Eleventh through Seventeenth Topics*, 511–17.

too, entails unconditional election. In chapter 6 I offered a full vindication of my conviction that God savingly loves everyone.

Here, in chapter 7, I offered a reconciliation or rapprochement between universal benevolence and sovereign election. How can both of these biblical affirmations be true? My answer to this all-important question is fourfold:

1. The Arminian faces the same problem as the Calvinist, since on his model God creates people while being prescient of their eventual damnation.

2. Given the transcendence of God, along with the reliability of the Bible, we are justified in thinking these truths are logically possible, even if we ourselves have no answer to the dilemma.

3. Molinist unconditional election creates more problems than it solves, since (a) in contrast to the biblical view of divine election, Molinist election is too impersonal; (b) it implies a divine sting operation, rendering divine benevolence less than universal; (c) it compromises the biblical view of human freedom; and (d) it turns God into a moral monster, since on this view God selects one good person over another for salvation.

4. Reformed Thomists are, indeed, able to reconcile universal benevolence with divine predilection via a distinction between the divine antecedent and consequent wills, manifested as they are in sufficient and efficient grace. As we read in the Westminster Larger Catechism: "All the elect, and they only, are effectually called: although others may be, and often are, outwardly called by the ministry of the Word, and have some common operations of the Spirit; who, for their wilful neglect and contempt of the grace offered to them, being justly left in their unbelief, do never truly come to Jesus Christ" (Q. 68). This text captures the essence of the antecedent-consequent/sufficient-efficient distinction. Recalcitrant unbelief comes wholly from us, resistant as we are to God's gracious overtures; saving grace is found in God alone (Ps 3:4; Jonah 2:9; Hos 13:9; Acts 7:51; John 6:44; Eph 2:8–9). If this option is even *possible*, the Reformed perspective on election proves to be more plausibly

true than either Arminianism or Molinism. In light of the evidence for this doctrine's truth, I have come to see in this distinction a genuine theodicy for the soteriological problem of evil. Indeed, God is fully morally justified in his allowance of evil and his permission of recalcitrant unbelief.

AN EPILOGUE

We began our study with a quotation of Charles Spurgeon, who affirmed both unconditional election and the universal divine benevolence. Spurgeon rightly says that it is better to be biblical than to insist, for the sake of consistency with your own system of theology, that only one side of that equation—i.e., sovereign grace or universal love—is true. To those who feel like there is no other choice but to agree with the "prince of preachers," I offer good news—i.e., there is a way to reconcile these biblical truths. God genuinely desires the redemption of every single human being and therefore graciously gives everyone, dead in sin as they are, sufficient grace to believe the gospel; yet, for the sake of a greater good, God sovereignly chooses to permit many persons to continue in their recalcitrant unbelief—and hence he permits his sufficient grace to not accomplish the end for which it is given (i.e., the salvation of all souls); yet for many other persons, who are no more worthy of saving grace than those whom he has passed by, God brings his sufficient, prevenient, grace into full flower whereby it efficaciously quickens the hearts of otherwise resistant sinners—who, in turn, freely trust in Christ as Savior. To those passed by and condemned, they receive the good of God's justice. To those whom he elects and redeems, they receive the good of God's grace.

As Spurgeon noted in our prologue, his Calvinism is not new. It is the doctrine of Clement of Rome, Augustine, Anselm, Aquinas, and the Magisterial Reformers. It is the teaching of the great Reformed confessions. The Thomistic distinction between God's antecedent and consequent will, along with the concomitant distinction between the divine sufficient and efficient grace, goes a long way in offering a coherent account of what we clearly read in the Reformed creeds. Thus I commend Reformed Thomism to the reader, which, among other things, offers the Roman Catholic a consistent understanding of the cardinal doctrine of *sola gratia* (via its doctrine of justification by faith alone), while also making good the common Christian confession that God genuinely desires the salvation of everyone.

As we began our study with a preacher, we end it with a creed—the very confession that gave birth to the so-called five points of Calvinism—which makes little sense if my basic thesis is not true.

CANONS OF DORT (CONCLUSION)

And so this is the clear, simple, and straightforward explanation of the orthodox teaching on the five articles in dispute in the Netherlands, as well as the rejection of the errors by which the Dutch churches have for some time been disturbed. This explanation and rejection the Synod declares to be derived from God's Word and in agreement with the confessions of the Reformed churches. Hence it clearly appears that those of whom one could hardly expect it, have shown no truth, equity, and charity at all in wishing to make the public believe:

> that the teaching of the Reformed churches on predestination and on the points associated with it by its very nature and tendency draws the minds of people away from all godliness and religion, is an opiate of the flesh and the devil, and is a stronghold of Satan where he lies in wait for all people, wounds most of them, and fatally pierces many of them with the arrows of both despair and self-assurance;

> that this teaching makes God the author of sin, unjust, a tyrant, and a hypocrite; and is nothing but a refurbished Stoicism, Manichaeism, Libertinism, and Mohammedanism;

> that this teaching makes people carnally self-assured, since it persuades them that nothing endangers the salvation of the chosen, no matter how they live, so that they may commit the most outrageous crimes with self-assurance; and that on the other hand nothing is of use to the reprobate for salvation even if they have truly performed all the works of the saints;

that this teaching means that God predestined and created, by the bare and unqualified choice of his will, without the least regard or consideration of any sin, the greatest part of the world to eternal condemnation; that in the same manner in which election is the source and cause of faith and good works, reprobation is the cause of unbelief and ungodliness; that many infant children of believers are snatched in their innocence from their mothers' breasts and cruelly cast into hell so that neither the blood of Christ nor their baptism nor the prayers of the church at their baptism can be of any use to them; and very many other slanderous accusations of this kind which the Reformed churches not only disavow but even denounce with their whole heart.

Therefore this Synod of Dort in the name of the Lord pleads with all who devoutly call on the name of our Savior Jesus Christ to form their judgment about the faith of the Reformed churches, not on the basis of false accusations gathered from here or there, or even on the basis of the personal statements of a number of ancient and modern authorities—statements which are also often either quoted out of context or misquoted and twisted to convey a different meaning—but on the basis of the churches' own official confessions and of the present explanation of the orthodox teaching which has been endorsed by the unanimous consent of the members of the whole Synod, one and all.

Finally, this Synod urges all fellow ministers in the gospel of Christ to deal with this teaching in a godly and reverent manner, in the academic institutions as well as in the churches; to do so, both in their speaking and writing, with a view to the glory of God's name, holiness of life, and the comfort of anxious souls; to think and also speak with Scripture according to the analogy of faith; and, finally, to refrain from all those ways of speaking which go beyond the bounds set for us by the genuine sense of the Holy Scriptures and which could give impertinent sophists a just occasion to scoff at the teaching of the Reformed churches or even to bring false accusations against it.

May God's Son Jesus Christ, who sits at the right hand of God and gives gifts to men, sanctify us in the truth, lead to the truth those who err, silence the mouths of those who lay false accusations against sound teaching, and equip faithful ministers of his Word with a spirit of wisdom and discretion, that all they say may be to the glory of God and the building up of their hearers. Amen.[1]

---

1. Joel R. Beeke and Sinclair Ferguson, eds., *Reformed Confessions Harmonized* (Grand Rapids: Baker, 1999), 35–36.

Appendix 1

ANSWERING OBJECTIONS TO ORIGINAL SIN

W e seem to live in a Pelagian society, with the innate goodness of humans (more often than not) taken as a given by the movers and shakers of our culture. As we saw in chapter 2, Pelagianism turns God into a moral monster insofar as it rejects the doctrine of original sin, which entails that God decided to place inherently good persons in a world wherein he knew they would be damned. In short, in electing persons unto redemption, God chooses one good person over another. Orthodox Christianity's way out of this dilemma is the doctrine of original sin, which (at least) teaches that every human inherits the sinful disposition of our first parents. By selecting a possible world wherein everyone is fallen into sin, God can exercise his freedom to choose one evil and sinful person over another. Those who are elect receive the goodness of divine grace, while those who are reprobate receive the goodness of divine justice.

Of course, the doctrine of original sin itself raises a number of difficulties. Here are a few of them:

1. HUMAN BEINGS, IF THEY ONLY KNEW THE FULL CONSEQUENCES OF THEIR ACTIONS, WOULD ALWAYS TAKE THE RIGHT COURSE OF ACTION (OR BEHAVIOR)

Indeed, some philosophers (such as Plato) believe that humanity's problem is its lack of education. By educating a person, we can change the basic predisposition of his or her nature. For many in our modern world, human nature is inherently good, but for want of a full comprehension of the consequences of our actions, we often go astray. To give examples: Had the Native Americans and/or ancient Canaanites known enough about this universe and the way it works, they would have never engaged in child sacrifice; if men only knew the full consequences of their behavior (e.g., depression, psychological disorders, [potential] death of their victims), they would never beat their wives; if Hitler had only known the truth about the Jews, as well as the full consequences of his "Final Solution" (i.e., the devastation and suffering it caused), he would never have implemented it. In light of this insight, we should not see humanity's fundamental problem as moral; rather, it is intellectual. With knowledge comes goodness; and so the more humans know, the better they will be. We are naturally good—or, at least, morally neutral—not evil!

Response. My experience tells me that this objection just isn't true. There is no necessary connection between being well educated and being a good person. To starkly illustrate the notion that education and knowledge of the consequences in no way cause a person to be moral or do the right thing, consider these chilling words of Ted Bundy (which he delivered to one of his victims):

> Then I learned that all moral judgments are "value judgments," that all value judgments are subjective, and that none can be proved to be either "right" or "wrong." I even read somewhere that the Chief Justice of the United States had written that the American Constitution expressed nothing more than collective value judgments. Believe it or not, I figured out for myself—what apparently the Chief Justice couldn't figure out for himself—that if the rationality of one value judgment was zero, multiplying it by millions would not make it one whit more rational. Now is there any reason to obey the law for anyone, like myself, who has the boldness and daring—the strength of character—to throw off its shackles. ... I discovered that to become truly free, truly unfettered, I had to become truly uninhibited. And I quickly discovered that the greatest obstacle to my freedom, the greatest block and limitation to it, consists in the insupportable "value judgment" that I was bound to respect the rights of others. I asked myself, who were these "others"? Other human beings, with human rights? Why is it more wrong to kill a

human animal than any other animal, a pig or a sheep or a steer? Is your life worth more to you than a hog's life to a hog? Why should I be willing to sacrifice my pleasure more for the one than for the other? Surely you would not, in this age of scientific enlightenment, declare that God or nature has marked some pleasures as "moral" or "good" and others as "immoral" or "bad"? In any case, let me assure you, my dear young lady, that there is absolutely no comparison between the pleasure I might take in eating ham and the pleasure I anticipate in raping and murdering you. That is the honest conclusion to which my education has led me—after the most conscientious examination of my spontaneous and uninhibited self.[1]

Hitler himself once said: "I freed Germany from the stupid and degrading fallacies of conscience and morality. We will train young people before whom the world will tremble. I want people to be capable of violence— imperious, relentless, and cruel."[2] These words, along with Bundy's, are not those of madmen. These are both intelligent men who thought through their own ethic. They were not crazy, but they were evil; and their problem was not a lack of education, nor too much of it, but a corrupt nature that desired to twist the truth for its own gain—pleasure for the one, power for the other.

---

1. Quoted in Louis P. Pojman, *Ethics: Discovering Right & Wrong* (5th ed.; Belmont, CA: Wadsworth, 2006), 30. Some may rejoin that Bundy, because he appeals to education, is clearly a product of a bad environment. But notice that his education is no different from anyone else who has grown up in twentieth-century America. What is the difference between Bundy and the average liberal who, though embracing his premises, would never take Bundy's presuppositions to the same conclusion? The answer seems to be that Bundy, though taught to think one way, knowingly corrupted the intent of his teachers. Only an evil disposition can explain this—which, when acknowledged, exposes the lie that if we all only knew the right path we would follow it.

2. Quotation of Hitler (the words hanging on a wall at Auschwitz), cited in Ravi Zacharias, *Can Man Live without God* (Nashville: Word, 1994), 23.

2. THE DOCTRINE OF ORIGINAL
SIN IS UNJUST; AND NOT ONLY
THAT, IT IS PESSIMISTIC

It is not fair for God to allow a sinful disposition to be transmitted from Adam to his posterity, for on this notion we are all being punished for a crime we didn't commit; and it is pessimistic to see human nature as evil, for such a doctrine leaves us without any hope in the world.

Response. Even in our modern era, which so often prides itself on its "rugged individualism," we have examples of groups of people being justly punished for the infraction of one person. For example, during a football game, when a single lineman jumps off sides, it's not as though he alone must step back ten yards—rather, it is the entire team that must lose yards with him. If a father is thrown into prison because he is guilty of a crime, his family will suffer for his guilt, whether they are in prison or not. A congresswoman, who represents her district, can determine its fate through a single vote. A president, who represents his people, can seal their fate by going to war. To be sure, critics of these analogies will note that we choose our presidents and congressional representatives and sports activities, but we did not choose Adam to represent us. However, (a) this is not necessarily true—for many in a district are represented by a person they did not choose; and presidents are never ushered into office with a unanimous vote. Nevertheless, those who either did not vote at all or voted for a different person are just as represented by our leaders as those who ensured their election. No one complains about this form of federalism, since it is unavoidable. In any case, (b) we need to remember that those who complain that they did not vote for Adam are actually suggesting that they—finite sinners that they are—could have made a better choice than the infinite and holy God! We, however, think that the appropriate course is to maintain faith in God—i.e., that he selected the best human representative possible, placed him in the most ideal of circumstances, gave him a perspicuous command, and clearly noted the consequences of his action if he were to disobey. No fairer test could ever be imagined, and no greater mistake has ever been recorded.

In all of this we need to appreciate our corporate solidarity with one another. Thomas Aquinas likens the human race to a single body—many of us comprise the feet of the body, others the hands, still others the arms, and so on. But, just as the feet do not move themselves, but are moved by the soul of the body, so also the human race, regardless of time and place, must share the fate of its soul—its federal head, Adam. The doctrine of original sin, because it so stresses the corporate solidarity of us all, reminds us that, when we inflict pain on another, we are not just hurting one person. Our immoral actions toward one another will damage the victim, his family and friends, *and even us*—often for years to come![3]

As for the notion that original sin is an unattractive and pessimistic doctrine that leads us to despair, we need to, first of all, remember the insight of J. I. Packer; namely, to despair of oneself is not a bad thing[4]—indeed, we ought to despair of ourselves and turn our gaze to God. What could be a better tool to cast away our own (pretended) self-sufficiency than the realization that we are all sinful wretches, desperately in need of a Savior? The Pelagian gospel of Joel Osteen and T. D. Jakes has done little for our self-esteem; for just as the man who feeds the crocodile must come to realize that he's on the menu, so also the preacher who feeds the mind of the sinner with nothing but a sense of his own goodness and sufficiency is bound to see an increase of sin and a decrease of faith. And so I close this response with the winsome insights of G. K. Chesterton:

> This, therefore, is, in conclusion, my reason for accepting the religion [of Christianity] and not merely the scattered and secular truths out of the religion. I do it because the thing has not merely told this truth or that truth, but has revealed itself as a truth-telling thing. All other philosophies say things that plainly seem to be true; only this philosophy has again and again said the thing that does not seem to be true, but is true. Alone of all the creeds it is convincing where it is not attractive; it turns out to be right, like my father in the garden. Theosophists for instance will preach an obviously attractive idea like reincarnation; but if we wait for its logical results, they are spiritual superciliousness and the cruelty

---

3. Aquinas, *ST* I-II.81.1.

4. J. I. Packer, "Introductory Essay," in John Owen's *Death of Death in the Death of Christ* (Carlisle, PA: Banner of Truth Trust, 1959), 2.

of caste. For if a man is a beggar by his own pre-natal sins, people will tend to despise the beggar. But Christianity preaches an obviously unattractive idea, such as original sin; but when we wait for its results, they are pathos and brotherhood, and a thunder of laughter and pity; for only with original sin we can at once pity the beggar and distrust the king. ... The unpopular parts of Christianity turn out when examined to be the very props of the people. The outer ring of Christianity is a rigid guard of ethical abnegations and professional priests; but inside that inhuman guard you will find the old human life dancing like children, and drinking wine like men; for Christianity is the only frame for pagan freedom. But in modern philosophy the case is the opposite; it is its outer ring that is obviously artistic and emancipated; its despair is within.[5]

3. THE DOCTRINE OF ORIGINAL SIN IS ANTI-JEWISH[6]

If original sin were true, one would think that such a biblical doctrine would have made its way into Judaism, just like it did in Christianity. But Jews unanimously reject original sin, insisting that we are born into this world as neutral agents and are thus able to improve our lot through the performance of good deeds. Why, if original sin is taught in the Bible, would these doctrines be rejected by Jews?

Response. Actually, more than a few Jews, many living in the centuries before Christ, did adhere to the doctrine(s) of original sin and total depravity. Indeed, the ancient rabbi Kafvenaki once remarked: "How shall I avoid sinning? My original is corrupt, and from thence are those sins." And, commenting on Psalm 51:5, Manasseh ben Israel concluded that "not only David, but all mankind, ever since sin was introduced into the world, do sin from their original." There is even an account in the Talmud, where it is asked, "From what time does concupiscence rule over man?" To this

---

5. G. K. Chesterton, *Orthodoxy: The Romance of Faith* (1908; repr., New York: Doubleday, 1959), 156–57.

6. This is one of the arguments Kirk MacGregor gives against original sin. See his *A Molinist-Anabaptist Systematic Theology* (Lanham, MD: University Press of America, 2007), 21–37. My comments here only offer a partial response to the points MacGregor has made.

Rabbi Hakkadosch answered, "From his formation," meaning his birth.[7]
Also, a number of quotations from various apocryphal works, most notably 2 Esdras, demonstrate that Jews were not unfamiliar with the doctrine
of original sin:

> For the first Adam, burdened with an evil heart, transgressed and
> was overcome, as were also all who were descended from him. Thus
> the disease became permanent; the law was in the hearts of the
> people along with the evil root; but what was good departed, and
> the evil remained. (2 Esdras 3:21-22 NRSV)

> For a grain of evil seed was sown in Adam's heart from the begin-
> ning, and how much un-godliness it has produced until now—and
> will produce until the time of threshing comes! (2 Esdras 4:30 NRSV)

> From a woman sin had its beginning,
>   and because of her we all die. (Sirach 25:24 NRSV)

Thus, the doctrine of original sin has deep roots in the Jewish tradition,
preceding Christianity by centuries.[8]

4. ORIGINAL SIN PRESUPPOSES THE
EXISTENCE OF ADAM AND EVE, WHO ARE
CLEARLY MYTHICAL CHARACTERS

Response. First, even if Adam and Eve are mythical literary characters, it
may very well be the case that the biblical creation stories are giving us a
mythical account of an historical occurrence. Thus, it is not impossible to
reconcile the doctrine of original sin with modern evolutionary theory.
Swinburne, himself a theistic evolutionist, does just that in the following
insight:

---

7. All quotations of these rabbis are taken from Jonathan Edwards, *Original Sin* (vol. 3
of *The Works of Jonathan Edwards*; ed. Clyde A. Holbrook; New Haven, CT: Yale University
Press, 1970), 429-31n3.

8. For more on this issue, see Michael L. Brown, *Theological Objections* (vol. 2 of *Answering
Jewish Objections to Jesus*; Grand Rapids: Baker, 2000), 198-208.

At some stage in the history of the world, there appeared the first creature with hominoid body who had some understanding of the difference between the morally obligatory, the morally permissible (i.e. right), and the morally wrong; and an ability freely to choose the morally right. So much is obvious; since on modern evolutionary views, as well as on all views held in Christian tradition, once upon a time there were no such creatures and now there are some, there must have been a first one. It seems reasonable to consider such a creature the first man; and we may follow biblical tradition and call him "Adam." (The Hebrew word means "man.")[9]

A few lines later he says, "The acquisition of some moral beliefs about what is obligatory would also ... constitute any actions of the first man contrary to obligation as objectively sinful (whether or not he believed them to be so). Adam was very probably also therefore the first sinner."[10] To be sure, Swinburne rejects the notion that we inherit the guilt of Adam. Our proneness to sin, however, plausibly resulted from Adam's bad example, immoral beliefs, and the sort of society created in the wake of his dawning conscience. He alone is not responsible for our genetically acquired propensity to sin, but he did begin "the process to which so many of us had subsequently contributed."[11]

Of course, another option is to offer good reasons to think Adam and Eve actually existed. This is the position I take; and so I commend the work of Fuzale Rana and Hugh Ross, who present a strong case for the historicity of our (purported) first parents.[12]

---

9. Richard Swinburne, *Responsibility and Atonement* (Oxford: Clarendon, 1989), 141.

10. Swinburne, *Responsibility and Atonement*, 142.

11. Swinburne, *Responsibility and Atonement*, 143.

12. Fazale Rana with Hugh Ross, *Who Was Adam? A Creation Model Approach to the Origin of Humanity* (2nd ed.; Covina, CA: Reasons to Believe, 2015); and Ross, *Navigating Genesis*, 37–122.

Appendix 2

SCIENTIA MEDIA IN THE LIGHT OF SCRIPTURE, DIVINE SOVEREIGNTY, AND THE DIVINE ASEITY

I believe the current revival of Molinism has advanced, and even enhanced, the doctrines of providence and the divine decree—e.g., by couching the issue in terms of world ensembles instead of a linear delineation of the order of decrees, Molinists have paved a way for us to better understand and articulate the relationship between divine sovereignty and divine love (a point we explore in more detail elsewhere in this work, especially in chapter 7). That said, I have offered a detailed critique of the doctrine of middle knowledge elsewhere. Not that my critique is unique in any way, for both the Thomistic and Reformed traditions have, by and large, rejected the doctrine because it (1) is nowhere taught in Scripture, (2) compromises the aseity of God, (3) entails environmental determinism (and, thus, fails to reconcile itself to libertarian freedom), (4) compromises the sovereignty of God, and (5) is superfluous.[1] This appendix highlights some of these criticisms.

The most important issue for us is whether or not (1) middle knowledge is taught or (at least) suggested in Scripture. For Scripture is our ultimate authority; and so if the Bible does not teach a doctrine, such is one good reason not to accept it. In a recent dissertation on this very issue, Sze Sze Chiew gives a close analysis of both the doctrine of the *scientia media* and the hermeneutical issues surrounding Molinists' use of various biblical

---

1. See Campbell, "Middle Knowledge: A Reformed Critique," 1–22; and Campbell, "The Beautiful Mind," 263–301. For more reasons to reject middle knowledge, see Reginald Garrigou-Lagrange, *God: His Existence and Nature (A Thomistic Solution to Certain Agnostic Antinomies)* (5th ed.; trans. Dom Bede Rose; St. Louis: B. Herder, 1945), 2:81–95.

texts. In particular, she scrutinizes how this tradition has used 1 Samuel 23:6–13 and Matthew 11:20–24 in support of the doctrine of middle knowledge. Her conclusion is quite straightforward: "I have come to the conclusion that Scripture does not warrant middle knowledge; and that to accept the Molinists' account of God's knowledge and their metaphysical definition of freedom leads to sacrificing and downplaying the overall biblical-theological account of God—the sovereign and saving God who creates, redeems, and consummates His creation."[2]

This chapter has illustrated several times how the *scientia media* (4) compromises the sovereignty of God. As we established in chapter 4, the Thomistic analysis of possible worlds begins with the presupposition that whatever is possible is grounded in what is actual. Justification for this notion is found in the fact that bare possibilities are nothing unless they are grounded in something. Pure potentials do not actually exist, and so, in and of themselves, they cannot cause anything. Indeed, if nothing then there cannot be something. Less carefully worded, if nothingness were to ever obtain, there would be nothing right now. For "nothing" is the absence of anything whatsoever; hence, a state of complete *nothing* would be the absence of matter, energy, time, space, or even states or states of affairs and so on, and hence *even the potential for something to be*. So, again, if nothing then there is no potential for something; if nothing, then there can never be something; or, *ex nihilo nihil fit* ("out of nothing nothing comes"). Hence the possible is grounded in the actual. In fact, we see all around us beings that are existent or actual, but have the potential to be something other than what they currently are—e.g., I exist, but I have the potential to be taller, shorter, fatter, or even nonexistent. Now, whatever admits of a composition between actuality and potentiality must be caused by another; and since there cannot be an infinite regress of act-potency beings, there must be a cause of all such beings that is pure actuality with no potentiality. But the "One who is Pure Act" is what we mean by God. Hence God is the foundation for whatever is possible.[3]

---

2. Sze Sze Chiew, *Middle Knowledge and Biblical Interpretation: Luis de Molina, Herman Bavinck, and William Lane Craig* (Contributions to Philosophical Theology 13; Frankfurt am Main: Peter Lang, 2016), 205.

3. For more on this see Gaven Kerr, *Aquinas's Way to God: The Proof in* De Ente et Essentia (Oxford: Oxford University Press, 2015). One is also encouraged to acquire an edition of

In chapter 5, we noted how Molinists distinguish between possible and feasible worlds, with the latter being a subset of the former. For the Molinist, human free will renders some worlds infeasible for God, indicating that, contrary to Thomism, there is a realm of possibility beyond his control. God simply cannot bring a world into being wherein no one sins, for all of us suffer from transworld depravity; and, for some Molinists, there are those who suffer from transworld damnation, meaning that he who is all-powerful cannot bring a world into being in which they freely choose to be saved. In short, there are those who are inaccessible to God, and are therefore unredeemable. This mitigates both the sovereignty of God and the gospel of Christ, as we have noted. To preserve divine sovereignty, *God* must the one who determines what is feasible for him; and, for us, the only gospel worth taking into the world is one that proclaims a God who can always reach us. Indeed, Van Til's words bear repeating: "The prodigal thought he had clean escaped from the father's influence. In reality the father controlled the 'far country' to which the prodigal had gone."[4] How so? Because, the consistently scriptural worldview rejects the notion that bare possibility precedes actuality; rather, the "biblical position holds God to be the source of all possibility."[5] Hence, Van Til's parabolic point is actually a metaphysical one; for just as the prodigal journeyed to a far country that was, in reality, still controlled by his father, there is no possible, plausible, or feasible world the sinner can wander into that allows her to hide from God. Indeed, regardless of the circumstances she finds herself in, the sinner always remains accessible to her Creator. The sinner who wants to hide from her Creator will not, at first glance, find comfort in this truth; but those of us who have tasted the goodness of the Lord, and have even discovered the many hidden treasures of the Reformed tradition, have found the absolute sovereignty of God to be a balm for our aching souls.

Yet, as important as divine sovereignty is, by far, an even more important issue is (2) the divine aseity. For sovereignty addresses *how God relates*

Aquinas's *De Ente et Essentia*.

4. Cornelius Van Til, "Why I Believe in God," in Greg L. Bahnsen, *Van Til's Apologetic: Readings and Analysis* (Phillipsburg, NJ: Presbyterian & Reformed, 1998), 139.

5. Cornelius Van Til, *A Survey of Christian Epistemology* (vol. 2 of *In Defense of the Faith*; Phillipsburg, NJ: Presbyterian & Reformed, 1980), 88.

to the creature; aseity addresses *what God is*. There is little doubt that the *scientia media* compromises the aseity of God. By "aseity" I mean that God's existence is not in any way caused *extra se* (i.e., by something or someone outside himself), but that he exists wholly of himself (*a se*) and is therefore totally self-existent and wholly uncaused. As such, God receives absolutely nothing from the creature, which (given the divine simplicity)[6] includes his cognition. Wisdom, understanding, and knowledge flow *from* the Creator and never *to* him. So like his existence, the divine *scientia* is wholly uncaused.[7] However, if the doctrine of middle knowledge is true, then it is the creature, not the Creator, who determines the content of the *scientia media*. Since this clearly contradicts the biblical claim that God receives nothing from the creature, including his knowledge, we are compelled to either accept the infallible proclamations of Scripture or accept the doctrine of middle knowledge. We cannot *consistently* accept both.

The Molinist Response. Luke Van Horn, who leans in favor of Molinism, has responded to this critique as follows: "It should be pointed out that Bavinck apparently did not understand MK [middle knowledge] accurately, since he mistakenly charges Molinists with believing that God's MK is derived from the will of creatures."[8] "On the contrary," he says, "Molinists reject such a misunderstanding, since on their view God has MK prior to creating anything, including any creaturely wills. Campbell makes the same mistake in his 'Middle Knowledge: A Reformed Critique' 16."[9] Craig concurs:

> Some opponents of middle knowledge incorrectly charge that free creatures cause God's middle knowledge of various actualizable worlds. But such an allegation is obviously mistaken, since in that logically prior moment nothing but God exists, so that there can

---

6. For an excellent defense of this wonderful truth, see James E. Dolezal, *God without Parts: Divine Simplicity and the Metaphysics of God's Absoluteness* (Eugene, OR: Pickwick, 2011). See also chapter 2 above.

7. For biblical support, see Campbell, "Middle Knowledge: A Reformed Critique," 17–18; and Chiew, *Middle Knowledge and Biblical Interpretation*, 140.

8. See Herman Bavinck, *God and Creation* (vol. 2 of *Reformed Dogmatics*; ed. John Bolt; trans. John Vriend; Grand Rapids: Baker Academic, 2004), 179.

9. Luke Van Horn, "On Incorporating Middle Knowledge into Calvinism: A Theological/ Metaphysical Muddle?," *Journal of the Evangelical Theological Society* 55, no. 4 (2012): 814n31.

be no talk of a causal relation. Rather Molinists have consistently asserted that there is no cause of God's cognitions *extra se*, but that He knows counterfactuals of freedom through His own essence, that is to say, innately.[10]

A Reformed Rejoinder. However, as I point out in "Middle Knowledge: A Reformed Critique," Bavinck is just one of many Reformed theologians who offer such a criticism of the divine *scientia media*;[11] and, at least on this score, this common Reformed objection has also been articulated and defended by many Catholics who embrace a Thomistic metaphysic. Of course, I recognize that Molinists resist the notion that the creature determines the content of the divine middle knowledge. That Molinists have *constantly* asserted that nothing determines the divine cognition to be what it is *extra se*, there can be no doubt; but whether they have *consistently* asserted as much is dubitable!

To the question of how God can comprehend what a creature would do in any given circumstance, Craig posits two possibilities—one offered by Molina and another offered by Francisco Suarez. Concerning the former, Craig is not willing to affirm everything Molina does, and yet still wonders, "Why can we not affirm that God comprehends an individual essence so completely that He knows what its exemplification would freely do under any circumstance?"[12] Concerning the latter, "Suarez thinks of God as positing a possible creature in His mind in certain circumstances and then observing what the creature would do; the creature may thus be said to have a *habitudo* to do something were it to be put in such circumstances, and the corresponding counterfactual is thus true and known by God."[13] Craig endorses both possibilities as ways in which God *can* know counterfactuals of creaturely freedom prior to the divine creative decree, since "neither Molina nor Suarez's account of how God knows such counterfactuals has

10. William Lane Craig, *Divine Foreknowledge and Human Freedom: The Coherence of Theism; Omniscience* (Brill's Studies in Intellectual History 19; New York: E. J. Brill, 1991), 272.

11. For an analysis of Bavinck's perspective on the authority of Scripture, theological method, and the grounds (or lack thereof) for middle knowledge, see Chiew, *Middle Knowledge and Biblical Interpretation*, 77-106.

12. Craig, *Divine Foreknowledge and Human Freedom*, 268.

13. Craig, *Divine Foreknowledge and Human Freedom*, 269.

been shown to be impossible."[14] It would seem that Molina and Suarez are virtually saying the same thing in their accounts of how the divine omniscience can infallibly know such counterfactuals—namely, he simply comprehends the essence and/or habits and/or character of the creature so well that he is able to know what the created being would do in any given circumstance. And it would seem that this is the best move a Molinist could make in order to reconcile middle knowledge with aseity. In the words of MacGregor, the individual essences of every hypothetical, libertarianly free creature God can make "exist neither independently of God nor outside of God but only as designs within the mind of God. In other words, these individual essences are solely the product of God's imagination— mental patterns or designs for things he knows in his infinite creativity and artistry he could create if he so willed." Therefore, "God obtains no knowledge at all from the creatures that could or would be created from these patterns or designs."[15]

What does it mean to say that the comprehension and/or imagination of a hypothetical creature's essence gives one the ability to know what that creature would do in any given circumstance? By way of analogy, such a divine comprehension is similar to me studying the activities of a person or animal and being able to predict what the person or animal would do if, say, she were offered a free ticket to a concert and/or he were offered a new chew toy. The difference between my prediction and the divine cognition is (1) I am fallible while God is not, (2) I must take time to study the creature(s) while the deity comprehends creatures' essences timelessly, and (3) I must look outside myself to gain knowledge of what the creature would do, while the content of such subjunctive conditionals eternally resides in the divine mind. But the analogy I have given nevertheless holds, since a similarity between the two modes of cognition is located in the fact that, in both my musings and God's imaginings, the truth-value of the proposition "p would do a in c" is determined by the creature being contemplated, and not by God or me. That the proposition is located in the divine

---

14. Craig, *Divine Foreknowledge and Human Freedom*, 269.

15. Kirk R. MacGregor, *Luis de Molina: The Life and Theology of the Founder of Middle Knowledge* (Grand Rapids: Zondervan, 2015), 101. MacGregor explicitly tells us that he is answering the Reformed criticism that middle knowledge compromises the divine aseity; see *Luis de Molina*, 101n61.

mind instead of a world of concrete objects—or, for that matter, a world of abstract objects—is irrelevant to the issue at hand. No matter what model of divine cognition we adopt—perceptualist or conceptualist—God must either "wait and see" what his creatures would do in the feasible circumstances in which they are placed, or he must contemplate the essence of the creature in order to figure out how that being would behave if placed in a particular state of affairs. Because that is in fact what Molinism teaches, we must conclude that the creature, not God, determines the content of the divine middle knowledge. Indeed, how else could it be that some logically possible worlds remain infeasible for God? If the creatures making up these world ensembles did not determine the truth-value of their respective counterfactuals, then there would be no basis for distinguishing between natural and middle knowledge.

In light of what we have said so far, we find the following two assertions of Molina, when placed alongside each other, to be incoherent:

> God does not get His knowledge from things, but knows all things *in* Himself and *from* Himself.[16]

> Therefore, it should be said (i) that *middle* knowledge partly has the character of *natural* knowledge, since it was prior to the free act of the divine will and since God did not have the power to know anything else, and (ii) that it partly has the character of *free* knowledge, since the fact that it is knowledge of the one part rather than the other derives from the fact that free choice, on the hypothesis that it should be created in one or another order of things, would do the one thing rather than the other, even though it would indifferently be able to do either of them.[17]

The first assertion is, to his credit, Molina's affirmation of a divine cognition that is wholly *a se*. In the words of MacGregor, "So, for Molina all God's

---

16. Molina, *Foreknowledge*, 4.14.15.49.12, emphasis original, quoted in MacGregor, *Luis de Molina*, 101.

17. Molina, *Foreknowledge*, 4.14.15.52.10, emphasis original, quoted in MacGregor, *Luis de Molina*, 93n38.

knowledge is self-contained, a doctrine which redounds to the aseity—the
absolute self-existence, self-sufficiency, independence, and autonomy—
of God."[18] However, Molina's second assertion contradicts his first; for, as
he clearly says, middle knowledge is both like and unlike natural and free
knowledge. It is like natural knowledge in the sense that it is necessary
for God to possess both natural and middle knowledge, while it is not necessary for God to possess free knowledge. Indeed, God could have chosen
not to create any world whatsoever, in which case God would have lacked a
scientia libera.[19] Also, natural and middle knowledge are logical moments in
the life of God which precede the divine creative decree, while free knowledge is posterior to the divine decision that a logically possible and feasible
world becomes actual. However, like free knowledge, and unlike natural
knowledge, the content of the scientia media "is not essential to God. Since
libertarian creatures could choose differently ..., [and] God's knowledge
would be different if they were to do so."[20] Hence Molina has taken away with
his left hand what he has given with his right—namely, on the one hand
he insists that God's knowledge is wholly a se, being in no way determined
by the creature—in his own words, "God does not get his knowledge from
things"—and on the other hand he insists that the content of the scientia
media is contingent on how the creature would act were he placed in this
or that circumstance. In short, it is creaturely freedom that determines
the divine middle knowledge to be what it is—not God. Thus, the classical
Thomistic and Reformed critique of middle knowledge still stands. Indeed,
while listing the many theological and philosophical problems inherent to
the concept of a divine scientia media, Garrigou-Lagrange tells us that such
a doctrine "ascribes passivity to Pure Act, that is, the divine intelligence is
measured by the determination of our free will, which it must ascertain

---

18. MacGregor, Luis de Molina, 101.

19. While we will not make a major issue out of this technical point, we are compelled to
note that this Molinistic assertion is not necessarily true. True, had God not created any world,
he would have never possessed a free knowledge of all temporal contingents in any creaturely
world. However, he would have still possessed free knowledge—for even the decision to never
create a world is, in effect, an eternal decree on the part of God; and so it follows that God
would still have had a scientia libera grounded in that eternal decree, not of the goings-on of
a creation that never existed, but of the eternal and loving fellowship between the members
of the triune Godhead.

20. MacGregor, Luis de Molina, 93, italics added.

and wait upon."[21] The idea of "waiting upon" the creature to know the truth-value of its hypothetical actions is, even on Molinism, clearly a *façon de parler*, since "waiting" is a temporal notion. Indeed, even if God were not timeless, his omniscience guarantees that he knows what he knows omni-temporally. Yet, on Molina's hypothesis, "waiting upon," like "ascertaining," correctly captures the fact that God is depending on the creature—or, even worse (and less coherently, but more accurately) *the idea of the essences of hypothetical creatures*—for the purpose of ascertaining the content of his own *scientia media*.

This same tension can be found in Arminius, who (on the one hand) tells us that all "the things which God knows, He knows neither by intelligible [*species*] images, nor by similitude, (for it is not necessary for Him to use abstraction and application for the purpose of understanding;) but He knows them by his own essence, and by this alone."[22] On the other hand, as the opening quotation of chapter 5 demonstrates, Arminius also tells us that middle knowledge depends on the liberty of the created will.[23]

---

21. Reginald Garrigou-Lagrange, *Grace: Commentary on the Summa Theologica of St. Thomas,* *I*ª*II*ᵃᵉ, q. 109–114 (trans. Dominican Nuns of Corpus Christi Monastery in Menlo Park, CA; St. Louis: B. Herder, 1952), 255. For a defense of "pure actuality" as an appropriate term for the divine self-existence or aseity, see Thomas Aquinas, ST Ia.3.1–4; Edward Feser, *Five Proofs of God* (San Francisco: Ignatius Press, 2017), 29–37, 67, 82, 206, 250; and James E. Dolezal, *All That Is in God: Evangelical Theology and the Challenge of Classical Christian Theism* (Grand Rapids: Reformation Heritage, 2017), 11–17.

22. James Arminius, *Disputations on Some of the Principle Subjects of the Christian Religion* (1828; repr., vol. 2 of *The Works of James Arminius*; trans. James Nichols and William Nichols; Grand Rapids: Baker, 1986), 120.

23. Kirk MacGregor thinks that the major difference between Arminius's and Molina's doctrine(s) of middle knowledge is that Arminius, in contrast to Molina, places the *scientia media* subsequent to the divine decree. This is the key to interpreting the difference between these two theologians, and it opens up the charge that Arminius, by rendering middle knowledge dependent on the creature, compromises the divine perfection in a way that Molina's doctrine does not. However, as MacGregor rightly points out, Arminius himself never enters into a full discussion of the divine decree and its relationship to middle knowledge, and so his reconstruction of Arminius's thought is itself built on an ambiguity left behind in the writings of the sixteenth-century divine. See *A Molinist-Anabaptist Systematic Theology* (Lanham, MD: University Press of America, 2007), 69–73. In any case, one could argue that, if MacGregor's exegesis of Arminius is correct, then Arminius's doctrine, from the standpoint of Perfect Being theology, is more plausible than Molina's; for if the *scientia media* comes logically posterior to the decree then one is *ultimately* grounding counterfactuals of creaturely freedom in the divine will rather than the creaturely will (or nothing at all). This means that the *scientia media*, similar to the *scientia libera*, is contingent on the creature only insofar as the divine will has determined it to be, in which case the divine aseity is preserved. To be sure, this interpretation of Arminius wreaks havoc on his doctrine of conditional election,

Of course, Craig all but admits the very point we're trying to make—i.e., that the creature, not God, determines the content of the divine middle knowledge. After giving us with his right hand a concept of divine omniscience wherein the knowledge of the deity is wholly *a se*, Craig, like Molina, MacGregor, and Arminius, takes it away with his left hand. Indeed, while addressing the core Reformed-Thomist objection to a *scientia media*, Craig writes:

> That leads us to the second half of Garrigou-Lagrange's objection, that middle knowledge posits passivity in God. *Despite Molinist protests, I think we will have to admit that this is true.* But at the same time ... this seems to me of no great consequence. As I argued earlier, God's simple foreknowledge can be understood as determined in its content by what will in fact occur. *This sort of determinacy or passivity on God's part seems to me altogether innocuous,* and if this sacrifices the Thomistic view of God as Pure Actuality, then so be it.[24]

Craig is clearly saying that God's *simple foreknowledge* is determined by the creature; and there is no explicit statement here of middle knowledge being so determined. Yet in the opening lines of the quotation, Craig explicitly says that middle knowledge does introduce passivity in God. Indeed, in an earlier chapter of his work Craig says "that on the Molinist account, there may be degrees of counterfactual dependence, God's middle knowledge

---

thereby accentuating the problems we have already discussed. But it may prove fruitful for a Reformed theologian who desires to construe the divine decree along the lines of possible worlds rather than as a logical ordering of divine thoughts, although one is left wondering whether middle knowledge does not become superfluous at precisely this point. Indeed, if MacGregor's exegesis is correct, Arminius's doctrine of middle knowledge may preserve divine aseity at the cost of utility. One might just as well call this entire episode in the divine life "the decree" rather than "middle knowledge"! In any case, one cannot use this distinction between Arminius and Molina as a reason to think that Molina avoids the standard Reformed Thomist critique of middle knowledge in a way Arminius does not; for every Reformed and Thomistic theologian cited in this appendix (and more besides) presupposes that the *scientia media* is *prior* to the divine decree. Hence, it is Molina's view that is being rejected, not Arminius's (assuming MacGregor has correctly located the difference between the two). So it is Molina's view, not Arminius's, that compromises the divine aseity (again, assuming MacGregor's exegesis of Arminius is correct).

24. Craig, *Divine Foreknowledge and Human Freedom*, 272–73, italics added. I am disheartened by Craig's cavalier rejection of the doctrine of the God's pure actuality, since it is not merely Thomistic or Reformed but biblical (see Dolezal, *All That Is in God*, 11–17).

being *directly* counterfactually dependent upon the course of future events and other past events being *indirectly* dependent upon future events, based on whether God would have acted differently if He had had different middle knowledge than He did."[25] Notice that God could have had different middle knowledge than he in fact possesses. How so? On Molinism, the creature does not have *causal* power over the past, since it does not make any sense to think that the creature *causes* God to have the knowledge he does (whether natural or middle) before the creation of the universe; but the creature does have *counterfactual* power over the past in the sense that, if his actions in any given circumstance would have been different than the divine middle knowledge understands them to be, then the content of the *scientia media* would be different than it in fact is.[26] This, of course, further proves that, on Molinism—and, for that matter, *any* theory postulating a middle knowledge in the mind of God (e.g., congruism)[27]—the creature, at least partially, determines the content of the divine mind (i.e., his middle knowledge) which, in turn, renders God less than wholly *a se*. If Molinism is true, then the creature has a say in what God *knows* and thus, to some degree, what God *is*—which *just is* the *confusion*, albeit ever so subtle, *of the*

---

25. Craig, *Divine Foreknowledge and Human Freedom*, 197, emphasis original.

26. Craig, *Divine Foreknowledge and Human Freedom*, 197–98.

27. As I demonstrate in "Middle Knowledge: A Reformed Critique," 16.

creature with the Creator. In the words of Garrigou-Lagrange, "Molinism is a kind of dream in which the creature forgets that he is a creature."[28]

---

28. Garrigou-Lagrange, *Grace*, 249. Van Horn offers another criticism of my exposition of the nature of counterfactuals and their relationship to middle knowledge. In my essay I wrote the following: "Another way to understand middle knowledge is to suggest that God knows via the *scientia media* all counterfactual states-of-affairs. A counterfactual is a state-of-affairs that is counter to what actually takes place in the real world. To put it another way, a counterfactual proposition is a subjunctive conditional which presupposes the falsity of the antecedent" ("Middle Knowledge: A Reformed Critique," 4). While I clearly offered a correct definition of counterfactuals, Van Horn states that many "counterfactuals are included in either natural or free knowledge. *If God were to create a Martian, it would be a temporal being* is a necessarily true counterfactual (and so known naturally), whereas *If Calvin had been an Israelite, he would have been a member of God's chosen people* is contingently true, since it is true only because God chose the Israelites (and hence is known freely)" (Van Horn, "Incorporating Middle Knowledge," 812n24, italics original). Horn's assessment seems correct. I should have worded my exposition more carefully. That said, I am not alone in my error. To quote just one advocate of middle knowledge, "In short, middle knowledge is God's prevolitional knowledge of all true counterfactuals" (MacGregor, *Luis de Molina*, 79). Perhaps a more careful way to summarize the doctrine of middle knowledge is to say that God knows all true counterfactuals of *contingent events*, including those resulting from *creaturely freedom*, via his middle knowledge; any counterfactual that is necessarily true is known via the divine natural knowledge, and any counterfactual that is contingent on the divine creative decree is known via the divine free knowledge. See Thomas Flint, *Divine Providence: The Molinist Account* (Ithaca, NY: Cornell University Press, 1998), 42–43. This, for me, exacerbates the problems inherent to middle knowledge; for if God can know counterfactuals via natural and free knowledge, then the *scientia media* is rendered superfluous.

Appendix 3

ISAIAH 45:7 AND THE ORIGIN OF EVIL

S keptics and hyper-Calvinists commonly insist that the Bible clearly teaches that God is the creator of all that is, including evil: "I am the LORD, and there is none else. I form the light, and create darkness: I make peace, and create evil: I the LORD do all these *things*" (Isa 45:6b–7 KJV). Commenting on this text, the great Old Testament scholar Claus Westermann rhetorically asks, "But what kind of God is this who created evil as well as good, woe as well as weal?"[1] Not all theologians are so upset at Isaiah's words. Some are only upset with those who do not have the stomach to trust in a God who created evil. Gordon Clark is one such thinker who, after making his case, based on this text in Isaiah, that God really is the cause of evil, laments, "O, Arminian, Arminian, thou that distortist the prophets and misinterpretest them that are sent unto thee; how often have I told your children the plain truth ... and ye would not let them understand!"[2]

---

1. Claus Westermann, *Isaiah 40–66: A Commentary* (trans. David M. G. Stalker; Philadelphia: Westminster, 1969), 162.

2. Gordon H. Clark, *Predestination* (Phillipsburg, NJ: Presbyterian & Reformed, 1987), 187–88. However, hyper-Calvinists such as Clark and Sproul Jr., who are themselves Presbyterians, should know that the Westminster Confession of Faith clearly states that God has foreordained everything that comes to pass, yet not in such a way that he is the author of sin (3.1). So how do they reconcile the Confession's statement with their view that God is the cause of evil (or sin)? I could not find Sproul Jr. offering any cogent answer to this question. Clark, on the other hand, does offer an answer in the following way: "Summarizing the Scriptures, the Confession says here that God is not the author of sin; that is, God does nothing sinful. Even those Christians who are not Calvinists must admit that God in some sense is the cause of sin, for he is the sole ultimate cause of everything. But God does not commit the sinful act, nor does he approve of it and reward it. Perhaps this illustration is faulty, as most illustrations are, but consider that God is the cause of my writing this book. Who could deny that God is the first or ultimate cause, since it was he who created mankind. But although God is the cause of this chapter, he is not its author. It would be much better, if he were." Gordon H. Clark, *What Do Presbyterians Believe?* (Phillipsburg, NJ: Presbyterian & Reformed, 1965), 37.

But it is not at all clear that Isaiah is claiming that YHWH created evil.
The word translated "evil" by the King James Version is the Hebrew word
רַע (ra') and, though it does (more often than not) convey the meaning of
"evil" (as in moral corruption or wickedness) throughout the Hebrew Bible,
it often means "calamity" or "disaster" in various passages throughout the
TaNaKh. As J. Alec Motyer notes, "Out of the 640 occurrences of the word
ra' (which ranges in meaning from a 'nasty' taste to full moral evil) there
are 275 instances where 'trouble' or 'calamity' is the meaning."[3] Thus, most

---

There are several problems with Clark's argument and illustration. First, part of the
problem in much of this is that Clark famously rejected the Thomistic doctrine of analogy
and adhered to the univocity of theological language. See Herman Hoeksema, *The Clark-Van
Til Controversy* (Unicoi, TN: Trinity Foundation, 2005), 17-24. But on this univocal doctrine
God causes things in the same way the creature causes them. But we only know of and/or
are only able to utilize mechanistic, efficient, causes in order to bring about various effects
(e.g., the movement of the food to my mouth; the movement of billiard balls on the table; the
movement of my body from A to Z). And so we are back to the domino effect, wherein—even
if God is a trillion places back pushing things in motion—my consciousness of being the
cause of the typing of these words is pure illusion. In short, given Clark's own presuppositions regarding our language about God and, by extension, his relationship to the world, the
distinction between "cause" and "author" is vacuous. Second, even granting his univocism,
Clark's argument does not follow through. Indeed, God is the cause of everything; but evil is
not a thing; therefore God is in no way the cause of evil.

If one rejects univocism and embraces the classical Thomistic doctrine of analogy, then
perhaps Clark's illustration, distinguishing "author" from "cause," would be coherent. Indeed,
on the doctrine of analogy, God causes events to obtain in our world in a *similar* way as we
do. Hence, God's causal activity is neither wholly like nor wholly unlike our bringing about
effects in this world. Given Thomistic analogy, then, we can at least see how it would be possible to "cause" an event without "authoring" it. A better analogy would be our earlier DVD
illustration, whereby God exhaustively comprehends every thing or essence or nature and
event on the DVD, and simply says "*Be,*" thereby ensuring that everything will occur just as it
was laid out on the DVD. Since, on the DVD, God is not causing any sins to happen, his bringing
about the states of affairs where sinful acts take place is merely an act whereby he "weakly"
actualizes their occurrence. To put it another way, on the DVD the actions of his creatures
are their own, arising from their own desires and powers of movement. God's rendering the
merely logically possible world, represented on the DVD, an actual world does not change
the integrity and freedom of creaturely agency. It simply ensures that these genuinely free
actions will take place. Indeed, given the *analogia entis* between God and creation, it seems
quite plausible to think that God is not merely able to foreordain *what* his creatures do, but
even the *way* they do it. On this model of theological language, there is nothing incoherent
in the Westminster Confession of Faith's claim that God has foreordained everything that
comes to pass, "yet so, as thereby neither is God the author of sin, nor is violence offered to
the will of the creatures; nor is the liberty or contingency of second causes taken away, but
rather established" (3.1). For a helpful modern defense of Thomistic analogy, see Norman L.
Geisler and Winfried Corduan, *Philosophy of Religion* (2nd ed.; Grand Rapids: Baker, 1989),
part 3; and Kreeft, *Summa of the* Summa, 123-33.

3. J. Alec Motyer, *The Prophecy of Isaiah: An Introduction & Commentary* (Downers Grove,
IL: InterVarsity Press, 1993), 359.

modern versions translate רָע variously as "calamity" (NASB, NET), "disaster" (NIV, HCSB), and "woe" (NRSV, NJPS).[4] Context determines which version, the KJV or a modern translation, is correct.[5]

---

4. That the NJPS gives this rendering—i.e., "I form the light and create darkness, I make weal and create woe—I the Lord do all these things" (Isa 45:7 NJPS)—is interesting in light of Rabbi Tovia Singer's critique of so-called Christian mistranslations; namely, "The translators of several Christian Bibles, however, sought to conceal Isaiah's message. They accomplished this task by mistranslating the Hebrew word as 'a calamity' or 'natural disaster,' rather than 'evil.'" See Singer, *Let's Get Biblical: Why Doesn't Judaism Accept the Christian Messiah?* (Forest Hills, NY: Outreach Judaism, 2014), 1:352. I say this is interesting because the NJPS itself renders רע as "woe." Thus it is unfair for Singer to suggest that Christian translations, in some nefarious or conspiratorial way, are trying to conceal the genuine meaning of the text when a very competent *Jewish* translation renders רע in much the same way as other modern Christian versions do. Singer then says, "Many conservative Christian Bibles, including the King James Version and the New American Standard, resisted the temptation to tamper with this unambiguous passage in the Book of Isaiah" (*Let's Get Biblical*, 1:353). To call other modern versions "tampering" with the true meaning of the text is simply unfair. Singer is also mistaken. True, the KJV renders רע as "evil," but not the NASB—which renders רע as "calamity." Singer may be confusing the early twentieth-century ASV with the NASB, which did indeed render רע as "evil."

Amazingly, Singer is another theologian who insists that God is the creator of evil: "God created both good and evil and presented these two powerful forces to mankind, so that man could then freely choose his spiritual path. This cardinal principle is clearly expressed in the Torah" (*Let's Get Biblical*, 1:353). Where in the Torah do we find such a teaching? It is written in Deut 30: "**See, I have set before you today life and good, death and evil.** ... I call heaven and earth as witnesses today against you, that I have set before you life and death, blessing and cursing. Therefore, choose life, that both you and your descendants may live' [Deut 30:15, 19]. ... It is a core teaching in the Jewish faith that man can attain virtue only if he possesses the free will to reject it and choose evil" (*Let's Get Biblical*, 1:353, *emphasis* original). Notice that Singer calls the doctrine of the divine creation of evil a "cardinal principle" of Judaism. Unfortunately for Singer, the Jewish theologians who edited *The Jewish Study Bible* did not draw the same inference from Deut 30 that he did. First, note their translation: "See, I set before you this day life and prosperity, death and adversity" (Deut 30:15 NJPS). Second, note their commentary on this verse: "**The necessity of choice.** If 'life' meant only biological life, there would be no choice. The choice is rather between life in the covenant and life not in the covenant. From this viewpoint, biological existence, and even prosperity, if not in the covenant, constitutes death." See *The Jewish Study Bible* (ed. Adele Berlin and Marc Zvi Brettler; Oxford: Oxford University Press, 2004), 436n30:11–20, *emphasis* original.

5. To be sure, the KJV is not the only version to translate רע as "evil." As pointed out in the prior footnote, the ASV agrees with the KJV here. Also, the 1599 Geneva Bible, which was the first English translation of the Scriptures to reach North America, renders the text as follows: "I form the light and create darkness: I make peace and create evil: I the Lord do all these things" (Isa 45:7). That said, the study notes originally accompanying this translation offer the following interpretive paraphrase: "I send peace and war, prosperity and adversity." See *1599 Geneva Bible: Calvin Legacy Edition* (ed. Peter A. Lillback et al.; White Hall, WV: Tolle Lege, 2008), 722. This may imply that the English word "evil" had a wider range of meaning during the sixteenth and seventeenth centuries than it does today. It is interesting to note that Calvin, who taught the editors of the Geneva Bible (even writing the preface to the 1560 edition), offered the following commentary on Isa 45:7: "Fanatics torture this word evil, as if God were the author of evil, that is, of sin; but it is very obvious how ridiculously they abuse this passage of the Prophet. This is sufficiently explained by the contrast, the parts

of which must agree with each other; for he [Isaiah] contrasts 'peace' with 'evil,' that is, with afflictions, wars, and other adverse occurrences. If he contrasted 'righteousness' with 'evil,' there would be some plausibility in their reasoning's, but this is a manifest contrast of things that are opposite to each other. Consequently, we ought not to reject the ordinary distinction, that God is the author of the 'evil' of punishment, but not of the 'evil' of guilt." The Genevan Reformer goes on to say, "But the Sophists are wrong in their exposition; for, while they acknowledge that famine, barrenness, war, pestilence, and other scourges, come from God, they deny that God is the author of calamities, when the Lord raises up wicked men to chastise us by their hand, as is evident from various passages of Scripture (1 Kings ix.14, 23.) The Lord does not indeed inspire them [i.e., wicked men] with malice, but he uses it [i.e., the wicked men's malice] for the purpose of chastising us, and exercises the office of a judge, in the same manner as he made use of the malice of Pharaoh and others, in order to punish his people (Exod. i.11 and ii.23.) We ought therefore to hold this doctrine, that God alone is the author of all events; that is, that adverse and prosperous events are sent by him, even though he makes use of the agency of men, that none may attribute it to fortune, or to any other cause." See John Calvin, *The Book of the Prophet Isaiah: Volume 2* (Calvin's Commentaries 8; trans. William Pringle [1850]; Grand Rapids: Baker, 1996), 403. The distinction between "evil of guilt" and "evil of punishment" is reasonable. If I am a creator of the former, then evil or wickedness arises from me as its cause and hence I am guilty of sin. If I am the creator of the latter, then I have caused bad things to happen to another as a punishment of their immoral actions—that is, my actions in this case are not evil in themselves, but they are evil to the one receiving the punishment. For example, a murderer is the author of the evil of guilt, while the judge is the author of the evil of the criminal's punishment. The punishment is not evil in and of itself; but it is a less than optimal state of affairs from the murderer's point of view.

Interestingly, Thomas Aquinas offers the same interpretation of Isaiah as Calvin does. Commenting on Isa 45:7, along with Amos 3:6 (i.e., "Shall there be evil in a city, and the Lord hath not done it?"), Thomas informs us that "these passages refer to the evil of penalty, and not to the evil of fault" (*ST* Ia.49.2). Jonathan Edwards, too, denies that Isaiah teaches us that God is the cause of evil: "This will justify us in understanding only of an effectual permission when God in Scripture is represented as causing the sins of men." See *The Blank Bible* (vol. 24.1 of *The Works of Jonathan Edwards*; ed. Stephen J. Stein; New Haven, CT: Yale University Press, 2006), 679.

In light of the foregoing, how did Calvinists become associated with absurd idea that the infinitely holy God is the cause of evil? One source of this unfortunate state of affairs is hyper-Calvinists such as Clark and Sproul Jr. Another source is those who caricature Calvin's teachings, thereby laying this heresy at the feet of the Reformer. For example, Chesterton, who obviously adores Aquinas, tells us that Calvinism "held that God had indeed made the world, but in a special sense, made the evil as well as the good: had made an evil will as well as an evil world." See G. K. Chesterton, *Saint Thomas Aquinas: The Dumb Ox* (1933; repr., New York: Doubleday, 1956), 106–7. Would Chesterton the Thomist agree with the "father of Neo-Thomism" when he writes: "Evil cannot happen without the divine permission, and God permits evil for some greater good, as He permits persecution for the sake of the patience and glory of martyrs. Moreover, from God's viewpoint, nothing happens by chance, for from eternity God willed or permitted the accidental conjunctions of second causes. Similarly, two servants of the same master meet each other by chance, but it is not a matter of chance for the master who sent the servants to the same place." Reginald Garrigou-Lagrange, *The Trinity and God the Creator: A Commentary on St. Thomas' Theological Summa, Ia, q. 27–119* (trans. Frederic C. Eckhoff; St. Louis: B. Herder, 1952). 441. If so, then he must also agree with the Calvinist A. A. Hodge: "God did neither cause nor approve Adam's sin. He forbade it, and presented motives which should have deterred from it. He created Adam holy and fully capable of obedience, and with sufficient knowledge of his duty, and then left him alone to his trial. If it be asked why God, who abhors sin, and who benevolently desires the excellence and happiness of his

The contextual evidence suggests that the modern versions give us the more accurate translation. Isaiah's purpose in giving us 45:7 is to round out his discussion of the coming of Cyrus, YHWH's anointed one who will allow the Hebrew people to go back to their homeland and rebuild the city of Jerusalem and her temple (see 44:28; 45:1-3).[6] The question may be asked, *How is it possible for the God of the Hebrews to use a Persian king to do his bidding?* Such a question does not fully appreciate the fact that YHWH alone is God—all other so-called gods are vain or nonexistent. YHWH is sovereign over the nations (40:17) and sits on the circle of the earth (40:22), and thus is the one who brings all princes and judges to ruin (40:23). The nations of the earth must listen to YHWH in silence, for he alone can speak with authority (41:1). YHWH alone is God, for he alone is living (41:4; 43:9; 44:9-20); and so he challenges the gods of the nations to speak anything, or do something (whether good or evil), so that the world may know that they are alive (41:23). Isaiah predicts that no other god will speak, for YHWH alone is the God who can foretell the future, since he alone knows the end from the beginning (40:21; 41:21-24; 43:8-13; 44:6-11). Because he is the sole

---

creatures, should sovereignly determine to permit such a fountain of pollution, degradation, and misery to be opened, we can only say with profound reverence, 'Even so, Father; for so it seemed good in thy sight.'" See *The Confession of Faith* (1869; repr., Carlisle, PA: Banner of Truth, 1958), 108. And so the Thomists and the Calvinists are agreed over against the hyper-Calvinists—i.e., God merely permits evil and sin, he never causes it. Any bad or less-than-optimal state of affairs that comes directly from his hand is punishment for sins committed by the creature. God is not guilty of any form of malice or evil, for he is in no way its cause.

6. That Isaiah, an eighth-century BC prophet, mentions Cyrus, who became king of Persia during the sixth century BC—thereby allowing the Jews to return to their homeland from Babylon ca. 536 BC—is at one and the same time one of the best arguments for the divine inspiration of Scripture (for it is surely impossible for a prophet to name a king roughly two hundred years in advance without divine guidance) and one of the classical arguments for the modernist approach to Scripture. That is to say, for many, if not most, OT scholars, Isa 45 appears in a section of the book (i.e., 40-66) that was not written until the sixth century BC. One of the main reasons for thinking this is the presupposition that predictive prophecy is impossible. Regardless of where one stands on the authenticity of Isaiah, one point that should not go unnoticed is that the prophet is portraying YHWH here as a deity who, unlike any other god, is able to predict the future (see Isa 43:8-13; 44:6-8). In short, the God of (Second) Isaiah cannot be the contingent god of open theism, who possesses merely a limited prescience of future contingents! For a classic defense of the modernist view of Isaiah, see Otto Eissfeldt, *The Old Testament: An Introduction* (trans. Peter Ackroyd; New York: Harper & Row, 1965), 301-46. For a more conservative, traditionalist approach to Isaiah, see Gleason L. Archer, *A Survey of Old Testament Introduction* (rev. and expanded ed.; Chicago: Moody Press, 2007), 307-31; and Oswald T. Allis, *The Unity of Isaiah: A Study in Prophecy* (Phillipsburg, NJ: Presbyterian & Reformed, 1980).

Creator of all that is, he is able to guarantee his own predictions; and he is therefore able to use any of his creatures for his own purposes—even a pagan king from Persia (44:24–27; 45:11–13).

Isaiah, then, is not giving a metaphysical dissertation on the origin of evil, but offering comfort to his people who, though in exile, will experience a corporate and national redemption. The Hebrew people will be allowed to return to their homeland via a decree of a Persian king named Cyrus. The reason Isaiah is trustworthy is that his message comes from YHWH; and the reason YHWH is trustworthy is that he is righteous, faithful, and sovereign over every event that transpires in this world—including the actions of pagan kings. He provides peace and blessing to those who obey his intrinsically holy commands, and he creates calamity and cursing to those who sin against his holy law. Thus, Blenkinsopp's translation of Isaiah 45:7.

> I am Yahveh; there is no other.
> I form light and create darkness.
> I bring about well-being and create woe;
> It is I, Yahveh, who do all these things.[7]

This translation brings out the parallelism of the Hebrew poetry nicely, with "light" parallel with "well-being," and "darkness" parallel with "woe." The contrast, as Calvin rightly notes, is between שָׁלוֹם (shalom) or "well-being" or "peace" and רַע or "woe" or "calamity." Had the word טוֹב (tov) or "righteousness" or "goodness" been used instead of שָׁלוֹם, then רַע might appropriately be translated as "evil" or "sin." But that is not what we find in the text.[8] Hence, Isaiah 45:7 does not teach that God creates evil.

---

7. Joseph Blenkinsopp, *Isaiah 40–55: A New Translation with Introduction and Commentary* (AB 19A; New York: Doubleday, 2002), 250.

8. However, while the word שׁלוֹם ("peace") is found in the Massoretic Text of Isa 45:7, טוֹב ("goodness") is found in a Qumran or Dead Sea scroll of Isaiah (i.e., 1QIsaᵃ). To be sure, the other Isaianic scrolls found at Qumran do not have this verse, and so it is difficult to know whether this reading was universally accepted at Qumran. Also, for what it is worth, the LXX translates the Hebrew word here as εἰρήνην, which implies that the manuscript of Isaiah used by the LXX translators had the word שׁלוֹם instead of טוֹב. Accepting the Qumran reading would not destroy our rather traditional interpretation of Isa 45:7, but it would weaken it significantly—for the argument drawn from the parallelism and contrast of the Hebrew terms would surely be mitigated.

Appendix 4

ON THE VERY FIRST FALL

Classical Christianity teaches that evil is singularly personified in one specific creature who was the very first being to sin. I am, of course, speaking of Lucifer, the anointed cherub who, not long after he was created, sought to ascend into the very realm of God and usurp the divine authority. There are two basic reasons Christians have traditionally believed this: First, even if there were no biblical texts to support it, we must believe that at least one of the angels introduced evil and sin into this universe, since God can in no way cause evil, and hence his original creation has to have been wholly good and lacking in any evils whatsoever. Second, there are several biblical texts that explicitly tell us of Satan's fall into sin, wherein he led one-third of God's angels into rebellion against the Almighty (Isa 14:12-21; Ezek 28:11-19; Rev 12:3-4, 7-12; see 2 Pet 2:4).

Of course, we should not be surprised to learn that this traditional Christian view has its detractors, both inside and outside the church. John Loftus, for example, informs us that "the only way Isaiah 14:12-17 and Ezekiel 28 can be seen as referring to Satan is by reading him back into the text."[1] Singer concurs, expanding on Loftus's assertion with two basic points:

> First, if Christians maintain that the "morning star" [of Isaiah 14:12] is a reference to Satan, how do they explain Revelation 22:16 where Jesus is called the "morning star" as well? Secondly, a cursory reading of the fourteenth chapter of Isaiah reveals that the "morning star" spoken of in Isaiah 14:12 is referring to Nebuchadnezzar, the wicked King of Babylon, and not to Satan. The prophet explicitly

---

1. John Loftus, *Why I Became an Atheist: A Former Preacher Rejects Christianity* (Amherst, NY: Prometheus, 2008), 385.

identified the king of Babylon as the subject of the prophecy [in Isa 14:4].[2]

Similarly, most readers will immediately notice that the referent of Ezekiel 28:11 is the king of Tyre. Hence, these two texts are obviously talking about the fall of the proud kings of Babylon and Tyre respectively. Consequently, even Christian scholars such as Calvin have insisted that Isaiah 14:12–20 must refer to the king of Babylon, whoever he may be.[3] We can only assume that, had Calvin lived long enough to finish his commentary on Ezekiel, he would have said something similar about chapter 28.

However, matters are not so simple when one delves a little more deeply into these texts. Indeed, while it is clear that Isaiah is prophesying against a Babylonian king, the identity of this figure has been notoriously difficult to ascertain.[4] Ironically, Singer's glib assertion that the identity is none other than Nebuchadnezzar happens to be the least likely of all the candidates. For while "Lucifer" or the "Morning Star" of Isaiah 14:12 will end in utter ruin (14:19–21), Nebuchadnezzar—who, to be sure, fell into ruin due to his hubris—was eventually restored into a right standing before God (see Dan 4:34–37). And what is true of Lucifer is also true of the anointed cherub of Ezekiel 28. While the prophet is clearly speaking about the king of Tyre, no one can be sure as to precisely which king is being discussed.[5] On the other hand, Christians have never been taken aback by these observations, for the traditional view is that, while the primary referents of these prophecies are the aforementioned kings, the secondary referent is the spiritual force standing behind them. Indeed, Scripture provides us with examples of celestial beings ruling through secular powers, as well as humans being a referent in a discourse with Satan himself (see Dan 10:1–21; Matt 16:23).

---

2. Tovia Singer, *Let's Get Biblical: Why Doesn't Judaism Accept the Christian Messiah?* (Forest Hills, NY: Outreach Judaism, 2014), 2:253.

3. See John Calvin, *The Book of the Prophet Isaiah: Volume 1* (Calvin's Commentaries 7; trans. William Pringle [1850]; Grand Rapids: Baker, 1996), 442.

4. See Joseph Blenkinsopp, *Isaiah 1–39: A New Translation with Introduction and Commentary* (AB 19; New York: Doubleday, 2000), 286–87.

5. See Daniel I. Block, *The Book of Ezekiel: Chapters 25–48* (NICOT; Grand Rapids: Eerdmans, 1998), 33–42, 102–21.

As for Revelation 22 — "It is I, Jesus, who sent my angel to you with this testimony for the churches. I am the root and descendent of David, the bright morning star" (Rev 22:16 NRSV) — this is a fulfillment of messianic prophecy, wherein the Messiah is called "the root of Jesse" (Isa 11:10) and "the star of Jacob" (Num 24:17). If we are right, and the "Morning Star" or "Lucifer" of Isaiah 14:12 is a reference to Satan, then we need not be bothered by the fact that Jesus is also "the Morning Star." For just as Jesus is the second Adam, who overturns the ruin which came to us through Adam's fall (1 Cor 15:22), Christ is also the *true* Morning Star, who fulfills everything Satan was originally created to be (see 2 Pet 1:19).

There are several lines of evidence favoring the traditional Christian reading of these texts. First, as more than a few scholars have noted, these passages are clear allusions to various ancient myths describing a rebellion of a god against the rest of the pantheon. As one commentary states:

> [In Isa 14:12-14] The King's aspirations to god-like status are mocked. Isaiah refers ironically to the king as *Shining One, son of Dawn*, applying to him the name of a character from ancient Canaanite myth. ... This character seems to have attempted to join the head of the pantheon, whether this was El (who was known in Canaanite texts as Most High) or Baal (whose palace was located on the *summit of Mount Zaphon*); Isaiah seems to mix the characteristics of these two Canaanite deities in his allusion to the myth. Similar references to a Canaanite myth in which an overreaching god is expelled from heaven occur in Ezek. ch. 28 and Ps. 82, and possibly Gen. 6.1-4.[6]

Notice that, just as there is no clear human referent in these prophecies, so also the mythical allusion is clear, even though no specific god precisely identifies with these poems. "Once again, the indications are that the prophet was not dependent upon any one story, but used a number of current motifs to fit his own point."[7] The more plausible interpretation,

---

6. *Jewish Study Bible*, (ed. Adele Berlin and Marc Zvi Brettler; Oxford: Oxford University Press, 2004), 812-13n14.1-23; see Blenkinsopp, *Isaiah 1-39*, 288.

7. John N. Oswalt, *The Book of Isaiah: Chapters 1-39* (NICOT; Grand Rapids: Eerdmans, 1986), 322.

then, seems to be that Isaiah and Ezekiel are reading the fall of these kings through Adam's fall from grace in Eden, which serves as the archetype of any tale wherein the creature assumes the prerogatives of the Creator. Note in this regard Ezekiel's explicit reference to Eden (28:12). Archetypal Adam helps us to look downward and understand the fall of the mighty men of the earth, and to look upward and understand of the fall of the mighty celestial ones of the heavenly realm. Pride in either sphere leads to the fall. Thus, it is quite reasonable to see these prophets addressing the spiritual forces standing behind the thrones of these kingdoms. Indeed, the noted similarities between Isaiah and Ezekiel here suggest a single spirit behind both powers—one originally created perfect, but who fell through excessive pride, believing that he could be like God.

Second, and in light of the foregoing, we can hardly blame Jesus when, after seventy-two disciples return and report all of the miracles they performed in his name, he says, "I watched Satan fall from heaven like a flash of lightening" (Luke 10:18 NRSV). The Greek here closely resembles the LXX version of Isaiah 14:12. Thus, Jesus (at least) believed Satan is being addressed in Isaiah's prophecy. The linguistic and thematic links between Isaiah 14 and Ezekiel 28 indicate that Satan is being addressed in Ezekiel's prophecy as well.

The following argument, inspired by Aquinas's discussion of Satan's fall, warrants the traditional Christian claim that Satan was the highest of God's creatures: (1) any act must have some motivation; (2) hence, any sinful act must have some motivation; (3) the anointed cherub's sin was motivated by pride (Ezek 28:17); (4) but where there is no excellence there is no basis for pride; (5) and the more excellent a creature is, the greater potential for hubris; (6) the height of hubris is to think that one can be like God; (7) as one who was "full of wisdom" the anointed cherub would have known the excellencies of all other angels; (8) had he been conscious of another angel who is greater than or equal to him, his hubris would have been checked; (9) it stands to reason, then, that Lucifer's hubris emerged out of his awareness that his excellence surpassed all other creatures; therefore, (10) Satan was originally the highest of God's creatures.[8]

---

8. Aquinas, *ST* Ia.63.7.

Loftus offers another, more philosophical critique of the traditional Christian doctrine of Satan's fall in the following way:

> The bottom line is that if Satan was the brightest creature in all of creation, and he knew of God's immediate presence, absolute good-ness, and omnipotent power like no one else, then to rebel against God makes him pure evil, suicidal, and dumber than a box of rocks. How is it that any creature in the direct unmediated presence of God would want to rebel against the absolute goodness and love of an infinitely powerful being? Even if a creature wanted to rebel, he would know that such a rebellion would be absolutely futile. But since no one can be that evil or stupid, he doesn't exist at all.[9]

This argument was answered by Thomas Aquinas nearly eight hundred years before Loftus set his pen in motion. For Aquinas, the angels had no access to the beatific vision (i.e., the intellectual apprehension of the divine essence) during their time of testing. While Thomas insists that the angels fell within moments of their creation, such need not be true for this model to be reasonable. Indeed, given this insight of the angelic doctor, two plau-sible theories emerge as to how Lucifer could have committed the first act of sin, even though he was fully aware of the divine presence: (1) While it was clearly revealed to him that YHWH alone is God, Lucifer may not have believed this, thinking that his amazing wisdom, beauty, and perfection proved that he had the right to that title—or, at least, he believed that it could be shared between himself and YHWH. It needs to be remembered that there are several schools of thought among Satanists (aka Luciferians) themselves, one of which thinks Satan is *greater* than God and another that thinks Satan is *equal* to God.[10] Assuming for a moment that Satan actually exists, perhaps he inspired his followers to believe such things because that is precisely what he himself believes. (2) Lucifer both received *and* believed the revelation of YHWH's supremacy; however, his own hubris led him to fight against God just the same. His sin, on this view, would

---

9. Loftus, *Why I Became an Atheist*, 386.

10. Walter Martin, Jill Martin Rische, and Kurt Van Gorden, *The Kingdom of the Occult* (Nashville: Thomas Nelson, 2008), 398.

be that he could attain ultimate happiness (beatitude) wholly apart from divine grace. This is precisely the view of Thomas.[11] Was this sin, on either view, foolish on Satan's part? Of course! Asinine, stupid, moronic, and just plain dumb? Yes, indeed! Implausible? No, for we have a lot of examples of really smart people doing really stupid things. For example, there are really smart atheists out there who give really bad arguments against the existence of Satan! Indeed, as the old saying goes, the greatest trick the devil ever pulled was convincing the world that he didn't exist!

---

11. Aquinas, *ST* Ia.63.3.

Appendix 5

THE DIVINE CREATIVE DECREE

The eternal creative decree of God is the divine act whereby he covenants with himself to (1) select a universe consisting of (among other beings) corporately fallen creatures, all of whom are evil sinners deserving nothing less than divine wrath; (2) order his desires and decrees in such a way that election and reprobation are decreed and a plan of redemption consistent with itself and the divine nature is set forth; and (3) bring this cosmos into being out of nothing except his power and wisdom, as well as keep it from perishing into oblivion.

There are two qualifications I must offer here: First, the selection of this universe and not another *just is* a decree of all that comes to pass. Since it is a *world-ensemble* that is decreed, as opposed to a *logical ordering* of one decree after another, an *historical order* is already comprehended and set in motion. Thus what we have here is an *order of the divine free knowledge*, wherein God comprehends all events that are foreordained to fall out in time, all in accordance with the manner in which they are originally comprehended in the *scientia naturalis*. Hence, while I will preserve many of the concerns of the infralapsarians (and even one concern of the supralapsarians), I am, for the most part, dispensing with decretal theology. That is to say, I am more comfortable moving from a layering of the divine omniscience (i.e., moving from natural to free knowledge) than a layering of the divine will (i.e., moving from the will to create humans, allow them to fall, redeem them, etc.).[1]

Second, not only does God select this universe to come into existence, knowing that it would fall into sin, but he also decides to infuse it with grace so as to redeem it. This means that there is an interesting interaction

---

1. See Kenneth Keathley, *Salvation and Sovereignty: A Molinist Approach* (Nashville: Broadman & Holman, 2010), 150.

between the divine will and the divine free knowledge such that, in desiring to redeem the good creation that falls, God actually makes certain counterfactual propositions true. Thus all counterfactual truths that are contingent are grounded in the decree.

I submit that the order of the one divine decree simply follows the historical order of the DVD (by way of analogy) or the divine natural knowledge of one logically possible world selected for redemption which, in turn, is comprehended via the *scientia libera*. Here is that decree:

(1) The selection of a logically possible world over all others, one that originates as a metaphysically good and morally pure cosmos, but wherein soon after free creatures are created, they reject and disobey the moral law, thereby introducing evil into the universe. This cosmos is therefore a fallen universe wherein every free creature misuses his or her free will and rebels against God. Hence, every free creature in this chosen cosmos will ultimately perish in the lake of fire (aka hell). God selects a world that becomes evil, wholly apart from any sort of divine influence to do so, in order to draw from it even greater goods that would not otherwise obtain (e.g., the manifestation of the widest array possible of his attributes; redemptive incarnation, courage, patience, etc.).

(2) God decides to redeem this wholly destitute world from its fallen state. In so deciding, God thereby makes various counterfactual states of affairs true. For example, had God decided not to redeem the universe, Michael the archangel would have perished into the lake of fire. Also, for example, had God not decided to redeem human beings, the human race would have destroyed itself by its own sin. (This is an interesting thought: What would have happened had God created this universe and, consistent with his sustaining providence, simply allowed the flow of sin and destruction to take its course? On this assumption, the following counterfactual is plausibly true: had God decided not to give any sort of grace to his creation, the human race would have wholly perished in the great flood and thus in the lake of fire. In any case, it is virtually certain that fewer human beings would have existed had God not chosen to redeem

this world.) Grace, or the unmerited mercy and favor of God, truly effects events in history. Had God not given grace, no one would be redeemed. "For God has shut up all in disobedience [so] that He might show mercy to all" (Rom 11:32).

(a) That the divine creative decree literally makes various counter-factual propositions true also gives us the rationale for prayer. Had God not decided to redeem this universe, prayer would not exist—for there would be no one to seek after God and hence no one to pray. But the divine decree ensures there will be redemption, and yet the only way a fallen person can receive mercy is to ask for it. Indeed, God's decree lays down one, and only one, condition for redemption—i.e., faith. Prayer is the quintessential act of faith. Notice that the thief on the cross did not say the words, "Jesus, I believe in you as the Christ and Son of the Living God!" No, all he asked for was a token of mercy—"Jesus, remember me when you come in your kingdom" (Luke 23:42). That simple prayer was an acknowledgment that Jesus is Lord, and so it in itself was an act of faith in the authority and mercy of Jesus. That very small act of faith saved the penitent thief. What is true for the penitent thief is true for all—"for 'WHOEVER WILL CALL ON THE NAME OF THE LORD WILL BE SAVED'" (Rom 10:13). The calling on the name of the Lord is both an act of faith and an act of prayer—since prayer, by definition, is speaking with and making requests to God. Hence divine grace renders the following counterfactual true—had the penitent thief not prayed to Christ for mercy, he would not have been saved. Here are two more absolutely true counterfactual propositions—had Moses not prayed for YHWH to show mercy to the people of Israel, the entire nation would have perished in the wilderness (Exod 32:11–14); had Hezekiah not prayed for YHWH to heal him, he would have died years earlier than he actually did (2 Kgs 20:1–5). Several important inferences can be drawn from these insights:

(i) Because grace literally creates a context whereby prayer exists, and since prayers are the first acts of faith of the adopted children of God, as well as the means whereby the children of God communicate with their Lord, the Lord will act as a loving and faithful Father by answering the prayers of his children—"If you then, being evil, know how to give good gifts to your children, how much more shall your Father who is in heaven give what is good to those who ask Him!" (Matt 7:11).

(ii) Prayer never changes God, but rather changes the way we relate to God. Those texts that speak of God changing his mind in light of prayer must be interpreted in light of all the Scriptures, especially those that clearly tell us that God never actually changes his mind (Num 23:19; 1 Sam 15:29; Mal 3:6; Jas 1:17). The change here is real, but it's not in God so much as it is in the way God relates to his creatures. In redemption there is a change in relationship between God and the creature from wrath to blessing—but notice that in this God never changed; only the sinner has changed in the way he or she relates to God.

(iii) That said, prayer truly affects the *plan* of God in various ways. Without mercy, there is no redemption. With mercy, there is. Without prayer, God dispenses his wrath. With prayer, his wrath is appeased. Prayer, then, is one of the means God uses to redeem this fallen world and literally rewrite the story of this universe. With the decree to select this universe, the story of this cosmos was literally heading in a specific direction. With the decree to redeem it, the story changed; and more changes still came about when the children of God prayed. In short, God is literally writing his story of redemption through the prayers of his people.

(iv) Obviously, God is not bound by our prayers—either negatively (as in, if we don't pray nothing gets done) or positively (as in, if we pray God is obligated to answer those prayers in the exact way we ask). No good father is beholden to his children, much less does he always honor their requests. The same is true with God. Hence prayer should never be analogous to us speaking with a servant or a genie in a bottle. Prayer is not the means whereby God serves us, but is the means whereby we serve God—and, amazingly, have the privilege to contribute to the divine plan. Hence, we should never say, "Prayer doesn't matter, since God will fulfill his decree whether I pray or not." No, we should instead say, "As a good Father, God wants to answer my prayer. But if I don't pray he won't answer. Therefore, I should pray, trusting that he will answer my request whenever and however he sees fit!"[2]

(3) The reason God selects this fallen world to exist, then, is so that he can bring much good out of the evil contained therein *via a plan of redemption*. In saying this, we do not presume to know why specific persons suffer particular kinds of evil. Indeed, God's decree to select this fallen world to obtain precedes any decree he gives concerning particular persons in this world. So, why we live in a world where diseases such as cancer exist is due to the fact that, without this and other kinds of suffering, particular goods—e.g., perseverance

---

2. Question: How is it that God, in deciding to infuse grace into a possible world that becomes fallen, and thereby creates true counterfactuals through his providence, creaturely freedom, prayer, etc., is not just choosing yet another logically possible world? That is, there is one DVD with a story wherein creation remains in its fallen condition, and another one that is redeemed, which thereby has a different story and ending from the other. That, of course, is one way to look at it. There is a logically possible world that possesses all of the elements (and more besides) of our ordering of the decree, and God just chooses that world to be. Since God does not need time to order a world, much less does he think sequentially (as we do), the choice of one world over another is instantaneous. Yet another way to look at it is in terms of this logically possible world God has chosen. To give yet another illustration: We all know that a director of a movie is not always pleased with the end result of his filming. So he, as they say, cleans everything up in postproduction—adding a scene here and there, which creates a need for yet more scenes and voiceovers and CGI characters that none of the actors could see while filming, etc. After editing the film to look like his vision of what he wants it to be, the director releases it to a theater for public viewing. Analogously, God takes a DVD that is absolutely nothing like what he wants it to be—e.g., there is sin and evil, and every character perishes into hell in the end. He edits it into a profound story wherein a number too great for any creature to count is redeemed, and his Son receives all the glory for that redemption. But how is this different than open-view theism? In the following way: Like George Lucas, the open-view deity changes his mind and edits the way the story unfolds even after he releases the film to the public; on the contrary, like Clint Eastwood, the God of Reformed Thomism sees no need to change anything after the story is edited. His is an *eternal* "edit," foreordaining all events (logically) before even one of them comes to pass; and all events in history fall out in time in exactly the same manner as his natural knowledge conceives them, as his decree ordains them, and as his free knowledge comprehends them.

and patience—would never obtain; however, why God allows one mother to be taken from this world by leukemia, while also allowing another to thrive while raising her children, remains unknown. Hence we can know the "why" of evil and suffering on the macro level, but on the micro level (i.e., why *this* person suffers from *this* evil) we confront a mystery.

(4) This fallen world, as we say, includes celestial (angelic) beings— led by one whose power, goodness, and wisdom surpasses all creatures—who freely and individually choose to rebel against God; as well as a mass of humanity all involved in one common and corporate ruin; thereby ensuring the greater good of God's glory via a world in which all of his attributes are manifest—e.g., justice to those evil persons who never repent; grace, which, among other things, effects the repentance of other evil persons.

(5) God decrees to send extrinsically efficacious graces to every celestial being, along with the first humans, to ensure that their obedience to him is a genuine possibility.

(6) These extrinsically effectual graces are accompanied with an antecedent desire that no creature falls into sin, as well as a consequent permissive will that many angels, along with the first humans—and thus the whole human race—fall into sin and hence are condemned.

(7) God antecedently desires that all fallen celestial beings repent of their sin and be redeemed; and he consequently, albeit permissively, wills that all fallen angels remain in their condemned state, with no chance to repent—which consequently entails the will to punish all fallen angels in the lake of fire. God also manifests a consequent and simple will to keep his elect angels from falling into sin—hence it is the will of God that all redeemed angels are saved by their own works.

(8) The fall of humankind having been permissively decreed, God antecedently desires that everyone in the human race repents of his sins via trust in God.

    (a) To fulfill and make good this antecedent desire, God decrees that a sufficient amount of grace and revelation is given to every human being, which, while restraining them from harm, tells them of God's existence, his moral law, their sin against him, and their desperate condition. Hence all human beings receive the gifts of *common grace*—for without this restraining grace given to all, every human being would be as bad as he could be, but with this gift of mercy human beings are restrained from the full exercise of the wickedness in their hearts and are even able to use their personal gifts and talents for their own enjoyment and benefit—and *general revelation*, which tells them of an eternal and good and powerful deity who desires that they do good and avoid evil; and they learn from this revelation that a day of judgment is coming to them, where their deeds will be weighed by the righteous Judge.

(b) General revelation consists, at a minimum, of several observations everyone knows even from birth: the fundamental intuition of being (wherein nothingness is inconceivable); the order of the universe, displayed in its beauty and elegance, pointing all humans to an Orderer of the cosmos; the intuition of absolute dependence, pointing to a being who is independent; the moral law of conscience, pointing all humans to a Moral Lawgiver; echoes of paradise lost, found in various human traditions (as well as the human subconscious), which speak of an original goodness lost by our first parents; the inescapability of the eternal nature of the human soul; and so on.

(c) Common grace consists, at a minimum, of extrinsically efficacious graces that make it really possible to fulfill the demands of God's sufficient revelation to humans. Such graces include the power of free agency, reason, human traditions that illustrate the moral law, marriage, family, and (eventually in human history) human governments to restrain evil, and so on.

(d) To fulfill and make good this antecedent desire, God decrees to give a sincere and genuine conditional offer to every member of the human race (which remains such, even after the decree of election is given)—i.e., if anyone repents through believing God and his truth, that person will be saved. This promise is true and genuine, even for those who have no access to explicit special revelation (discussed in (e) below). Remember, special revelation existed even in the garden of Eden; and its echo still resounds (implicitly) deep within the human spirit. Thus, anyone living far removed from special revelation ought nevertheless to reason as follows: I have failed to live up to the demands of the moral law; I therefore deserve condemnation; therefore, I cast myself on the mercy of the Creator-God to save me on the day of judgment. Anyone who does such a thing will be saved. Unfortunately, humans, being the totally depraved sinners they are, never do this. They spurn the natural revelation of God, twisting it into a different god or philosophy in order to excuse themselves from judgment. All truth from God is suppressed in unrighteousness. Thus, while general revelation renders a robust natural theology *possible in principle*, human depravity renders such a knowledge of the divine *implausible in practice*. And so,

(e) To fulfill and make good his antecedent desire, God decrees to give to humankind a special revelation that not only confirms the prior general revelation of his own existence and his moral law, but also progressively lays down the prehistory of humankind—explaining how the race fell, and even how it has already been judged via a flood, which is a guarantee of the future judgment to come—as well as the redemptive history of the corporate body God chooses to receive his special revelation; also, this supernatural revelation reveals God's desire to create a nation to implement justice, worship the divine being via sacrifices and offerings and psalms and preaching, and also serve as the ethnic people from whom the Savior comes, and so on.

(f) To fulfill and make good his antecedent desire, God decrees to establish various persons and institutions throughout history— broadly speaking, this refers (but is not limited) to the prophets of the patriarchal era, the prophetic school and sacrificial system during the Israelite era, and the apostolic college and church during the Christian era. These persons and/or institutions are "havens of revelation" for anyone to listen to and/or enter and hear the way of salvation that God has decreed. Hence these institutions are extrinsically effectual means of grace—i.e., when a person during the patriarchal era, or a Jew (or gentile) of the Israelite era, or a gentile (or Jew) of the Christian era enters such a sanctuary as is offered during these respective epochs, there is a sense in which she is preparing herself for salvation; for the message she receives is "trust the prophetic message that the Lord is Righteous and will not acquit the guilty, and fall upon the mercy of God for redemption," or "taste, see, observe, and hear that the Lord is good, and trust in YHWH so that it will be accounted to you as righteousness," or "rely upon or trust in the Lord Jesus Christ, and in him alone, and you will be saved."

(g) To fulfill and make good his antecedent desire, God sends his Son to earth to live a sinless life, thereby doing what no other human being could ever do (i.e., fulfill the demands of the law), provide an atonement for sin that is infinite in value—i.e., an atonement that is sufficient to save an infinite number of people on an infinite number of planets—and then raise him from the dead as proof that the divine imprimatur rests on his person, his doctrine, and his redemptive work.

(h) To fulfill and make good his antecedent desire, God the Holy Spirit struggles with the hearts of human beings in an attempt to open their eyes to the revelation concerning Christ and his sufficient atonement. The normative (*but certainly not the only*) means by which this is done are the institutions discussed in (f), and so this strife between humans and the Holy Spirit is normally a special, albeit extrinsic, efficacious grace that makes faith genuinely possible for anyone who is in hearing distance of the gospel.

(9) Accompanying his antecedent desire for everyone in the human race to be saved is the divine consequent will that only some particular persons are saved.

(a) This will is rendered effectual by the divine election—i.e., the act of God whereby he chooses to save a massive number of specific[3] fallen sinners, thereby making a covenant of grace with them to provide all the means necessary for the accomplishment of that end.

(b) This will also (logically) entails a permissive reprobation—i.e., the act of God whereby he chooses to pass over many fallen sinners, thus does not choose them unto salvation, and hence permits them to resist his sufficient grace, thereby ensuring their just condemnation unto the wrath of God.

(c) This consequent will regarding the reprobate does not entail any pleasure on God's part that the reprobate remain condemned, for God never takes pleasure in the death or condemnation of the wicked. God is pleased with *his plan* of redemption *as such*—which includes his act of reprobation—though he is never pleased with the damnation of particular reprobate persons. Like an author who weeps over the death of one of her characters, while also remaining content with her story,[4] God is saddened over the damnation of the reprobate, and yet pleased with his eternal plan.

(d) Nor does the consequent will regarding the reprobate entail God's creation of unbelief within the hearts of those whom he has passed over. Rather, throughout their lives God continues

---

3. It is precisely at this point where our order of the divine omniscience intersects with decretal theology. Molinists want to locate electing grace in the *scientia media*. However, that option being closed to us, we must locate electing grace in the decree itself, which is grounded in the *scientia naturalis* and comprehended in the *scientia libera*. For no good can be realized apart from its particular circumstances; therefore, the decree of election must concern actual persons and not merely hypothetical ones.

4. One can find several interviews on the web where J. K. Rowling, author of the famous Harry Potter series, informs her fans that she genuinely wept over the death of Sirius Black (among other characters). Notice that she is absolutely sovereign over her book series—she can write her story any way she wants. As far as her books are concerned, she is omnipotent with respect to the universe she has made. So why allow Sirius to die if she did not want him to? Because she determined that his death would be used to for a greater good. Rowling's experience here offers us a helpful analogy that renders our perspective quite reasonable. For just as Rowling wrote a story that often made her sad, due to a genuine concern over the characters she created, so also God often decrees what he does not desire. He genuinely loves everyone and desires their salvation; thus his permissive decree to allow many to perish is not something he savors.

to hold his hands out, as it were, welcoming them into his covenant kingdom. All any reprobate person needs to do in order to be saved is trust in the divine Savior alone for his redemption and he will be justified in the sight of God. This offer is genuine—so genuine that if, per chance via a narrow possibility, a reprobate person were to defy the secret decree of election and trust in Christ as his Savior, he would be saved. This will never happen, of course (i.e., it is not broadly possible). But the reason it will never happen is the recalcitrant heart of the reprobate person, not the pleasure God takes in seeing a reprobate person condemned—that is, it's not the case that the reprobate person will not believe because he cannot; rather, he cannot because he will not.

(e) This consequent will regarding the elect *does* entail a pleasure on God's part that the elect are, at some point in their lives, moved from a state of wrath and condemnation to a state of blessing and justification. All elect persons are born into this world as condemned sinners, and the wrath they bear is no less dangerous than the wrath borne by the reprobate. If, per chance (or by a narrow possibility), an elect person were to die the day, or even the second, before he was foreordained to trust in Christ, he would perish in the lake of fire, along with all other reprobate creatures. Of course, this will never happen. But it could. The only reason it doesn't is the grace of God. Hence, every saved person is elect, but not every elect person is currently saved—although all elect persons will eventually be saved at some point before death.

(f) The consequent will of God should therefore never be used as an excuse not to believe. A person should never say, "I am elect, therefore I needn't believe." No, she should instead say, "Am I elect? Well, I can never know until I am saved. And the only way I can be saved is to believe in Christ—therefore I should believe in Christ!"

(g) The consequent will of God should therefore be a motivation for all people to press into the kingdom of God—to enter the church and experience the word of God by hearing it preached and seeing it offered in the sacraments. Only through the word of God can a person have faith. Therefore, every person should constantly avail himself to the word so that he might have his eyes and ears opened and believe.

(h) The consequent will of God is no mere choice on his part that a certain number of people will be saved. Rather, it logically entails specific acts on the part of God to accomplish the redemption of those whom he has chosen. The Triune God covenants with himself—Father, Son, and Holy Spirit—to accomplish the redemption of his people. This is called the eternal covenant of redemption (or the *pretemporal Pactum Salutis*). So, in light of this eternal covenant of redemption, the Father eternally chooses a multitude of human sinners, which no creature can number, to be redeemed. The Father elects us in "eternity past," guaranteeing our future salvation from damnation.

(i) The consequent will of God therefore entails that the Son comes to earth to actually redeem his people from their sins—rather than make their redemption a mere possibility. So, while the atonement of Christ is *sufficient* to save an infinite number of people on an infinite number of planets, it is *efficient* only for the elect. Hence the redemptive work of Christ is for everyone in the sense that all are called and welcomed to partake in it—i.e., the atonement is sufficient to save all in that, if a reprobate person were, per chance, to cling to the atonement by a sincere act of faith, he would be saved (i.e., Christ need not return and die a second death for such a believer). But while the atonement enlightens even reprobate persons regarding God's truth, draws them into churches, and even brings many such people to a mental assent to the truths of the gospel and even a changed life for the better, such effects of the atonement are incidental to its one great purpose, which is to redeem the elect. The atonement of Christ makes salvation not merely possible but actual for the elect in the sense that it procures for them all of the spiritual blessings God has reserved for anyone who will be saved—including faith, which is the first spiritual gift of God. Hence the Son redeems us in the historical past (or the historical future, as was the case for those living before the advent of Christ), thereby securing our salvation from the effects of sin.

(j) The consequent will of God thus entails that the Holy Spirit, while striving with many (both elect and reprobate) in order to help them to see their miserable condition and believe, will at some point stop wrestling with any given human. To some, he departs and leaves them in their sin, thereby hardening their hearts for the day of wrath. To be sure, while the wrestling with reprobates sometimes ends, the posture of invitation always remains. Like the father of the prodigal, God gives some reprobates over to their sins and allows them to harden their hearts; but just as the father sat on his porch, yearning for the prodigal's return, so also God holds his hands out to every disobedient and recalcitrant sinner. As the parable of the prodigal son teaches us, God sometimes gives elect persons over to their own sins as well, thereby allowing even them to harden their hearts. That said, whether it be the chosen prodigal who wastes his life in extravagant debauchery or the chosen legalist who prides herself concerning her own (so-called) works-righteousness, there comes a time when God the Holy Spirit provides the elect person with the intrinsic and effectual grace of the new birth, which opens their hearts to the truth of the gospel. Seconds before the new birth, an elect person finds himself ignoring, doubting, arguing with, laughing at, or striving against the message of the gospel and the internal witness of the Holy Spirit (as the case may be); but the very instant he is born again (regenerated) he trusts in Christ as his Savior. The second such a sinner places his faith in the theanthropic person, God the Father justifies him (i.e., declares him righteous). The second a person places his faith in Christ, God the Son becomes his Advocate, representing him before the Father as the Great High Priest. The second a person places his faith in the Lord, God the Holy Spirit seals him for the day of judgment and adopts him into the covenant kingdom of

God's family, guaranteeing that nothing will separate him from the redemptive love of God. Hence, the Holy Spirit quickens us in our personal past, sustains our faith in the present, and seals us for the future.

(10) With his plan of redemption, as well as his design for all of cosmic, angelic, biological, and human history, in place, God decrees to bring this logically possible world into being from nothing, thereby making it actual rather than merely possible. This powerful and effective decree sustains this actual world in being and guarantees that all that is in the decree falls out in time, in order, and in accordance with the nature of that which is decreed—i.e., necessary events fall out necessarily, contingent events contingently, free actions freely, and so on.

While this model of the ordering of the divine knowledge is not exhaustive, I think it is sufficient as a vindication of the coherence of theism, along with universal benevolence and unconditional election. To be sure, some will still complain, saying, "Why does God find fault with those who are reprobate? Had he given the same gifts to them that he gives to the elect, everyone would be saved!" The answer to this objection, of course, is that the reprobate damn themselves by sinning against God, denying his revelation, and resisting his grace. This is why he finds fault with them. True, God could have made things different than they actually are. But he was never obligated to do so. Nor does this divine choice to not give effectual grace to everyone remove the responsibility and culpability of the reprobate.

The reader will recall the Molinist dictum I have quoted several times throughout this study: "It is up to God whether or not we find ourselves in a world in which we are predestined to salvation; but it is up to us whether or not we are predestined to salvation in a world in which we find ourselves."[5] We have already seen many problems with this proposition. However, I think that the biblical sentiment behind this statement—i.e., *that God is in no way the author of a person's unbelief*—can be preserved when we distinguish between the way God relates to his elect and the way he relates

---

5. William Lane Craig, "'No Other Name': A Middle Knowledge Perspective on the Exclusivity of Salvation through Christ," *F&P* 6 (April 1989): 181–82.

to the reprobate. In making this distinction, we preserve the asymmetry of election and reprobation. Thus, I word my rather infralapsarian distinction as follows:

Election: It is up to God whether a person finds herself in a world in which she is elect; and it is also up to God whether a person is elect and justified in the world in which she finds herself.

Reprobation: It is up to God whether a person finds herself in a world in which she is reprobate; but it is up to each reprobate person whether she is reprobate and condemned in the world in which she finds herself.[6]

---

6. One will often hear Arminians say something like the following: "The only reason any person goes to hell is because he chooses to do so." By this they do not mean that the option between heaven and hell is explicitly and audibly offered by God to everyone, and some just choose hell over heaven. Rather, there are some persons, referred to in the classical Christian tradition as reprobates, who upon receiving divine revelation (via nature if not both nature and holy writ) spurn it and reject it, indicating that they want nothing to do with God. This choice to reject God and his offer of salvation *just* is a choice to damn themselves for all eternity. Throughout our study we have seen that, from the Pelagian and Arminian and Molinistic points of view, this notion of the reprobate condemning themselves is actually incoherent. Ironically, only on the strong foundation of Reformed theology can one assert that the reprobate are *wholly* responsible for their self-condemnation! Hence, on the one hand Paul can say to those who reject his message that they have condemned themselves (or counted themselves unworthy of eternal life), even while Luke explains that only those who were ordained to eternal life believed the apostolic message (see Acts 13:46, 48). Indeed, Christ comes into the world not to condemn it, but to save it; and humans condemn themselves via their evil deeds (John 3:17, 19). Again, only the Reformed Thomist can consistently say, "The only reason any person goes to hell is because he or she chooses to do so."

BIBLIOGRAPHY

Abbott, Edwin A. *Flatland: A Romance of Many Dimensions*. Edited by
Philip Smith. Reprint, Mineola, NY: Dover, 1992.

Adler, Mortimer J. *How to Think about God: A Guide for the 20th-Century
Pagan*. New York: Macmillan, 1979.

Agnes, Michael, ed. *Webster's New World College Dictionary*. 4th ed.
Cleveland: Wiley, 2002.

Allis, Oswald T. *The Unity of Isaiah: A Study in Prophecy*. Phillipsburg, NJ:
Presbyterian & Reformed, 1980.

Aquinas, Thomas. *Commentaries on St. Paul's Epistles to Timothy, Titus,
and Philemon*. Translated by Chrysostom Baer. South Bend, IN: St.
Augustine's Press, 2007.

———. *Commentary on the Letter of Saint Paul to the Romans*. Translated
by F. R. Larcher. Edited by J. Mortensen and E. Alarcon. Latin/
English Edition of the Works of St. Thomas Aquinas 37. Lander,
WY: The Aquinas Institute for the Study of Sacred Doctrine, 2012.

———. *Commentary on Saint Paul's Epistle to the Ephesians*. Translated by
Matthew L. Lamb. Aquinas Scripture Series 2. Albany, NY: Magi
Books, 1966.

———. *Summa Contra Gentiles*. 5 vols. Translated by James F. Anderson.
Notre Dame: University of Notre Dame Press, 1975.

———. *Summa Theologica*. Translated by Fathers of the English
Dominican Province. Allen, TX: Thomas More, 1948.

Archer, Gleason L. *Encyclopedia of Bible Difficulties*. Grand Rapids:
Zondervan, 1982.

———. *A Survey of Old Testament Introduction*. Rev. and expanded ed.
Chicago: Moody Press, 2007.

Arminius, James. *The Works of James Arminius*. 3 vols. Translated by James
Nichols and William Nichols. Grand Rapids: Baker, 1986.

Asselt, Willem J. van, J. Martin Bac, and Roelf T. te Velde, eds. *Reformed Thought on Freedom: The Concept of Free Choice in Early Modern Reformed Theology*. Grand Rapids: Baker Academic, 2010.

Asselt, Willem J. van, and Eef Dekker, eds. *Reformation and Scholasticism: An Ecumenical Enterprise*. Grand Rapids: Baker Academic, 2001.

Audi, Robert, ed. *The Cambridge Dictionary of Philosophy*. Cambridge: Cambridge University Press, 1995.

Augustine. *Augustin: Anti-Pelagian Writings*. Edited by Philip Schaff. Translated by Peter Holmes and Robert Ernest Wallis. Rev. translation by Benjamin B. Warfield. Vol. 5 of *Nicene and Post-Nicene Fathers*. Peabody, MA: Hendrickson, 1994.

Bahnsen, Greg L. *Van Til's Apologetic: Readings and Analysis*. Phillipsburg, NJ: Presbyterian & Reformed, 1998.

Barth, Markus. *Ephesians: Introduction, Translation and Commentary on Chapters 1–3*. AB 34. New York: Doubleday, 1974.

Basinger, David, and Randall Basinger, eds. *Predestination and Free Will: Four Views of Divine Sovereignty and Human Freedom*. Downers Grove, IL: InterVarsity Press, 1986.

Bauer, Walter, Frederick William Danker, W. F. Arndt, and F. W. Gingrich. *A Greek-English Lexicon of the New Testament and Other Early Christian Literature*. 3rd ed. Chicago: University of Chicago Press, 2000.

Bavinck, Herman. *Reformed Dogmatics*. 4 vols. Edited by John Bolt. Translated by John Vriend. Grand Rapids: Baker Academic, 2004.

Beckwith, Francis J., Carl Moser, and Paul Owen, eds. *The New Mormon Challenge: Responding to the Latest Defenses of a Fast-Growing Movement*. Grand Rapids: Zondervan, 2002.

Beckwith, Roger. *The Old Testament Canon of the New Testament Church*. Grand Rapids: Eerdmans, 1985.

Beeke, Joel, and Sinclair B. Ferguson, eds. *Reformed Confessions Harmonized*. Grand Rapids: Baker, 1999.

Beilby, James K., and Paul R. Eddy, eds. *Divine Foreknowledge: Four Views*. Downers Grove, IL: InterVarsity Press, 2001.

Berkhof, Louis. *Systematic Theology*. Rev. and enl. ed. Grand Rapids: Eerdmans, 1996.

Berlin, Adele, and Marc Zvi Brettler, eds. *The Jewish Study Bible*. Oxford: Oxford University Press, 2004.

Bignon, Guillaume. *Excusing Sinners and Blaming God: A Calvinist Assessment of Determinism, Moral Responsibility, and Divine Involvement in Evil*. Eugene, OR: Pickwick, 2018.

Blenkinsopp, Joseph. *Isaiah 1–39: A New Translation with Introduction and Commentary*. AB 19. New York: Doubleday, 2000.

———. *Isaiah 40–55: A New Translation with Introduction and Commentary*. AB 19A. New York: Doubleday, 2002.

Block, Daniel I. *The Book of Ezekiel: Chapters 1–24*. NICOT. Grand Rapids: Eerdmans, 1997.

———. *The Book of Ezekiel: Chapters 25–48*. NICOT. Grand Rapids: Eerdmans, 1998.

Blomberg, Craig L., and Stephen E. Robinson. *How Wide the Divide? A Mormon and an Evangelical in Conversation*. Downers Grove, IL: InterVarsity Press, 1997.

Bock, Darrell L. *Acts*. BECNT. Grand Rapids: Baker, 2007.

Boethius, Anicius. *The Consolation of Philosophy*. 2nd ed. Translated by Victor Watts. New York: Penguin, 1999.

Boice, James Montgomery, and Philip Graham Ryken. *The Doctrines of Grace: Rediscovering the Evangelical Gospel*. Wheaton, IL: Crossway, 2002.

Boyd, Gregory A. *God of the Possible: A Biblical Introduction to the Open View of God*. Grand Rapids: Baker, 2000.

Brand, Chad Owen, ed. *Perspectives on Election: Five Views*. Nashville: Broadman & Holman, 2006.

Bratcher, Dennis, ed. "The Five Articles of the Remonstrants (1610)." Accessed June 25, 2018. http://www.crivoice.org/creed-remonstrants.html.

Brown, Francis, et al., eds. *The New Brown-Driver-Briggs-Gesenius Hebrew and English Lexicon*. Peabody, MA: Hendrickson, 1979.

Brown, Michael L. *Answering Jewish Objections to Jesus*. 5 vols. Grand Rapids: Baker, 2000–2010.

Brown, Raymond E. *The Gospel according to John (XIII–XXI)*. AB 29A. New York: Doubleday, 1970.

Bruce, F. F. *The Book of Acts*. NICNT. Grand Rapids: Eerdmans, 1988.

Buswell, J. Oliver. *A Systematic Theology of the Christian Religion*. 2 vols. in 1. Grand Rapids: Zondervan, 1962.

Cabal, Ted et al. eds. *The Apologetics Study Bible*. Nashville: Holman Bible, 2007.

Calvin, John. *Calvin's Commentaries*. 22 vols. Reprint, Grand Rapids: Baker, 1996.

———. *Institutes of the Christian Religion*. Edited by John T. McNeill. Translated by Ford Lewis Battles. Library of Christian Classics 22. Philadelphia: Westminster, 1960.

Campbell, Travis James. "The Beautiful Mind: A Reaffirmation and Reconstruction of the Classical Reformed Doctrines of the Divine Omniscience, Prescience, and Human Freedom." PhD diss., Westminster Theological Seminary, 2004.

———. "Middle Knowledge: A Reformed Critique." *Westminster Theological Journal* 68, no. 1 (Spring 2006): 1–22.

———. "Should Ole Aquinas Be Forgot and Never Brought to Mind: A Response to Dewey Roberts' 'Aquinas Not a Safe Guide for Protestants.'" https://www.the-aquilareport.com/ole-aquinas-forgot-never-brought-mind/.

Carson, D. A. *The Difficult Doctrine of the Love of God*. Wheaton, IL: Crossway, 2000.

———, ed. *Right with God: Justification in the Bible and the World*. Reprint, Eugene, OR: Wipf & Stock, 2002.

Cassuto, Umberto. *A Commentary on the Book of Exodus*. Translated by Israel Abrahams. Jerusalem: Magnes, 1967.

Chemnitz, Martin. *Examination of the Council of Trent: Part 1*. 1578 Frankfurt ed. Translated by Fred Kramer. St. Louis: Concordia, 1971.

Chesterton, G. K. *Orthodoxy: The Romance of Faith*. Reprint, New York: Doubleday, 1959.

———. *Saint Thomas Aquinas: The Dumb Ox*. Reprint, New York: Doubleday, 1956.

Chiew, Sze Sze. *Middle Knowledge and Biblical Interpretation: Luis de Molina, Herman Bavinck, and William Lane Craig*. Contributions to Philosophical Theology 13. Frankfurt am Main: Peter Lang, 2016.

Childs, Brevard S. *The Book of Exodus: A Critical, Theological Commentary*. Old Testament Library. Louisville: Westminster, 1974.

Clark, David K., and Norman L. Geisler. *Apologetics in the New Age: A Christian Critique of Pantheism*. Grand Rapids: Baker, 1990.

Clark, Gordon H. *Predestination*. Phillipsburg, NJ: Presbyterian & Reformed, 1987.

———. *What Do Presbyterians Believe?* Phillipsburg, NJ: Presbyterian & Reformed, 1965.

Clark, Kelly James, ed. *Philosophers Who Believe: The Spiritual Journeys of 11 Leading Thinkers*. Downers Grove, IL: InterVarsity Press, 1993.

Cobb, John B., Jr., and David Ray Griffin. *Process Theology: An Introductory Exposition*. Philadelphia: Westminster, 1976.

Cobb, John B., Jr., and Clark H. Pinnock, eds. *Searching for an Adequate God: A Dialogue between Process and Free Will Theists*. Grand Rapids: Eerdmans, 2000.

Collins, C. John. *Genesis 1–4: A Linguistic, Literary, and Theological Commentary*. Phillipsburg, NJ: Presbyterian & Reformed, 2006.

Copan, Paul. *"That's Just Your Interpretation": Responding to Skeptics Who Challenge Your Faith*. Grand Rapids: Baker, 2001.

Copan, Paul, and William Lane Craig. *Creation Out of Nothing: A Biblical, Philosophical, and Scientific Exploration*. Grand Rapids: Baker, 2004.

Copan, Paul, and Paul K. Moser, eds. *The Rationality of Theism*. London: Routledge, 2003.

Copi, Irving M., and Carl Cohen. *Introduction to Logic*. 12th ed. Upper Saddle River, NJ: Prentice Hall, 2005.

Corduan, Winfried. *In the Beginning God: A Fresh Look at the Case for Original Monotheism*. Nashville: B&H, 2013.

Craig, William Lane. *Divine Foreknowledge and Human Freedom: The Coherence of Theism; Omniscience*. Brill's Studies in Intellectual History 19. New York: E. J. Brill, 1991.

———. *God over All: Divine Aseity and the Challenge of Platonism.* Oxford: Oxford University Press, 2016.

———. "'Lest Anyone Should Fall': A Middle Knowledge Perspective on Perseverance and Apostolic Warnings." *International Journal for Philosophy of Religion* 29 (1991): 65–74.

———. "Middle Knowledge, Truth-Makers, and the 'Grounding Objection.'" *F&P* 18 (July 2001): 337–52.

———. "'No Other Name': A Middle Knowledge Perspective on the Exclusivity of Salvation through Christ." *F&P* 6 (April 1989): 172–88.

———. *The Only Wise God: The Compatibility of Divine Foreknowledge and Human Freedom.* Grand Rapids: Baker, 1987.

———, ed. *Philosophy of Religion: A Reader and Guide.* New Brunswick, NJ: Rutgers University Press, 2002.

———. *The Problem of Divine Foreknowledge and Future Contingents from Aristotle to Suarez.* Edited by A. J. Vanderjagt. Brill's Studies in Intellectual History 7. New York: E. J. Brill, 1988.

———. *Time and Eternity: Exploring God's Relationship to Time.* Wheaton, IL: Crossway, 2001.

Craig, William Lane, and J. P. Moreland, eds. *The Blackwell Companion to Natural Theology.* Chichester, West Sussex, UK: Blackwell, 2009.

———, eds. *Naturalism: A Critical Analysis.* London: Routledge, 2000.

Cranfield, C. E. B. *A Critical and Exegetical Commentary on The Epistle to the Romans.* 2 vols. ICC. Edinburgh: T&T Clark, 1979.

Crockett, William, ed. *Four Views on Hell.* Grand Rapids: Zondervan, 1996.

Cunningham, William. *The Reformers and the Theology of the Reformation.* Reprint, Carlisle, PA: Banner of Truth Trust, 1967.

Dabney, Robert L. *Systematic Theology.* 2nd ed. Carlisle, PA: Banner of Truth Trust, 1996.

Davies, Brian. *An Introduction to the Philosophy of Religion.* 3rd ed. Oxford: Oxford University Press, 2004.

———, ed. *Philosophy of Religion: A Guide and Anthology.* Oxford: Oxford University Press, 2000.

Dekker, Eef. *Middle Knowledge.* Leuven: Peeters, 2000.

Dennett, Daniel C. "Thank Goodness." Updated Dec. 6, 2017. https://www. huffingtonpost.com/daniel-c-dennett/thank-goodness_b_33207. html.

Dever, William G. *Did God Have a Wife? Archeology and Folk Religion in Ancient Israel.* Grand Rapids: Eerdmans, 2005.

Dolezal, James E. *All That Is in God: Evangelical Theology and the Challenge of Classical Christian Theism.* Grand Rapids: Reformation Heritage Books, 2017.

———. *God without Parts: Divine Simplicity and the Metaphysics of God's Absoluteness.* Eugene, OR: Pickwick, 2011.

Dunn, James D. G. *Romans 9–16.* WBC 38A. Dallas: Word Books, 1988.

———. *The Theology of Paul the Apostle.* Grand Rapids: Eerdmans, 1998.

Edwards, Jonathan. *The Works of Jonathan Edwards.* 26 vols. New Haven, CT: Yale University Press, 2006.

Eissfeldt, Otto. *The Old Testament: An Introduction.* Translated by Peter Ackroyd. New York: Harper & Row, 1965.

Elwell, Walter A., ed. *Evangelical Dictionary of Theology.* 2nd ed. Grand Rapids: Baker, 2001.

Erickson, Millard J. *Christian Theology.* 2nd ed. Grand Rapids: Baker, 1998.

Fee, Gordon D. *The First Epistle to the Corinthians.* NICNT. Grand Rapids: Eerdmans, 1987.

Feinberg, John S. *The Many Faces of Evil: Theological Systems and the Problems of Evil.* 3rd ed. Wheaton, IL: Crossway, 2004.

Ferguson, Sinclair B., and David F. Wright, eds. *New Dictionary of Theology.* Downers Grove, IL: InterVarsity Press, 1988.

Feser, Edward. *Five Proofs of God.* San Francisco: Ignatius Press, 2017.

———. *The Last Superstition: A Refutation of the New Atheism.* South Bend, IN: St. Augustine's Press, 2008.

Fitzmyer, Joseph A. *The Acts of the Apostles.* AB 31. New York: Doubleday, 1998.

———. *Romans: A New Translation with Introduction and Commentary.* AB 33. New York: Doubleday, 1993.

Flint, Thomas. *Divine Providence: The Molinist Account.* Ithaca, NY: Cornell University Press, 1998.

Flowers, Leighton. *The Potter's Promise: A Biblical Defense of Traditional Soteriology*. N.p.: Trinity Academic Press, 2017.

Fragapane, Carmen. "Salvation by Christ: A Response to Credenda/Agenda." Accessed May 27, 2019. http://orthodoxinfo.com/inquirers/frag_salv.aspx.

Frame, John M. *No Other God: A Response to Open Theism*. Phillipsburg, NJ: Presbyterian & Reformed, 2001.

Garrigou-Lagrange, Reginald. *God: His Existence and Nature (A Thomistic Solution to Certain Agnostic Antinomies)*. Translated by Dom Bede Rose. 2 vols. 5th ed. St. Louis: B. Herder, 1945.

————. *Grace: Commentary on the Summa Theologica of St. Thomas, I^aII^æ, q. 109–114*. Translated by Dominican Nuns of Corpus Christi Monastery in Menlo Park, CA. St. Louis: B. Herder, 1952.

————. *The One God: A Commentary on the First Part of St. Thomas' Theological Summa*. Translated by Dom Bede Rose. St. Louis: B. Herder, 1946.

————. *Predestination: The Meaning of Predestination in Scripture and the Church*. Translated by Dom Bede Rose. Reprint, Rockford, IL: Tan Books, 1998.

————. *The Trinity and God the Creator: A Commentary on St. Thomas' Theological Summa, I^a, q. 27–119*. Translated by Frederic C. Eckhoff. St. Louis: B. Herder, 1952.

Geisler, Norman L. *Chosen But Free: A Balanced View of God's Sovereignty and Free Will*. 3rd ed. Minneapolis: Bethany, 2010.

————. *Christian Apologetics*. 2nd ed. Grand Rapids: Baker, 2013.

————, ed. *Inerrancy*. Grand Rapids: Zondervan, 1980.

————. *Thomas Aquinas: An Evangelical Appraisal*. Grand Rapids: Baker, 1991.

————, ed. *What Augustine Says*. Reprint, Eugene, OR: Wipf & Stock, 2003.

Geisler, Norman L., and Winfried Corduan. *Philosophy of Religion*. 2nd ed. Grand Rapids: Baker, 1988.

Geisler, Norman L., and Wayne House. *The Battle for God: Responding to the Challenges of Neotheism*. Grand Rapids: Kregel, 2001.

Geisler, Norman L., and William D. Watkins. *Worlds Apart: A Handbook on World Views*. 2nd ed. Eugene, OR: Wipf & Stock, 2003.

Geivett, Douglas R. *Evil and the Evidence for God: The Challenge of John Hick's Theodicy*. Philadelphia: Temple University Press, 1993.

Girardeau, John L. *Calvinism and Evangelical Arminianism Compared as to Election, Reprobation, Justification, and Related Doctrines*. Reprint, Harrisonburg, VA: Sprinkle, 1984.

Gould, Paul M., ed. *Beyond the Control of God? Six Views on the Problem of God and Abstract Objects*. New York: Bloomsbury, 2014.

Groothius, Douglas R. *Confronting the New Age*. Downers Grove, IL: InterVarsity Press, 1988.

———. *Unmasking the New Age*. Downers Grove, IL: InterVarsity Press, 1986.

Grudem, Wayne. *Systematic Theology: An Introduction to Biblical Doctrine*. Grand Rapids: Zondervan, 1995.

Gruenler, Royce Gordon. *The Inexhaustible God: Biblical Faith and the Challenge of Process Theism*. Grand Rapids: Baker, 1983.

Habermas, Gary R. *Forever Loved: A Personal Account of Grief and Resurrection*. Joplin, MO: College Press, 1997.

Hartshorne, Charles. *Omnipotence and Other Theological Mistakes*. Albany, NY: SUNY Press, 1984.

Hasker, William. *God, Time, and Knowledge*. Cornell Studies in the Philosophy of Religion. Ithaca, NY: Cornell University Press, 1989.

Hawking, Stephen, and Roger Penrose. *The Nature of Space and Time*. Princeton Scientific Library. Princeton, NJ: Princeton University Press, 1996.

Helm, Paul. "Jonathan Edwards and the Parting of the Ways?" *JES* 4, no. 1 (2014): 42–60.

———. "Turretin and Edwards Once More." *JES* 4, no. 3 (2014): 286–96.

Hodge, A. A. *The Confession of Faith*. Carlisle, PA: Banner of Truth, 1958.

Hodge, Charles. *Commentary on Romans*. Rev. ed. Carlisle, PA: Banner of Truth Trust, 1986.

———. *Systematic Theology*. 3 vols. New York: Charles Scribner's Sons, 1872–73.

Hoehner, Harold W. *Ephesians: An Exegetical Commentary*. Grand Rapids: Baker, 2002.

Hoekema, Anthony A. *Saved by Grace*. Grand Rapids: Eerdmans, 1989.

Hoeksema, Herman. *The Clark-Van Til Controversy*. Unicoi, TN: Trinity Foundation, 2005.

The Holy Bible: The Net Bible® (The New English Translation™). Biblical Studies Press, 2001.

Horton, Michael, ed. *Christ the Lord: The Reformation and Lordship Salvation*. Grand Rapids: Baker, 1992.

Hunt, David. *What Love Is This? Calvinism's Misrepresentation of God*. Sisters, OR: Loyal, 2002.

Jastrow, Robert. *God and the Astronomers*. 2nd ed. New York: W. W. Norton, 1992.

Keathley, Kenneth. *Salvation and Sovereignty: A Molinist Approach*. Nashville: B&H Academic, 2010.

Keener, Craig S. *Acts: An Exegetical Commentary*. Vol. 2, 3:1–14:28. Grand Rapids: Baker, 2013.

———. *The Gospel of John: A Commentary*. 2 vols. Peabody, MA: Hendrickson, 2003.

Kelley, J. N. D. *A Commentary on the Epistles of Peter and of Jude*. Peabody, MA: Hendrickson, 1969.

Kenny, Anthony. *God of the Philosophers*. Oxford: Clarendon, 1979.

Kerr, Gaven. *Aquinas's Way to God: The Proof in* De Ente et Essentia. Oxford: Oxford University Press, 2015.

Kittel, Gerhard, and Gerhard Friedrich, eds. *Theological Dictionary of the New Testament*. Translated by Geoffrey W. Bromiley. 10 vols. Grand Rapids: Eerdmans, 1972.

Klein, William W. *The New Chosen People: A Corporate View of Election*. Eugene, OR: Wipf & Stock, 2001.

Kreeft, Peter. *Summa of the* Summa. San Francisco: Ignatius Press, 1990.

Kruger, Michael J. *Canon Revisited: Establishing the Order and Authority of the New Testament Books*. Wheaton, IL: Crossway, 2012.

Laing, John D. *Middle Knowledge: Human Freedom in Divine Sovereignty*. Grand Rapids: Kregel, 2018.

Lapide, Pinchas. *The Resurrection of Jesus: A Jewish Perspective.* Translated by Wilhelm C. Linss. Reprint, Eugene, OR: Wipf & Stock, n.d.

Leftow, Brian. *God and Necessity.* Oxford: Oxford University Press, 2012.

Leith, John H., ed. *Creeds of the Churches.* 3rd ed. Louisville: John Knox, 1982.

Lennox, John C. *Determined to Believe? The Sovereignty of God, Freedom, Faith, & Human Responsibility.* Grand Rapids: Zondervan, 2017.

Letham, Robert. *Through Western Eyes (Eastern Orthodoxy: A Reformed Perspective).* Fearn, Ross-shire, UK: Christian Focus, 2007.

Lewis, C. S. *A Grief Observed.* San Francisco: HarperCollins, 1989.

———. *Mere Christianity.* 2nd ed. New York: Macmillan, 1952.

Lewis, David. *Counterfactuals.* Oxford: Blackwell, 1973.

———. *On the Plurality of Worlds.* Oxford: Blackwell, 1986.

Lillback, Peter A., et al., eds. *1599 Geneva Bible: Calvin Legacy Edition.* White Hall, WV: Tolle Lege, 2008.

Limborch, Philipp van. *A Complete System, or Body of Divinity, Both Speculative and Practical, Founded on Scripture and Reason.* Vol. 1. Translated by William Jones. Reprint, London: Forgotten Books, 2015.

Lincoln, Andrew T. *Ephesians.* WBC 42. Dallas: Word Books, 1990.

Lisle, Jason. *Keeping Faith in an Age of Reason: Refuting Alleged Bible Contradictions.* Green Forest, AR: Master Books, 2017.

Loftus, John. *Why I Became an Atheist: A Former Preacher Rejects Christianity.* Amherst, NY: Prometheus, 2008.

MacGregor, Kirk R. *Luis de Molina: The Life and Theology of the Founder of Middle Knowledge.* Grand Rapids: Zondervan, 2015.

———. *A Molinist-Anabaptist Systematic Theology.* Lanham, MD: University Press of America, 2007.

Machen, J. Gresham. *The Christian View of Man.* Reprint, Carlisle, PA: Banner of Truth Trust, 1965.

———. *What Is Faith?* Reprint, Carlisle, PA: Banner of Truth Trust, 1991.

Mackie, J. L. *The Miracle of Theism: Arguments for and against the Existence of God.* Oxford: Clarendon, 1982.

Manning, Russell Re, ed. *The Oxford Handbook of Natural Theology.* Oxford: Oxford University Press, 2013.

Martin, Michael. *Atheism: A Philosophical Justification*. Philadelphia: Temple University Press, 1990.

Martin, Walter, Jill Martin Rische, and Kurt Van Gorden. *The Kingdom of the Occult*. Nashville: Thomas Nelson, 2008.

McDowell, Josh, and Sean McDowell. *Evidence That Demands a Verdict: Life Changing Truth for a Skeptical World*. 4th ed. Nashville: Thomas Nelson, 2017.

Miley, John. *Systematic Theology*. 2 vols. New York: Hunt & Eaton, 1892–93.

Molina, Luis de. *On Divine Foreknowledge (Part IV of the* Concordia*)*. Translated by Alfred J. Freddoso. Ithaca, NY: Cornell University Press, 1988.

Moo, Douglas J. *The Epistle to the Romans*. NICNT. Grand Rapids: Eerdmans, 1996.

Moreland, J. P., and William Lane Craig. *Philosophical Foundations for a Christian Worldview*. 2nd ed. Downers Grove, IL: InterVarsity Press, 2017.

Morris, Leon. *The Epistle to the Romans*. Grand Rapids: Eerdmans, 1988.

———. *The Gospel according to John*. 2nd ed. NICNT. Grand Rapids: Eerdmans, 1995.

Morris, Thomas V. *Anselmian Explorations: Essays in Philosophical Theology*. Notre Dame, IN: University of Notre Dame Press, 1987.

———, ed. *The Concept of God*. Oxford Readings in Philosophy. Oxford: Oxford University Press, 1987.

Motyer, Alec. *The Prophecy of Isaiah: An Introduction & Commentary*. Downers Grove, IL: InterVarsity Press, 1993.

Muller, Richard A. *God, Creation, and Providence in the Thought of Jacob Arminius*. Grand Rapids: Baker, 1991.

———. "Jonathan Edwards and Francis Turretin on Necessity, Contingency, and Freedom of Will. In Response to Paul Helm." *JES* 4, no. 3 (2014): 266–85.

———. "Jonathan Edwards and the Absence of Free Choice: A Parting of Ways in the Reformed Tradition." *JES* 1, no. 1 (2011): 3–22.

———. *Post-Reformation Reformed Dogmatics*. 4 vols. 2nd ed. Grand Rapids, Baker Academic, 2003.

Murray, Iain H. *Spurgeon v. Hyper-Calvinism: The Battle for Gospel Preaching*. Carlisle, PA: Banner of Truth, 1995.

Murray, John. *The Epistle to the Romans*. 2 vols. in 1. Grand Rapids: Eerdmans, 1968.

Myers, J. D. *The Re-Justification of God: An Exegetical and Theological Study of Romans 9:10–24*. Dallas, OR: Redeeming Press, 2017.

Nash, Ronald H. *The Concept of God: An Exploration of Contemporary Difficulties with the Attributes of God*. Grand Rapids: Zondervan, 1983.

———, ed. *Process Theology*. Grand Rapids: Baker, 1987.

Nolland, John. *The Gospel of Matthew: A Commentary on the Greek Text*. New International Greek Testament Commentary. Grand Rapids: Eerdmans, 2005.

Ockham, William. *Predestination, God's Foreknowledge, and Future Contingents*. Translated by McCord Adams and Norman Kretzmann. 2nd ed. Indianapolis: Hackett, 1983.

Olsen, Roger E. *Arminian Theology: Myths and Realities*. Downers Grove, IL: InterVarsity Press, 2006.

Oswalt, John N. *The Bible among the Myths*. Grand Rapids: Zondervan, 2009.

———. *The Book of Isaiah: Chapters 1–39*. NICOT. Grand Rapids: Eerdmans, 1986.

Ott, Ludwig. *The Fundamentals of Catholic Dogma*. Translated by Patrick Lynch. 4th ed. Edited by James Canon Bastible. Rockford, IL: Tan Books, 1974.

Owen, John. *Death of Death in the Death of Christ*. Carlisle, PA: Banner of Truth Trust, 1959.

———. *The Works of John Owen*. Edited by John Goold. 10 vols. Carlisle, PA: Banner of Truth Trust, 1967.

Packer, J. I. *Knowing God*. 2nd ed. Downers Grove, IL: InterVarsity Press, 1993.

Pelagius. *Commentary on St. Paul's Epistle to the Romans*. Oxford Early Christian Studies. Oxford: Clarendon, 1993.

Pelikan, Jaroslav. *The Riddle of Roman Catholicism*. New York: Abingdon, 1959.

Perszyk, Ken, ed. *Molinism: The Contemporary Debate*. Oxford: Oxford University Press, 2011.

Picirilli, Robert E. *Grace, Faith, Free Will—Contrasting Views of Salvation: Calvinism & Arminianism*. Nashville: Randall House, 2002.

Pink, Arthur W. *The Sovereignty of God*. 3rd ed. Pensacola, FL: Chapel Library, 1999.

Pinnock, Clark H., ed. *The Grace of God and the Will of Man*. Minneapolis: Bethany House, 1995.

———, ed. *Grace Unlimited*. Minneapolis: Bethany, 1975.

Pinnock, Clark H., et al. *The Openness of God: A Biblical Challenge to the Traditional Understanding of God*. Downers Grove, IL: InterVarsity Press, 1994.

Piper, John. *God's Passion for His Glory: Living the Vision with Jonathan Edwards (With the Complete Text of* The End for Which God Created the World*)*. Wheaton, IL: Crossway, 1998.

———. *The Justification of God: An Exegetical and Theological Study of Romans 9:1-23*. 2nd ed. Grand Rapids: Baker, 1993.

Piper, John, Justin Taylor, and Paul Kjoss Helseth, eds. *Beyond the Bounds: Open Theism and the Undermining of Biblical Christianity*. Wheaton, IL: Crossway, 2003.

Plantinga, Alvin C. *Does God Have a Nature?* Milwaukee: Marquette University Press, 1980.

———. *God, Freedom, and Evil*. Grand Rapids: Eerdmans, 1974.

———. *The Nature of Necessity*. Oxford: Clarendon, 1974.

———. "On Ockham's Way Out." In *The Concept of God*. Edited by Thomas V. Morris. Oxford Readings in Philosophy. Oxford: Oxford University Press, 1987.

Pojman, Louis P. *Ethics: Discovering Right & Wrong*. 5th ed. Belmont, CA: Wadsworth, 2006.

Qureshi, Nabeel. *Seeking Allah, Finding Jesus: A Devout Muslim Encounters Christianity*. Grand Rapids: Zondervan, 2014.

Rana, Fazale, with Hugh Ross. *Who Was Adam? A Creation Model Approach to the Origin of Humanity*. 2nd ed. Covina, CA: Reasons to Believe, 2015.

Reymond, Robert L. *A New Systematic Theology of the Christian Faith.* 2nd ed. Nashville: Thomas Nelson, 1998.

Rhodes, Ron, and Marian Bodine. *Reasoning from the Scriptures with the Mormons.* Eugene, OR: Harvest House, 1995.

Ridderbos, Herman N. *The Gospel of John: A Theological Commentary.* Translated by John Vriend. Grand Rapids: Eerdmans, 1997.

Ross, Hugh. *Beyond the Cosmos: The Transdimensionality of God.* Covina, CA: Reasons to Believe, 2017.

————. *The Creator and the Cosmos.* 4th ed. Covina, CA: Reasons to Believe, 2018.

————. *The Fingerprint of God.* 2nd ed. New Kensington, PA: Whitaker House, 1989.

————. *Navigating Genesis: A Scientist's Journey through Genesis 1–11.* Covina, CA: Reasons to Believe, 2014.

Ross, Hugh, and Kathy Ross. *Always Be Ready: A Call to Adventurous Faith.* Covina, CA: Reasons to Believe, 2018.

Schaeffer, Francis A. *How Should We Then Live?* Vol. 5 of *The Complete Works of Francis A. Schaeffer.* 2nd ed. Wheaton, IL: Crossway, 1985.

Schreiner, Thomas. *Faith Alone: The Doctrine of Justification.* Five Solas Series. Grand Rapids: Zondervan, 2015.

————. "Notes on 2 Peter." In *The Apologetics Study Bible.* Edited by Ted Cabal et al. Nashville: Holman Bible, 2007.

————. *Romans.* BECNT. Grand Rapids: Baker, 1998.

Schreiner, Thomas, and Bruce A. Ware, eds. *The Grace of God, The Bondage of the Will.* 2 vols. Grand Rapids: Baker, 1995.

Serapion. "The Divine Transforming Grace." *The Ecumenical Review* 56, no. 3 (July 2004): 312–21.

Shank, Robert. *Elect in the Son: A Study of the Doctrine of Election.* Minneapolis: Bethany, 1989.

Singer, Tovia. *Let's Get Biblical: Why Doesn't Judaism Accept the Christian Messiah?* 2 vols. Forest Hills, NY: Outreach Judaism, 2014.

Smith, George. *Atheism: The Case against God.* Buffalo, NY: Prometheus, 1976.

Sprinkle, Preston, ed. *Four Views on Hell.* 2nd ed. Grand Rapids: Zondervan, 2016.

Sproul, R. C. *Chosen by God*. Wheaton, IL: Tyndale House, 1986.

———. *Explaining Inerrancy*. Orlando: Ligonier Ministries, 1996.

———. *Faith Alone: The Evangelical Doctrine of Justification*. Grand Rapids: Baker, 1995.

Sproul, R. C., John Gerstner, and Arthur Lindsley. *Classical Apologetics: A Rational Defense of the Christian Faith and a Critique of Presuppositional Apologetics*. Grand Rapids: Zondervan, 1984.

Sproul, R. C., Jr. *Almighty over All: Understanding the Sovereignty of God*. Grand Rapids: Baker, 1999.

Spurgeon, Charles H. *Spurgeon's Sermons*. 10 vols. Grand Rapids: Baker, 1996.

Stalnaker, Robert C. *Ways a World Might Be: Metaphysical and Anti-Metaphysical Essays*. Oxford: Clarendon, 2003.

Storms, Samuel. *Chosen for Life: The Case for Divine Election*. Wheaton, IL: Crossway, 2007.

Sungenis, Robert A. *Not by Faith Alone: The Biblical Evidence for the Catholic Doctrine of Justification*. Santa Barbara, CA: Queenship, 1997.

Swinburne, Richard. *Responsibility and Atonement*. Oxford: Clarendon, 1989.

Tappert, Theodore G., ed. *The Book of Concord: The Confessions of the Evangelical Lutheran Church*. Philadelphia: Fortress, 1959.

Thieme, Robert B., Jr. *The Integrity of God*. 2nd ed. Houston: R. B. Thieme, Jr. Bible Ministries, 1987.

Thompson, J. A. *The Book of Jeremiah*. NICOT. Grand Rapids: Eerdmans, 1980.

Tiessen, Terrence. *Who Can Be Saved?* Downers Grove, IL: InterVarsity Press, 2004.

Trueman, Carl R. *Grace Alone: Salvation as a Gift from God*. Five Solas Series. Grand Rapids: Zondervan, 2017.

Turek, Frank. *Stealing from God: Why Atheists Need God to Make Their Case*. Colorado Springs: NavPress, 2014.

Turretin, Francis. *Eleventh through Seventeenth Topics*. Vol. 2 of *Institutes of Elenctic Theology*. Edited by James T. Dennison Jr. Translated by George Musgrave Giger. Phillipsburg, NJ: Presbyterian & Reformed, 1994.

———. *First through Tenth Topics*. Vol. 1 of *Institutes of Elenctic Theology*. Edited by James T. Dennison Jr. Translated by George Musgrave Giger. Phillipsburg, NJ: Presbyterian & Reformed, 1992.

Van Horn, Luke. "On Incorporating Middle Knowledge into Calvinism: A Theological/Metaphysical Muddle?" *Journal of the Evangelical Theological Society* 55, no. 4 (2012): 807–27.

Van Til, Cornelius. *A Survey of Christian Epistemology*. Vol. 2 of *In Defense of the Faith*. Philipsburg, NJ: Presbyterian & Reformed, 1980.

Venema, Cornelius P. *Heinrich Bullinger and the Doctrine of Predestination: Author of "The Other Reformed Tradition"?* Grand Rapids: Baker, 2002.

Voltaire. *Candide or Optimism*. Translated and edited by Robert M. Adams. 2nd ed. New York: W. W. Norton, 1991.

Wallace, Daniel B. *Greek Grammar beyond the Basics*. Grand Rapids: Zondervan, 1996.

Wallace, Stan W, ed. *Does God Exist? The Craig-Flew Debate*. Burlington, VT: Ashgate, 2003.

Walls, Jerry L. *Does God Love Everyone? The Heart of What's Wrong with Calvinism*. Eugene, OR: Cascade Books, 2016.

———. *Hell: The Logic of Damnation*. Notre Dame, IN: University of Notre Dame Press, 1992.

———. "Is Molinism as Bad as Calvinism?" *F&P* 7, no. 1 (January 1990): 85–98.

Walls, Jerry, and Joseph R. Dongell. *Why I Am Not a Calvinist*. Downers Grove, IL: InterVarsity Press, 2004.

Ware, Bruce A. *God's Lesser Glory: The Diminished God of Open Theism*. Wheaton, IL: Crossway Books, 2000.

Warfield, Benjamin B. *The Inspiration and Authority of the Bible*. Edited by Samuel G. Craig. Phillipsburg, NJ: Presbyterian & Reformed, 1948.

———. *The Plan of Salvation*. Reprint, Eugene, OR: Wipf & Stock, 2000.

Westermann, Claus. *Isaiah 40–66: A Commentary*. Translated by David M. G. Stalker. Philadelphia: Westminster, 1969.

White, James R. *The Potter's Freedom: A Defense of the Reformation and a Rebuttal to Norman Geisler's* Chosen but Free. 2nd ed. Merrick, NY: Calvary, 2009.

Whitehead, Alfred North. *Process and Reality*. Corrected ed. Edited by David Ray Griffin and Donald W. Sherborne. New York: Free Press, 1978.

Worthing, Mark William. *God, Creation, and Contemporary Physics*. Minneapolis: Fortress, 1996.

Young, Edward J. *The Book of Isaiah*. Vol. 1, *Chapters 1–18*. Grand Rapids: Eerdmans, 1965.

Zacharias, Ravi. *Can Man Live without God?* Nashville: Word, 1994.

INDEX OF NAMES

INDEX OF SUBJECTS

SCRIPTURE REFERENCES

OLD TESTAMENT

357

NEW TESTAMENT